PAN THE GOAT-GOD

HARVARD STUDIES IN
COMPARATIVE LITERATURE
Founded by William Henry Schofield

30

PAN THE GOAT-GOD

HIS MYTH IN MODERN TIMES

by Patricia Merivale

HARVARD UNIVERSITY PRESS

CAMBRIDGE, MASSACHUSETTS

1969

TO MY PARENTS

PREFACE

"But when I saw him from behind I was certain he was an animal, and when I saw him in front I knew he was a god."

"Pan," said the Professor dreamily, "was a god and an animal..."

"Pan again!" said Dr. Bull irritably. "You seem to think Pan is every-thing."

"So he is," said the Professor, "in Greek. He means everything."

"Don't forget," said the Secretary, looking down, "that he also means Panic."

G. K. Chesterton, The Man Who Was Thursday, chapter xiv

Chesterton here alludes to a curious philological accident that made Pan not merely the god of Arcadia, but of the whole of nature; he could have added another, by which Pan became not merely the god of shepherds, but, in Christian myth, either the devil, as might be expected, or, both more important and more surprising, Christ, as shepherd-god himself.

The present book is a study of this most distinctive, charming, and unusually varied motif from classical mythology. It assumes no particular theory of the nature, validity, or meaning of myth in literature; it is not "myth criticism," but the literary history of a mythical theme. Most previous study of Pan has been from the point of view of anthropology, archaeology, or art history (to all of which Reinhard Herbig's monograph *Pan der griech-ische Bocksgott* provides a very valuable introduction); these approaches, as well as the technical study of mythography, will all be subordinated here to literary analysis. But perhaps this book will help some myth critic to answer more fully, in social, cultural, and mythological terms, than I have been able to do in literary terms, the key question: why was there, between 1890 and 1926, that astonishing resurgence of interest in the Pan motif, and that rich harvest of its varied possibilities? And why was it so largely an English and American phenomenon? For so relatively unconcerned with Pan do continental authors seem to be, that I could scarcely make this book "comparative," in the narrow sense, at all.

Even in the chief area of concern, completeness of course eluded me. Presumably very few readers would have noticed the (inadvertent) omission of Warwick Deeping's "The Pool of the Satyr," but any reader with a less stringent definition of Pan than mine might be puzzled by the omission of John Fowles, John Updike, and especially John Barth, whose Giles Goat-Boy may well be the best-known contemporary goatish superman. I can only conclude with an assertion borrowed from Ezra Pound: "I have seen the God Pan and it was in this manner."

The illustrations, chiefly from Renaissance and later art, amplify and comment on the literary text, while telling a very different story of their own. Readers with a special interest in the iconology of the theme should correlate the selection given here with the illustrations in Herbig's *Pan*, especially valuable for classical Pans.

I am happy to acknowledge my gratitude to Harry Levin, for his assistance and encouragement at each stage of my work, including, of course, his willingness to recommend its acceptance for this series. To Douglas Bush, my debt is both deep and obvious; I would be very proud if he were willing to accept this book as a tiny footnote to the magnificent works in which, effectively, he developed the field of mythical thematics. My debts to both are personal as well as intellectual; the confidence they expressed in the value of this study provided me with much of the impetus for its completion, and especially for its revision for publication.

A general, but nonetheless heartfelt acknowledgment is due to all those friends and colleagues who helped with inquiries, with books and study space, and particularly with clues to the fortunes of Pan, saying "of course you know X's Pan" — when I very often did not — and putting up with my behaving, over the last few years, as if "Pan was everything." I want also to thank Janet Dolman for her work on the index.

I am grateful to the editors of *Philological Quarterly, Victorian Newsletter,* and *Texas Studies in Literature and Language* for their permission to reprint here material that first appeared in their journals.

Unless otherwise indicated, translations from the Greek are from Loeb Classical Library editions, by permission of Harvard University Press, and translations from other languages are my own.

To Wellesley College for an Alice Freeman Palmer Fellowship, and to the American Association of University Women for a Special Fellowship, which together made possible the basic research for this book, and to the President's Research Council of the University of British Columbia for a grant to cover subsequent research, revision, and incidental publication expenses, my gratitude and thanks.

Finally, the book is dedicated to my parents, who made it all possible.

Vancouver
October 1968

CONTENTS

ILLUSTRATIONS

follow page 144

PAN THE GOAT-GOD

Chapter I

FROM THE ARCADIAN TO THE AUGUSTAN

Pan, first worshiped in Arcadia, was the god of woods and shepherds, and he had the feet and legs of a goat. This is the irreducible statement of his identity from which all other statements of his role in literary history must be seen to proceed. However abstractly intellectual, however farfetched, however contradictory some of the uses to which, as we shall see, the Pan motif has been put, this concrete, individual figure lies behind them all. The meanings may vary widely, but the pictorial characteristics do not. The paradox of a being half goat and half god is the very core of his nature.

For literary purposes the actualities of the Arcadian religion, whatever they may have been, scarcely matter in comparison with the Athenian, Alexandrian, and Roman versions of that worship.[1] Pan's career in literature begins, as far as can be ascertained, with the Homeric Hymn to Pan, "a hymn in form [but] an idyll in spirit," uncertain in date and authorship, but certainly post-Homeric.[2] It is the first of many sources to broach the question of etymology, achieving the singularly unconvincing answer that "Pan" is called "all" because he charmed or delighted all the gods. Its chief significance — apart from setting down in an early and basic form the commonly agreed upon and ever recurring attributes of Pan, his natural setting, his pastoral activities, his music-making and dancing — is in its presentation of a comic-grotesque godling who is a second-class citizen and a non-Homeric latecomer among the Olympians.

There are fleeting references to Pan in Pindar,[3] in the Greek tragedians,[4] in Aristophanes[5] and Plato,[6] but only Herodotus, of the major fifth-century Greek writers, had a story to tell of Pan. He narrates the legendary background to the official introduction of Pan worship in Athens, and gives a conveniently precise date for the event and therefore, by extension, for the availability of Pan as a literary subject. Just before the Battle of Marathon (490 B.C.), Pan appeared to Pheidippides, the Athenian messenger, and asked," 'Why is it that ye take no thought for me, that am your friend, and ere now have oft been serviceable to you, and will be so again?' This story the Athenians believed to be true" and after the victory "they founded a temple of Pan beneath the Acropolis" (VI, 105).[7]

The first literary cult of Pan appears in the epigrams and dedications of the *Greek Anthology*, which, while varying in (presumed) date from the third century B.C. to the sixth century after Christ, present a fairly uniform picture of a pastoral deity to whom the tools of hunter and fisher and the products of agriculture are dedicated, in hopes of success in those pursuits. One example, more obviously poetic than many, will serve to illustrate the relatively simple figure of the Arcadian goat-god, as yet unclouded by allegory and ruler over only a very narrow kingdom: "Charicles by the wooded hill offered to Pan who loves the rock this yellow, bearded goat, a horned creature to the horned, a hairy one to the hairy-legged, a bounding one to the deft leaper, a denizen of the woods to the forest god." [8] This is not really country rusticity at all, but the literary exercise of a city dweller. Pan as the country god imagined by city dwellers, the nearest approach to the original Arcadian Pan, will recur as often as the pastoral itself, though seldom in as shaggy a form as here.

The Pan of Theocritus, more influential by far than the Pans of the *Greek Anthology*, is likewise the object of the shepherds' worship. They allude to his piping and guarding sheep, and to his effigies; they swear oaths by him. But Pan himself is a verbal ornament who takes no part in the action. The one exception is the Pan supposed to strike terror into the shepherds, who is too much of a fellow Arcadian countryman to convey effectively the primitive fear, mixed with wonder, that no doubt lay behind the superstition: "It is not right, good shepherd, it is not right for us to pipe at mid-day: we are afraid of Pan; for in truth it is then he reposes wearied from the chase: and he is crabbed, and sharp anger ever rests upon his nostril." [9] The brief allusions of Euripides convey true terror better.

The prose romances give the earliest examples of Pan as a participant in a plot, as a character among human characters, and thus the earliest solutions to the problems that arise at the points where myth and fiction are combined. Apuleius, in *The Golden Ass* (ca. A.D. 155), creates a Pan characterized as old, kindly, and helpful, which, while never seriously challenging, in later times, the commoner view of him as old, shaggy, and lecherous (one likelier to pursue nymphs than to counsel them), has yet fathered a considerable number of fictional Pans. However, Apuleius avoids the other fictional problem of congruity between mythical and human characters by placing Pan in the purely mythical inner narrative of Cupid and Psyche inserted into the main romance plot. When Psyche, having attempted suicide, was washed ashore,

Pan, the goat-legged country god, happened to be sitting near by, caressing the mountain nymph Echo and teaching her to repeat all sorts of pretty songs. A flock of she-goats roamed around, browsing greedily on the grass. Pan was already aware of Psyche's misfortune, so he gently beckoned to the desolate girl and did what he could to comfort her. "Pretty dear," he said soothingly. "Though I'm only an old, old shepherd and very much of a countryman, I have picked up a good deal of experience in my time . . . Your sad eyes show that you're desperately in love . . . Stop crying, try to be cheerful, and open your heart to Cupid, the greatest of us gods." [10]

Longus, in his *Daphnis and Chloe*, starts with much the same material as Theocritus. On one level of representation Pan is seen in the country effigies on which little sacrifices are placed, in the oaths "by Pan" and the prayers to Pan. These are worked smoothly into the plot and given psychological justification in the moods and beliefs of Daphnis and Chloe, but Pan's attributes remain Theocritean. On another level, Pan appears in dreams and visions; and on still another level of reality, he can actually be seen, not in himself, but in the actions he causes. Panic terror is a reality to stampeding crowds, whether of goats or of pirates, and the Pan who causes their stampedes, although invisible, is strongly personified. Longus' method of shifting smoothly from one of these levels to another represents, for fictional purposes, a great technical advance over the static decorative icons of Theocritus.

Although the Arcadian frame of reference is elaborated with Theocritean detail, and Pan's normal pastoral role is constantly before us, Longus also allows two aspects of his nature to emerge that are difficult to reconcile with this role. One, the savage destruction of Echo by the maddened shepherds, Longus does not even try to explain; it is put into the frame of Daphnis' narration. The other, the anomaly of Pan as a warrior, is handled more neatly by Longus than by any of the other classical authors who attempted it. Herodotus simply announces the legend of Pan's aid to the Athenians, making no attempt to describe his part in the battle. Silius Italicus (A.D. 26–101) makes Pan's role doubly odd — Jupiter sends Pan into battle as a peacemaker (*Punica* XIII, 326f). Nonnus (ca. A.D. 450) produced a specimen of the very sort that Lucian had satirized three centuries earlier. He exploits a whole troop of Pans for their freakish picturesqueness in an elaborate epic battle procession; one Pan might have been more effective than thirteen (*Dionysiaca* XIV, 67–96, and elsewhere). Longus' Pan, unlike these epic Pans, retains his Arcadian quality: he fights in defense of his fields and his worshipers and uses, not the inappropriate weapons of the epic warrior, but his own weapons of stampeding herds and pipings that cause panic. Several elements of the terror story are present here, but the point of view is different: Pan is on "our" side, and we are not expected to share the terror of those whom he is rightfully punishing.[11]

Lucian, on the other hand, simply laughed at the Warrior Pan, whether at Marathon, in India with Dionysus (the theme of Nonnus' plodding epic), or in Egypt fighting the Titans (III, 169). "That Pan came from Arcadia to Marathon to take a hand in the battle" ("The Lover of Lies," III, 325) is an instance of "cities and whole peoples tell[ing] lies unanimously and officially."[12] In "The Double Indictment" (ca. A.D. 165) Pan, living in the Cave of Pan under the Acropolis and "paying the usual tax as a resident alien" (III, 101), has some satiric comments to make, from his rural point of view, on Athenian philosophers. Apart from a single touch in Apuleius, "I am an old, old shepherd and very much of a countryman," Lucian is alone in making Pan "human." Further, he is the first to use a Pan figure to comment satirically on the real world, mocking mythology while turning it to literary advantage. In Apuleius' Psyche myth, as in *Daphnis and Chloe*, Pan is an accepted part of a world which is all of a piece; here Pan, a fragment of another world (that of familiar tradition and myth), wanders into a "realistic" context; Pan mocks himself as well, for he is aware of himself as a myth.[13]

Still, for most of the pre-Romantic Pans in English literature (and many thereafter), no Greek source need be supposed. Two stories from Ovid and a few lines from Virgil provided actions and attributes enough to fill the Elizabethan pastoral lyric and drama not only with icons of the pastoral scene but with the lovesick Pans of many a vain pursuit and with Pans emblematic of such incompatibles as rustic ignorance and poetic creativity. The essence of Theocritus' pastoral Pan is compressed into these lines from Virgil's second Eclogue:

> mecum una in silvis imitabere Pana canendo.
> Pan primum calamos cera coniungere plures
> instituit, Pan curat oves oviumque magistros. (II, 31–33)

(With me in the woods you shall rival Pan in song. It was Pan who first undertook to join together many reeds with wax; Pan cares for the sheep and the guardians of the sheep.) "Panaque Silvanumque senem Nymphasque sorores" (*Georg.* II, 493–494), Pan and old Silvanus and the sister Nymphs, are in the cast of many a pastoral ritual, dance, or festival.[14] But Ovid's story of Pan and Syrinx (*Met.* I, 689–714) is certainly the best-known Pan story in existence; perhaps it would be worthwhile transcribing it in its most colorful and influential, though neither most concise nor most accurate, translation:[15]

> And after other talke he [Argus] askt (for lately was it founde)
> Who was the founder of that Pype that did so sweetely sounde.

Then sayde the God, [Hermes], there dwelt sometime a Nymph
of noble fame
Among the hilles of *Arcadie*, that *Syrinx* had to name.
Of all the Nymphes of *Nonacris* and Fairie farre and neere,
In beautie and in parsonage thys Ladie had no peere.
Full often had she given the slippe both to the *Satyrs* quicke
And other Gods that dwell in Woods, and in the Forrests thicke,
Or in the fruitfull fieldes abrode. It was hir whole desire
Too follow chaste *Dianas* guise in Maydenhead and attire.
Whome she did counterfaite so nighe, that such as did hir see
Might at a blush have taken hir, *Diana* for to bee,
But that the Nymph did in hir hande a bowe of Cornell holde,
Whereas *Diana* evermore did beare a bowe of golde.
And yet she did deceyve folke so. Upon a certaine day
God *Pan* with garland on his heade of Pinetree, sawe hir stray
From Mount *Lyceus* all alone, and thus to hir did say.
Unto a Gods request, O Nymph, voucesafe thou to agree
That doth desire thy wedded spouse and husband for to bee.
   There was yet more behinde to tell: as how that *Syrinx* fled
   Through waylesse woods and gave no eare to that that *Pan*
   had sed,
Untill she to the gentle streame of sandie *Ladon* came,
Where, for bicause it was so deepe, she could not passe the same,
She piteously to chaunge hir shape the water Nymphes besought:
And how when *Pan* betweene his armes, to catch y Nymph
   had thought,
In steade of hir he caught the Reedes newe growne upon the brooke,
And as he sighed, with his breath the Reedes he softly shooke,
Which made a still and mourning noyse, with straungnesse of the
   which
And sweetenesse of the feeble sounde the God delighted mich,
Saide certesse *Syrinx* for thy sake it is my full intent
To make my comfort of these Reedes wherein thou doest lament:
And how that there of sundrie Reedes with wax together knit,
He made the Pipe which of hir name the Greekes call *Syrinx* yet.

For the two centuries (1580–1780) for which I assume primarily Latin sources for Pan, the story of Pan and the Judgment
of Midas (*Met.* XI, 146–193) is nearly as important, especially
for the eighteenth century, which read the sequel to the story of
Midas and the Golden Touch in the following elegant form: [16]

   Now loathing wealth, th' occasion of his woes,
   Far in the woods he [Midas] sought a calm repose;

In caves and grottos, where the nymphs resort,
And keep with mountain *Pan* their sylvan court.
Ah! had he left his stupid soul behind!
But his condition alter'd not his mind.

For where high *Tmolus* rears his shady brow,
And from his cliffs surveys the seas below,
In his descent, by *Sardis* bounded here,
By the small confines of *Hypaepa* there,
Pan to the nymphs his frolick ditties play'd,
Tuning his reeds beneath the chequer'd shade.
The nymphs are pleas'd, the boasting sylvan plays,
And speaks with slight of great *Apollo's* lays.
Tmolus was arbiter; the boaster still
Accepts the tryal with unequal skill.
The venerable judge was seated high
On his own hill, that seem'd to touch the sky.
Above the whisp'ring trees his head he rears,
From their encumbring boughs to free his ears;
A wreath of oak alone his temples bound,
The pendant acorns loosely dangled round.
In me your judge, says he, there's no delay:
Then bids the goatherd God begin, and play.
Pan tun'd the pipe, and with his rural song
Pleas'd the low taste of all the vulgar throng;
Such songs a vulgar judgment mostly please,
Midas was there, and *Midas* judg'd with these.

The mountain sire with grave deportment now
To *Phoebus* turns his venerable brow:
And, as he turns, with him the listning wood
In the same posture of attention stood.
The God his own *Parnassian* laurel crown'd,
And in a wreath his golden tresses bound,
Graceful his purple mantle swept the ground.
High on the left his iv'ry lute he rais'd,
The lute, emboss'd with glitt'ring jewels, blaz'd
In his right hand he nicely held the quill,
His easy posture spoke a master's skill.
The strings he touch'd with more than human art,
Which pleas'd the judge's ear, and sooth'd his heart;
Who soon judiciously the palm decreed,
And to the lute postpon'd the squeaking reed.

All, with applause, the rightful sentence heard,
Midas alone dissatisfy'd appear'd;
To him unjustly giv'n the judgment seems,

For *Pan's* barbarick notes he most esteems.
The lyrick God, who thought his untun'd ear
Deserv'd but ill a human form to wear,
Of that deprives him, and supplies the place
With some more fit, and of an ampler space:
Fix'd on his noddle an unseemly pair,
Flagging, and large, and full of whitish hair;
Without a total change from what he was,
Still in the man preserves the simple ass.

But the Roman Pans were not all so elegant. An anonymous nine-line poem, "Incerti ad Panem," made up of forty-eight epithets (for example, "Saltator") in the vocative, presents a Pan unwashed, hairy, goatish, fierce, inconstant, and noisy — an unusually frank glimpse at the logical result of postulating a god half-animal, in and of the countryside, and probably closer to the Pan that the Arcadians (or the Roman country folk) actually believed in than the well-scrubbed deity of Virgil.[17]

The Latin god Faunus has a role in Roman legend quite independent of the Greek Pan traditions, yet the Romans apparently believed him to be identical with Pan[18] and, as a result, Pan and Faunus have many overlapping functions. Many of the references to Faunus in Ovid's *Fasti* and in the *Aeneid*, for instance, have little or no connection with Pan. But a reference to Faunus lying in the fields at noon (*Fasti* IV, 762) has Theocritean overtones, and in a line like Horace's "Faune nympharum fugientum amator" (O Faunus, lover of the fleeing nymphs; *Odes* III, 18, 1), meter rather than distinction of meaning might have dictated the choice. In the second book of the *Fasti*, Faunus is given, for almost the only time in the history of Pan figures, a role both comic and undignified. Ovid can only fit it into Faunus' more typical roles of prophet and ruler by making a farfetched but amusing link between the tale of Faunus, Hercules, and Omphale (presumably based on a Greek original) and the Roman rituals he is discussing:

Veste Deus, lusus, fallentes lumina vestes
Non amat; et nudos ad sua sacra vocat. (II, 353–355)

(The god, betrayed by clothing, does not love deceiving garments and summons [only] the naked to his ceremonies.) When the story of Faunus' encounter with the transvestite Hercules and his humiliating expulsion is retold by Sidney, at the end of his masque *The Lady of May*, he restores the more appropriate designation of "Pan."

Within the classical framework the image of Pan, in spite of the wide variety of literary treatment, remained, as we have seen, relatively consistent. Yet parallel with the main stream of Greek, Alexandrian, and Roman literature, a "literarisch[er] Denkbegriff" [19] developed which was startlingly incompatible with the image of the Arcadian goat-god. At least as early as the Homeric Hymn to Pan, writers had been struggling, with varying degrees of implausibility, to account for the apparent derivation of "Pan" from *pān* meaning "all," [20] whereas the correct derivation appears to be from *pa-on* (grazer). The history of the Pan motif would gain as much in logic as it would lose in variety and charm if this etymology had been recognized from the beginning. The author of the Orphic Hymn to Pan made the "allness" of Pan essential and the pastoral characteristic peripheral. The Pan of the Orphic Hymn, as Roscher points out, [21] joins elements of the traditional popular beliefs to the abstract pantheistic conceptions of the philosophers; the two modes are not entirely blended, yet it is a fairly successful attempt to translate the latter into visual terms. Roscher subscribes in part to the usual theory that etymological confusion made possible this extension of Pan's form to include the heavens, the sea, earth, and fire — universal Nature — and the extension of his function, becoming Supreme Governor or "soul" of the World. [22]

A more consistent picture was developed by the Stoic philosophers with the aid of a schematic allegorical anatomy of Pan that becomes wearisomely familiar when followed from one medieval or Renaissance encyclopedist to the next. [23] According to Roscher, it is first found in the works of the Stoic philosopher Cornutus (fl. A.D. 39–65). The essence of the allegorical anatomy is contained in these lines of Cornutus: "Inferior pars hujus dei hispida est, & hircum refert, ad designandum asperitatem terrae. Superior autem pars similis est homini, nam aether, propterea quod in ipso ratio sita sit, tenet totius mundi imperium." (The lower part of this god is hairy, and recalls a goat, to designate the roughness of the earth. The upper part, however, is like a man, for heaven holds sway over the entire world, because in heaven itself reason is placed.)[24] The versions familiar in the Renaissance, based probably on Servius (A.D. 400)[25] rather than Cornutus, were more detailed. Here, for instance, is Isidore of Seville (A.D. 636), who follows Servius almost verbatim:

> Pan . . . deum rusticorum, quem in naturae similitudinem formaverunt; unde et Pan dictus est, id est, omne. Fingunt enim eum ex universali elementorum specie. Habet enim cornua in similitudinem radiorum solis et lunae. Distinctam maculis habet pellem, propter caeli sidera. Rubet eius facies, ad similitudinem aetheris. Fistulam septem calamorum gestat, propter harmoniam caeli in qua septem sunt soni et septem discrimina vocum. Villosus est, quia tellus est convestita et agitur ventis. Pars eius inferior foeda est, propter arbores et feras et pecudes. Caprinas ungulas habet, ut soliditatem terrae ostendat, quem volunt rerum et totius naturae deum: unde et Pan quasi omnia dicunt.

> Pan . . . the god of the rustics, whom they have formed in the shape of Nature; wherefore he is called Pan, that is, All. For they form him out of every kind of element. For he has horns in the shape of the rays of the sun and the moon. He has skin marked with spots, because of the stars of the sky. His face is red, in the likeness of the upper air. He carries a pipe with seven reeds, because of the harmony of heaven in which there are seven notes and seven distinctions of tones. He is hairy, since the earth is clothed and is stirred by the winds. His lower part is filthy, because of trees and wild beasts and herds. He has goat hoofs, to show forth the solidity of the earth, he whom they desire as the god of things and of all nature: whence they call him Pan, as if to say Everything.[26]

Many details have been added; some, such as Cornutus' emphasis on Pan's lasciviousness (allegorically interpreted) have been abandoned. But Cornutus' conception, adumbrated by Plato, of Pan's twofold nature as an emblem of the universe, which is made up of (goatish) earth and (human or divine) heaven (or the heavens), remained surprisingly constant.

The Renaissance encyclopedists attempted to present a variety of aspects and interpretations of Pan rather than to further a single point of view, yet the allegorical interpretation is generally given the most prominent position. Bacon's "Pan, or Nature," in *The Wisdom of the Ancients*, is the chief literary monument in English of the encyclopedic tradition.[27] He is concerned with presenting a particular point of view rather than an eclectic gathering of information. But he has relied chiefly on the allegorists both for sources (most of the Pan stories to be found in an independent reading of the mythical sources have been omitted) and for method: "Pan's horns touch heaven" since "universal forms of nature do ... reach up to God" (p. 290). The episode of Pan's battle with Cupid, beloved of Servius and the other allegorists, is taken to mean that matter seeks chaos, but is restrained by concord (p. 292).

The two streams, the Stoic (or schematically allegorical) and the Orphic, are, in most Renaissance sources, not easy to distinguish, although at times signs are given of the latter's separate existence. Lilius Gyraldus, for example, quotes Macrobius ("non sylvarum dominum, sed universae substantiae materialis dominatorem" — not the lord of the woods, but the ruler of universal material substance), in addition to the more usual "Phurnutus" (Cornutus) and Servius.[28] Natalis Comes quotes the first few lines of the Orphic Hymn to Pan and comments: "Nihil vero est aliud Pan quam natura ipsa a divina providentia, menteque; proficiscens ac procreata" (Truly Pan is nothing other than nature itself, coming forth and begotten from divine providence and intelligence).[29] On the whole, the Orphic "All," who is the ruler and soul of the universe, takes second place to the allegorical "All" who, anatomized and reunited, forms its emblem.

The Italian neo-Platonists developed a Pan based more directly on the Orphic Hymn and paired him, the "universal," with his opposite, the "particular," symbolized by Proteus. This symbolic Pan, conceived of in lofty philosophical terms, is difficult to employ in the workaday literary world which thrives on "Proteus," on what can be differentiated, individualized, and pictured on a human scale. Yet there is a painting of such a Pan; while attempting to confute the difficulty of visualizing him, Luca Signorelli's painting of a universal Pan, youthful and senti-

mental, with a half-moon for horns and traces of goats' feet, loses
the vivid if grotesque concreteness of the allegorical conception
without achieving the grandeur of the Orphic conception.[30]

The second great philological accident to alter the history of
the Pan motif occurred in the reign of Tiberius, and was recorded by Plutarch in his *Moralia* ("De Defectu Oraculorum,"
xvii).

As for death among such beings, I have heard the words of a man
who was not a fool nor an impostor. The father of Aemilianus the
orator, to whom some of you have listened, was Epitherses, who lived
in our town and was my teacher in grammar. He said that once
upon a time in making a voyage to Italy he embarked on a ship
carrying freight and many passengers. It was already evening when,
near the Echinades Islands, the wind dropped, and the ship drifted
near Paxi. Almost everybody was awake, and a good many had not
finished their after-dinner wine. Suddenly from the island of Paxi
was heard the voice of someone loudly calling Thamus, so that all
were amazed. Thamus was an Egyptian pilot, not known by name
even to many on board. Twice he was called and made no reply, but
the third time he answered; and the caller, raising his voice, said,
"When you come opposite to Palodes, announce that Great Pan is
dead." On hearing this, all, said Epitherses, were astounded and
reasoned among themselves whether it were better to carry out the
order or to refuse to meddle and let the matter go. Under the circumstances Thamus made up his mind that if there should be a
breeze, he would sail past and keep quiet, but with no wind and a
smooth sea about the place he would announce what he had heard.
So, when he came opposite Palodes, and there was neither wind nor
wave, Thamus from the stern, looking toward the land, said the words
as he had heard them: "Great Pan is dead." Even before he had
finished there was a great cry of lamentation, not of one person, but
of many, mingled with exclamations of amazement. As many persons
were on the vessel, the story was soon spread abroad in Rome, and
Thamus was sent for by Tiberius Caesar. Tiberius became so convinced of the truth of the story that he caused an inquiry and investigation to be made about Pan; and the scholars, who were numerous at his court, conjectured that he was the son born of Hermes
and Penelopê.

Moreover, Philip had several witnesses among the persons present
who had been pupils of the old man Aemilianus.[31]

The tale, as Plutarch tells it, is one of the best mystery stories

ever written: his matter-of-fact narrative method, unimpeach-
able witnesses, historical setting, and corroborative details all
seem to certify to its truth, and yet, as the scholars at the court of
Tiberius were the first to discover, it is very difficult to explain.

An evident, and odd, chronological coincidence made possible
the long series of interpretations, beginning with Eusebius (d.
A.D. 340), that placed Pan, at last, within the Christian frame of
reference. "So far Plutarch. But it is important to observe the
time at which he says that the death of the daemon took place.
For it was the time of Tiberius, in which our Saviour, making
His sojourn among men, is recorded to have been ridding human
life from daemons of every kind." [32] As the pagan deities were
demons, in the Christian view, Eusebius' explanation, equating
Pan with the daemon, seems natural and unforced; he is no more
precise about the date of the event than Plutarch himself had
been. Another tradition, less logical and more spectacular, grew
up as well:

> Viri sanctissimi afferunt eam vocem auditam e paxis ea nocte . . .
> xix anno tiberii: quo quidem christus passus est: qua voce miracula
> quodam ex sollitudiem desertorum scopulorum edita nunciabat illus
> dominum . . . passum. Quid non pan significat: nisi totum. Sic
> totius et universae naturae dominus passus erat . . . nos vero de Pane
> agimus, de quo melius apud Theodosium [Macrobius] cum dicat
> . . . non sylvarum dominum, sed universae substantiae materialis
> dominatorem . . . Cujus naturae vis universorum corporum sive illa
> divina sive terrena sint: componit essentiam: . . . quam licet ad
> Solem referat.

The holiest men declare that this voice was heard from Paxis that
night . . . in the nineteenth year of Tiberius' reign: at which time
indeed Christ died: who, with a voice miraculously issuing forth from
the solitude of the deserted rocks, was announcing that the Lord . . .
was dead. Now what does Pan mean, if not all. Thus the lord of all
and of universal nature had died . . . Truly we are dealing with the
Pan of whom better [is said] by Theodosius [Macrobius] when he
says [he is] not the lord of the woods, but the ruler of the material
substance of the universe . . . The strength of whose nature forms
the essence of universal bodies whether they are divine or earthly
. . . It is proper for this name to refer to the Sun.

Here Paulus Marsus (commentary on Ovid's *Fasti* I, 397, ca.

1482), writes as one repeating received tradition, but the identity of the "viri sanctissimi" who made this significantly more precise assertion of the date of the event is still unknown.

Two completely incompatible interpretations were now possible, and an army of commentators, taking their text from Plutarch and their gloss from Eusebius (Pan–demon) or from the tradition represented by Paulus Marsus (Pan–Christ), opted for one or the other, often with more literalism and fervor than their sources warrant.

But literary men found little advantage in the Pan–demon equivalence; when it occurs, as in Ronsard's *Hymne des Daimons* and Milton's *Paradise Regained*, it seems to owe more to the general Christian identification of pagan gods with devils than to the special case propounded by Eusebius, which was left to the commentators. The precedent for the Renaissance was probably set by Rabelais' elaboration of the Pan–Christ figure in *Le Quart Livre*, xxviii, where several arguments are skillfully blended: the chronological, "car cestuy très bon, très grand Pan, notre unique Servateur, mourut les Jérusalem, régnant en Rome Tibère César" (for this most good, most great Pan, our only Savior, died near Jerusalem, while Tiberius Caesar was reigning in Rome); the etymological "à bon droit peut il être en langage grégeois dit Pan, vu qu'il est le nôtre Tout" (in the Greek language he can quite rightly be called Pan, seeing that he is our All); the Orphic, in the manner of Macrobius and Paulus Marsus, "tout ce que sommes, tout ce que vivons, tout ce qu'avons" (all that we are, all that we live by, all that we have) — all derivable from the commentary on the *Fasti*, which he may well have known. But Rabelais introduces pastoral elements, new in this connection, with the mourning of universal nature, and with the explicit reference to Virgil (*Ecl.* II, 33), inviting comparison of Virgil's Pan the great shepherd, who loves both sheep and their shepherds too, with the biblical Good Shepherd of John 10:11. Further, Rabelais may have been the first to add "Dieu" to the Plutarchan formula "pan megas," "the great Pan," thus originating the form in which it re-echoes to the present day: "the great god Pan is dead." [33]

The two Christian schools of explication held the field for a long time, despite the occasional sniping of skeptics, of whom Reginald Scot is an early representative, at once cynical and ingenious in his rationalism: "*Thamus* having little to doo, thought to plaie with his companie, whom he might easilie overtake with such a jest . . . he being an old pilot, knew where some noise was usuall, by meanes of some eccho in the sea." But such skepticism was more characteristic of eighteenth-century mythography, as in the Abbé Banier's view that the story was a hoax perpetrated on Tiberius by his courtiers.[34]

The nineteenth century was the heyday in literature of Plutarch's theme of the Death of Pan, and of purely symbolic explanations for it. The richness of the symbolism depends for the most part on an opposition of Pan and Christ, in the Eusebian manner, although the Eusebian equivalence of Pan and the great Demon is rare. Toward the end of the nineteenth century, though, in accordance with the needs of a new mythography, literal explanations again seemed necessary, and some more satisfying to the modern temperament were devised, testifying not only to the ingenuity of the anthropologists, but also to the power of this story to compel attempts at rational explanation. Reinach's view, the most cogent and acceptable one, is that the event indeed occurred: however, the voices from the Isle of Paxi announced not the death of Pan ("O [human] Thamus, the great Pan is dead"), but the yearly ritual death of the god Thammuz ("Thammuz [who is] the all-great, is dead"). If this is true, a philological accident even odder than the one that made Pan "All" lies behind the whole tradition that "the great god Pan is dead."[35]

The literary importance of the controversies over Plutarch's story does not, fortunately, depend on the dozens of versions[36] provided in stodgy and undigested lumps by the information gatherers and polemicists. The condensed approximations of Plutarch's own words that most of them employed often resonate oddly, both stylistically and logically, in the contexts in which they are placed; one feels that it was too good a story to leave out, yet too odd a story to blend in.[37] Yet it was no doubt as the result of their efforts that the story became part of the well-read gentleman's intellectual store: both Sir Philip Sidney and Sir Thomas Browne, for example, sixty years apart, refer gracefully and in passing to the original story in a way that implies familiarity with the interpretations; [38] the story was not entirely the obscure property of the annotators by the time Spenser, Milton, and Marvell elevated it into poetry of the first rank.

ELIZABETHAN AND JACOBEAN MISCELLANY

Allusions to Pan are not very common in English literature before the 1580's, and those that do occur are likelier to derive from encyclopedic than from classical sources. One such example is Chaucer's allusion to "Pan, that men clepe god of kynde"; [39] another is Gower's "Pan, which is the god of kinde / With love wrastlede and was overcome," [40] both in the formulas of Servius. Our subject begins, for practical purposes, with the publication of Geoffrey Whitney's *Choice of Emblemes* in 1586. His version, in Poulter's Measure, of Ovid's Judgment of Midas set a pattern for the long sequence of emblematic-satiric interpretations in which Pan always represents the wrong, the stupid, the prejudiced choice, Midas' "perversum iudicium":

> Presumptuous Pan, did strive Apollos skill to passe:
> But Midas gave the palme to PAN: wherefore the
>   eares of asse
> Apollo gave the Iudge: which doth all Iudges teache
> To iudge with knowledge, and advise, in matters
>   paste their reache.[41]

Thomas Campion compresses the whole narrative into his lyric "To His Sweet Lute Apollo Sung." Lyly's lyric, "Pan's Syrinx Was a Girl Indeed" (like Shelley's "Hymn of Pan"), argues Pan's case, based largely on Ovid's Pan and Syrinx story, in the larger dramatic context of Ovid's Midas story. Lyly's play *Midas* (1592) thus unites two of the most typically Elizabethan variants of the Pan motif. But where Wyatt and most of the authors who adapted Whitney's "Perversa Iudicia" saw only one reasonable outcome to the competition, Lyly's lyric and dialogue make a vigorous and not unsuccessful defense of Pan's whole way of life and, in particular, of his "popular" art, before the nymphs make the inevitable decision in favor of the "highbrow" art of Apollo: "Beleeve me Apollo, our groves are pleasanter than your heavens, our Milk-maides than your Goddesses, our rude ditties to a pipe than your sonnets to a lute," says Pan, and Apollo himself admits that "seeing it happens in earth, we must be judged of those on earth" (IV, 1).

About forty years later, George Sandys, in his commentary on the *Metamorphoses*, developed the Pan–Midas story into a three-fold allegory, cultural, religious, and political. The chief satirical point drawn by Lyly, and most later authors, corresponds to Sandys' cultural allegory: Midas stupidly chooses "illiterate rusticity," of which Pan is the emblem, in preference to the profounder delights offered by Apollo and the Muses.

The same point is made more sharply and coherently in Thomas Heywood's *Love's Mistris* (1636). Midas' choice of entertainment in preference to art determines the structure of the entire play: the story of Cupid and Psyche, handled seriously and lyrically, is a play-within-a-play, the masque. In the course of the comic episodes which frame this masque, Midas rejects it in favor of the antimasque, a burlesque competition between two clowns, representing Pan and Apollo, in which the Apollonian clown sings doggerel barely more elevated than that of his opponent. The real moral is not contained in this parody of the traditional pastoral singing contest, but in the contest waged for Midas' allegiance and, by extension, the audience's, between the whole of the masque, representing the artistic taste of "Apuleius," and the whole of the antimasque, representing the crude entertainment appreciated by the uncultivated Midas.[42]

Of course the Cupid and Psyche story itself allows Pan a minor role, but having chosen to employ a comic Pan in the subplot, Heywood had to forgo the use of an Apuleian Pan in the main plot.[43] Likewise, Thomas Shadwell, in his feeble version of the same theme (*Psyche, A Tragedy*, 1673), replaces Pan by an unnamed "River-God," who saves Psyche from suicide. Pan has another role in Shadwell's play, that of introducing the entertainment in which Psyche's story is told, and, as in Heywood, he can hardly play a part in both frame and inner plot.

Pan's role as a master of ceremonies in pastoral drama can be explicit, as in Shadwell, or implicit, as in all the shepherds' festivals and other pastoral frolics of which he is either the patron saint (Jonson, Fletcher, Shirley) [44] or at least a conspicuous participant (Heywood, even Marmion). This largely ornamental and dramatically trivial function was a tradition more deeply rooted in the nonsatiric drama than was any classical Pan story. Yet his ceremonial functions justify Pan, if not as a character or even an idea, at least as a rhetorical device, "a genius loci or patron saint, whom everybody worships, but nobody hears or sees." The best example of the dramatic use of Pan as "an icon or a name" [45] to generate pastoral atmosphere is found in John Fletcher's *The Faithful Shepherdess*. Pan directs the action through his agent, the Satyr. The latter, a happy blend, as it were, of Puck (with his Oberon perpetually offstage) and the Guardian Spirit of Milton's *Comus*, has as his chief function the protection of chastity — a role which clashes curiously with the accepted (though at this period neglected) connotation of both "satyr" and "Pan." "Pan, the father of our sheep . . . Thou that keepst us chaste and free" (I, ii). There is obviously some accretion of Christ qualities here. Fletcher had trouble pouring the new wine of the Christian ethic into the old bottle of the pastoral convention, but he gave an admirable hint to Milton of how the pastoral drama might be combined with the morality play.

But oaths, prayers, and rites, in the manner of Theocritus,[46] can neither clothe the icon in divinity nor quicken him into life, any more than can festivals to Pan that are merely the excuse for song and dance. There was, nevertheless, one way to make Pan seen and heard, as well as believed in, and that was to place him not on stage, but in the audience, and at its center. Pan as master of ceremonies links the inner ceremony of the shepherds' festival with the outer ceremony of the dramatic performance itself. When identified with the real master of the ceremony, that is, the king, Pan links the whole dramatic performance with the real world in which it is played. Ben Jonson's *Pan's*

Anniversarie, while seeming to refer to a narrow, invented pastoral world, in fact refers more generally to the world at large, and most specifically to the court itself, where King James, on his birthday, was to be honored as poet and hunter, as molder of manners, as the protector of "shepherds." [47] Ceremonial identifications of James I and Pan were almost as common as the equally conventional identifications of Queen Elizabeth with pastoral Diana had been; the allegory is less satisfactory partly because Pan had by that time been used to symbolize so many different people, both lesser and greater than James I, and partly because the resemblance, if the mind were allowed to stray ever so slightly from the strict terms of the allegory, was a considerably less flattering one. Decorum could only be maintained by neglecting numerous inconvenient aspects of the Pan symbol, including any connected with the goat-god's shaggy, animal, material presence.

If one takes a broader literary context than the Jacobean masque, the question of ceremonial identifications becomes very complicated indeed. As Ovid's Midas story supplied the basic material for the satiric Pans, so elaborations of two Virgilian concepts (both from the second Eclogue) provided the starting points for the long ladder of ceremonial identifications; the same two concepts, of course, were of central importance in nonallegorical pastoral as well. At the top the ladder starts from Pan's fundamental character as a shepherd — "Pan curat oves oviumque magistros" (*Ecl.* II, 33) — and makes possible Pan's identification with God the Father, with Christ, and, by analogy, with their earthly representatives, kings and popes. Synthesis with the Plutarchan Pan–Christ identification of the theologians is, of course, possible at any point in this part of the scale, but is, in pastoral contexts, curiously difficult to demonstrate with certainty.

The ladder begins at the other end with Pan's character as a pastoral piper — "Pan primum calamos cera coniungere plures / Instituit" (32–33); thus, on the ascending scale, "Pan" becomes a suitable hyperbolic compliment for a poet, for a patron of poets, and then, overlapping with the "shepherd" analogy, for a king as chief patron of poets. The poems of William Browne, and especially the commendatory verses written to Browne by his fellow poets, are a mine of examples of this second category. Taking the ladder as a whole, Spenser's *Shepheardes Calender* is unrivaled in English literature for its joyous profusion of ceremonial identifications. The problem of sorting out Spenser's Pans is greatly simplified by considering not the irreconcilable differences in meaning [48] but the remarkable similarity in function. Precedent for almost all the different identifications can be found in the poems of Marot, Spenser's chief source, or in other continental authors, though none of them put as many different meanings into any one work as Spenser did.

In "Aprill," lines 50–54 and 90–94, we find the royal identification of the sort used in Jonson's masques. As Pan and Syrinx are the parents of "fayre *Eliza*, Queene of shepheardes all" (line 34), Pan must be (as E. K. points out) King Henry VIII. An analogous identification is found in Marot's "Eglogue de Marot au Roy soubz les noms de Pan et Robin" (1539), which gives an extensive pastoral allegory relating the king (Francis I) to the shepherd-god Pan.[49] In an age of the divine right of kings, it was not surprising that a supplication to "Pan, dieu souverain" (sovereign god), an earthly monarch guarding "Parcz, et brebis, et les maistres d'iceulx" (sheepfolds, and sheep, and the masters thereof; p. 343), should closely resemble in mood and wording a prayer to "Dieu soubz la personne de Pan, dieu des Bergiers" (God in the character of Pan, god of the Shepherds), responsible, likewise, for "conservant noz loges et noz parcz" (caring for our huts and our sheepfolds; p. 391). But in the former poem, Marot is asking Francis I for patronage, while in the latter he is complaining to God of the "faux pasteurs . . . qui . . . ton sainct temple ont pollu" (false shepherds . . . who . . . have polluted thy sacred temple; p. 394). Spenser's lines in "Maye" (51–54) offer a close parallel to Marot's:

> I muse, what account both these will make,
> The one for the hire, which he doth take,
> And th'other for leauing his Lords taske,
> When great *Pan* account of shepeherdes shall aske.

In both cases "God" rather than Christ seems to be "buried in the authors conceipt"; if so, E. K.'s long and erudite note at this point on Plutarch's story of the Death of Pan is irrelevant. Indeed "Maye," line 111, "For *Pan* himself was their inheritaunce," is glossed by E. K. as "God." There are two places in later Eclogues where the identification of Pan and Christ is unequivocal:

> And wonned not the great God *Pan,*
>> upon mount *Olivet*:
> Feeding the blessed flocke of *Dan,*
>> which dyd himselfe beget?

> O shepheard great,
>> that bought his flocke so deare . . .
>> ("Julye" 49–54)

and, similarly:

> Marrie that great *Pan* bought with deare borrow,
>> To quite it from the blacke bowre of sorrowe.
>> ("September" 96–97)

E. K.'s gloss about the Death of Pan would have been a possible one for either of those passages, but even there it would not have been an essential one. Neither these passages nor any other Pan passage in *The Shepheardes Calender* contain evidence of a knowledge of the Plutarchan story. If the lines derived from Rabelais, as seems likely, Spenser subtracted all of the lengthy reference to the Plutarchan story, which Rabelais was in fact explicating. Marot's "Complaincte d'un Pastoreau Chrestien à Dieu soubz la personne de Pan," mentioned earlier, has also been suggested as a source, but, like Boccaccio's fourteenth Eclogue (lines 23 and 77), it identifies not Pan and Christ, but "the Christian and the Arcadian divinities." [50]

Having established the Pan–Christ identification in the July Eclogue, Spenser goes on to use "mighty *Pan*" in line 144 in a way that might mean God, if we accept E. K.'s gloss of "the brethren twelue" in the preceding line as the twelve sons of Jacob; Spenser might have had in mind the twelve apostles as well,[51] which interpretation would permit a delicate balance of

God and Christ identifications in one image. But a few stanzas later, by a logical antithesis of Christ and anti-Christ, the Pope at Rome can be referred to as "theyr Pan" ("Julye" 179), that is, the false Pan.[52] Thus the imagery of this eclogue can be read in terms of relatively consistent Pan–Christ identifications.

Theological and pastoral meanings merge in the December eclogue. It gracefully elaborates Virgil's "Pan curat oves" (Pan cares for the sheep), as E. K. points out, in its plea to "soueraigne *Pan* thou God of shepheards all," which parallels Marot's plea to Francis I to protect the poet from the storms of poverty, and seems to refer, on a deeper level, to the Christian divinity ("over-arching Providence," as M. Y. Hughes put it), who alone can soften the winter of old age and death. Once the autobiographical section which follows this initial plea begins, Pan becomes merely the god of pastoral poetry, with whom — as in Virgil's "Pan etiam Arcadia dicat se iudice victum" (Even Pan, with Arcady judging, would declare himself beaten; *Ecl.* IV, 59) — the poet has a right to compare himself.

> To *Pan* his owne selfe pype I neede not yield.
> For if the flocking Nymphes did folow *Pan*,
> The wiser Muses after *Colin* ranne.
> ("December" 46–48)

In "June" (65–70) Colin had been more modest about his poetic achievement:

> Of muses *Hobbinol*, I conne no skill . . .
> For sith I heard, that *Pan* with *Phoebus* strove . . .
> I neuer lyst presume to Parnasse hyll . . .

But Pan is a useful patron saint at this point: Colin comes from the cheerless northern hills down to the sunny south, where Pan (perhaps a fellow poet, as occasionally in Marot) performs in court entertainments for Queen Elizabeth.

The lesser art of "homely shepheards quill," Pan's poetic standard, is rejected in December; Pan's divinity is rejected as well: "Perdie God was he none." The initial situation set out in January has, in the long run, been reversed. Pan has not pitied Colin's pains as a lover,[53] and Colin's piping does not continue

to please "rude Pan" indefinitely. "December" strongly reinforces the bare hints given in "November" 8 and 10 that there are more important things in art and life than pastoral songs and pastoral emotions. The Pan who continues to matter and the Pan who must be rejected, one from each end of the allegorical scale, dwell side by side in the same eclogue.

The apparent variety of Spenser's chameleon Pan is in fact limited to the relatively dignified ceremonial or pastoral functions that we have seen in the *Shepheardes Calender*. When Spenser needed a goat-god as the hero of an erotic pursuit, he twice used the name "Faunus."[54] At several points in *The Faerie Queene* the exemplars of lustful, terrifying brutishness are designated "satyrs," and the leader of such a band is once called "Sylvanus" (I, vi, 7–33).[55] Twice Spenser seems deliberately to avoid a Pan reference: in the *Epithalamion* he follows Servius, rather than Virgil, in replacing Pan with Endymion, but leaves in a reference to the wool with which Pan lured Cynthia; in "Virgils Gnat" the words "O Faunes" (line 145) correspond to "O Panes" in line 94 of the *Culex*.

It seems curious, in an age so fond of emblem and allegory, that the possibilities offered by Andrea Alciati's emblem "Natura" should be relatively neglected:

> Men worship nature by the name of Pan
> A man half goat withal a goat half man
> Above a man, where sacred reason raignes;
> Borne in the heart and toured in the braines
> Below a Goat, since nature propagates
> By coiture, in all whom life instates.
> Rough goats, as other animals, expresse
> Ranke luxury, and brutish lusts excesse
> Some say that wisdome governes in the heart;
> Some in the braine: none in the nether part.[56]

The allegories which made Pan "All" or "Nature," of which the above is an example (although the encyclopedists' lofty interpretations are debased here to the level of the proverbial), were presumably familiar. Indeed Lyly and Jonson (and doubtless many others) make brief and frivolous references to Pan as

"All" — though it seems to be more an etymological joke than an Orphic one. Yet Pan is used chiefly as the emblem of rustic ignorance, and his allegorical role is, for the most part, limited to the cold ceremonial convention. At their best, these allegories drew from an extremely limited list of Pan's attributes, since neither monarch nor poet could be endowed with hoofs, shaggy legs, or (least of all) horns. Further, the convention never returns to touch the earth of a mythical source, and inevitably becomes ever thinner. It will never be better than at its cheerfully vigorous beginning in the *Shepheardes Calender;* it fades quietly from sight in the pages of Norris of Bemerton and Dryden.

So that, well into the seventeenth century, the situation is this: Orphic Pan belongs only to scholars; the shaggy Pan of sex and terror is likely to be replaced by a satyr; Plutarchan Pan has perhaps been found by Spenser, but has only demonstrably been found by E. K. Spenser, at any rate, always gives some intellectual content to his Pans; his successors use chiefly the brief, stereotyped, emptily decorative pastoral allusion, a mere device (like Warner's title, *Pan His Syrinx or Pipe*) for bringing in Virgilian or other pastoral associations. Some nineteenth-century versions of pastoral Pan oddly enough give a richer and deeper picture of the goat-god than was apparently possible in this most pastoral of literary centuries. Yet the process of enriching the limited scope of the "pure" pastoral begins with Milton, whose coming appears to be prophesied in these lines from the *Arcadia*:

> Who doubts but Pas' fine pipe again will bring
> The ancient praise to Arcad shepherds' skill?
> Pan is not dead, since Pas begins to sing.[57]

MILTON AND OTHERS

Pan was not a helpful poetic concept for most seventeenth-century poets. For the Metaphysicals he was, of course, part of the "goodly exiled train of gods and goddesses"; the Cavaliers preferred to use Cupid in their mythological conceits. But Milton, as we see in *Arcades* (ca. 1633), could turn a ceremonial compliment more gracefully than the Jacobeans:

> Though *Syrinx* your *Pans* Mistres were,
> Yet *Syrinx* well might wait on her. (106–107)[58]

More than that, while playing on its ceremonial connotations, he could give such a compliment dramatic motivation and relevance:

> . . . Hail forren wonder
> Whom certain these rough shades did never breed
> Unlesse the Goddes that in rurall shrine
> Dwell'st here with *Pan*, or *Silvan* . . . (*Comus* 265–268)

The Lady can assess this compliment at its true worth, for she knows how "prosperous growth" (270) can become the excuse for orgies of sensual excess. "Bounteous Pan" (176) might be in himself morally neutral or beneficent, but in the context of Comus' rhetoric he seems to become of the wassailers' party; Pan's worshipers cannot be expected to honor virtue. Milton wisely transferred to Jove and his agent, the Guardian Spirit, the function of guarding chastity that Fletcher had somewhat incongruously assigned to Pan and the Satyr. "Pan's holiday," innocent enough in most pastorals, almost a true Christian rite in *The Faithful Shepherdess*, becomes, more logically, the occasion when "In wanton dance they praise the bounteous Pan, / And thank the gods amiss" (*Comus* 176–177).

In the *Epitaphium Damonis* (1640), Pan asleep under an oak in the summer noon (51–52) is simply an element of the pastoral scene (as is the Faunus of line 32), but in the fifth Elegy (1629), Nature's bounty and Nature's rapine are inextricably entangled:

> Per sata luxuriat fruticetaque Maenalius Pan,
> Vix Cybele mater, vix sibi tuta Ceres. (125–126)

(Through grain fields and through copses Maenalian Pan runs riot: Mother Cybele and Ceres can scarcely find safety for themselves.) The point is made even clearer in the parallel example of Faunus (127): "Atque aliquam cupidus praedatur

Oreada Faunus" (lustful Faunus would gladly seize upon some Oread). In this same Elegy, Sylvanus, not Pan, is described as "Semicaperque Deus, semideusque caper" (the God half-goat, the goat half-god; 122), in a phrase which corresponds to Alciati's formula for Pan in his emblem "Nature": "semicaprumque hominem, semivirumque Deum" (the man half-goat, the God half-man). The significant differences are that Milton omits the middle ground of humanity that Alciati places between goat and god, and that Milton, at this point, is not interested in passing moral judgment. It is also clear that, unlike Spenser, Milton does not intend to draw a sharp distinction between one goat-god and another, between pastoral Pan and lustful Faunus. Here as in *Comus* ("Pan or Silvan" 268), as in *Paradise Lost* IV, 707–708, as in *Paradise Regained* II, 190–191, the terms "Pan," "Faunus," and "Sylvanus" are virtually interchangeable.

In Book IV of *Paradise Lost*, Milton exploits Pan's pastoral associations on two distinct levels of truth, one poetic, one religious. In lines 266–268, Pan is a pictorial metaphor in a "real," theologically acceptable Garden of Eden:

> Universal *Pan*
> Knit with the *Graces* and the *Hours* in dance
> Led on th'Eternal Spring.

At once the type of reference shifts, and Daphne and Bacchus, among others, form part of an extended negative mythical comparison designed, as so often in Milton, to add the poetic richness of myth while maintaining its falsehood. A few hundred lines later in this same book, Pan himself is reduced to a similar level of merely complimentary comparison: the beauty of the "feignd" bower of Pan, Faunus, and Sylvanus is used to highlight the greater beauty of Eve's real bower. The pastoral allusions (cf. *Ep. Dam.* 52–53) are familiar from Renaissance poetry; it is the key adjective "universal," vital to the Orphic Hymn and to the encyclopedists, but hitherto rare in English poetry, that makes it possible virtually to juxtapose a "true" Pan and a "false" one. In essence, in *Paradise Lost* Milton has enriched the idea of Pan as a universal deity [59] by combining it with more vividly pictorial details from classical poetry (perhaps as interpreted in much Renaissance painting), and then associating it with the natural bounty that Pan represented, less beneficently and more sensually, in *Comus* and the fifth Elegy.

An entirely different literary development lies behind the equation of Pan in *On the Morning of Christ's Nativity* (1629, thus at about the same time as Elegy v), not with a universal deity but, more specifically, with Christ himself:

> The Shepherds on the Lawn,
> Or ere the point of dawn,
> 　Sate simply chatting in a rustick row;
> Full little thought they than,
> That the mighty *Pan*
> 　Was kindly com to live with them below. (viii, 85–90)

The influence of Plutarch is much clearer here than it was in the case of Spenser; it is especially clear in parts of the Ode that do not relate to Pan — stanzas xix to xxii, which detail the deaths of the pagan gods. Pan is the one god whose death cannot possibly be included; for the purposes of a Nativity ode, Milton has to change the occasion of the Pan–Christ identification from the Crucifixion[60] to the Nativity. Milton's version differs from most previous interpretations (and from most later ones) in that it does not attempt even consistency with the Plutarchan story, let alone an explanation of it. The actual event "in the reign of Tiberius" could not in any case have been the birth of Christ; an identification of Pan and Christ renders impossible the only logical connection that could be made between the birth of Christ and the death of Pan, that is, a Pan–demon identification.

Of course it is perfectly possible to separate the Cessation of Oracles from the Death of Pan, even though Plutarch gives the latter as his chief exemplum of the possibility of the former. Many people discussed one without the other,[61] but it was very uncommon to associate the two again without mentioning their joining link as found in Plutarch's argument. In effect Milton has merged Spenser's Pan–Christ, the god of shepherds, with E. K.'s gloss on the Death of Pan. He could have done this without the help of a precedent, but in one of the sources commonly cited for this part of the *Nativity*, Giles Fletcher's *Christs Victorie and Triumph* (1610), the elements that distinguish Milton's account from earlier ones are in fact present. Most important, the Cessation of Oracles is associated with the Nativity:

> The cursed Oracles were all struck dumb;
> To see their SHEPHERD, the poor shepherds press. (II, lxxvi)

The Pan–Christ identification is only made explicit in a later passage, and there it is more figurative than Milton's would be:

> Ah, foolish Shepherds! who were wont t'esteem,
> Your God all rough, and shaggy-hair'd to be;
> And yet far wiser Shepherds than ye deem,
> For who so poor (tho' who so rich) as HE,
> When sojourning with us in low degree,
> He wash'd his flocks in *Jordan's* spotless tide. (IV, xxxvii)

The gap between these two passages, like the gap in the Nativity Ode between the Cessation of Oracles and the Pan–Christ identification, forestalls detailed examination of their relation to the original story and to each other. Fletcher, unlike Milton and Spenser, sees and exploits the paradox inherent in identifying Christ with a shaggy goat-god, although his solution, introducing another, less relevant paradox, "For who so poor (tho' who so rich) as HE," lacks the point and pungency of the best metaphysical conceits.

It is a long step from the Pan–Christ of Milton's earliest allusion to the Pan–devil of his latest; the whole series of Milton's allusions to Pan gives evidence, not of a unified development from the one concept to the other, but of a continued willingness to accept mythical material from varied and mutually incompatible sources. In *Paradise Regained*, Pan is again associated with sexuality, but the notion of beneficent fecundity that moderated Milton's judgment of him in the fifth Elegy and to some extent even in *Comus* is no longer present. Pan, like the other woodland gods, is a disguise in which devils may perpetrate sexual crimes, as Satan makes clear in his charge against Belial:

Too long, then layst thy scapes on names adored
Apollo, Neptune, Jupiter, or *Pan*,
Satyr or Faun or Silvan. (II, 189–191)

Pan is, of course, a fitting emblem of the devil's sexual nature,
but in this passage his special fitness is nullified; he is not more
libidinous than Jupiter or Apollo. Milton's Pan–demon has to
be explicated in terms of the traditional equivalence of all pagan
deities with devils. The passage is an allusion, "without much
strangeness added to it," [62] to the Ovidian amours of the gods,
as seen through Puritan eyes jaundiced by Patristic interpretations, rather than a comment, in the manner of the fifth Elegy,
on the sexual aspect of Pan's devil nature. The rather obscure
poems of Milton's contemporary Henry More show traces of
a much more "Gothic" Pan–demon, part of a tradition that
conceived of Pan as having a special claim to devildom, sur-
passing that of such elegant Olympians as Apollo and Neptune.

Eusebius' equation of Pan with a master demon has already
been mentioned; equally relevant is his recounting of Porphyry's tale that nine worshipers of Pan died of fright after behold-
ing the god (*Praep. Ev.* 208a, 189c–d, 190b). Mantuan sees Pan
as a diabolical pagan deity:

At neque nos tempus soli praevidimus illud:
Praevidere alii lemures quoque . . .
Scimus et ex gelidis tepidum manasse cruorem
Fontibus, et noctu medias ululasse per urbes
Pane truces agitante lupos rabiemque ferente.

Nor do we alone foresee that time:
Others have foreseen specters too . . .
We know that warm blood has dripped from the frozen
                                                         fountains,
And that fierce wolves have howled in the middle of cities at night,
Driven on by frenzy-bringing Pan.[63]

Ronsard's *Hymne des Daimons* (1555) gathers together a
variety of demon lore including

Les uns aucunes fois se transforment en Fées,
En Dryades des bois, en Nymphes, & Napées,
En Faunes bien souvent, en Satyres, & Pans,

Qui ont le corps pelu, marqueté comme Fans,
Ils ont l'orteil de Bouc, & d'un Chevreil l'oreille,
La corne d'un Chamois, & la face vermeille
Comme un rouge Croissant: & dançent toute nuict
Dedans un carrefour, ou prés d'une eau qui bruict. (331–338)

Some are transformed at times into Fairies,
Into woodland Dryads, into Nymphs of field and dell,
Often into Fauns, into Satyrs and Pans,
Whose bodies are hairy and speckled like Fawns,
They have the hoofs of a he-goat and the ears of a roebuck,
The horns of a chamois and faces crimsoned
Like a red crescent-moon, and they dance through the night
At a crossroads, or near a murmuring brook.

In his concluding lines, oddly reminiscent of the *Orphic Hymn* to Pan, Ronsard endows all demons with one property of Pan:

O Seigneur Eternel, en qui seul gist ma foy . . .
Donne moy, que jamais je ne trouve en ma voye
Ces Paniques terreurs, mais O Seigneur, envoye
Loing de la Chrestienté, dans le païs des Turcz,
Ces Larves, ces Daimons, ces Lares, & Lemurs.[64]

O Lord Eternal, in whom alone dwells my faith . . .
Grant that I never find in my path
These Panic terrors, but, O Lord, send
Far from the Christian world, into the land of the Turks,
These specters, these demons, these spirits and hobgoblins.

The *Orphic Hymn* concludes (in Thomas Taylor's translation):

Fanatic Pan, thy humble suppliant hear . . .
Drive panic Fury too, wherever found,
From human kind, to earth's remotest bound.

Henry More's equation of Pan and demon in his *Praeexistency of the Soul* (ca. 1647) is more explicitly sexual than Mantuan's or Ronsard's. More makes Pan emblematic of the beastly element in human nature, as if only half of Alciati's Pan emblem had seemed relevant to him:

So we as stranger Infants elsewhere born
Can not divine from what spring we did flow
Ne dare these base alliances to scorn,
Nor lift our selves a whit from hence below,

Ne strive our Parentage again to know;
Ne dream we once of any other stock,
Since foster'd upon *Rheas* knees we grow,
In Satyres arms with many a mow and mock
Oft danc'd, and hairy *Pan* our cradle oft hath rock'd.

But *Pan* nor *Rhea* be our Parentage
We been the Of-spring of all-seeing *Jove*.

One scene in this poem is a Witches' Sabbath presided over by the "Goat," Satan; More looks forward to the time when "filthy lust" and "sinfull dust" cease to be part of the human condition, for

Pans pipe shall then be mute, and Satyrs heel
Shall cease to dance ybrent in scorching fire.

More's most "Gothic" interpretation is in *The Argument of Psychozoia or, the Life of the Soul*:

I hear such sounds as Adams brood would fright.
The dolefull echoes from the hollow hill
Mock howling wolves: the woods with black bedight
Answer rough Pan, his pipe and eke his skill,
And all the Satyr-routs rude whoops and shoutings shrill.[65]

Such interpretations are extremely uncommon in English poetry, dominated as it was by the more positive view of Pan induced by the pastoral tradition. Milton's slight hints and More's explicit statements of such possibilities are the only precursors that I know of in English for the "Gothic" mode of interpretation, later so important in prose fiction.

Similarly, extended allegories of Christ as Pan are rare in English; there is nothing comparable to the *auto sacramental* of Calderón, *El Verdadero Dios Pan* (1670), in which the story of Pan and Luna becomes Christ's loving pursuit of the human soul (not unlike some medieval allegorizations of Apollo and Daphne). Calderón of course takes advantage of the pun on "Pan" and "bread" available in Spanish. He concludes with a Plutarchan "El dios Pan es el que ha muerto" (He who has died is the god Pan; line 2269) and a Rabelais-like "pues si es el Todo el que ha muerto" (indeed, he who has died is All; 2273). Andrew Marvell, perhaps, comes closest to such an allegory, in his *Clorinda and Damon*, where the claims of spirituality, represented by "great *Pan*," the god of shepherds, triumph over the temptations of carnality; but it is one level of artificial literary pastoral triumphing over another, since Marvell does not follow Spenser, Giles Fletcher, and Milton in their use of rustic "simple shepherds" to accompany Christ's entry into Pan's pastoral world. Marvell concludes, however, with a hint of a "universal" Pan in his pastoral setting:

> Of *Pan* the flowry Pastures sing . . .
> For all the World is our *Pan's* Quire.

A more original contribution to the Pan tradition appears in Marvell's *The Garden*, where the neat turn in the fourth stanza provides the best "metaphysical" Pan in English:

> The *Gods*, that mortal Beauty chase,
> Still in a Tree did end their race.
> *Apollo* hunted *Daphne* so,
> Only that She might Laurel grow.
> And *Pan* did after *Syrinx* speed,
> Not as a Nymph, but for a Reed.[66]

Lines 201–214 of Marvell's *The First Anniversary of the Government Under O.C.* (1655) invite comparison with the *Nativity* as a treatment of the Plutarchan story of the Death of Pan. Like Cowley and Norris, the other two poetic contemporaries of Milton who refer to Plutarch, Marvell returns to the orthodox interpretation. The "Panique groan, / As if that Natures self were overthrown" (lines 203–204) relates the near death of Cromwell to the death of Christ, at which time this and other portents are supposed to have taken place. "The vaulted Marbles rent" echoes the verse in the Gospel of Matthew (27.51) that biblical commentators tended to gloss at this time with a reference to Plutarch; the "dying Chorus" (line 211) and the imagery of shipwreck echo the "resounding shore" and "loud lament" into which Milton had transmuted Plutarch's coastal geography. The Death of Pan is by now suitable imagery for the death of great men ("kings and potentates," as E. K. put it); a rough ceremonial identification of Cromwell and Pan is established through this half panegyric, half mock-heroic device.

In his *Pastoral on the Death of his Sacred Majesty King Charles the Second* (1685), John Norris of Bemerton employed this device with devastating literalism and ineffectiveness, simply returning to the imagery of the pastoral elegy, in which Pan is the king:

> Nature her self perceivd Pan's mighty Fate . . .
> And almost sympathiz'd with him to Death.[67]

The flowering of the Plutarchan panegyric, however, came not in England, but in Germany, where, in 1679, the words "der grosse Pan ist todt!" (the great Pan is dead!) introduced a long and wordy funeral oration in honor of the great man of Breslau, Christian Hoffman von Hoffmanwaldau. "Wolte GOTT! diese Unglueckstimme were nur auff dem das Ionische Meer durchstreichenden und laengst verfaulten Egyptischen Schiffe gehoeret nicht aber den 18 April letzthin das Schif dieser Stadt durch ein Panisches Schrecken erschuettert worden. Unser Pan . . . ein Bild der Natur . . . so viel als Alles heisset." (Would to GOD! that this voice of misfortune had only been heard on that Egyptian ship, crossing the Ionian Sea and now long decayed, and had not, indeed, shattered the ship of this city with a Panic terror on April 18 this year. Our Pan . . . a picture of Nature . . . rightly called All.[68]

Abraham Cowley's brief allusion to the Death of Pan in his *On the Death of Mr. Crashaw* (ca. 1649) gives clearer evidence than Milton's or Marvell's allusions as to how the story could be made useful to English poets. Unlike Marvell, Cowley uses it in a cultural rather than a personal context: for the first (but not the last) time, it becomes a symbol in intellectual history. As the death of Pan (Christ) "long since all Oracles broke," there is no longer any justification for the regrettable continuance of mythical poetry — compare Mrs. Browning's epochmaking version of the same idea, couched in very different poetic diction.

It will soon become apparent that Milton is the most important single figure in the pre-Romantic development of the Pan motif. He can exploit the ceremonial, complimentary Pan and the Virgilian or Theocritean resonances of the name as well as any Elizabethan poet can, though he sometimes does so only to refute them. He remembered that a sylvan deity could be "semicaperque Deus; semideusque caper"; his Pan–Christ identification gains significance and poetic value from its association with the Cessation of Oracles. In addition Milton establishes Pan's role as an emblem of fecundity and bestial sexuality, extending the latter concept by making him the cloak for a devil. Then, in a contrast which makes the clash of Pope and Henry VIII within the "chameleon" Pan of Spenser seem mild in comparison, Milton provides an Orphic Pan as well (of particular interest to the Romantic poets), a Pan both "universal" and beneficent. In short, later English authors now have virtually the whole scale of possible Pan references to play upon. It is a minor oddity, symptomatic, of course, of much larger trends in literary history, that for a hundred and thirty years no one takes up the challenge.

THE RESTORATION AND THE EIGHTEENTH CENTURY (1670–1810)

It is hardly surprising that no period of literature since the Middle Ages shows less variety, abundance, and originality in its Pan figures than does the Restoration and the eighteenth century. The Neo-Classicists were curiously uninterested in classical mythology and curiously wooden in their use of it. Thus my first generalizations will be negative ones: during this period we will hear next to nothing of Plutarchan Pan, of allegorical or Orphic Pans, of the Pan of sex and terror; a century and a half passes before the Romantics pick up the threads left by Milton and Spenser. But there are still three facets of the motif that will repay a brief investigation: the terminal traces of the ceremonial and pastoral Pans, more congenial to eighteenth-century taste; developments in cultural history and mythography which affect literature at one point; and the interesting further cultivation of the emblematic Pan (especially by way of the Midas myth) for satiric purposes.

Augustan mythology in general, as Douglas Bush rightly says, is largely to be found in "travesties; mock-heroic poems; translations and paraphrases . . . mythological allusions equally numerous and frigid";[69] this is also true of the Pan figure in particular, with the modification that the allusions, although frigid, are not numerous. A few examples will serve to illustrate the superficial nature of the remains of pastoral Pan. He fared worse than did the pastoral convention as a whole; apparently he lacked the gracefulness necessary for a character in the world of Chloe and Strephon and the Dresden shepherdesses.

Pan appears most often in the brief allusions of descriptive formulas, like Pope's "rough satyrs dance, and Pan applauds the song" (*Pastorals*, "Summer," line 50), or in pastoral oaths, as in the *Westminster Drollery*, where the rustic couple (not, of course, the court lovers), " 'Fore God Pan did plight their Troth; So to the church [!] away they hie."[70] Dryden combines reminiscences of the pseudo-Theocritean oath with a standard low joke of Elizabethan comedy (used of Pan surprisingly rarely): "I swear by *Pan* (tho' he wears horns you'll say)/ Cudgell'd and kick'd, I'le not be forc'd away"[71] ("Daphnis: Theocritus, Idyll xxvii," ca. 1685).

More forceful than these empty stereotypes are the erotic Pans of *Windsor Forest* and of John Gay's *The Story of Cephisa*, which capture, if not the uniquely goatish vigor of the god, at least a sensation of his speed in the chase. In both poems, passions are only skin deep; both lovers rely on the same sighs, prayers, and pantings as do the more orthodox eighteenth-century lovers. Pope's Pan could be any ardent swain who "saw and lov'd and burning with desire / Pursu'd" were it not for the metamorphosis which turns the nymph, in the manner of Renaissance topological poems, into a recognizable part of the landscape — the river Loddon, a tributary ("offspring") of the Thames (lines 170–218).[72] Gay gives more detail, though Pan's strongest self-advertisement is a curiously commercial one:

> PAN is my name; — the herds on yonder plains,
> My herbage fattens and my care sustains;
> To me the woodland empire is decreed.[73]

The dominant note is the sentimental; when the metamorphosis is accomplished, Pan is left to bestow "a lover's cares" upon the Sensitive Plant. We are still a long way from the shaggy eroticism of Browning's Pans, though Gay knows of another side to Pan's nature, one commonly left out of English Pan poems: "Let vig'rous *Pan* th'unguarded minute seize, / And in a shaggy goat the virgin please" (*The Fan*, II, 149–50; 1713).

Later in the century, pastoral develops a fashionable "melancholy" mode, serving as a setting for reflections about human life loosely attached to observations of carefully chosen natural scenes. Joseph Warton writes, in his "Ode to Evening" (1746), very much as Thomas Gray might have written about Pan:

> Hail, meek-eyed maiden, clad in sober grey . . .
> When Phoebus sinks behind the gilded hills . . .
> The panting Dryads, that in day's fierce heat
> To inmost bowers and cooling caverns ran,
> Return to trip in wanton evening dance,
> Old Sylvan too returns, and laughing Pan.
> To the deep wood the clamorous rooks repair . . .
> Now every passion sleeps: desponding Love,
> And pining Envy, ever-restless Pride;
> And holy calm creeps o'er my peaceful soul,
> Anger and mad Ambition's storms subside.[74]

This might almost be a poetic description of a painting by Poussin. The "caverns," the "deep wood," and the highly artificial action hint at a "Picturesque" scene; by 1786, Thomas Warton, writing a very similar Theocritean poem, emphasizes the picturesque elements in a scene worthy of Salvator Rosa:

> Theocritus, forsook awhile
> The graces of his pastoral isle . . .
> And Pan's own umbrage, dark and deep,
> The caverns hung with ivy-twine,
> The cliffs that waved with oak and pine,
> And Etna's hoar romantic pile.[75]

William Lisle Bowles, in 1789, speaks of "The Visionary Boy" as

> By many a haunt of Pan, and wood-nymph's cave,
> Lingering and listening to the Doric strain

Of him, the bard whose music might succeed
To the wild melodies of Pan's own reed!

In another poem he recommends illustrating Theocritus in the manner of Rubens, making explicit the debt of this particular type of poem to pictorial art:

And catch the beauties of the pastoral bard
Shadowing his wildest landscapes! Aetna's fires,
Bebrycian rocks, Anapus' holy stream,
And woods of ancient Pan; the broken crag
And the old fisher here; the purple vines
There bending.

"The Visionary Boy" combines the notion of Pan as a suitable deity for picturesque landscape with Pan the patron of a poet in a way which reminds one of the early Keats.[76]

On the other hand, William Cowper (*The Task*, 1785), negates such pastoral scenes more forcibly than even Milton had done; at the same time he negates Milton's "universal Pan" by neglecting to mention him.

The Lord of all, himself through all diffused,
Sustains and is the life of all that lives.
Nature is but the name for an effect
Whose cause is God . . .
Him blind antiquity profaned, not served,
With self-taught rites, and under various names,
Female and male, Pomona, Pales, Pan,
And Flora and Vertumnus; peopling earth
With tutelary goddesses and gods
That were not; and commending as they would
To each some province, garden, field or grove. (VI, 221–237)

This lacks the concision and dramatic effectiveness of the Lady's brief criticism in *Comus* (line 176), "and thank the gods amiss," but the sentiment is the same. Cowper, however, is more consistent and literal than Milton; he never gives "Pan" a special status as a universal deity, for Christ rules universal nature under his own name. The pastoral picture that Cowper attacks (like Milton comparing Eden with the bower where "Pan nor Sylvanus never slept") is formed by adding to a scenic description a tired alliterative formula of its tutelary deities, in a way derived remotely from Virgil (*Georgics*, II) and Ovid.[77] Cowper (unlike Milton) knocks down a poetical straw man when he denies the validity of the eighteenth-century pastoral Pan.

The "ceremonial" Pans, whether royal or theological, did not survive even so long. Dryden in 1691 brings to a conclusion the series of tributes to English monarchs under the guise of Pan with a fleeting reference to William of Orange [78] and the lively doggerel of "The Lady's Song," a pastoral allegory of the exile of James II that reverses the message of *Lysistrata* while supplying the most vigorous royal Pan since *Pan's Anniversarie*:

> But if you dare think of deserving our Charms,
> Away with your Sheephooks and take to your Arms;
> Then Lawrels and Myrtles your Brows shall adorn,
> When *Pan*, and his Son, and fair *Syrinx*, return.

Dryden's other Pans appear to owe more to Spenser than to any other source. As in Spenser, a royal identification does not preclude a more solemn identification on pastoral grounds (without evident Plutarchan influence) with Christ himself. In *The Hind and the Panther* (1687), one reference is satiric:

> Not so the blessed *Pan* his flock encreas'd
> Content to fold 'em from the famish'd beast:
> Mild were his laws; the Sheep and harmless Hind
> Were never of the persecuting kind. (I, 284–287)

Another reference combines a Spenserian moral with perhaps a hint from the *Nativity Ode*:

> Nor yet despise it, for this poor aboad
> Has oft receiv'd, and yet receives a god . . .
> This mean retreat did mighty *Pan* contain;
> Be emulous of him, and pomp disdain. (II, 707f)

Most of the other Augustan Pans can be subsumed under Bush's headings of "travesty" and "translation," and, at that, Venus, Mars, Vulcan, Cupid, and Bacchus, appearing in their dozens, were far more popular subjects for burlesque than Pan. The only two burlesques on vaguely classical themes in which Pan seems to play a prominent role are both mock-heroic poems on outdoor sport. In one, Matthew Concanen's *A Match at Foot-Ball* (Dublin, 1720), Pan is the patron deity of one team in these "mimick Wars" of rustic life. He suffers an epic temper tantrum, interpolates, digressively, the story of Syrinx, but appears in the story to be chiefly a sentimental pastoral lover, who "pensive . . . sighed . . . now big with hope, and now dismay'd with fear." (The justly far more famous version of the grotesque sentimental lover, related to the Satyr of pastoral drama, is of course the Polyphemus of Handel's *Acis and Galatea*). In Thomas Mathison's *The Goff* (Edinburgh, 1743) angry Pan defends his rural kingdom by kicking the golf ball into a bunker, where, epically, "deep sunk in sand the hapless orb remained." [79]

A thorough discussion of the Pans in eighteenth-century translations would tell us more about translation than about Pan: translators and paraphrasers were of course limited by their classical sources, which consisted, for our purposes, largely of Virgil's *Georgics* and *Eclogues* and Ovid's *Metamorphoses*. Dryden's translations of the *Eclogues*, for example, would give several instances of the epigrammatic effect encouraged by the couplet form. The implications of his addition to Virgil's story of Pan and Luna (*Georgics* III, 601–602) are amusing: "nor didst thou disdain / When call'd in woody shades, *to cure a Lover's pain*" (italics mine). His translation of the story of Syrinx (*Met.* I, 950–988) provides a distinct non-Ovidian interpretation: Pan is "a Lustful God" who "burns with new Desires." Dryden's conclusion is a cruder, less subtle version of Marvell's "and Pan did after Syrinx speed / Not as a Nymph but for a reed." Metaphysical paradox is replaced by Augustan antithesis: "Who canst not be the Partner of my Bed / At least shalt be the Consort of my Mind."

Meanwhile the eighteenth-century mythographers, English and continental, like their predecessors, the Renaissance encyclopedists, were discovering or compiling many more variations of the Pan myth than literary men were willing to exploit. At the end of the seventeenth century, Pan was still likely to be a pawn in theological controversy, whether on the side of skepticism (Fontenelle, van Dale) or of dogmatic but farfetched orthodoxy (Huetius). While never ceasing to be primarily compendia of mythological information, mythographical works developed the various rational modes of interpretation, such as euhemerism and historical allegory.[80] Thomas Blackwell, for instance, in his *Letters Concerning Mythology* (London, 1748), interprets an emblem of a virgin seeking refuge from Pan in Vesta's temple to represent the historical triumph of civilization over the rocks and shaggy wilds of nature (p. 62), an interpretation which parallels on a much larger scale the typical Augustan use of Pan to represent rustic, uncultivated ignorance. As Gibbon said of the Feast of Lupercalia (compare Ovid's account in the *Fasti*), "The savage and simple rites were expressive of an early state of society before the invention of arts and agriculture. The rustic deities who presided over the toils and pleasures of the pastoral life, Pan, Faunus and their train of satyrs, were such as the fancy of shepherds might create, sportive, petulant and lascivious, whose power was limited and whose malice was inoffensive. A goat was the offering the best adapted to their character and attributes" (*Decline and Fall*, chapter 36). By the end of the eighteenth century, the interpretations tended to be similarly rational and matter-of-fact, as in Lemprière (who presumed, following Banier, that the story of the Death of Pan was a hoax perpetrated upon Tiberius by a courtier), "antiquarisch," as in Knoblauch, or showing signs of recognizably scientific archaeological and anthropological researches, in the more modern fashion, as in Payne Knight. A new element enters in the work of Joseph Spence (*Polymetis*, 1747), who is reminded by some drawing of an ancient artifact that Pan brings fears and frightful dreams, that his face can be "more terrible than that of Mars," with a horror in it like the Devil's, and that he is so lascivious that "for a very obvious reason" his face only could be represented.[81]

These clues will not be followed up for a long time. With the exception of one line from Pope's *Dunciad*, the whole body of eighteenth-century Pans could have been compiled without any reference to nonliterary sources.

"Pan to Moses lends his pagan horn," in Pope's description of the Destruction of Learning, represents the victory of Gothic Dulness over classical civilization:

> See . . .
> Streets paved with heroes, Tiber choked with gods:
> Till Peter's keys some christened Jove adorn,
> And Pan to Moses lends his pagan horn;
> See, graceless Venus to a virgin turned,
> Or Phidias broken, and Apelles burned. (III, 108–112)

The variorum note explains the passage as a whole by saying that the popes, "demolishing the Heathen Temples and Statues [spared] some of the Statues, by modifying them into Images of Saints," and the Moses reference in particular by alluding to the Vulgate translation of the Book of Exodus. The Vulgate reads as follows: "Cumque descenderat Moyses de monte Sinai, tenebat duas tabulas testimonii; et ignorabat quod cornuta esset facies sua ex consortio sermonis Domini. Videntes autem Aaron et filii Israel cornutam Moysi faciem, timuerunt prope accedere" (34.29–30). "And it came to pass, when Moses came down from mount Sinai with the two tables of testimony in Moses' hand . . . that *Moses wist not that the skin of his face shone* while he talked with him. And when Aaron and all the children of Israel saw Moses, behold, the skin of his face shone; and they were afraid to come nigh him." (Italics mine.) The Hebrew word for "ray" apparently also means "horn," and St. Jerome so translated it; the King James version given here is less sonorous but more accurate. Thus Michelangelo was given license to make his statue of Moses with horns rather than with an aureole.[82]

There is no tradition of a statue of Pan actually being altered to a statue of Moses, as there was of some of the other changes Pope lists. But some sort of equivalence of Pan and Moses, encouraged by the accident of the horns, flourished in the theological writings of P. D. Huetius, Bishop of Avranches. In his *Demonstratio Evangelica* (1679), Huetius combines the last of the "theological" interpretations with one of the first of the "rational" interpretations, to reach a conclusion of a rare and absorbing absurdity. His primary thesis is that "Graeci Mosaicam doctrinam infinitis fabulis obduxerant" (the Greeks hid the Mosaic doctrine under endless fables), and his secondary thesis is that virtually every Greek deity can be identified with Moses. The most solid evidence for identifying Moses with Pan is provided by their both possessing horns (though Huetius acknowledges the original mistranslation); but other criteria among his encyclopedic variety of Pan references include their reputations in battle, their similar associations with hills and "solis locis et sterilibus" (solitary and barren places), Moses' association with the Creation and Pan's with "Mundi harmoniam" (the harmony of the world). Then, by an elaborate system of syllogisms with undistributed middles, Silvanus, Priapus, Faunus, Jupiter, and other gods associated with or loosely identified with Pan are similarly equated with Moses. Elsewhere Huetius identifies Pan with Christ in the traditional Plutarchan fashion,[83] but I cannot find that he ever states the logical corollary, an equivalence of Moses and Christ. Even so, there seems no reason to dispute Knoblauch's judgment (1794) of Huetius' Pan–Moses identification that "seine Argumente dafür kann man ohne Lachen kaum lesen (one can hardly read his arguments for it without laughing). Whether Pope knew Huetius' work or not, it seems reasonable to suppose that in writing this line of the *Dunciad* he recalled some more specific and extensive identification of Pan with Moses than could be provided by any horned statue of Moses, or even by the original Vulgate passage.

At this point it seems as if we should run aground for lack of material. But the ways of using Pan suggested by the Renaissance emblem books presented eighteenth-century authors with much greater opportunities for originality than any of the highly derivative types that I have been discussing, presumably because the method of the emblem and the principal Pan story conveyed by emblems — that of Midas (in Whitney's "Perversa Iudicia") — were particularly susceptible to being turned into satire.

The Pan in John Gay's "Pan and Fortune: To a Young Heir," however, owes nothing to Whitney. He is an emblem of something scarcely hinted at up to now, the value to be found in country life. Such a meaning is justified, of course, by the associations of the pastoral Pan, god of woods and countryside, and incidentally reminds us of the "Arcadiac" Pan of the nineteenth century, participator in the endless dialectic between the wicked city and the idyllic country. Lest one think that Gay, of all people, has become a Romantic out of his time, it must be emphasized that he is commenting satirically on a concrete social situation, the tendency of young heirs to gamble away the solid patrimony of a country squire. Pastoral sentiment runs financial interest a very poor second.

Gay's *Fables* were published in "two parts, beautified with seventy elegant engravings." The elegant engraving which beautifies this fable clearly shows its emblematic base;[84] it is a picture of winged Fortune on a wheel, with Death, the headsman, in the background. The Fool, the young heir, is being lured by knaves to ruin his forest and park to pay his gambling debts, as a carefully draped Pan looks on.

> To see the desolation spread,
> *Pan* drops a tear, and hangs his head:
> His bosom now with fury burns,
> Beneath his hoof the dice he spurns;
> Cards too, in peevish passion torn,
> The sport of whirling winds are borne.

To the Heir's claim that "Fortune . . . meditates my ruin," Fortune herself rejoins

> 'Tis *Folly*, *Pan*, that is thy foe.
> By me his late estate he won,
> But he by *Folly* was undone.

The opposition of Folly and Pan here differentiates Gay's treatment sharply from the emblematic Midas stories, where (following Whitney) Midas' "perversa iudicia" are equated with folly, and Pan, whom Midas chooses over Apollo, is equated with the rusticity that is ignorance (rather than, as here, the pastoral rusticity appropriate to the landed gentry).

Swift's "Fable of Midas" (1711–1712) is a short satire on the

Duke of Marlborough, whose skill at turning "dung itself to gold," by way of contractors' graft, was reckoned by the author to be second only to Midas'. Both jokes and satire fall rather flat; they show something less than Swift's usual genius for universalizing the topical:

> None e'er did modern Midas chuse
> Subject or patron of his muse
> But found him thus their merit scan:
> That Phoebus must give place to Pan:
> He values not the poet's praise
> Nor will exchange his plums for bays.
> To Pan alone rich misers call
> And there's the jest, for Pan is ALL.
> Here English wits will be to seek
> Howe'er 'tis all one in the Greek.

Christopher Smart's "The Judgment of Midas" (1752) is a very short masque, in style more like Heywood (*Love's Mistris*) and Lyly (*Midas*) than like Swift. His political satire, although topical, is very much broader in scope than is Swift's muck-raking, but it is subordinated to the simple comic lyricism of the masque. We know that Midas is biased, "for with Pan / He tends the sheep-walks all the live-long day," but Smart has some sympathy for his position, which he sums up gnomically: " 'Tis hard to judge, whene'er the great contend." Smart's Pan sings a song (like Lyly's) which puts up a reasonable lyric defense of his own way of life, in terms of the English climate (in winter he "keeps our restless souls in tune"):

> O'er cots and vales, and every shepherd swain,
> In peaceable pre-eminence I reign;
> With pipe on plain, and nymph in secret grove,
> The day is music, and the night is love.
> I, blest with these, nor envy nor desire
>   Thy gaudy chariot, or thy golden lyre.

The nymphs approve Midas' choice, but Apollo's view of it is quickly given: "Such rural honors [ass's ears] all the gods decree, / To those who sing like Pan, and judge like thee."

Blake's "Imitation of Spenser" is an early lyric interesting to

the commentators for its inefficient metrical experimentation
rather than for its content; but it becomes much more meaningful in the context of the eighteenth-century Midas story.
Like his poem "The Muses," it contains a criticism of modern
poetry,[85] aimed at "brutish Pan" whose "tinkling sounds . . .
[are] Sound without sense." If Pan is the modern poet, the
modern critic is

> Midas [who] the praise hath gain'd of lengthen'd ears,
> For which himself might deem him ne'er the worse
> To sit in council with his modern peers,
> And judge of tinkling rimes [Pan's] and elegances
>   terse [Apollo's].[86]

Clearly "Golden Apollo" writes poetry as it should be written,
and "brutish Pan," fortunately, attacks him in vain.

The Midas story made an appeal to a wider segment of eighteenth-century taste in the rather less elegant form of Kane
O'Hara's burletta *Midas*, performed in 1764, 1804, and 1814. It
is a cross between a burlesque and a comic opera; its rhythms
and rhyme schemes at their best have a Gilbert and Sullivan
quality; its plot and characterizations make no great demands
upon the imagination. The episode of the judgment itself becomes part of the rustic romance plot, in a compression made
necessary by the relatively slow unfolding of a story set to music.
This compression blurs the outlines of any definite Pan character or Pan idea, even if such were possible in a form where
the words are so decisively dominated by the tunes. Pan is a
bachelor "Tippling, Sir, at th'alehouse." Midas and Apollo
(disguised as a shepherd) are rivals for the affections of the
same country lass. Despite Midas' obvious interest in Apollo's
defeat, when the contest actually takes place, he has to be bribed
to choose "the drowsy drone" of Pan's bagpipe. Apollo throws
off his disguise and condemns Midas to "wander with *Pan* / He
a stinking old goat, thou an ass." The one touch (apart from
the bribe) that links this frivolity in a superficial way with the
Midas of satire is the epilogue addressed to the critics telling
them to "remember the fate of *Midas*" and not hiss the performance. It seems probable that the musical criticism contained

in this "parody on Italian opera seria" may well be more penetrating than anything in the unpretentious libretto.[87]

Probably the best Midas satire since Heywood's *Love's Mistris* is a virtually unknown but lively polemic by an unknown (and probably pseudonymous) author, of eighteenth-century tastes and anti-Romantic disposition, which appeared in 1808: Anthony Fisgrave's *Midas, or a Serious Inquiry Concerning Taste and Genius, Including a Proposal for the Certain Advancement of the Elegant Arts, to which is added, by way of illustration, a Fragment of Ancient History*.[88] This wordy but humorously effective satire has poor taste as its general target, like the other cultural satires, but in hitting its specific target of Romantic poetry, it becomes literary satire as well. The fault lies with "connoisseurs" and with the "ignorant" who prefer "genius in the rough" (p. 149) to polished and practiced artistry. As in the comic operas, Pan is represented as a "facetious rustic" (p. 104), whose performances are largely inspired by drink. He charms Midas, the connoisseur, as well as the ignorant audience with

> A variety that resembled the gambols of a wild calf on the mountains and seemed to be composed of small portions of all the airs he had ever practised . . . [Pan played "Dainty Davy," and the audience, which loved dancing, approved, then] "Lumps of Pudding," — an air, if possible, still more exquisite than the former . . . The cadences he here introduced were perfectly romantic: beautiful episodes, wherein the performer in a kind of playful digression appeared to have lost all remembrance of the air.

Apollo's song, on the other hand, had a plot, and characters; it was "not without design and a specific character . . . had too much of art and contrivance, and wanted the wild irregularity that surprises and the boldness that elevates." It could not compete with the charms of pure novelty, for Pan ascended "higher in the musical scale by many notes than ever instrument or human voice had gone before" (pp. 150–153). Fisgrave goes on to satirize, in a similar way, academies, bluestockings, architecture, the Picturesque, and much else, but Pan's music remains the chief exemplum of ignorant or popular taste (to Fisgrave the two are synonymous), and Midas' choice of Pan is a type of "the prejudices, the vices and the follies of mankind" (p. 208).

Pan, when not simply a decorative icon, is to the eighteenth century — fascinated by questions of "taste" and critical judgment — chiefly a clumsy plebeian god, distinctly unimposing and, at his best, merely energetically amusing — the emblem of Ignorance, presumptuously aiming for a sphere far above his reach. This comic-satiric mode was the only aspect of the Pan motif that the eighteenth century developed, instead of simply imitating, and even that development was not altogether an improvement. The best comic-satiric Pans are still to be found in the richer allegories of Lyly and Heywood, where the point is reinforced rather than weakened by allowing the god to retain some shreds of dignity.[89]

Chapter II

ROMANTIC PAN

Hazlitt, speaking of "the natural genius of the country" in the first of his *Lectures on the Age of Elizabeth* (1820), replies almost defiantly as if to some charge of Romantic irregularity, like those accusations that Fisgrave had concealed under the emblem of Pan: "Our literature, in a word, is Gothic and grotesque; unequal and irregular . . . It aims at an excess of beauty or power . . . Our understanding is not . . . smooth . . . but full of knotty points and jutting excrescences, rough, uneven, overgrown with brambles; and I like this aspect of mind . . . where nature keeps a good deal of the soil in her own hands. Perhaps the genius of our poetry has more of Pan than of Apollo; 'but Pan is a God, Apollo is no more!' " [1] The last phrase, taken from Lyly's *Midas* (IV, 1), shows that Hazlitt had found useful as a critical metaphor that very contest between Pan and Apollo which had hitherto been the weapon of the "Apollonians." Hazlitt remembers the Pans of Lyly and of Beaumont and Fletcher; he imagines them on the stage, and then makes the astonishing comparison of Pan and the earthy, grotesque Caliban: "It is not indeed pleasant to see this character [Caliban] on the stage any more than it is to see the god Pan personated there." Similarly he catches and intensifies the spirit of an allegorical Pan, such as Bacon's, in this random yet vivid allusion: "Earth in Rembrandt's copies, is rough and hairy; and Pan has struck his hoof against it!" But the Romantic Pan in general, and most particularly Wordsworth's, is not to be the Pan of "knotty points and jutting excrescences" — quite the contrary. Hazlitt himself touches upon the more characteristic Romantic Pan in his frequent use of the Miltonic tag "Universal Pan," and especially in his comment on Coleridge, who, in his more Spinozistic stages, "beheld the living

traces and the sky-painting proportions of the mighty Pan . . .
but poetry redeemed him from this spectral philosophy." [2]

Coleridge's visionary, pantheist philosophy is only once exemplified in a "spectral" Pan, however; in *Biographia Literaria*
(1817), Coleridge describes in terms of Michelangelo's horned
statue of Moses a Pan who is clearly in the spirit of the Orphic
Hymn, thus giving the "mysterious Pan" an odd flavor of eighteenth-century mythography.

> As we were gazing on Michael Angelo's Moses . . . we called to
> mind . . . that horns were the emblem of power and sovereignty
> among the Eastern nations, and are still retained as such in Abyssinia;
> the Achelous [a bull-headed river god] of the ancient Greeks; and
> the probable ideas and feelings, that originally suggested the mixture
> of the human and the brute form in the figure, by which they realized
> the idea of their mysterious Pan, as representing intelligence blended
> with a darker power, deeper, mightier, and more universal than the
> conscious intellect of man — than intelligence. (Chapter xxi) [3]

It was probably by way of the Orphic Hymn, especially in
Thomas Taylor's translation (1787), that the Romantics found
the Orphic Pan, the Soul of All Things, rescued him from the
allegorists and encyclopedists, and made him a major poetic
motif, which at its best became both universal and pastoral.

Wordsworth's Pans are among the first in English literature
to be deliberately nonpictorial, or "invisible." Wordsworth's
Pan is so all-embracing, so indefinable an abstraction, that he
cannot be permitted more than a narrow range of specific limit-
ing qualities. The concept is more akin to that of the Orphic
Hymn than to the allegorical interpretations. To the allegorists,
Pan, though abstract, was never "invisible"; he was a clear visual
emblem, with each detail, from horns to hoofs, etched in and
labeled. Wordsworth's Pan is more like that of the Neo-Platonists (for example, Pico della Mirandola and Politian), who had
also sacrificed the image to the idea, and thus missed the stronger
possibilities of the motif. The "universal Pan" in "Poems Dedicated to National Independence" is a less exalted version of the
"something far more deeply interfused [in] the blue sky and in

the mind of man" of "Tintern Abbey." Pan is no longer a goat-god.

> O'er the wide earth, on mountain and on plain,
> Dwells in the affections and the soul of man
> A Godhead, like the universal PAN;
> But more exalted, with a brighter train. (II, xiv)

The more famous lines from *The Prelude* (VIII, 180–185) appear to be full of corroborative detail, but in fact declare Pan's invisibility again, this time explicitly:

> Of rich Clitumnus; and the goat-herd lived
> As calmly, underneath the pleasant brows
> Of cool Lucretilis, where the pipe was heard
> Of Pan, Invisible God, thrilling the rocks
> With tutelary music, from all harm
> The fold protecting.

Invisibility is necessary, presumably, to preserve mystery and universality; it is not a classical trait. But the picture that surrounds the invisible center is made up of Virgilian and Horatian associations.[4] The chief sensory impression is auditory: "the pipe was heard . . . thrilling the rocks / With tutelary music."

Similarly, Great Pan is a voice, rather than a vision, in "Grasmere Lake" (1807),[5] the first part of which, "a vivid repetition of the stars," is so strongly visual. Pan "low-whispering through the reeds" conveys a message similar to the "hope and steadfast promise" that the "more exalted" spirit of nature conveyed to man in "Independence and Liberty," xiv. "Whispering through the reeds" has a gamut of associations; it combines a naturalistic explanation of Pan's piping with a mythical explanation of the sound of wind in the reeds. Thus it reminds us, without needing a direct statement, that Pan is a spirit universal in nature; the whispering of reeds is simply a manifestation of nature which tells of her "tranquillity." The contrast of man's "unholy deeds" with Pan's "tranquillity" is rather like the escapist contrast of city and countryside which will afflict, in a cruder form, the poetry of the rest of the century, but here the "Orphic" overtones give it a greater depth and subtlety than is usual in "Arcadiac" verse.

"On the Power of Sound," stanza x (1828), again narrows Pan's scope to the auditory:

> The pipe of Pan, to shepherds
> Couched in the shadow of Maenalian pines,
> Was passing sweet.

Virgil's eighth Eclogue likewise deals with the "origin of music":

> Maenalus argutumque nemus pinosque loquentes
> semper habet semper pastorum ille audit amores
> Panaque, qui primus calamos non passus inertes. (22–24)

(Maenalus always has melodious groves and speaking pines; and always listens to shepherds' loves and to Pan, who first would not allow the reeds to lie idle.) Wordsworth, having alluded to Virgil, does not need to complete the reference to "primus calamos non passus inertes." Five and a half of the "eight most noble Pindaric verses" [6] which begin the poem — those describing the procession of Bacchus — are most vividly visualized; it is the two and a half relating to Pan that are not.

Only in the fourth book of the *Excursion* (lines 851–887) does Wordsworth allow us to see what there was to be seen of Pan; here it is in the course of a naturalistic explanation of the origins of myth. There is irony in "The simple shepherd's awe-inspiring God" being no more than a "goat's depending beard" seen through "withered boughs grotesque," but, like the shepherds of Milton and Giles Fletcher, though for a different reason, it seems that these shepherds are wiser than they know. This Pan is much closer to the merely mythological level of the "fleet Oreads" or the "lurking Satyrs" than is the Pan of, say, "Grasmere Lake"; he is one spirit among the many that infuse natural objects, rather than the one spirit that infuses all natural objects. This example simply confirms that there is nothing to be seen of Pan apart from the natural objects which are his outer manifestations. "The goat's depending beard" is the narrowest possible focus of these manifestations, and the whole universe is the widest; Wordsworth's Pans, although shown on several different levels of seriousness, are remarkably consistent.

The triple layer of simile in the *Excursion* (VII, 728–740) is puzzling. It denies myth at the very time that it exploits myth, as Milton's epic similes so often do, and declares as well that myths may contain truth. The truth may shine out from the "idle songs" as Pan might shine, though "veiled in human form," and as "the scholar's genius" and "the spirit of a hero" might shine "through a simple rustic garb's disguise." There are plenty of "such fables" concerning other gods, but it is highly uncharacteristic of Pan to appear in any form but his own, for it is through his form, half-goat, half-god, that he is known and defined. The "idle song" that Wordsworth had in mind for Pan was probably, then, the Homeric Hymn as misinterpreted by Andrew Tooke in his *Pantheon* (1698) where it is Pan (not Hermes, his father, as in the original) who "laid aside, as it were, his Divinity, and became a Shepherd" to win the love of the nymph Dryope.[7] The similar disguise motif in several eighteenth-century pastoral comic operas may provide other relevant parallels, though these are even less like the work of "old bards." Even if the source is accounted for, the simile is still puzzling. Apollo might well represent the spirit of scholarship, or conceivably of heroism, but I find it difficult to link Pan with either of those qualities, and to make the simile as a whole coherent. The notion of Pan as a spirit whose "disguise" alone is visible is, of course, consistent with the rest of Wordsworth's usage.

If Wordsworth is, to quote Douglas Bush, "the fountainhead of nineteenth-century poetry on mythological themes" (*Romantic Tradition*, p. 56), does it then follow that he will be the fountainhead of nineteenth-century poetic references to Pan? This is a special case of the more general problem for which this study as a whole should provide some relevant evidence: to what extent does the Pan theme mirror on a small scale the state of mythology at any one point, and its ebbs and flows from one literary age to another?

The three principal factors in Wordsworth's interpretation of Pan are the auditory emphasis, the dependence on Virgilian and Horatian echoes, and the muted "Orphic" quality, the equation of Pan with the spirit infusing natural phenomena. Although "piping" is always the key activity of Pan, and we have not heard the last of Clitumnus and Maenalus, only the Orphic quality had a pronounced influence on later poets, and largely on the minor poets at that. Ralph Waldo Emerson is a very distinguished, and very Wordsworthian, exception to this generalization. Keats and Shelley took some hints from Wordsworth, but, among the major Victorians, Matthew Arnold and Tennyson almost ignored Pan altogether, and new, non-Wordsworthian sources account for the most distinctive characteristics of Pan in Walter Savage Landor and the Brownings, and even in George Meredith and Swinburne.

Wordsworth quite deliberately refused to tie down the abstraction for which Pan seemed the appropriate designation by taking too literally Pan's shagginess, his goatiness, his grotesqueness. He created many fine lines of poetry around the "invisible Pan," but they gain their strength from other sources than the Pan figure itself. This formless Pan is as dangerous a guide for the minor authors in the Romantic vein as the conventionalized pastoral Pan (with whom he is often associated) had been; they managed to dilute Wordsworth's symbol beyond the point even of banality. To widen the image as far as Wordsworth does is drastically to narrow its possibilities.

Here, for the first time since Milton (whose view of Pan, unlike Wordsworth's, was frequently contradictory and often negative), Pan is found in major poems by a major author, poems of which no contemporary or later poet is likely to be unaware. Yet Bush's assessment of Wordsworth's crucial influence on mythological poetry in general has only a partial corollary in the case of the Pan figure.

Keats, for instance, avoided Wordsworth's intangible Pan and, like Hazlitt, learned from the Elizabethan dramatists. By expressing Pan's more local "Arcadian" significance in concrete and specific functions and phenomena, the Elizabethans had gained in vividness what they had lost in sublimity of concept. But Keats can, at the same time, improve upon the very half-hearted Elizabethan hints of universality, and show a Pan who "governs the Affairs of the Universal World by his Mind as he represents it by his Body." [8] It is perhaps the secret of the success of Pan as a symbol of universality (Orphic) that he can be vividly portrayed in the Arcadian or pastoral fashion at the same time, and only Thomas Love Peacock, at his most carpingly anti-Romantic, would worry about the distinctness and incompatibility of the two roles.

Keats's Pan imagery in the earliest poems is far less elaborate than it will be in *Endymion*, and is confined largely to the pastoral, although to Keats this is nothing like as "confining" a limitation as it was to Renaissance poets. Keats, like other Romantic poets, always means something more than and different from the conventional, codified pastoral, although he is happy to exploit its resonances as far as they will take him. In the "Dedication to Leigh Hunt, Esq.," the world of "glory and loveliness" is gone, and must be replaced as best it can by the consolations of poetry. Miltonically, the effect of "glory and loveliness" is gained by the rhetorical device of denying its presence while describing it: "No crowd of nymphs . . . Pan is no longer sought." But if Keats's equivalent to Milton's true religion is poetry, he cannot yet conceive of poetry as being better and truer than the glory it replaces; it is only "as high."

In "I Stood Tip-Toe," Keats likewise uses the mythical material at one rhetorical remove. The story of Syrinx appears in an epic simile relating Keats's subjective feelings to those of the original pastoral poet

> Who pull'd the boughs aside,
> That we might look into a forest wide,
> To catch a glimpse of Fawns, and Dryades. (151–153)

Keats then goes one stage further, and makes Pan's feelings subjective as well:

> . . . poor Pan, — how he did weep to find,
> Nought but a lovely sighing of the wind
> Along the reedy stream; a half heard strain,
> Full of sweet desolation — balmy pain. (159–162)

Taken out of context, these lines simply turn Pan into an anachronistic Romantic lover, somewhat as William Browne,

John Gay, and others had done earlier. The emotion is like the "melancholy loth" of the Syrinx lines in *Endymion* (I, 242–243), but in the earlier poem the feeling is less restrained and less skillfully blended into the poem as a whole. However, in this particular context, where both Keats and the "bard of old" depend in the same way upon Nature as a source of poetry, upon natural phenomena which may be transmuted into myth (compare Wordsworth's "Grasmere Lake"), it seems legitimate to complete the well-known story and draw a parallel between Pan, who created music from the sighing of the reeds, and the bard, who would be inspired by that same sighing to write of Pan. Like Wordsworth and Lucretius before him,[9] Keats could make mythic poetry that retained its mystery out of the same rationalistic explanation that seems to explain away the mystery.

In "Sleep and Poetry" Keats admits that pure pastoral is an early stage of his poetic development: he will pass "*First* the realm . . . Of Flora, and old Pan" (lines 101–102, italics mine), where these gods appear, almost in the eighteenth-century manner, simply as icons of the pastoral scene. It is a Horatian world, where nymphs' shoulders are there to be bitten; its artificiality is acknowledged in the implied parallel of "a lovely tale of human life we'll read" (line 110), and it must be abandoned for "a nobler life / Where I may find the agonies, the strife / Of human hearts" (lines 123–125), with which "Flora and old Pan," in their purely pastoral version, have nothing to do.

"The Hymn to Pan" (*Endymion*, I, 232–306), the climax of Keats's Pan imagery, broadens the concept far beyond that of the early poems. To be sure, Keats begins where the Elizabethan poets and especially the dramatists had left off. The setting of the hymn is a shepherds' festival to Pan, as in Michael Drayton, Ben Jonson, John Fletcher, William Browne. The stanzaic structure of Keats's "Hymn," giving a distinct function of Pan in each stanza, resembles Jonson's first "Hymn" in *Pan's Anniversary*; all the functions Keats lists in his first three stanzas — forester, hunter, shepherd, leader of fauns and satyrs, would-be lover of nymphs — have their analogues in Jonson. "Breather round our farms, / To keep off mildews, and all weather harms" is Keats's version of the time-honored Virgilian formula "ovium custos." In Jonson's elaboration it reads, Pan "keeps away all heats and colds, / Drives all diseases from our folds"; and in Fletcher's, Pan "doth keep / Our flocks from harm." Both Fletcher and Keats emphasize the trembling of Syrinx; Fletcher's "Whilst the hollow neighboring ground / Fills the music with her sound" (Act I) is very similar in wording, if not in effect, to "Strange ministrant of undescribed sounds / That come a swooning over hollow grounds." [10] The "willing service" of Keats's satyrs resembles that of the Satyr in *The Faithful Shepherdess*: the former "by mysterious enticement draw / Bewildered shepherds to their path again"; the latter must

> stay
> To see what mortals lose their way,
> And by a false fire, seeming bright,
> Train them in and leave them right. (Act III)

Numerous other parallels, both of word and of idea, could doubtless be found. Keats certainly knew the Homeric Hymn to Pan, in Chapman's translation (1616), but in fact the parallels are not nearly as close as with the Elizabethans, for "Homer" emphasized Pan's direct actions, whereas Keats's Pan, like Fletcher's, only acts through others.

Keats draws away from the Elizabethans in the meaning that he gives to the equivalence of Pan and All. (This can be seen most clearly in the last two stanzas, where the Arcadian shades over into the Orphic.) Jonson, among others, had equated them thus: "Pan is our All, by him we breathe, we live," but this is simply an etymological variant on "the best of shepherds, Pan"; Orphic influence, if any, is extremely halfhearted. Thomas Taylor translated the opening lines of the Orphic Hymn as follows:

> I call strong Pan, the substance of the whole,
> Etherial, marine, earthly, general soul,
> Immortal fire; for all the world is thine,
> And all are parts of thee, O pow'r divine. [11]

Whether Wordsworth knew this hymn or not could not be determined from the texts of his Pan references alone, but that Keats knew the hymn either directly or through some intermediary version of the Orphic Pan seems extremely probable.

Thus Keats had the whole treasury of pastoral imagery to choose from in delineating his ideal of earthly, of human and social life, of which Pan is here the suitable deity:

> Pan will bid
> Us live in peace, in love and peace among
> His forest wildernesses. (IV, 634–636)

Endymion is, among other things, the representative or deputy of Pan: "Through me the shepherd realm shall prosper well" (IV, 863), even if more is said of pastoral pleasures — "pipes will I fashion of the syrinx flag" (IV, 686) — than of pastoral duties. The Pan festival, the generic act of worship appropriate to this convention, with its strong emphasis on "the rites of true society," as Jonson put it, is here imbued with far more actual religious feeling than it is in the play-acting ceremonies of Jonson and Fletcher, who see it half-mockingly and from a distance. But Keats gives numerous hints in the early stanzas that his Pan will be more complex. The "undescribed sounds / That . . . wither drearily on barren moors," where, as Keats might have added later, "no birds sing," the epithets in the Syrinx stanza, "solemn," "dreary," "desolate," "dank," "strange," and "melancholy loth," followed by the golden harvest imagery of the next stanza, and the mysteriousness of the lure to lost shepherds — so different from the *ignis fatuus* of Fletcher — show that we are not in the sharply outlined sunshine world of the *Eclogues* or the pastoral drama, but in a world where sun and shadow are strangely mingled, as if by Coleridge's "darker," "deeper" power. Thus we are not entirely unprepared for the shift from Arcadia to the universe; there is something of an unknown in Pan's simplest and most local actions.

In the context of the entire poem, however, Pan is soon seen to represent the whole only in a certain way. Endymion must leave the Pan world of the shepherds to approach the Diana world, or even that halfway stage, the Neptune world. Idealized as the society is in which Endymion hopes to "nurse the golden age 'mong shepherd clans" (II, 896), this society is clearly at a lower level of perfection than "the great dream" of Diana's world; at times Endymion fears to reach beyond this natural sphere where there is a "tie / Of mortals each to each," for, as in fairy tales, supernatural love requires man to stay in a world of "too thin breathing" (IV, 638–650), which will be fatal to him. Pan is both the first stage of the development and the "Dread opener of the mysterious doors / Leading to [the] universal knowledge" which comes in the succeeding stages. At the same time he is the incarnation of that knowledge in actual phenomena: "the leaven / That spreading in this dull and clodded earth / Gives it a touch ethereal." He is Earth, imaging heaven by means of the sea: "a firmament reflected in a sea" (compare "Grasmere Lake": "a vivid repetition of the stars"), and thus, as the author of the Orphic Hymn would agree, he is All, all aspects of the universe (except, oddly, the "fire" of the Orphic hymn). Both Keats and the hymnist differ from such allegorists as Bacon in not equating each part of Pan schematically with the corresponding aspect of the universe, but blending them all into one.

Keats's "Sonnet to Homer" (1818) may be compared with the "pastoral poet" section of "I Stood Tip-Toe." "But then the veil was rent" (compare "So did he feel, who pulled the boughs aside"), and both the world of myth, including Pan, and the way in which he was to "see" it were revealed to Homer. The sonnet form enforces a certain impersonality as well as an invaluable compression of a conceit which had rambled somewhat in the earlier poem. The slight confusion in "I Stood Tip-Toe" between the poet writing and the poet written about is eliminated in the sonnet, even though the mythical subjects are those that Keats himself uses elsewhere, rather than the epic subjects more characteristic of the real Homer. The tripartite division of the mythic material under the aegis of the three deities, Pan, Jove, and Neptune, is very like the division into earth, sky, and sea that structures *Endymion*; the triple functions of "Dian, Queen of Earth, and Heaven, and Hell," though not perfectly symmetrical with Pan, Jove, and Neptune, are likewise paralleled in *Endymion*. It is faintly amusing that Keats, with the Homeric Hymns in front of him, still credited to Homer in Chapman's translation, may not have realized that Homer was the one major Greek poet for whom Pan did not in any literal sense make "sing . . . his forest hive." Yet Keats need have known only these hymns to make his list of "Homeric" material.

In *The Fall of Hyperion*, Keats mentions Pan for the last time, and, not unnaturally, considering the epic context, these lines (added at the end of 1819 to the poem *Hyperion*) resemble those in *Endymion*. In the original version of *Hyperion* no natural setting is provided for Saturn's opening speech, and he has no audience. The location described in *The Fall of Hyperion* (I, 404–411) is like the dank area where Pan mourned the loss of Syrinx, and although it is, strictly, Saturn's speech that "pervade[s]" the whole natural setting very much as Pan "leavened" it in the earlier poem, it seems that the "solitary Pan" is omnipresent in the natural earth to hear Saturn's "strange musings," as he was the omnipresent "ministrant of undescribed sounds" in *Endymion*. The word "solitary" reminds us of the Orphic descriptions of Pan withdrawn to a cave or a height.[12] "Solitary" is not in itself an epithet more concrete than Wordsworth's "invisible," but Keats describes the natural world that Pan seems to be filling so as to give a much sharper sense of Pan's pervasiveness.

Keats profited from his close study of "Homer," and, more important, of Orphic material and of the Elizabethans, to combine the pastoral and the Orphic into a blend more pungent than Wordsworth's. Like Wordsworth, Keats was too awe-inspired to be very specific about the center of Pan's mystery, but he is much clearer on the details that surround it; he gives it an outline, if not an image. As in the stanzas of the "Hymn to Pan," concrete details prepare us for abstract conceptions.

Shelley can also "universalize" Pan in the characteristic Romantic fashion; as it happens, his best-known Pan poem opens rather different possibilities. His "Hymn of Pan" (1820) forms a pair with his "Hymn of Apollo"; in both cases the preposition is significant, for these are not hymns *to* their respective deities, as in the Greek originals and their Elizabethan analogues, but hymns *by* them, and thus, perhaps, not properly hymns at all. I have said that they are a pair; their relationship might be surmised, though not easily, from seeing them out of their original context in collections of Shelley's poetry. But the matter is resolved by seeing them in place in Mary Shelley's playlet *Midas* (1820)[13] where they serve as Pan's and Apollo's contributions to the competition with which we are so familiar from Elizabethan and eighteenth-century sources. They are thus analogous in function to the poems of Lyly, Heywood, Smart, and Bach's librettist, rather than to the Homeric and Orphic hymns or to Jonson and Keats, although they are closer to the last four in inspiration and poetic power.

Printed as a lyric apart from the admittedly very inferior and (like Lyly's) little-read drama that framed it, the "Hymn of Pan" is virtually the first lyric in English solely devoted to Pan the musician, and thus forms a bridge between all the Pans in the "Midas" contexts, where he has hitherto had his best chance to display musical talent, and the innumerable plotless lyrics of Pan piping which will follow through the rest of the century. The latter genre reached its high point here at its very beginning.

The Pan of this poem — and, again, the juxtaposition with Apollo should not be forgotten — although a god of nature, is not "universal" and does not claim to be. In fact it is only for the variety and scope of his subject matter and the power of his music to move his auditors that he makes any claims at all; in this respect he is more like Orpheus than like the usual versions of Pan. The pretentious Pan of the singing contests reveals himself in the repeated claim that Apollo is envious of his "sweet pipings," and that age has frozen Tmolus' blood; Pan cannot account otherwise for their failure to weep at his story of Syrinx.[14]

The "Hymn of Pan," taken out of context, is a pleasant nature lyric with intermittent mythical evocations: these two elements are not nearly as well blended as in Keats's "Hymn to Pan." But then Shelley's poem is more a rendering of the "sweet pipings" in verbal music than a carefully formulated poetic explication of Pan. The lines on Syrinx, however, demand closer scrutiny:

> Singing how down the vale of Maenalus
> > I pursued a maiden and clasped a reed.
> Gods and men, we are all deluded thus!
> > It breaks in our bosom and then we bleed.

It is the same conceit as Marvell's "And Pan did after Syrinx speed / Not as a Nymph, but for a reed," in a different, less compact, poetic idiom and with a romantic, and much more explicit, moral. "We are all deluded thus," for the pursuit of ideal beauty ends in disillusionment and suffering. Marvell, on the other hand, expressed a more "classical" view that art and permanence, symbolized by the reed (and by Apollo's laurel), matter more than the transient pleasures of the nymph's body, a view developed romantically by Coleridge in his sketch for an allegorical interpretation: "Pan, Syrinx / Disappointment turning sensual into purer pleasures — disapp: Lust by regret, refining into Love & ending in Harmony." [15]

While Keats, more in the Ovidian manner of the Elizabethans, uses the Syrinx story largely for its emotive value, Marvell and Shelley have manipulated the facts of the story into images expressive of a complex of thought as well as feeling.

The Pan of Shelley's *Witch of Atlas* (1820) is of the "universal" type brought into English poetry by Milton and sanctified by Wordsworth and Keats. Shelley's Pan has no visible characteristics at all, not even the Miltonic propensity to dance with "Graces and Hours":

> And universal Pan, 'tis said, was there,
> > And though none saw him, — through the adamant
> Of the deep mountains, through the trackless air,
> > And through those living spirits, like a want,
> He passed out of his everlasting lair
> > Where the quick heart of the great world doth pant,
> And felt that wondrous lady all alone, —
> And she felt him, upon her emerald throne. (stanza ix)

Even the natural setting in *The Witch of Atlas* does not make the universality of Pan nearly as palpable as do Keats's "enmossed realms" and "ragged precipices." The "deep mountains" and "trackless air" of Shelley are much more reminiscent of Wordsworth's "wide earth, on mountain and on plain." [16]

Although there is nothing in the lines dealing with Pan himself that could not have been developed from Wordsworth — and some of the phrasing, if not the total content, almost certainly was — the context of the whole poem makes it clear that Shelley had other sources. Carl Grabo, in his account of Shelley's neo-Platonism, omits the evident parallels with Wordsworth, and derives the Pan directly from Macrobius' "Arcadic Pan . . . the Lord or dominator over all material substance" by way of Taylor, whom Shelley is known to have read, or Ralph Cudworth.[17] Grabo interprets the allegory of this passage as follows: "Universal Pan, god of all material substance, feels then the influence of the goddess of love and beauty in nature, of her who shapes living forms in the likeness of their divine archetypes" and the influence is reciprocal (p. 42).

Shelley's vague "universal Pan" contrasts strongly with the grotesque concreteness of his catalogue of the woodland deities, many of whom are given emblematic characteristics in the manner of a Spenserian procession (stanzas vi–ix).

> And old Silenus, shaking a green stick
> > Of lilies, and the wood-gods in a crew
> Came, blithe . . .
> And Dryope and Faunus followed quick,
> > Teasing the God to sing them something new. (stanza viii)

Milton, who was never troubled by baroque incongruities, had no qualms about putting a woodland Pan into the same book of *Paradise Lost* as a "universal Pan" (IV, 707, 266), but Shelley, more congruously, left the goat-footed Pan out of his procession of wood gods; Faunus takes Pan's place as an appropriate partner for Dryope (Pan's mother).[18]

The only well-known Romantic poem even to touch upon the Plutarchan Pan story is Shelley's Chorus from *Hellas*, beginning "Worlds on worlds are rolling ever" (1821), which clearly owes more to Milton's description of the death of pagan gods in the Nativity Ode than to any fresh discovery of Plutarchan material.

> So fleet, so faint, so fair,
>   The Powers of earth and air
> Fled from the folding-star of Bethlehem:
>   Apollo, Pan, and Love,
>   And even Olympian Jove
> Grew weak, for killing Truth had glared on them;
>   Our hills and seas and streams,
>   Dispeopled of their dreams,
> Their waters turned to blood, their dew to tears,
>   Wailed for the golden years.

Pan is just one member of a group of the best-known deities, neither equated with Christ, in the Miltonic manner, nor, as an individual, diametrically opposed to Christ; "Great Pan is dead!" was not yet a catchphrase in English poetry. The departing gods have more of Shelley's sympathy than they had of Milton's, for the dominant emotion is that of nostalgia for lost myth, the typically Romantic attitude first expressed in Schiller's *Götter Griechenlands* and, in English, in Coleridge's adaptation of Schiller's *Die Piccolomini*.[19]

The Plutarchan story was, of course, perfectly familiar to the Romantic poets in some form more direct than that supplied by Milton. Leigh Hunt, for instance, alludes to it as follows: "I hope you paid your devotions as usual to the Religio Loci, and hung up an evergreen. If you all go on so, there will be a hope some day that old Vansittart & others will be struck with a Panic Terror, and that a voice will be heard along the water saying 'The great God Pan is alive again,'—upon which the villagers will leave off starving, and singing profane hymns, and fall to dancing again."[20] Hunt's quite unserious hope for redemption and revenge by way of the resurgence of pagan worship is interesting for its association of the death of Pan with the triumph of Christianity and concomitant misfortunes, as well as for its extension of the "nostalgic" view of the death of the gods, including specifically (unlike Shelley) the death of Pan, to embrace the possibility of their revival. It was some decades before any poetic capital was made out of this extended conception (Byron and Peacock continued the Schilleresque formula of a hopeless nostalgia), and when it came it owed nothing to Hunt.

Hunt's letter has further significance as being one of a cluster of epistolary references to a Pan cult among a group of Romantic poets, including Shelley. On one level the cult seems to have involved a private verbal fetish, of a lightly conversational nature; on another, a sort of shorthand for a mutually shared and deeply felt esteem for paganism and the values imputed to it.

On September 7, 1818, Thomas Love Peacock, writing to Thomas Jefferson Hogg from Marlow, signed himself, "In the name of Pan, Yours most sincerely." The letter's other rhetorical flourishes included this: "when I hope I shall see your Homeric physiognomy in this gelid valley which we have consecrated to the only true gods, to whom I hope you continue to pour Libations and sing Dithyrambics." [21] To Shelley, less than three months later, Peacock wrote, "And were I not fearful of the risk of such a malediction, I would say, 'May Pan never be propitious to me if I be not in all coming fortnights as regular as the dial.'" [22]

Hogg and Shelley exchanged letters containing similar reports in 1821. Hogg began (June 15) by mentioning a walk with Peacock: "I need hardly add that we propitiated the far-darting King by a garland and an inscription, in Bisham Wood, which we hope to show you some day: SMINTHEEI." [23] On October 12, Shelley replied to this account of the propitiation of Apollo: "How much I envy your walks . . . I am glad to hear that you do not neglect the rites of the true religion. Your letter awakened my sleeping devotion, & the same evening I ascended alone the high mountain behind my house, & suspended a garland, & raised a small turf-altar to the mountain-walking Pan (pan oreibateis)" [24] The cumulative effect of these remarks is greater than their individual significance, since they convey a sense of interaction, of ritual jokes and gestures repeated frequently over a period of time. These would be of purely biographical interest, for none was published until very much later, were it not that each of these authors, with the exception of

Hogg — who is especially prominent in the exchanges, and may even have been in some sense their instigator — demonstrated "fondness for Pan" [25] in published works.

The contrast of public seriousness and private jocularity is nowhere more evident than in Leigh Hunt's "The Universal Pan" (1820), which is a classic example of a minor poet's over serious imitation of his betters. The theme of the Orphic Pan in the hands of Keats, Wordsworth, and Shelley has not only force but discretion, whereas Hunt never knows when to stop. The remarks in his letter have, by their very offhand concision, more to tell us about the importance of the Pan symbol than his fifty-three lines of wordy blank verse. In the poem Hunt has nothing to say about the death of Pan, or about Panic terror. He first sets up the antithesis of country and city more explicitly than Wordsworth had done:

> Not in the Town — not in the busy Town
> Am I, but come amongst the woodlands here
> And thou shalt find me.

Like Wordsworth, Keats, and Shelley, Hunt feels obliged to say

> I am the universal Spirit, around
> Whose habitations the great Sun is proud
> To run his journey . . . the pervading and surrounding power
> Of the great earth.

In an even more forceful reminder of *Endymion*, he adds, "the moon at night . . . leaves / Her cold bright kiss upon my forehead green." Pan is likewise the source of poetic inspiration, as to Keats and Wordsworth; thus it is the poet, rather than Pan himself, as in classical tradition, who is described as sleeping at noon (so that he may hear Pan). As Hunt is more specific about Pan's attributes than the other Romantics, so he is more specific in his application of Pan as a remedy for the world's ills, in a serious version of the flippant suggestion in his letter. His pantheism is passive, and confessedly escapist: "Come then to me, ye who are tired of life, / Noise, and the trouble of cities." He concludes with a few more strident imperatives and a string of personifications: "Here is . . . Happiness with roses 'round her hair . . . and Melancholy without Sorrow," to quote a few of the fourteen available. This is Romanticism with the eighteenth century still clinging to it. The core of Hunt's thought was expressed much better in three lines of "Grasmere Lake"; the poem's chief significance is that it shows the Wordsworthian Pan undergoing the process of dilution that made him vapid enough for the lesser Victorians.

Peacock, the inventor and sole proprietor of the anti-Romantic Pan, seized the opportunity for sarcasm at Hunt's expense:

> Pan, it may be necessary to tell the citizens, is the author of "Panic Terrors." The Cockney poet, who entitled a poem *The Universal Pan*, which began with "Not in the town am I"; a most original demonstration of his universality; has had a good opportunity, since he wrote that poem, of seeing that Pan can be in town sometimes. Perhaps, according to his Mythology, the Pan in town was the Sylvan Pan; a fashionable arrival for the season.[26]

This, the first (and nearly the last) modern piece of Pan criticism, skillfully exposes the contradiction inherent in Pan's two functions in Romantic poetry, the one Arcadian and the other Orphic. Yet this observation would have better suited the mood of the eighteenth century. Many a greater poet dodged the question more neatly than Hunt; many a minor poet would be as clumsy or clumsier; but no nineteenth-century poet could go behind the Romantic assumptions and include the anti-Arcadian modern city in Pan's Orphic orbit, or make fun of the Arcadian Pan for being countrified.

Peacock did not simply criticize Hunt's Pan; to take advantage of Hunt's lapses, both poetic and financial, he wrote his own lyric, "Pan in Town," to which the remarks quoted are his footnote of justification. Unfortunately it does not live up to its title; Pan simply sings a song warning of the dangers of Paper Money, one of Peacock's favorite subjects of satire throughout his whole literary career. The word "Panic" is of course appropriate alike to the country Pan of tradition and to his manifestations in City life, and thus demonstrates a side of Pan's universality concealed from Hunt as he wrote "The Universal

Pan." Despite this excellently farfetched jest, there is nothing Pan-like in the lyric itself.

A "Lucianic" Pan occurs as early as 1816, in Peacock's unpublished fragmentary romance *Calidore*. This may well be the first (nondramatic) fictional Pan character in English: the figure begins with, but is not limited to, the Pan of mythology. Peacock's aim, like Lucian's before him, is to create a comic-satiric effect by playing off the idealized gods familiar from mythology against these gods reduced to a limited human level.[27]

When Arthur's knights were defeated by Mordred, they were exiled to the island set aside for the representatives of mythologies that could no longer command belief; there they found their predecessors, the Olympians who had been defeated by Christ. Their first glimpse reveals a Pan far more "Homeric" or Lucianic than Romantic (the Orphic Pan, at least, does not lend himself to fiction): "Two very singular persons were walking on the sea-shore: one in appearance a young and handsome man with a crown of vine-leaves on his head . . . the other a wild and singular figure in a fine state of picturesque roughness, with goat's horns and feet and a laughing face" (VIII, 323). These gods know that men call them by the names of devils and worship other gods gloomily where the Olympians were once worshiped cheerfully. The class distinctions among the deities, which Lucian also noted, apply even to this afterlife: Pan and the woodland gods live in the valleys, while the Olympians are on the mountain; Bacchus divides his time between the two. Pan performs incidental actions that remind us of his associations with nymphs and music, but, apart from the initial vignette, his principal contribution is a drinking song, heavy with classical allusions, but possessing no more dramatic function than do the similar lyrics that decorate so liberally the pages of Peacock's later novels.

In *Melincourt* (1817), Peacock finally gets into his typical satiric stride. He no longer shows us Pan reveling, as in *Calidore*; he tells us that according to the findings of modern scholarship, Pan ought to revel. A generalized satire has become a focused intellectual satire. The hero of *Melincourt*, that most attractive child of nature, the dumb Baronet, Sir Oran Haut-Ton, is perhaps the only character in Peacock's works whose charm does not depend on his dialogue. Sir Oran is a "specimen of the natural and original man . . . caught by an intelligent negro very young, in the woods of Angola"; to the extent that he is a satire on Monboddo's view of the humanity of the apes, he is no concern of ours. But having once established Oran's claim to humanity, Peacock raises him even higher "in the scale of being." Another character, rephrasing "Rousseau and the author of 'Philosophie de la Nature,'" identifies Oran with "a god of the woods": "It is all the more curious to think that modern travellers should have made beasts, under the names of Pongos, Mandrills, and Oran Outangs, of the very same beings whom the ancients worshipped as divinities under the names of Fauns and Satyrs, Silenus and Pan" (II, 63).

At this point, the guying becomes more specific. Thomas Taylor the Platonist, to whose translation of the Orphic Hymn we have already referred, is the original of Peacock's "learned mythologist, who has long laboured to rebuild the fallen temple of Jupiter . . . [who] immediately conceived a high veneration [for Sir Oran] and would never call him by any name but Pan." He addresses Sir Oran in the words of the Orphic Hymn to Pan (although the translation that the mythologist is said to have made bears no relation to Taylor's) and continues

It alludes to the happy existence of the dancing Pans, Fauns, Orans *et id genus omne*, whose dwellings are the caves of rocks and the hollows of trees, such as undoubtedly was, or would have been the natural mode of life of our friend Pan among the woods of Angola. It alludes, too, to their musical powers, which in our friend Pan it gives me indescribable pleasure to find so happily exemplified [in a Pan-like melancholy fluting]. The epithet *Bacchic*, our friend Pan's attachment to the bottle demonstrates to be very appropriate; and the epithet *Kosmokratos*, king of the world, points out a striking similarity between the Orphic Pan and the Troglodyte of Linnaeus' . . . he concluded by saying, he had known many profound philosophical and mythological systems founded on much slighter analogies.[28]

And indeed, if we remember Huetius' *Demonstratio Evangelica*, we must admit that the learned mythologist has at least as firm a basis for his deductions as had the learned cleric.

For all Oran's Pan-like actions,[29] he is no more a fictional character identified as Pan than is the Pan of *Calidore*. Not until the end of the century does Pan become sufficiently free of his mythical identity to take part, as himself, in newly devised fictions.

By an irony fundamental in Peacock's literary makeup, he could produce not only several anti-Romantic Pans, but a fine specimen of a Romantic Pan as well. His narrative poem of 1818, *Rhododaphne*, has several references, perhaps over scrupulously annotated by the author, derived directly from classical sources. Usually, whatever the source, they appear in highly Romantic contexts: "Vainly have their vows been paid / To Pan" for Calliroë's recovery from her mysterious illness; nor can "Arcadian Pan" dissolve the chain of the Thessalian spell. Lines like "Divine / No less than our own Pan must be / To us Love's bounteous deity," combine a Miltonic echo (cf. *Comus* 176) with a sentiment that might have come from eighteenth-century pastoral.

The longest and most crucial passage dealing with Pan in this poem is a genuine contribution to the Romantic conception:

> By living streams, in sylvan shades,
> Where winds and waves symphonious make
> Sweet melody, the youths and maids
> No more with choral music wake
> Lone Echo from her tangled brake,
> On Pan, or Sylvan Genius, calling,
> Naiad or Nymph, in suppliant song.[30]

So far the theme is similar to Keats's line (written at about the same time) "Pan is no longer sought." Peacock shares Keats's keen sense of loss, of vanished beauty. He says of one of his fictional characters that his "fancy peopled [certain scenes] at pleasure with nymphs and genii, fauns and satyrs" (*Gryll Grange*, p. 98). The remark could apply equally well to Peacock himself or to Keats.

Peacock goes on, however, to define this loss in terms of the Plutarchan Death of Pan, for the first time in English poetry:

> The streams no sedge-crowned Genii roll
> From bounteous urn: great Pan is dead:
> The life, the intellectual soul
> Of vale, and grove, and stream, has fled
> For ever with the creed sublime
> That nursed the Muse of earlier time.[31]

Peacock combines here the Plutarchan Pan and the usual "Orphic" Pan of the Romantic poets, to reinforce the emotional loss by alleging a metaphysical one.

Shelley's comments on *Rhododaphne*, in a critique first published in 1879, overemphasize its classicism; only a Romantic could see this poem as "essentially antique." "We are led forth from the frequent pomp of sacrifice into the solitude of mountains and forest where Pan 'The life, the intellectual soul of grove and stream' yet lives and yet is worshipped." [32] Shelley prefers to emphasize here the Pan of the narrative part of the poem; he makes no comment upon the "dead" Pan of the introductory passage from which he is quoting. Nor does he comment on the most striking feature of the passage, its nostalgic sense of loss.

This nostalgia Peacock shared with so many of his poetic contemporaries, including the Shelley of *Hellas*, that it may not have seemed necessary to comment on it. It is tempting, as so many critics have found, to trace this mood of "neo-Hellenism" back to Schiller's *Die Götter Griechenlands*, or, oftener and, I think, less helpfully, to Coleridge's translation (1799–1800) of Schiller's play *Die Piccolomini*:

> The intelligible forms of ancient poets,
> The fair humanities of old religion,
> The Power, the Beauty, and the Majesty,
> That had their haunts in dale, or piny mountain,
> Or forest by slow stream, or pebbly spring,
> Or chasms and wat'ry depths; all these have vanished.
> They live no longer in the faith of reason!
> But still the heart doth need a language, still
> Doth the old instinct bring back the old names. (II. iv 123f)

This passage is quoted or referred to with great frequency in the literature of the time: to give a few random examples, Sir Walter Scott quotes it toward the end of the third chapter of *Guy Mannering*; Felicia Hemans gives it as the epigraph of her poem "The Streams"; and as late as 1875 it is given as the motto for an edition of Thomas Taylor's *Eleusinian and Bacchic Mysteries*.[33]

The mood of nostalgia in the passage from *The Piccolomini* is frequently emphasized by omitting the lines that give clues to the context. Only Scott, whose purpose in quoting the lines is closer to Schiller's own, gives a fuller perspective: *Guy Mannering* is subtitled *The Astrologer*.

The Romantics undoubtedly owed a general debt to Schiller, and to Schiller via Coleridge, for ways of expressing a powerful and important Romantic mood. Yet when we have noted that neither Schiller, nor Coleridge on his behalf, mentions the death of Pan, or even includes him among those "that had their haunts in dale, or piny mountain,"[34] assessing the precise degree of indebtedness of Wordsworth, Keats, Peacock, Byron, or Felicia Hemans to Schiller and Coleridge is not really our concern, even though all five embedded references to Pan in passages of generalized mythological nostalgia.

There are varying degrees of embedment, however. Wordsworth's nostalgia (especially strong in *The Prelude*, VIII, 128f) is never as explicit as that of the others named; Pan's share in it, as an Arcadian deity, is slightly modified by his Orphic functions. Keats gives Pan simply as one more example of vanished myth; it is an especially potent one because of Pan's pastoral, Arcadian associations. Felicia Hemans refers to "Pan's deserted haunts"; this is both a picturesque pastoral reference at the appropriate moment, as in Keats, and one more reference to a vanished deity, as in Shelley's "Chorus" from *Hellas*. Scattered through her poem are several allusions to the Cessation of Oracles, an episode commonly associated (as in Plutarch's "De Defectu Oraculorum" itself) with the Death of Pan, which might lead one to suppose that she had that episode in mind as well. But the line is not sufficiently specific to make it clear; and sources were available which discussed the Cessation of Oracles without mentioning the death of Pan.[35]

Another passage that has been traced back, and with good reason, to Schiller and Coleridge is Byron's fragment "Aristomenes," written in 1823, but unpublished until 1901.[36] I quote it in its entirety.

> The Gods of old are silent on their shore.
> Since the great Pan expired, and through the roar
> Of the Ionian waters broke a dread
> Voice which proclaimed "the Mighty Pan is dead."
> How much died with him! false or true — the dream
> Was beautiful which peopled every stream
> With more than finny tenants, and adorned
> The woods and waters with coy nymphs that scorned
> Pursuing Deities, or in the embrace
> Of gods brought forth the high heroic race
> Whose names are on the hills and o'er the seas.

The first four lines of Byron's fragment contain the closest, most specific re-telling of the Plutarchan story yet written in English poetry. Milton and Spenser both required commentators to find the Plutarchan references in their lines on Pan; both Hunt and Peacock used the story allusively, assuming that their audience (consisting, in Hunt's case, entirely of T. J. Hogg) would have the Plutarchan story clearly in mind. Byron, on the other hand, gives the essence of Plutarch's narration, including the new and significant details of the "Ionian waters" and "the dread voice." From the story he proposes to draw the conclusion that the other "Gods of old" died at the same time. Byron then makes his link between the death of Pan and the death of myth; the poem pivots in a rather obvious fashion on the line "How much died with him." [37] Pan's death is a type or representative death: causality is not emphasized, and the last, Schilleresque, part of the poem is an elaboration of the "how much" of the pivotal line.

Byron's poem very much resembles Peacock's in general sentiment, but his structural skill is inferior, and his interpretation of Pan is very different. Byron does not state that Pan is any more "universal" than the other gods. Pan is part of the beautiful dream, he might perhaps be a "pursuing Deity," but he is nothing like Peacock's "intellectual soul of vale and grove"; Byron will not commit himself to Peacock's almost paradoxical blend of the Orphic and the Plutarchan.

Byron's sources for this poem are by no means as clear as are Shelley's, say, for the "Chorus" from *Hellas*. Material was available in Plutarch's own version, in E. K.'s notes on Spenser and Thomas Warton's on Milton; although eighteenth-century mythographers were not obsessed with Plutarchan Pan as their predecessors had been for over a century, Lemprière and Cudworth are also possible sources. Byron clearly read more than what Peacock and Felicia Hemans provided — but it need not have been very much more.

Byron and Peacock both leave the way open for attributing the demise of Pan to the agency of Christ, but they are concerned with the loss of the old rather than with the dichotomy between old and new. Schiller and Felicia Hemans each assess briefly the antithesis of pagan and Christian, and display opposite loyalties; in both the contrast of "then" and "now" is implicit throughout. Of the responsibility of Christianity Schiller says only

> Alle jene Blüten sind gefallen
> Von des Nordes schauerlichem Wehn. (xiii)

> All those blossoms have been killed
> By the chilly drifts from the north.

Mrs. Hemans' predilections, despite her playing with mythic nostalgia throughout many stanzas, are made clear in the line "While yet the light of heaven-born truth was not" (stanza lxiii). Neither Schiller nor Mrs. Hemans is talking about Pan at this point, but here, in embryo, is the conflict in which Christ and Pan become polar opposites. Even in Hunt's "The great God Pan is alive again," the conflict which will dominate Elizabeth Barrett Browning's "The Dead Pan" (1844) — and, through her, much nineteenth-century prose and poetry — has not yet emerged clearly.

The parallel between "Aristomenes" and "The Dead Pan" did

not escape E. H. Coleridge, who links them allusively by quoting the latter in his note. It would be tempting to see in "Aristomenes" the missing link between Schiller's Pan-less "Gods of Greece" and Plutarch's Christ-less "On the Cessation of Oracles" on the one hand, and Mrs. Browning's clear Pan–Christ opposition on the other, as if she were "replying" to Byron as well as to Schiller. But, like Hunt's epistolary reference to the revival of a happy pagan religion, Byron's fragment cannot have had a very wide circulation.

Even though we have devoted considerable space to the Plutarchan Pans of the Romantic period, it should be clear that what references there were, with the exception of Shelley's adaptation of Milton, were either unpublished or, like *Rhododaphne*, not widely circulated. The major Romantics, Wordsworth, Keats, and Shelley, had nothing to gain from identifying Pan with Christ, or opposing him to Christ. For them Pan was Orphic, or pastoral, or most commonly some blend of the two. He came directly from classical sources, or from Milton (note the phrase "universal Pan" used by Shelley, Wordsworth, and Hunt, implied by Keats and Coleridge, and repeatedly quoted by Hazlitt) with additions from the Homeric and Orphic Hymns (especially in Keats) and a strong infusion of neo-Platonist ideas through such possible intermediaries as Cudworth and Thomas Taylor. Although many Victorian Pans do follow on logically from these Romantic Pans, they form too narrow a base to be the whole source of the astonishing proliferation and variety which will be discussed in the next chapter.

There are two principal ways of giving solidity to a Pan figure: one is by providing concrete visual details which emphasize Pan's characteristic attributes, his form and his functions; the other is by allying the reference with one or another of the Pan stories which seize the imagination most effectively. For the eighteenth century, the Judgment of Midas was such a story; for the Victorians it was, without any doubt, Plutarch's story of the Death of Pan, in which the Romantics had taken only this fleeting interest.

Only Hazlitt, among the Romantics, employs the crudely

vigorous and eminently visual Pan who could be both an idea and a picture at the same time, a Pan allied to the grotesqueness and exaggeration, the "Gothic" qualities, which were a part of the Romantic movement. Of those who used Pan extensively, perhaps Keats's Pans are the most satisfying, according to Hazlitt's criteria, for he provides details of function, if not of form, and gives a "local habitation" to what might otherwise be an abstract mysteriousness.

The possibilities of the Pan motif are best realized, I feel, when some idea or point of view is given concrete expression in the *form* of the goat-god, while the paradox of his double nature is preserved, as it is in the best of the original myths. The ideas that Pan has symbolized at one time or another are astonishingly (though not randomly) varied, but his form remains, by definition, relatively constant. If either picture or idea must, for some reason, be sacrificed, the essence of the figure will be far less damaged by the sacrifice of the idea.[38]

Chapter III

VICTORIAN PAN

The Victorian genius for using the traditional fabric of myth and legend to set free topically relevant and psychologically valid meanings is well exemplified in their exploration and development of the possibilities of the Pan motif. The major Victorian poets, especially Landor, the Brownings, and Meredith, restored the figure of Pan the Arcadian goat-god to his classical role as a participant in actions, endowed him with elements of individuality and of personality, whether human, bestial, or divine, and stressed the paradox that he was both a goat and a god. They owed little to their immediate predecessors, the Romantic poets, for whom Pan had been an abstract concept; "invisible" or "universal" were the characteristic Romantic epithets for Pan, who was an all-infusing spirit of the landscape, most often benevolently pastoral, occasionally heard, but almost never seen. For most of earlier English literature he had not been even a spirit, but only an emblem or icon of the pastoral scene. Among the major Victorians, Swinburne, to be sure, follows Emerson's development of the Romantic tradition and continues to use Pan as an abstract, infusing spirit; but he, too, widens the concept of Pan significantly by stressing not his benevolence, but his power to terrify.

THE MAJOR POETS

As early as 1815 and 1820, Walter Savage Landor made a concrete and sharply visualized Pan the chief character in two long narrative poems, both in Latin. English versions appeared long afterwards in his *Hellenics* of 1847. "Pan and Pitys" and "Cupid and Pan" [1] relate two relatively obscure Pan stories of no previous (or subsequent) interest to English poets.

"Cupid and Pan" tells the story of Pan's defeat and blinding at the hands of Cupid. Although with roots deep in Alexandrian art and poetry, this tale was familiar to English authors, if at all, chiefly through Bacon's contribution to the long allegorical tradition of the encyclopedic mythographers ("Pan," in *Of the Wisdom of the Ancients*, 1609).[2] A succinct summary of Landor's detailed and cumbersome plot is provided in Swinburne's "Song for the Centenary of Walter Savage Landor" (1880). Where Landor rigidly eliminated the allegorical elements which had provided the story's chief *raison d'être*, Swinburne, sensing perhaps the pointlessness of the combat when reduced to purely narrative terms, restores some hints of its allegorical import:

> [Landor] sang the strife of strengths divine that strove . . .
> Who should be friends forever in heaven above
> And here on pastoral earth: Arcadian Pan,
> And the awless [sic] lord of kings and shepherds, Love:
>   All the sweet strife and strange
>   With fervid counterchange
> Till one fierce wail through many a glade and grove
>   Rang . . .
> Nor might god's hurt find healing save of godlike hand.
>   (stanza 29)

With references in five separate poems, Landor has a virtual monopoly of the "Pan and Pitys" tale in English poetry. He rejected the more familiar metamorphosis story, alluded to by Propertius and Longus, in which Pitys is turned into a pine to escape Pan's lust, in favor of an obscurer and more complex version: Boreas, the rejected rival, kills Pitys in a fit of anger; Pan wears the pine wreath henceforth in token of mourning. Landor's account is both more detailed and more realistic than his sources. He does not claim that Pitys *became* a pine: in the version of 1847 he leaves the association quite obscure, and in the conclusion of the later version of the same poem (1859) he simply refers to "the pine-tree darkened with her gore." Earlier sources disagree on whether Boreas pushed Pitys "onto" the rocks or "off from" the rocks;[3] Landor's Boreas, behaving more like a "real" North Wind, hurls a rock at her. Landor's elaborations of the plot seem even more gratuitous in this idyl than in "Cupid and Pan"; two long digressive versions of Pan's love affair with Luna, neither of which Virgil would have recognized, contribute nothing to the plot and muddle the characterization. Again, Swinburne's brief summary of "Pan and Pitys" is in some ways superior to its original: "And his love smitten in their dawn of joy / Leave[s] Pan the pine-leaf of her change to wear" (stanza 18). This collaboration, unwitting on Landor's part, was beneficial to both parties. Landor's themes anchor Swinburne's lyric flights which, elsewhere in the poem, tend to soar into "fire" and "lightning," "night" and "darkness," while Swinburne's compressions give the essence of the solid and tortuous narrative as well as a much-needed interpretation of its import.

In several shorter poems, Landor continues to widen the scope of his allusions to the classical Pan. In the first two of his *Final Poems* (1863), he uses the phrase "Pan and Pitys" as a convenient summarizing symbol of his own poetic output. "A Friend to Theocritos in Egypt" uses the form of dramatic monologue and a historical setting to give an effect of impersonality, but the friend's gift to Theocritos of "two papyrus-leaves / Recording, one the loves and one the woes / Of Pan and Pitys, heretofore unsung" and his comment that "shepherds in their contests only try / Who best can puzzle" seem to relate the author both to contemporary English poetry and to the loftier company of the Alexandrian bucolic poets themselves. This impression is reinforced by Pan's own lines in the poem "Pan," which opens the *Final Poems*:

> I minded thee in Sicily with one
> I dearly love; I heard thee tell my loss
> Of Pitys; and he swore that none but thou
> Could thus contend with him, or ever should.

The daring hyperbole of "there is room / Just for us two" (that is, Landor and Pan himself) can readily be matched in Renaissance poetry (see Marot, for instance, or Spenser), but Landor probably had in mind Theocritus' "Pan only shall take place and prize before you" (I, 3), or Moschus' "Pan will fear to put lip to it lest he come off second to thee" (III, 55). "Friend to Theocritos" and "Pan" are more pointed and more consistent in mood than the idyls. The second one turns in on itself beautifully by ending with the same word with which it began: "Pan." The first turns, at the end, from speech to action:

> Come, Theocritos,
> Come, let us lend a shoulder to the wheel
> And help to lift it from this depth of sand.

Thus the reader's thoughts are carried on past the poem itself, and yet the lines seal off the mood of nostalgia of which the poem is an expression; this is a fine detail of Theocritean form, of no interest to later poets, who were concerned chiefly with Theocritean sentiment.

Allusions to lines in Greek tragedy, a most unusual source for Pans in English, allow Landor to define Pan as a divinely fearful avenger:[4]

> Little cares he for Pan: he scarcely fears
> That other, powerfuller and terribler,
> To whom more crowns are offered than to Zeus.

These lines, from "Lysander, Alcanor, Phanöe," are part of a short horror story in which a Pan "bitter to those who slight him or forswear" is presumed responsible for the disappearance of a maiden who had feared that "captious Pan / On one or other may look evil-eyed." Landor (later authors would be less discreet) leaves the horror implied in such lines as "Brief cries were heard ere long, faint and more faint / Pan! was it thou?" Swinburne's "how sharp is thine eye to lighten, thine hand to smite" ("A Nympholept") may owe something to Landor's mediation between English and Greek, but otherwise Pan the terrible avenger does not reappear until Arthur Machen, Saki, and others put him into prose.

More significant for later poetry is Landor's emphasis on certain less banefully grotesque aspects of Pan's being: Pan's "ruddy breast" like "corktree's bark," the frequent references to his goat-skin, the contrast of his "hairy shank" and Cupid's "soft thigh" in their battle scene ("Cupid and Pan," 1859), may have suggested or reinforced Robert Browning's strong sense of Pan's physical grotesqueness, as in the "goat-thigh to greaved thigh" of "Pheidippides" (1879), and Meredith's similar interpretation, "the shaggy brown skin of the beast" ("Day of the Daughter of Hades," 1863).

Landor, greatly elaborating hints found in the *Greek Anthology* and in *Daphnis and Chloe* that Pan was unhappy in love, attributes a romantic sensibility to Pan that blends uneasily with his comic grotesqueness. Pan is faithful and melancholy; he weeps repeatedly and blushes. Lonely and melancholy Pan figures, like Pans used as a focal point for pseudo-Theocritean nostalgia (in the manner of the first two Final Poems), are among the excesses of *fin-de-siècle* poetry, but I doubt if Landor deserves more blame for them than Keats or Walter Pater.

More than any of the Romantics, Landor attempted what have been called "psychologically valid versions of stories previously enshrined in conventional sentiment," one characteristically Victorian way of using the "liberating power of legend." [5] But Landor did not permit himself to be liberated very far, for to him the Greek "muses were sedate," the Greek "Nymphs . . . fear'd, or seem'd to fear" (XV, 166). The reservation, the distancing, conveyed by the familiar classical turn of the latter phrase summarizes Landor's method of preventing excessive intimacy between reader and subject. Landor sacrificed the wider symbolic interpretations of myth without gaining the psychological immediacy with which Browning or Meredith would replace or supplement "meaning" and "moral." We have not come as far from the "hard and brilliant surface of traditional substance" [6] that coats the emotions of John Gay's Cephisa and the other eighteenth-century victims of Pan's amorous pursuit as might at first be supposed, though, to be sure, Gay's rococo verve has given way to something more like Winckelmann's "edle Einfalt und stille Grösse" (noble simplicity and silent greatness).

Landor's remarkably varied and original introductions of Pan themes into English literature fell upon stony ground, partly because Landor's poetry as a whole was easier to admire than to imitate, and partly because he had chosen stories more notable for their obscure classical origins than for their applicability to

Victorian poetic and intellectual problems; where his principal form, the blank-verse idyl, was copied, the results were deplorable. Sturge Moore's are perhaps the best known of the later lengthy, chiseled Pan narratives, though Robert Bridges and William Morris, in their versions of "Cupid and Psyche," also have their slow, Landorian moments.

Chronology here provides a curious contrast. Landor's younger poetic contemporary, Elizabeth Barrett Browning, though hardly a better poet, was a most potent shaper of what future generations were to think of Pan. She first mentioned Pan in 1820, the year of Landor's "Cupido et Pan" and the last bumper year for Romantic Pans (Shelley, Hazlitt, Leigh Hunt). Like Landor (and English poets as a whole) she said no more of Pan until the 1840's. Whereas the Romantics tended to make Pan peripheral to their main subject, and all of them together had written fewer than two hundred lines on Pan, both Mrs. Browning and Landor wrote about four hundred lines of poetry in which Pan is the central subject in his own right.

Her "great 'epic' of eleven or twelve years old," [7] "The Battle of Marathon," retells Herodotus' account (VI, 105) in the manner of Pope's *Homer*. The Athenian herald narrates his frightening encounter with Pan:

> The monster Pan his form gigantic reared,
> And dreadful to my awe-struck sight appeared . . .
> Up to the hips a goat, but man's his face. (II, pp. 15–16)

The herald's terror is very quickly assuaged when Pan replies "in accents mild" with a cryptic offer of help, "Athens' fame I seek," and an ambiguous prediction of victory, "The fates conceal the rest." Even though she feels obliged to apologize in the preface for the mythological, non-Christian emphases of this poem, there are already hints of the stand she would eventually take in the dispute between "Christ" and "Pan." Pan's face was "grim, and stranger to celestial grace"; the herald was adjured to "learn submission to the will divine." The poem invites comparison with Felicia Hemans' *Modern Greece* (and not in this respect alone) as an early counterattack of "pietism" upon "paganism" (to use Douglas Bush's terminology) at a time when the pagans seemed to have the field to themselves.

The shift from an apparently terrifying Pan figure to an actually benevolent one can be observed again in the sonnet "Flush or Faunus" (1850). When her spaniel, Flush, places his "head as hairy as Faunus" over her weeping face, the epic simile that occurs to her is of "some Arcadian, / Amazed by goatly god in twilight grove." This is quite effective, in a Keatsian way; however the discovery that "as the bearded vision closelier ran / My tears off, I knew Flush" provides an anticlimax bordering on domestic bathos. Her concluding moral interpretation has a certain elegant compression:

> I . . . rose above
> Surprise and sadness, — thanking the true PAN,
> Who, by low creatures, leads to heights of love.

She contrasts, as it were, a pseudo-Pan called Faunus, a goatish and terrifying god, with a "true PAN" who might almost be Wordsworthian were he not so obviously Christian in inspiration.

On several occasions Mrs. Browning attempts to grasp bravely the nettle of Pan's crudely and frighteningly animal nature — for which she must be given full credit, since at this time hardly anyone else had thought of doing so — and then puts on gloves to protect her hands as she does here. The contrast with her husband's treatment of Pan will be very evident.

The Pans of *Aurora Leigh* (1856) are more genuinely Wordsworthian in their inspiration. Near the begining of the poem, "Pan's white goats, with udders warm and full / Of mystic contemplations" represent, in a sentimentally domestic way, the nourishing power of nature (p. 376). But further on, in Book V, a more complex argument is developed:

> Good love, howe'er ill-placed,
> Is better for a man's soul in the end,
> Than if he loved ill what deserves love well.
> A pagan kissing for a step of Pan
> The wild-goat's hoof-print on the loamy down,
> Exceeds our modern thinker who turns back

The strata . . . granite, limestone, coal, and clay,
Concluding coldly with, "Here's law! where's God?" (p. 465)

There is a double borrowing from Wordsworth here. She uses
his naturalistic explanation for the origin of myth: the "hoof-
print" yields "Pan" to the pagan imagination just as the "goat's
depending beard" yields "Pan himself, / The simple shepherd's
awe-inspiring God!" in Book IV of *The Excursion* (lines 883–
887). This she blends with a prosaic version of one part of Wordsworth's moral in "The World Is Too Much With Us": the "step
of Pan" bears the same relation to the "sight of Proteus rising
from the sea" as its antithesis, "turn[ing] back the strata," does
to "getting and spending." Evidence that she may have developed
this parallel deliberately is provided by her letter to John Kenyon (March 25, 1843) where she says " 'I would rather be / A
pagan, suckled in a creed outworn —' . . . Certainly *I* would
rather be a pagan whose religion was actual, earnest, continual
. . . than I would be a *Christian* who, from whatever motive,
shrank from hearing or uttering the name of Christ out of a
'church' . . . What pagan poet ever thought of casting his gods
out of his poetry?" [8]

In these interesting but easily forgotten pieces Mrs. Browning
has made very little original contribution to the development of
the Pan motif. "A Musical Instrument" (1859), however, whatever its defects according to higher critical canons, not only says
a great deal about Pan that had scarcely been said before, but
does so in vivid phrasing and a compulsively memorable meter
that have combined to make it an anthology piece for the widest
reading public. It is very probable that, for a large section of that
public, literary acquaintance with Pan begins with the question
"What was he doing, the great god Pan, / Down in the reeds by
the river?" and ends, if it goes further than those two lines, with
some fragment of Mrs. Browning's answer.

The poem resembles Shelley's "Hymn of Pan" (1820) in being
not only a description of Pan's song, but an attempt to render the
sounds of the song itself (see especially stanza six). It resembles
Lyly's "Pan's Syrinx Was a Girl Indeed" and even Marvell's

"The Garden" ("And *Pan* did after *Syrinx* speed, / Not as a Nymph, but for a Reed") in exploiting the Syrinx story to say something about the nature of art. But it is more pretentious than Lyly and less intellectually successful than Marvell. The philosophy of art that the poem claims as a *raison d'être*, that suffering is necessary to art, but art does not justify suffering, is far less impressive than the simple lyric which transmits the idea; indeed the two are to some extent at odds, for the cruelty she imputes to Pan is muffled by the honey of her verses. As in "Flush and Faunus," the simile is neatly worked out, but neither the spaniel nor Pan's action of stripping a river reed can quite bear the weight of the comparison: Pan is not to be domesticated so easily. Again, as in "Flush and Faunus," Pan is countered by the "true gods" who hold the ethical balance, who judge that "the cost and pain" of artistic creativity are too great. Her most successful evocation of Pan ends, like all her others, in a rejection of what he stands for; but, like greater poets before her, she gets full lyric value from her myth before rejecting it, and the rejection is correspondingly muted. She captures, better than anyone since Milton ("Semicaperque deus; semideusque caper" — The god half-goat; the goat half-god) the paradox of Pan's nature; her interpretation of it is that as a beast he is cruel, as a god he is creative. "Yet half a beast is the great god Pan."

These grave moral doubts as to the value of what Pan stands for, which are peripheral to the real impact of "A Musical Instrument," are the principal structuring element in the one most influential Pan poem ever written in English, "The Dead Pan" (1844). I do not consider it a better poem or even a better-known poem than "A Musical Instrument." It is overloaded with poetic jargon and with melodramatic excesses that nullify the very effects the poem seeks, and its moral — that Christianity should replace Greek myth as a subject for poetry now that "Pan, Pan is dead!" — is as uncongenially obtrusive as that refrain (repeated, with slight variations, thirty-nine times) is monotonous.[9] "The Dead Pan" does not seem to have been either as widely anthologized or as widely taught in schools as has "A Musical Instrument" (its length, two hundred and seventy-three lines, may

have been a factor). Yet the poets who read it were very likely to
write poems of their own about the significance of the Death of
Pan. This literary fashion and the catchphrase which was that
fashion's hallmark and its legacy will be discussed later; here it
is enough to say that Mrs. Browning and Pan made each other
famous.

Arnold and Tennyson do not concern themselves with the
subtler possibilities of the Pan motif; but they invoke with rare
grace the Arcady to which so many less skillful poets would try
to escape. Tennyson's pastoral scene in *In Memoriam* (1850) is
a nostalgic idealization of his youth with Hallam, analogous to
the "self-same hill" of "Lycidas."

> And crying, How changed from where it ran
>   Thro' lands where not a leaf was dumb;
>   But all the lavish hills would hum
> The murmur of a happy Pan. (XXIII, stanza 3)

> And many an old philosophy
>   On Argive heights divinely sang,
>   And round us all the thicket rang
> To many a flute of Arcady. (XXIII, stanza 6)

The influence of Wordsworth is perceptible, for "Pan" permeates
the landscape, and is heard rather than seen. More important is
the special Victorian pastoral of a world, like childhood itself,
different from and happier than the world the poet is writing
in. Here Arcady is tranquillity recollected in a time of turmoil,
and the Pan, in retrospect, was bound to be a "happy" one. The
more Browningesque elements in Pan, earthy, shaggy, potentially sinister, are given a different personification:

> Arise and fly
> The reeling Faun, the sensual feast;
> Move upward, working out the beast,
> And let the ape and tiger die. (CXVIII, stanza 7)

Likewise terrifying lustfulness and sexual disgust take on the
beastly form of "twy-natured" Faun or satyr — "Catch her, goat-
foot" — in the nightmare reverie of "Lucretius." It is probably

coincidental, but oddly enough Spenser makes a similar distinction, in practice, between pastoral Pan and lustful Faunus.

Matthew Arnold uses the "Arcadian" contrast of city and country, complex "civilized" turbulence and rural calm, for an effect very like Tennyson's, although Tennyson is concerned with the results of misfortune and Arnold with differences in temperament:

> In the huge world, which roars hard by,
> Be others happy if they can!
> But in my helpless cradle I
> Was breathed on by the rural Pan.[10]

Pan's world is better than the one we are imprisoned in; he who knows Pan's world is inevitably unhappy here.

But this *is* Pan's world, declared Robert Browning, rejecting the duality implied by the pastoral Pan in favor of another duality no less deliberately schematic, but more subtly attuned to human psychology. "The Bishop Orders His Tomb in St. Praxed's Church" was published in 1845, only a year later than Mrs. Browning's "The Dead Pan." Browning's happy juxtapositions of the sacred and the profane in this poem convey more of the essence of the Pan motif in six lines than do all Mrs. Browning's strident stanzas on the duality of Pan and Christ.

> Those Pans and Nymphs ye wot of, and perchance
> Some tripod, thyrsus, with a vase or so,
> The Saviour at his sermon on the mount,
> Saint Praxed in a glory, and one Pan
> Ready to twitch the Nymph's last garment off,
> And Moses with the tables.

These opposites are startlingly resolved in the Bishop's own paradoxical character. He is fully alive and aware of life's pagan claims upon the flesh at the very moment of ordering his tomb; the bronze frieze upon a black basalt background points the same contrast. The tomb is a significant artifact which, like Keats's Grecian Urn, assures a sort of immortality to its subject, not, in this case, a beautiful generic action, but a complex, highly individual human character. The Bishop sees himself, in part, as a Pan in pursuit of one last nymph throughout eternity; though we may well feel that the earthy outweighs the spiritual in the Bishop's makeup, it must not be forgotten that he sees himself as a Moses, of sorts, as well. His character is like Pan's own: it can hold goat and god in equilibrium.

Like the Bishop, Guido, in *The Ring and the Book* (1868), sees Pan as equivalent to the pagan claims of life, "the inexorable need"; but for him the Bishop's reconciliation is not possible. "The living truth / [was] Revealed to strike Pan dead" (XI, 1976). Here Browning's least concrete and most obscure "Pan" is a symbol in a less subtle intellectual equation than the Bishop's, and little is gained by the reference.

During the last decade of his life, Browning wrote three narrative poems in which Pan is once more, in the Landorian manner, a character in a story. The Pan of Browning's "Pheidippides" (1879), like many later Pans of prose fiction (for instance, Kenneth Grahame's *The Wind in the Willows*), bestows a vision of himself, "awful yet kind," upon the hero. Browning's treatment of Herodotus' story invites an unfair comparison with his wife's version of sixty years earlier (which he had apparently not read).[11] There is no point in enumerating the many excellences which distinguish the mature work of a great poet from the prolix and precocious first work of a minor poet. For our purposes it is worth noting that the concept of a Pan both awe-inspiring and benevolent occurs in each. In "The Battle of Marathon" the two moods are separated: Pan appears to be awe-inspiring at first and is then revealed to be kindly. Browning's Pheidippides does not shift his point of view; he sees the paradoxical combination of both qualities at once, "awful yet kind." In this context the kindness is more important. Pan, "grave-kindly . . . amused at a mortal's awe," not unlike the Apuleian Pan, has a very nearly human personality which is much more consistent than Landor's version in the *Idyls*, largely, I feel, because it takes more account of Pan's godhood. But there is much of Landor, nevertheless, in such concretely descriptive lines as these:

> There, in the cool of a cleft, sat he — majestical Pan!
> Ivy drooped wanton, kissed his head, moss cushioned his hoof:
> All the great God was good in the eyes grave-kindly — the curl

> Carved on the bearded cheek, amused at a mortal's awe,
> As, under the human trunk, the goat-thighs grand I saw.

Compare, for example, Landor's "Pan":

> Pan led me to a wood the other day,
> Then, bending both hoofs under him, where moss
> Was softest and where highest was the tuft . . . .

Browning also observes the grotesqueness of sending the shepherd-god into battle, the same oddity that had intrigued Lucian and Nonnus; he summarizes it in the Landor-like juxtaposition of "goat-thigh to greaved thigh."

In "Pan and Luna" (1880) Pan is given a personality very different from that of the wise befriender of Pheidippides. Again Browning sees a paradox that Mrs. Browning had seen earlier; again he follows out its implications and expresses it more compactly and powerfully. Here it is the paradox of "A Musical Instrument," much altered by its punctuation and its context: Pan is "half-god half-brute." The story is from Virgil (Georgics III, 391–393), and Browning explores the psychological and physiological consequences that might be supposed to follow from Virgil's cool premises, "Arcadia, night, a cloud, Pan, and the moon." Browning follows the goddess' own point of view as far as he can, then retreats ironically when her actions become incomprehensible:

> ". . . To the deep
> Of his domain the wildwood, Pan forthwith
> Called her, and so she followed" — in her sleep
> Surely? — "by no means spurning him." The myth
> Explain who may!

He cuts through the psychological knot simply by returning to the original poetic building blocks: "Arcadia, night, a cloud, Pan, and the moon." The importance of the poem lies in Browning's firm grasp of the vigorous crudity of Pan's animal sexual nature and his clear visualization of the resulting grotesquely comic scene:

> So lay this Maid-Moon clasped around and caught
> By rough red Pan, the god of all that tract . . .

Bruised to the breast of Pan, half-god half-brute,
Raked by his bristly boar-sward while he lapped
— Never say, kissed her! that were to pollute
Love's language — which moreover proves unapt
To tell how she recoiled — as who finds thorns
Where she sought flowers— when, feeling she touched — horns!

The basic theme of the tenth section of "With Gerard de Lairesse" (*Parleyings With Certain People*, 1887) is likewise that of a goatish monster in pursuit of feminine innocence, but the subjective feelings that concern Browning here are those of the satyr (compare the Polyphemus of opera) rather than those of his prey. The crux of the poem is the strong discrepancy between the "uncouth" terrifying appearance of the satyr in the eyes of the nymph, his comical appearance to the poet, and his own "heart . . . panting sick / Behind that shaggy bulwark of [his] breast," his "world of woe," and his "passion . . . that made those breath-bursts thick."

The neoclassical tenets of Gerard de Lairesse's *Art of Painting* demand that paintings exploit emblematic scenes for their surface emotions, those appropriate to terrified innocence, say, or to evil-doing with its "sweets and punishment." De Lairesse devises, for instance, a complicated practical joke, played upon three nymphs by a group of satyrs, labels it "Sweet Repose disturbed by Lewdness. An Emblem," and says, "Is not this now, though a feigned story, matter sufficient to furnish many landscapes?" Several of his engravings could illustrate Browning's line "Thy hot eyes reach and revel on the maid," and in at least one the figure is clearly Pan.[12] Browning, taking the same attitude that Mrs. Browning took in "The Dead Pan," rejects the attempt to

Recapture ancient fable that escapes,
Push back reality, repeople earth
With vanished falseness. (section XIII)

Yet he himself takes every opportunity here, as in "Pan and Luna," to discover what genuine emotions might lie beneath the emblematic surface of a painted scene. Gay's Pan pursued an allegedly terrified Cephisa; Landor's nymphs "fear'd, or seem'd to fear"; but Browning was the first to use mythical terms to underline rather than to obscure what feelings might "really" be involved in such a situation.

I have emphasized repeatedly the importance of visualizing the goat-god clearly and of coming to grips with the paradox of his double nature. Mrs. Browning tried valiantly to do so, but unfortunately, as we have seen, blurred the image of Pan's fierce animal nature into that of her tame spaniel Flush. Robert Browning obviously opened his eyes and took into account the propensities and characteristics of Pan that painters, unlike poets, had never forgotten. Where poets could rely upon verbal associations, and did so, the painters, in innumerable "Bacchanals" or "Pans and Syrinxes" or "Satyrs and Nymphs," had to show the contrast of "goaty thighs" and "great smooth marbly limbs," and had to provide Pan and his victim with facial and bodily expressions revelatory of emotions.[13] Browning's use of pictorial detail brings the themes of such paintings within the range of psychological interpretation.

Thus Browning's influence on the development of the Pan motif, though less spectacular than his wife's, was far more subtle. She gave great prominence to two immensely useful Pan stories; he provided new ways of using the motif, whether within the framework of a traditional story or in some story newly devised and adapted from hints in the classic sources. His emphasis upon the "goat" in Pan was a very necessary reversal of the Romantic emphasis upon an impalpable "god" at a time when the motif was fast etiolating into abstraction. Of course Browning's lessons were of little benefit to the most popular poetic forms of Pan: minor poets continued to produce Pans invisible, universal, and eternal, inherited more directly from Wordsworth and Emerson; lyrical, nostalgic Pans, the pastoral supernumeraries of "Arcadiac" verse; the Pans who "died" or "revived," as balance shifted on some intellectual seesaw. Browning's most important innovation was to see Pan, not as a goat-god outside ourselves, but as the goat-god within ourselves, not exclusively sexual, but largely so, because sexuality is, for poetic purposes, the most vivid aspect of our animal natures. This valuable

Verinnerlichung of the motif was to be developed not primarily in poetry but in prose fiction; D. H. Lawrence, forty-five years later, would give the most thorough explication of the goat-god within us.

In the 1840's, while Landor and the Brownings were laying the groundwork for a strongly visualized, individual Pan who, as a symbol, could represent almost anything *except* an "Orphic" totality of nature, Ralph Waldo Emerson in America was developing a Pan rather like Wordsworth's, although more seriously and elaborately symbolic. Emerson, too, was reluctant to admit that Pan had a very clearly defined outward image, dependent upon the dichotomy of beast and god. Because his Pan stands for an "eternal" process rather than a "universal" condition, he gives him qualities more appropriate to Proteus than to the pastoral piper: "the eternal Pan / . . . Halteth never in one shape" ("Woodnotes II," 1841). This "eternal Pan" is not readily distinguishable from Emerson's concept of the creating, ordering, infusing and inspiring "Oversoul." Poets are the "pipes through which the breath of Pan doth blow / A momentary music" ("Pan"); the breath which inspires the poet is the same as that which infuses the whole creation; his creativity is a microcosm of universal creation, and the syrinx pipes make the music of the spheres. All this is implied elliptically in the tribute to Wordsworth as "Pan's recording voice"; as Emerson seems to have been much impressed by Wordsworth's Pan images, it is a doubly appropriate acknowledgment of both general and specific poetic debts. No one came closer than Wordsworth to capturing "the sights and voices ravishing / The boy knew on the hills in spring" ("The Harp"), to "recording" the "momentary music." [14]

So pastoral Pan, poet and musician, is one with universal Pan, who not only infuses all nature but "layeth the world's incessant plan" ("Woodnotes II"); this creative ordering is conceived in terms of music: "these gray crags . . . but beads are of a rosary / On prayer and music strung . . . For the world was built in order, / And the atoms march in tune" ("Monadnoc," 1847). Poetic and mystic experience are almost equivalent

forms of the "intuition" by which one reaches the Oversoul;
thus "music and wine are one" ("Bacchus"). Pan "pour[s] of
his power the wine / To every age, to every race" ("Woodnotes
II"), but the intoxicating strain, the inspiration, of Pan's "shepherd's pipe" is "silent yet to most, for his pipes make the music
of the spheres, which, because it sounds eternally, is not heard
at all by the dull, but only by the mind" (XII, 32). Hence the
importance of the poet, the "well-beloved flower" of Pan ("The
Poet," 1844), to whom "the ideal shall be real" (III, 40). To him
Nature promises truer, more direct experience than the dull can
have:

> I [Mt. Monadnoc] will give my son to eat
> Best of Pan's immortal meat,
> Bread to eat, and juice to drain;
> So the coinage of his brain
> Shall not be forms of stars, but stars,
> Nor pictures pale, but Jove and Mars. ("Monadnoc")

"Pan's immortal meat" is a periphrasis for "berries," as in
Fletcher's *Faithful Shepherdess* (I, 90–91), where they are "that
luscious meat, / The great god Pan himself doth eat," [15] and
the juice (or "wine") from them inspires visions which are a
heightened reality, not the "picture pale" seen by the ordinary.
Wordsworth's "vivid repetition of the stars; Jove, Venus and
the ruddy crest of Mars" ("Grasmere Lake") has been intensi-
fied considerably. The inebriation of the poet's intellect by nec-
tar, its intoxication by experience of the nature of things, will
yield a near mystical state of passivity and ecstasy that will
resemble Pan's own:

> The patient Pan,
> Drunken with nectar,
> Sleeps or feigns slumber
> Drowsily humming
> Music to the march of time. ("Fragments on Nature")

So far Emerson's Pan images, though erudite and complexly
interrelated, are clear enough. But the relationship of Pan
("World-soul") to animal instinct forces Emerson ("Nature,"
1846) to contradict the received image of Pan: "A dilettanteism

in nature is barren and unworthy . . . Frivolity is a most unfit tribute to Pan, who ought to be represented in the mythology as the most continent of gods" (III, 145). The paradoxical effect of this definition comes from the reader's familiarity with Pan's well-documented lustfulness, to which Emerson himself alludes in "Woodnotes II": "he is free and libertine." Lest we think that "continent" has some special meaning here, there are other places where the point is made more clearly. The section of "Fragments on Nature and Life" which begins with the words "The patient Pan" concludes

> Well he knows his own affair,
> Piling mountain chains of phlegm
> On the nervous brain of man,
> As he holds down central fires
> Under Alps and Andes cold;
> Haply else we could not live,
> Life would be too wild an ode.

Emerson did not publish these lines, but in "Monadnoc" he attributes a very similar function to the "World-soul":

> The World-soul knows his own affair . . .
> He cools the present's fiery glow,
> Sets the life-pulse strong but slow:
> Bitter winds and fasts austere.

This curious inversion of Browning's rather more suitable equation of Pan with the central fires is perhaps symptomatic of Emerson's tendency to mistake "second nature for nature." [16]

Two further points complicate the interpretation of Emerson's Orphic Pan: one is the overlap of the abstractly Orphic and the concretely allegorical; the other is the Protean quality of the Pan image. In "Fragments" ("The patient Pan") Emerson's one poetic attempt to make Pan concrete fails to blend smoothly with the lofty metaphysical functions that Pan chiefly represents:

> This poor tooting, creaking cricket,
> Pan, half asleep, rolling over
> His great body in the grass,

Tooting, creaking,
Feigns to sleep, sleeping never.

The allegorists themselves, used as they were to yoking incompatibles, could not avoid a sense of strain as they joined concrete allegory and impalpable mysticism. Emerson, following his models closely, has the same difficulty.[17]

"The Natural History of Intellect" (1893) interprets Pan allegorically as "instinct," meaning not animal instinct but "that glimpse of inextinguishable light by which men are guided" (XII, 32); an unarticulated form of "inspiration" rather than a central fire in need of banking. He attributes this special definition to the Greeks: "the unscrutable force we call Instinct, or Nature when it first becomes intelligent."

> The mythology cleaves close to Nature; and what else was it they represented in Pan, god of shepherds, who was not yet completely finished in godlike form, blocked rather, and wanting the extremities; had emblematic horns and feet? [A circular argument; the horns and feet were as concrete as any other part of Pan before they were used emblematically.] Pan, that is, All. His habit was to dwell in mountains, lying on the ground, tooting like a cricket in the sun, refusing to speak, clinging to his behemoth ways! (XII, 32)

Although Emerson is slightly inconvenienced by the "emblematic horns and feet," he accepts without comment another allegorical characteristic: "he wears a coat of leopard spots or stars." This he uses again in a much clearer allegorical passage, from "The Method of Nature" (1841):

> The termination of the world in a man appears to be the last victory of intelligence . . . The great Pan of old, who was clothed in a leopard skin to signify the beautiful variety of things, and the firmament, his coat of stars, — was but the representative of thee, O rich and various Man! thou palace of sight and sound, carrying in thy senses the morning and the night and the unfathomable galaxy; in thy brain, the geometry of the City of God; in thy heart, the bower of love and the realms of right and wrong . . . (I, 167)

This passage strongly resembles the only other modern "allegorical" interpretation of Pan, Thomas Carlyle's comparison of Pan and Man in general, or James Boswell in particular: "is not man a microcosm . . . of that same Universe [under which the Ancients had figured Pan] . . . No wonder that man, that each man, and James Boswell like the others, should resemble it!" But Carlyle seizes the real point of the allegorical tradition, the very point which Emerson shoves to one side, namely that "the highest lay side by side with the lowest," in Pan, in Boswell, in Man, and in the Universe; "the cloven, hairy feet of a goat" cannot be lightly dismissed.[18]

The terms of the prose allegories, "thee, O rich and various Man!" and "Instinct," are rather more specialized than the primary Orphic interpretation in the poems, of Pan as the "Deity . . . pervading all things." It is particularly true of Emerson's poems that — unlike either Romantic or allegorical Pan, which emphasize stasis, a universal condition, by way of a "universal Pan" — they emphasize flux, an eternal process, in terms of "the eternal Pan." The better to do this, Emerson amalgamated certain aspects of the traditional "Proteus" image with his own Pan image, which may help to account for (if not eliminate) some of its more confusing aspects. The neo-Platonist Pico della Mirandola uses "Pan" and "Proteus" as two aspects of All, as the "one" and the "many," the stable and the ever shifting; this seems the legitimate and logical neo-Platonic extrapolation of the material given in classical mythology.[19] Emerson, however, attributes to Pan the essentially Protean characteristic: Pan "was only seen under disguises, and was not represented by any outward image," which becomes, in "Woodnotes II,"

> Onward and on, the eternal Pan . . .
> Halteth never in one shape,
> But forever doth escape,
> Like wave or flame, into new forms
> Of gem, and air, of plants, and worms . . .
> From form to form He maketh haste.

Pan was "in the secret of Nature and could look both before and after." Instinct, equated with Pan, was "a shapeless giant in the cave, massive, without hands or fingers or articulating lips or teeth or tongue; Behemoth, disdaining speech" (XII, 36).

Compare Bacon's definition of "Proteus, or Matter" in *The Wisdom of the Ancients*:

So excellent a prophet . . . for he knew not only things to come, but even things past as well as present: so that besides his skill in divination, he was the messenger and interpreter of all antiquities and hidden mysteries. The place of his abode was a huge vast cave, where his custom was every day at noon to count his flock of seacalves, and then to go to sleep. Moreover, he that desired his advice in any thing could by no other means obtain it, but by catching him in manacles, and holding him fast therewith: who, nevertheless, to be at liberty, would turn himself into all manner of forms and wonders of nature: sometimes into fire, sometimes into water, sometimes into the shape of beasts, and the like, till at length he was restored to his own form again.[20]

Thus Emerson's unwillingness to admit that Pan did have a very clearly defined "outward image," and that this image depended upon a dichotomy of beast and god (as Carlyle saw), is not so much evidence of an inherent reluctance to visualize Pan clearly as of a philosophical need to give Pan the Protean attributes incompatible with one fixed form. Occasionally Emerson needed a concrete detail, like the "leopard skin" or his own simile of the "tooting . . . cricket" or a more abstract capacity to inspire "earth-born fears called *panics*"; these are just frequent enough to jar with the Protean abstraction which, under the name of Pan, not only infuses all nature (as Pan was traditionally said to do) but also changes his shape. When Emerson needed some hints from the traditional "one fixed form," he used them without explanation. If pressed with inconsistency, he might have claimed (as, in a way, Wordsworth did) that Pan's best-known form was simply his best-known "disguise."

Swinburne's three major Pan poems, "Pan and Thalassius," "A Nympholept," and "The Palace of Pan," all late works (1887–1893), blend Emersonian meaning with Theocritean characteristics to produce emotions not always in proportion to their evident causes. These emotions are of the two extremes of ecstasy and terror, a division of the Emersonian "All" into two opposites in a way that is not Emersonian. In the most forceful of the three poems, "A Nympholept" (1891), terror is clearly the emotion emphasized, despite an appearance of symmetry. In earlier English poetry, only hints in Landor show the possibility of a terrifying Pan. Theocritus, although presumably the appropriate classical source, is scarcely an adequate one. Considerable expansion of lines 15–18 of the first idyll is needed to render them genuinely terrifying.[21]

Swinburne comes closest to Theocritus' Pan, who sleeps at noonday and must not be disturbed, in "Pan and Thalassius" (1887):

> Such wrath on thy nostril quivers
> As once in Sicilian heat
> Bade herdsmen quail.[22]

The opening line of "A Nympholept" brings together the three crucial elements of the Theocritean setting which recur, in different combinations, wherever Theocritus, directly or by way of Swinburne, has influenced the treatment of Pan: "Summer, and noon, and a splendour of silence, felt" are clues that "the place of the slumber of Pan" ("The Palace of Pan") may be near. But Swinburne's Pans are really only Theocritean in the sense that Wordsworth's are Virgilian: the outer clues are classical, but the central meaning, which adds mystery and terror to the Arcadian superstition, is no longer so.

"The terror that lurked in the noon" ("Palace of Pan") presents dangers much closer at hand than those implied by Theocritus in the shepherds' respect for Pan's slumbers:

> If I live, and the life that may look on him drop not dead . . .
> How sharp is thine eye to lighten, thine hand to smite.

> Yet man should fear lest he see what of old men saw
> And withered: yet shall I quail if thy breath smite me.

Landor hinted at this, but the key text for Pan's "smiting" with terror is not Theocritus, but Eusebius (quoting Porphyry) on the sudden death that came in the fields to nine people at the "blessed sight" of the "good daemon" Pan: "But at the sound of that strange song . . . / all in frozen terror gaz'd / Upon the Daemon's frantic course." [23] In Swinburne's view, this is a religious terror: "fear / So deep, so dim, so sacred, is wellnigh sweet." When a man's small soul is exposed to or merged with the soul of all things, whose unity, Pan, is made up of the duality of good and evil, the resulting emotions are terror and ecstasy, which blur together into the mystical emotion which might be called "Panic":

> It is rapture or terror that circles me round, and invades
> Each vein of my life with hope — if it be not fear?

Swinburne's originality, for English poetry, consists not only in his enlargement of a minor and generally forgotten aspect of Pan's "personality" into a dominant theme, but also, more important, in his combination of the notion of terror with that of a universal nature spirit, in the manner suggested by Carlyle and Robert Louis Stevenson in prose. These two had developed the Romantic "universal" Pan by adding the possibilities of malevolence and terror, for "all" nature, they said, must inevitably include terror as well as beauty and joy. "For Nature, as green as she looks, rests everywhere on dread foundations, were we farther down; and Pan, to whose music the Nymphs dance, has a cry in him that can drive all men distracted," said Carlyle.[24] Stevenson, in his essay "Pan's Pipes" (1878), extended the description to provide a remarkable parallel, indeed a possible source, for Swinburne's "A Nympholept."

> [Pan] with a gleeful and an angry look, [is] the type of the shaggy world . . . [The sounds of nature] are all airs upon Pan's pipe; he it was who gave them breath . . . Alas, if that were all! But oftentimes the air is changed; and in the screech of the night wind, chasing navies, subverting the tall ships and the rooted cedar of the hills; in the random deadly levin or the fury of headlong floods, we recognize the "dread foundation" of life and the anger in Pan's heart . . . the wise people who created for us the idea of Pan thought that of all fears the fear of him was the most terrible, since it embraces all.

Compare these lines from "A Nympholept" for Swinburne's interpretation of Carlyle's "dread foundations":

> We hear not the footfall of terror that treads the sea,
> We hear not the moan of winds that assail the pine:

We see not if shipwreck reign in the storm's dim shrine . . .
But in all things evil and fearful that fear may scan,
As in all things good, as in all things fair that fall,
We know thee present and latent, the lord of man.

Swinburne's is a most unphilosophical sort of pantheism; it emphasizes the subjective emotional reactions to a few colorful surface symptoms rather than the essential unity which underlies those symptoms. But if "A Nympholept" lacks the intellectual content and consistency of Emerson's Pan poems, it far excels them in vivid poetical expression.

It is significant that, of Swinburne's few words of physical description for Pan, the Emersonian "breath" should be the most frequent. In the second stanza of "A Nympholept," Pan could hardly be less palpable:

As the word that quickened at first into flame, and ran,
Creative and subtle and fierce with invasive power,
Through darkness and cloud, from the breath of the one God,
Pan.

In a later passage, "breath" is less Emersonian; it conveys a suggestion of the actual motion of air in a woodland, as a personified emanation of the Nature Spirit:

Is it Pan's breath, fierce in the tremulous maidenhair,
That bids fear creep as a snake through the woodlands, felt
In the leaves that it stirs not yet, in the mute bright air?

These poems, I suggest, served to channel an Emersonian Pan into a form serviceable not to later poets, who were as little concerned with a Pan of terror as earlier ones had been, but to writers of prose fiction, one of whose overriding themes is that of terror caused by merging with or seeing the All which is Pan. The horror writers (Machen, Saki, E. F. Benson, even William Faulkner and D. H. Lawrence) use Swinburne's clues to indicate Pan's awe-inspiring presence or approach, but the important similarity is in the extreme and ineffable emotions to which the experience gives rise. Swinburne's innovations have this in common with Browning's: they were both developed in prose fiction rather than in poetry.[25]

But it was possible to combine happily the concrete psychological and material detail of an interpretation like Browning's with the pantheistic spirit of Emerson's, making the best of both parts of the Victorian tradition. This was done in only one poem, to my knowledge, George Meredith's "The Day of the Daughter of Hades" (1863).

Meredith's rather better-known poem "The Woods of Westermain" (1883) contains one explicit reference to Pan; "pipings of the reedy Pan" have their place in these "enchanted woods," even if, like the other poetic concepts of Nature to which Meredith alludes, they are "under ban" elsewhere. This is an orthodox, Romantic way of relating myth and Nature. The diffused, nonpersonified sense of grotesque terror emanating from this very wood is something different. The poem concludes with a weirdly distorted version of a Bacchic procession in which Pan perhaps lurks between the lines; his place would be with "hideousness on hoof and horn," unless he is the "One whose eyes are out," that is, Pan blinded by Cupid. Meredith "hears the heart of wildness beat / Like a centaur's hoof on sward." We are halfway to Swinburne, who names his woodland terror "Pan."

In "The Day of the Daughter of Hades" we are shown Pan from the point of view of Skiágeneia, the daughter of Hades, a useful device for combining "human" feelings about the god with a nonhuman objectivity of interpretation. She asks Callistes to tell her of

> The frolic, the Goatfoot God,
> For stories of indolent noon
> In the pineforest's odorous nod.

Callistes replies with a much fairer rendition of Theocritus' Pan than any to be found in Swinburne:

> . . . he can
> Be waspish, irascible, rude,
> He is oftener friendly to man,
> And ever to beasts and their brood.

This Pan might be, potentially, terrifying, but it is through an uncertain temper rather than through intrinsic evil in his nature, through pettiness rather than majesty. On the whole, Pan is the benevolent guardian of men and sheep, and for this Skiágeneia, with her inborn understanding for the world of "beak and claw," did

> . . . love him well,
> She said, and his pipes of the reed,
> His twitched lips puffing to tell
> In music his tears and his need,
> Against the sharp catch of his hurt.

In these lines there is a most Landorian combination of the grotesque exterior and the sentimental inner emotion of Pan. In addition, Meredith's remarkable ellipsis conveys the interpretation of the Syrinx story (compare Shelley's), that through Pan's suffering art is created.

> Not as shepherds of Pan did she speak,
> Nor spake as the schools, to divert,
> But fondly, perceiving him weak
> Before Gods, and to shepherds a fear,
> A holiness, horn and heel.
> All this she had learnt in her ear
> From Callistes, and taught him to feel.

Skiágeneia rejects two interpretations of Pan, the shepherds' pastoral figure and the Orphic or allegorical abstractions of the schoolmen, though in fact both find some place in Meredith's final synthesis. Then she makes a most unusual juxtaposition of attributes: she not only perceives that Pan is "weak before Gods," a concept derived most probably from the Homeric Hymn to Pan, where he is an object of mockery to the Olympians, but also that he is a terror to shepherds: Theocritus, again, but this time the one quality of terror is abstracted from Theocritus' more balanced picture. Neither observation is unexpected in itself, but the close collocation of the two brings out Pan's status halfway between gods and men; he is something of an "outsider" to both. Pan is "a holiness, horn and heel"; this brief phrase gives the essence of Meredith's view. "Horn" and "heel" (or "hoof") are typical and frequent expressions throughout

Meredith's poetry for conveying the notion of the beast in nature; they contrast interestingly with Swinburne's word "breath," which provides a similar clue to *his* poetic intentions.

The paradox of "a holiness, horn and heel" is developed further in the next lines:

> Yea, the solemn divinity flushed
> Through the shaggy brown skin of the beast,
> And the steeps where the cataract rushed,
> And the wilds where the forest is priest,
> Were his temple to clothe him in awe,
> While she spake.

I know of no better poetic rendering of the Orphic philosophers' view that Pan is the spirit pervading the earth, or of the allegorists' view that the goat half of Pan represents the earth and his human half the heavens, than these lines of Meredith: "Yea, the solemn divinity flushed / Through the shaggy brown skin of the beast." The "shaggy brown skin" seems at first to relate only to Pan's goatish aspects; in connection with what follows it serves at the same time to describe the surface of the earth itself.

The concluding lines are very like parts of Keats's "Hymn to Pan" in the religious tone given to the connection between Pan and the phenomena of nature, but Meredith, unwilling to separate spirit and phenomena, compresses the notion into an almost metaphysical conceit. Yet Meredith is unabashedly eclectic; Keats would never have presumed to be "fond" of the god, or to scrutinize his character, as opposed to his manifestations, quite so closely. Indeed, although it can be shown at each point that Meredith is borrowing a traditional view of Pan, it is the height of originality to combine them in such a way that Pan is both an abstraction, like Keats's Pan, and a character, like Browning's. Meredith has preserved admirably both the paradox of Pan's dual nature and the concrete qualities of his essential form; he has succeeded in using them, together, in the service of the very interpretation of Pan which, from its inception, has been the one most likely to lapse into vagueness, to lose sight of these distinctive qualities and to turn Pan into a name only. Considerable subtlety, both of thought and of poetic technique, distinguishes these lines from that earlier and more familiar version of the Goat-God, Mrs. Browning's bald statement that "Half a beast is the great god Pan."

"PAN IS DEAD": THE INTELLECTUAL SEESAW

The theme of the death of Pan, which Mrs. Browning introduced into English literature with such éclat in 1844, was of very little interest to major Victorian poets or novelists. But the theme haunted minor authors, both of poetry and of prose argument, for the rest of the last century, and has been revived triumphantly more recently, for the last poem of any interest to deal with the subject was written by Ezra Pound in 1912; the last (and the best) prose work, by D. H. Lawrence in 1924.

Even though Mrs. Browning states her sources at the beginning of her poem "The Dead Pan," the word "partly" in her introduction, and some inconsistencies therein, leave scope for speculation:

> Excited by Schiller's *Götter Griechenlands*, and partly founded on a well-known tradition mentioned in a treatise of Plutarch (*De Oraculorum Defectu*), according to which, at the hour of the Saviour's agony, a cry of 'Great Pan is dead!' swept across the waves in the hearing of certain mariners, — and the oracles ceased.
> It is in all veneration to the memory of the deathless Schiller that I oppose a doctrine still more dishonouring to poetry than to Christianity.
> . . . Mr. Kenyon's graceful and harmonious paraphrase of the German poem was the first occasion of the turning of my thoughts in this direction.

As Plutarch does not mention Christ (though from Mrs. Browning's syntax, one might suppose that he had), and Schiller does not mention Pan, Mrs. Browning must have tapped the "well-known tradition" of the death of Pan at some other point or points in addition to the sources she specifies. Schiller's curious omission of Pan from his very long list of vanished deities is, to be sure, rectified in her friend John Kenyon's paraphrase.[26] The last lines of his final stanza are

Idalian smiles! Jove's lofty brow!
Pan! the Wood-nymphs! all are gone!
Bright as ye were, bright Fictions! — now —
Ye live in Poet's dream — alone.

Yet this version could not have suggested the structure or the incidents. Pan, for Kenyon, was one god among many, and in the title poem of his own book, he employs an unapologetically pagan "gay, goat-footed Pan."

As to the first point, Mrs. Browning has simply conflated her reading of Plutarch with her reading of the innumerable interpreters of Plutarch, most of whom give copious excerpts from the original. E. K., for instance, in the gloss to Spenser's "Maye," line 54, claims (as Plutarch does not) that "all Oracles surceased," and that the event took place "at about the same time, that our Lord suffered his most bitter passion for the redemtion of man." E. K.'s use of pronouns is such that one might well assume that Plutarch said these things, whereas in fact it is "Lauetere [sic] . . . in his booke of walking sprightes" who made these claims. E. K. supports the identification of Pan with Christ, as Spenser's text demands, but he gives great emphasis to the contrary identification with "the great Satanas," first found in "Eusebius in his fifte booke de Preparat. Euang." to whom E. K., however, erroneously attributes the Pan–Christ identification. As Mrs. Browning very obviously prefers the Pan–devil identification, it is clear that any "Spenserian" influence came from E. K.'s notes rather than Spenser's text. Another possible source, Thomas Warton's note on Milton's Nativity Ode, similarly glosses a Pan–Christ identification in the text with a Pan–devil identification. Warton quotes E. K. in part, ending with "Satanas" and not giving E. K.'s final choice of "Christ, the onely and very Pan." Mrs. Browning's extensive reading of the Church Fathers in the original Greek might well have included the appropriate passages from Eusebius, although no mention of him is made in her essay "Some Account of the Greek Christian Poets" (1842), where other details of her reading in this area are given.[27] Explanations for her introduction are easier to come by than explanations for the structure and episodes of her poem itself; the repeated refrain, using "Pan" as a summarizing symbol for all the Greek deities, and the elaborate dialectic between myth and Christianity are found neither in the sources she lists nor in previous English poetry.

The indignant moral which concludes "The Dead Pan" forms (in her own view) its raison d'être:

> Phoebus' chariot-course is run:
> Look up, poets, to the sun!
>   Pan, Pan is dead. (stanza xxxiv)

> God Himself is the best Poet,
> And the Real is His song. (xxxvi)

> Shame, to stand in His creation,
> And doubt truth's sufficiency! —
> To think God's song unexcelling
> The poor tales of our own telling —
>   When Pan is dead. (xxxvii)

This (minus the indignation) could almost be the work of a French Romantic, like Chateaubriand, the early Victor Hugo, and the many others who were partisans of the "merveilleux chrétien" (Christian supernatural) and opponents of "les couleurs usées et fausses de la mythologie païenne" (the worn-out and false colors of pagan mythology).[28]

More specifically, Mrs. Browning may have seen Heinrich Heine's "Heligoland Journal" (1839),[29] in which the nostalgia of Schiller, so congenial to the Romantics, had been rendered more genuinely melancholy and combined with a sharp sense of dualistic conflict, of the sort that recurs constantly in the poetry of the Victorians. Heine, like Mrs. Browning, emphasizes the Crucifixion itself ("Welch ein Heilquell für alle Leidende war das Blut, welches auf Golgatha floss!" — What a fountain of healing for all sufferers was the blood that flowed on Golgotha) as the direct cause of the death of the Greek gods. "Zuerst starb Pan" (First died Pan; p. 103). Thereafter the phrase "Pan ist todt!" (Pan is dead!) serves three times as a summarizing refrain, set off from and concluding three passages of heightened prose, each dealing with the death of gods.[30]

In the "Heligoland Journal" Heine postulates a different sort of survival for the pagan gods than he does in his better-known "Götter im Exil" (1853). "Und im Grunde erhielten sie sich ja bey uns bis auf heutigen Tag, bey uns, den Dichtern" (And in fact they have been preserved among us up to the present day, among us, the poets; p. 113). He feared, however, that "eine neue Götterverfolgung" (a new persecution of the gods) threatened; although Mrs. Browning did her best to fulfill his apprehension, most writers remained on the side of the gods. By the time Swinburne summarized the dispute in "Pan and Thalassius" (1887),

> Yea:
> Too lightly the words were spoken
> That mourned or that mocked at thee dead,

those who "mocked" with Mrs. Browning would have been found far fewer than those who joined Heine in feeling that Christ's cold, gray victory over Pan was the victory of morality over beauty. "Die öde Werkeltagsgesinnung der modernen Puritaner verbreitet sich schon über ganz Europa wie eine graue Dämmerung" (The gloomy workaday mood of the modern Puritans spreads itself over all Europe like a gray twilight), said Heine, echoing Schiller: "What blight-wind from our bitter North / Hath seared your hues and shrunk your flowers?"

The only really distinguished poem to deal in this way with the Plutarchan story, one equaled by no English poem, is Théophile Gautier's combination of forceful meaning and graceful verse in "Bûchers et Tombeaux" (1852):

> Des dieux que l'art toujours révère
> Trônaient au ciel marmoréen;
> Mais l'Olympe cède au Calvaire,
> Jupiter au Nazaréen;
>
> Une voix dit: Pan est mort! — L'ombre
> S'étend. — Comme sur un drap noir,
> Sur la tristesse immense et sombre
> Le blanc squelette se fait voir.
>
> Gods whom art always reveres
> Are throned in the marmoreal sky;

But Olympus is yielding to Calvary,
Jupiter to the Nazarean;

A voice says: Pan is dead!—The shadow
Stretches out.—As if on a black sheet
Upon immense and gloomy sadness
The white skeleton becomes visible.

A year later, Sir Richard Burton put Gautier's sentiments into swinging iambic tetrameters:

> And when, at length, "Great Pan is dead" uprose the loud
>   and dolorous cry,
> A glamour wither'd on the ground, a splendor faded in the sky
> Yea, Pan was dead, the Nazarene came and seized his seat be-
>   neath the sun,
> The votary of the Riddle-god, whose one is three and three is one,
> Whose saddening creed of herited Sin spilt o'er the world its cold
>   gray spell
> In every vista showed a grave, and 'neath the grave the glare of
>   Hell:
> Till all Life's poesy sinks to prose; romance to dull Reality fades:
> Earth's flush of gladness pales in gloom and God again to man
>   degrades.[31]

The most graceful tributes to the dead gods in English poetry, Swinburne's, do not follow Gautier in naming Pan, dead or alive, as the conquered victim of "the pale Galilean," but the imagery of the cold from the north causing the Death of Nymphs which is found in Schiller, Heine, and Mrs. Browning ("This cold feeble sun and breeze"), and suggested in Gautier and Burton, perhaps has its last echo in "The world has grown grey from thy breath."

Browning's Guido, on the other hand, is too violent to "mourn"; he attacks Mrs. Browning's case vigorously. Guido, "a primitive religionist" sprung "From fauns and nymphs," points out hypocrisy and incompleteness in the "living truth / Revealed to strike Pan dead." To him, the case for "Pan" is complete; to his author, of course, it can only be partial.

The Christian viewpoint had its supporters. Charles Mackay follows Mrs. Browning closely, both in time (1845), and in sentiments. His viewpoint is theological rather than aesthetic-theological, and he is not at all specific about the contents of the enemy creed which Pan represents. But Mrs. Browning would certainly agree with him that "an error has expired; / And the new Truth shall reign for evermore!" In Mackay the voice announcing the Death of Pan was somewhat louder than usual: "mariners . . . A month's long voyage from the nearest land" were able to hear it.[32]

The refrain of Roden Noel's "Pan" (1868) contradicts Mrs. Browning: "Pan is not dead!" He appeals to the evidence of Nature herself, "Ocean, thunder, rippling river, / All are living Presences," to the Naiads, and to the "World-Intelligence," to support his assertion, which depends ultimately on a more Emersonian definition of Pan than Mrs. Browning permitted herself. But then the Plutarchan story, with Mrs. Browning's explanation of it, occurs to him and he sees that

> . . . before the wondrous story
> Of loving, self-surrendering Man
> Paled the world's inferior glory,
> Knelt the proud Olympian.

In the end it is a Christian God who survives, as Mrs. Browning would hope. He does so, not by defeating the lesser deities, but by absorbing and transcending them:

> Till even the Person of our Lord . . .
> Will fade in the full summer-shine
> Of all grown Human, and Divine . . .
> Eternal God be all in all;
>   Pan lives, though dead! [33]

The same notion of transcendence rather than conflict is given a more evolutionary slant in Francis W. Bourdillon's agreeably allegorical pastoral romance, *A Lost God*. A shepherd youth grows from the worship of his natural environment, Pan, to the worship of Christ, the god who is above Nature and yet includes it: Christ, whose Crucifixion parallels Pan's Death, but on a higher plane, "accomplishes your dreams of Pan / In ways beyond your dreaming." [34]

The case of Robert Buchanan is complicated by the number

and variety of his references to the Death of Pan. He is not a poet with a very clear voice of his own, but he produces some interesting new combinations, at a rather higher level of poetic competence [35] than Noel, Mackay, or Bourdillon.

He answers Mrs. Browning in "Pan: Epilogue," from "London Poems" (1866–1870). "Pan, Pan is dead!" is given as the epigraph of this poem; the poet disputes it at once. Pan, though "bowed" and "ghost-like," still haunts the city streets, and reminds the poet of the "gleam of some forgotten life," and "waters clear." These enfeebled echoes of natural beauty are not so much a call to escape as they are a painful embarrassment in the circumstances of urban life:

> Christ help thee, Pan! canst *thou* not go
>> Now all the other gods are fled?
> Why dost thou flutter to and fro
>> When all the sages deem thee dead?
> Or, if thou still must live and dream,
> . . . Why quit the peace of wood and stream? (I, 185)

In the first of Buchanan's "Undertones" (1864), Proteus speaks of how he, in the form of the infant Christ, sees the dead Pan

> Float huge, unsinew'd, down a mighty stream . . .
> There was a sound of fear and lamentation,
>> The forests wail'd, the stars and moon grew pale
> The air grew cloudy with the desolation
>> Of gods that fell from realmless thrones like hail;
> But as I gazed, the great God Pan awaking,
>> Lookt in the Infant's happy eyes and smiled,
> And smiling died. (I, 25)

In the third of the "Undertones," Pan very much resembles "Le Satyre" of Victor Hugo (1859). He is made conscious of his ugliness by the Olympians; he defends himself vigorously against them; he asserts the wonders of Nature, which are part of him; he complains of the injustice of the Olympians, and predicts their downfall. "Ainsi les dieux riaient du pauvre paysan" (Thus the gods were laughing at the poor countryman) in the fashion of the "Homeric Hymn to Pan"; "Place à

Tout! Je suis Pan; Jupiter! à genoux" (Give way to All! I am
Pan; Jupiter! to your knees).³⁶ Buchanan's Pan must be transmuted into

> Some power more piteous, yet a part of me [that]
> Shall hurl ye from Olumpos [sic] to the depths,
> While I — I, Pan —
> The ancient haunting shadow of dim earths,
> Shall slough this form of beast, this wrinkled length,
> Yea, cast it from my feet as one who shakes
> A worthless garment off; and lo, beneath,
> Mild-featured manhood, manhood eminent,
> Subdued into the glory of a god.³⁷

In a poetic symposium called "The Earthquake" (1885), Pan
is used in three different ways by the supporters of three different points of view. A young poet celebrates a day in the
country, punctuating his narrative with choruses beginning "O
who will worship the great god Pan?" and ending it with

> 'Tis a happy world,' I said;
> 'Pan still pipes, though Christ is dead!'

"Dan Paumanok the Yankee pantheist" (Walt Whitman)
counters this "Arcadiac" point of view with

> But Christ is just as much alive as Pan,
> Not less or more,

but his hedonism is rebuked:

> Woe to the land wherein the Satyr reigns,
> And Pan usurps Apollo's ivory throne! (II, 22)

Particularly noteworthy in Buchanan's poetry is his frequent
coupling of the Death of Pan with the much broader subject
of the Death of the Gods, which, from "Prometheus Unbound"
and "Hyperion" to "Balder Dead" and the "Götterdämmerung"
and beyond, haunted the poets of the nineteenth century. It
would require another study to discuss adequately the meaning
and ramifications of this theme in Victorian intellectual history. Its general connection with the attacks of science upon
received faith, however, are clear enough: "Et les choses qu'on

crut éternelles s'écroulent" (And the things believed to be eternal are crumbling).[38]

There is no necessary connection between the specific Plutarchan story of the Death of Pan and the more general theme of the death of gods. Romantic deities often fade away without Pan; the Victorian dynasties of gods generally crumble cataclysmically without Pan. Yet in both cases, he may be a supernumerary, as so often in Buchanan.[39] Buchanan developed what might be called the moribund Pan (frequent in later minor verse), whose age, decrepitude, sadness, and loneliness are stressed. All of these qualities relate more to his status as a fallen god, like Heine's exiled Jupiter in *De l'Allemagne*, than to his previous reputation as an unhappy lover. This frailty is the reverse side of the "Titanism," derived from Hugo, that Buchanan often attributes to Pan. Titanism assimilates certain Orphic and allegorical qualities of Pan quite readily, but makes him rather more like Prometheus at times than like his traditional self.

Swinburne, in denying that Pan had died at all, assessed correctly the history of the literary cliché. Henry David Thoreau, perhaps, originated the Arcadiac quibble, which we have seen in the heavy hands of Buchanan. In 1849, only four years after "The Dead Pan," Thoreau, whose Pan worship was more serious than most, declared that "the great God Pan is not dead, as was rumored," implying that Thoreau was "most constant at his shrine" for the Arcadiac reason that Nature is not dead.

Meanwhile James Russell Lowell, using an idea better expressed by Wordsworth, and even by Mrs. Browning (*Aurora Leigh*, V, 1856), demonstrated that "Pan" was a counter of readily transferable meaning. In "The Foot-Path" (1868), "Pan," instead of holding a middle ground between the evils of scientific rationalism and the good of the true religion, is rather loosely equated with a "poetic" truth which includes God. And the enemy of Romance is not morality, as it was to Burton, but science.

> [I] envy Science not her feat
> To make a twice-told tale of God.
> They said the fairies tript no more,

> And long ago that Pan was dead;
> 'Twas but that fools preferred to bore
> Earth's rind inch-deep for truth instead.
> Pan leaps and pipes all summer long . . .
> Would we but doff our lenses strong
> And trust our wiser eyes' delight.

Most of the Arcadiac poets would simply omit both God and Science; otherwise these lines are a fair sample of a typical Arcadiac argument, attempting, in a mild way, to rehabilitate myth for the sake of its inner truth. In "Credidimus Jovem Regnare" (1887), a fairly ordinary rewriting of Coleridge's *Piccolomini* translation leads into this antithesis:

> Now Pan at last is surely dead,
> And King No-Credit reigns instead.

If for "King No-Credit" we read whatever manifestation or summary symbol of modern, urban, mechanized, soulless life the poet has in mind, we have the typical Arcadiac antithesis, which tended to replace the solemn religious antithesis of Pan and Christ. Lowell, unlike Mrs. Browning, is on Pan's side, but of course "Pan" means something different.[40]

With Lowell we stand on the watershed between the intellectual poetry of the mid-Victorians and the predominantly lyric adaptations of later poets. With Oscar Wilde and Lord Alfred Douglas the descent is well under way into the eternal Arcady, where Pan is no longer a thought (or the imitation of one) but an emotion (or the imitation of one). Douglas, in lines that echo Pan's pursuit of Daphnis through the pages of the Greek Anthology, as well as the poet's personal dilemma, is more specific than Wilde about what died with Pan:

> Dull fools decree the sweet unfruitful love
> In Hellas counted more than half divine,
> Less than half human now . . .
> Wither, red rose, the world is sad and brown,
> For Pan is dead.[41]

In "Santa Decca" (1881) Wilde characterizes the loss of romance and pagan beauty in terms of Theocritean pastoral:

And in the noon the careless shepherds sing,
For Pan is dead, and all the wantoning . . .
Great Pan is dead, and Mary's Son is King.

But "perchance . . . Some God lies hidden in the asphodel," and Pan is alive after all. That is the hope and the assumption of the Arcadiac poet, who brushes aside such residue of the intellectual conflict as remains in Wilde and Douglas and proclaims the living Pan. Perhaps it is just as well; the Pan of intellectual argument, a remote descendant of the Pan of the theologians and encyclopedists, is less comfortable in verse than he is as a poetic image in a prose argument.

Even in prose argument, an air of "the schools" clings to Pan for a long time. Heine, like Rabelais before him, tells the whole story almost in Plutarch's words before he can comment on and exploit it in his own fashion. But Robert Louis Stevenson, in the boldest counterattack upon the cold, gray facts of modern civilization — "Pan's Pipes," 1878 — need only say "Pan is not dead, but of all the classic hierarchy alone survives in triumph" to bring the Plutarchan story to mind. He claims Pan as the symbol of "Romance herself," in opposition to "the feint of explanation, nicknamed science . . . Science writes of the world as if with the cold finger of a starfish; it is all true; but what is it when compared to the reality of which it discourses?" This is a familiar way of relating Pan and science (compare Lowell and Mrs. Browning); only eighteen years later Georges Clemenceau, with Voltaire instead of Wordsworth for an ancestor, gives Pan exactly the opposite function. For neither Stevenson nor Clemenceau is Pan dead, but for one it is the scientist who would kill him, and for the other it is the scientist who brings him back to life. Of such permutations of thought is the Pan symbol expressive.

Clemenceau's *Le Grand Pan* (1896) gives a thorough, scholarly, historical survey of the Pan motif, of the sort found previously only in specialized works of archaeology and mythography.[42] Like Heine, he begins with Plutarch's story, though he gives a wordily atmospheric version of it instead of hewing closely to Plutarch's economical narrative. Pan, in the first place, stands for classical culture, civilization, and values, as expressed in an art that affirmed the joy of life on life's own terms. The Church killed the things Pan stood for (here the author's Gibbonesque bias is clear), but Christ's victory was only temporary. The voices that claimed Pan's death were in error; at the Renaissance artists began to express the beauty of life and nature once more. This rationalistic interpretation is only part of Clemenceau's vision of Pan: he sees also the Orphic Pan whose "members" are all things, and the transcendental Pan whose energy is in all things. Like Emerson, he sees Pan as "l'esprit invaincu . . . *l'ensemble du monde*, comme dit l'hymne orphique . . . le *Grand Pan* qui, par nous, se fait et *grandit*" (the unconquered spirit . . . the *unity of the world*, as the Orphic Hymn says . . . the *Great Pan* who, through us, creates himself and *grows*; pp. 72, 74). Clemenceau's emphasis on the need for individual effort to express and fulfill the universal spirit is, if anything, stronger than Emerson's, as well as being more explicitly evolutionary. His Pan is, likewise, "toujours un, toujours changeant" (always one, always changing), but the changes are all progressions toward "la vie toujours plus vivante par la beauté toujours plus belle, par la bonté toujours meilleure" (life ever more alive by way of beauty ever lovelier, by way of goodness ever better; p. 77). Any heir of the romantic Pan view would approve Clemenceau's demand for a return to the fount of universal energy, from which the evolution of self-consciousness has separated us (Lawrence, in "Pan in America," says much the same thing). But it would be an unusual romantic who could share his assumption that the increase of man's self-consciousness, the extension of his scientific explorations and knowledge, and the crowning of "le *Grand Pan* d'un organisme social de justice et d'amour" (the *Great Pan* of a social organism of justice and love; p. 80),[43] were the ways to achieve this goal. Like Mrs. Browning, Clemenceau finds "vérité" (truth) a better subject for art than "rêves" (dreams; p. 78), but his "vérité" is that of scientific revelation, which he holds in a truly religious veneration, and not that of Christian revelation, which to him bears not life but death.

Clemenceau's identification of Pan with human strivings and achievements is in close accord with the view of Hugo's Satyre,[44] who likewise exults in man's growing domination over matter. The attack of Science upon Faith in the name of reason could produce two sorts of mythology. Conceived of pessimistically as the overthrow of the gods, of secure, received belief, it yielded a "mythology of nihilism" (in Karl Guthke's phrase), of man alone in an uncaring or even malicious universe (as in Thomas Hardy). Conceived of optimistically, it yielded the "Saint-Simonian" myths of reason, humanity, and progress. Hugo's version of the latter shows the grotesque, earth-tied buffoon of a Satyr, tumbling the illusory Olympian tyrants of Church and Monarchy by the powerful oratory of his Orpheus-like song, and revealing himself to be Pan, all nature and humanity creatively evolving toward its own divinity, which will be the prophesied end of evil.

A rationalistic Pan was not common in England, where Stevenson's wonder and nostalgia set the dominant mood, but it burst out briefly in James Thomson's "free-thinking" polemic "Great Christ Is Dead!" (1875). Thomson's interests are less scholarly than Clemenceau's. He does give a brief, rather random, survey of the literary history of the motif,[45] and begins his essay, as is so usual, by recounting Plutarch (although he uses Rabelais' version rather than the original). Thomson sees three stages of history: the pagan dynasty, which died with Pan; the Christian dynasty, whose death has just been decreed by "Fate, in the form of Science"; and the scientific dispensation, where "Pan lives, not as a God, but as the All, Nature, now that the oppression of the Supernatural is removed . . . Miraculous voices are not heard in these days; but everywhere myriads of natural voices are continually announcing to us . . . Great Christ is dead!"

In the meantime Pan had become, more prosaically, a useful symbol for cultural history, to be equated with whatever the author thinks of as typically Greek. Friedrich Nietzsche, in *The Birth of Tragedy* (section xi), recounts Plutarch and then says "Die Tragödie ist tot!" (Tragedy is dead!); Douglas' Pan stands for "sweet unfruitful love"; Walter Pater uses the formula, at the beginning of "Hippolytus Veiled," to stand for the death of Greek religion; Stéphane Mallarmé (*Les Dieux antiques*, 1880) takes Pan to be "le paganisme tout entier dans son crépuscule" (all of paganism in its twilight), and dates Pan's death "aux dernières heures du monde impérial" (during the last hours of the imperial world). Herman Melville (in *Clarel*, ca. 1876) again makes the story part of an intellectual debate, a metaphor in his hero's search for religious truth. He showed originality in making the story stand not for one fixed position but for the change itself; he is the only one to consider the myth as such, and to ask why such stories might matter:

> When rule and era passed away
> With old Sylvanus (stories say),
> The oracles adrift were hurled,
> And ocean moaned about the world,
> And wandering voices without name
> At sea to sailors did proclaim,
> *Pan, Pan is dead!*
>   Such fables old—
> From man's deep nature are they rolled,
> Pained and perplexed — awed, overawed
> By sense of change? [46]

By 1910 the "Pan is dead" argument could be used much more allusively. G. K. Chesterton, like Thomson, uses the argument as a metaphor for defining stages of belief. In his book *William Blake*, Chesterton equates Pan with a primitive, Greek sense of wonder, associated with Dionysus, sex, wine, and the "mysticism of the forest." This was killed not by Christ, but by Roman common sense, and when Christ was born, "PAN for the first time began to stir in his grave" (p. 107). Only Christianity could fuse Roman order with pre-Roman instincts for the supernatural. With such a paradoxical twisting of the metaphor one might suppose that all utility had been squeezed out of it, and indeed it took rather hard wear in the seventy years I have been discussing. But the Victorians made good literary and symbolic use of the double metaphor "Pan is dead" and its Arcadiac offspring, "Pan is still alive," to express the dualities of which they were so painfully aware: Paganism or Christian faith; hedonism or morality; the truth of Romance or the truth of science; civilization or the retreat to Arcady. Pan, in whatever sense, would be on one end of an intellectual seesaw, and the writer would argue for one or the other pole of the duality, for "Pan" or, to take the case of his archetypal opponent, for "Christ." That the goat-god, emblematic in so many ways of Nature or the natural, should die is in itself an intriguing paradox, as the learned commentators had felt from the very beginning; this paradox has the power of good myth to survive the most curious literary transmutations. The metaphor that it was Christ, in effect, who killed Pan was especially appropriate for the purposes of the nineteenth century. And yet, as we shall see with the Pans of D. H. Lawrence, the finest achievement of the prose tradition was still to come.

The end of the Pan tradition, for all practical purposes, came earlier in poetry. Among the young authors whose Pan poems are in a very different mode from their mature work occurs, somewhat surprisingly, the name of Ezra Pound. As nobody, not even a minor poet, gave much thought to the Death of Pan after 1912 — at about that point it slipped back into the same relative obscurity it had enjoyed before 1844 — Pound's "Pan Is Dead" (*Ripostes*, 1915) seems a suitable link between the Arcadiac world of Wilde and Douglas and the almost Pan-less world of modern poetry:

> Pan is dead. Great Pan is dead.
> Ah! bow your heads, ye maidens all,
> And weave ye him his coronal.
>
> There is no summer in the leaves,
> And withered are the sedges;
> How shall we weave a coronal,
> Or gather floral pledges?
>
> That I may not say, Ladies.
> Death was ever a churl.
> That I may not say, Ladies.
> How should he show a reason,

That he has taken our Lord away
Upon such hollow season?

ARCADIACS AND OTHERS: 1880–1914

In dealing with the minor lyric poetry of the period 1880–1914, a semistatistical approach is unavoidable. Examples are so numerous, and the patterned family resemblances so strong, that it is better to weigh them by the pound or measure them by the yard, like cinnamon drops or Kelmscott wallpaper, than to analyze them individually in the same detail that I have devoted to their predecessors.[47] According to Helen H. Law's *Bibliography of Greek Myth in English Poetry*, it appears that Pan is the most popular of the Greek gods. She lists one hundred and six items under the heading "Pan"; his nearest competitors are Helen, Orpheus, Persephone, and Aphrodite, with sixty-eight, sixty-three, sixty, and fifty-seven references respectively. She includes poems of all periods in these lists, but it is the spate of Arcadiac poems between 1895 and 1914 that account for Pan's commanding lead.[48]

No doubt far greater poems have been written about Helen or Orpheus than about Pan; they never became the one fashionable subject on which every minor poet thought he could turn out a ditty. I feel safe in claiming that the whole of Arcadiac poetry is greater than the sum of its parts, the difference between the two being expressible in terms of Bush's useful dictum that "minor poets, because they are minor, may reflect the *Zeitgeist* more clearly than great ones." On the whole the Edwardian *Zeitgeist*, on the basis of these poems, seems to have all too much in common with the weaker aspects of English neo-Hellenism. Luckily Pan was rather more alive in the prose of the period than in its verse, and even more luckily, "Pan" as an image is many things other than a shorthand term for the dreams and "facile pagan joys" of the English Hellenists.[49] In 1881, the year of Oscar Wilde's Pan poems, W. S. Gilbert's *Patience* provided a formula for achieving a conducive atmosphere:

Let the merry cymbals sound,
Gaily pipe Pandaean pleasure,

With a Daphnephoric bound
Tread a gay but classic measure.

To detail the transformations of the phrase "Pan is dead," bequeathed to the minor poets by Mrs. Browning, would be to write the natural history of a cliché. As lyric structure has replaced the narrative or dialectic structure, and lyric mood the intellectual concepts of many of the poems discussed in the last chapter, there is seldom anything significant to distinguish the lyrics which use the phrase explicitly from those which omit it. The minor poets produced some astonishing permutations and combinations of the material that the major poets (and Mrs. Browning) had placed within their grasp. Numerically, and perhaps thematically as well, the most important classification of the minor poems is that which blends nostalgia and escapism. These Pans are invariably benevolent, when characterized sufficiently to have an attitude; when described sufficiently to have attributes, the pipes and the goat feet are likeliest to be mentioned; almost the only action is that of piping; almost the only concepts are those of nostalgia for an idealized (often Theocritean) past — it is generally this that has "died" — or escape from an unendurably ugly present. More often than not, Pan is simply part of the visual or auditory landscape, nothing more than a name with vague associations. What Pan represents lives on in the woods, is moribund in the cities, or, incapable of death, despite the rumors (the unspecified "they" who declare his death are among the commonest features of these poems), adapts himself in some fashion to our own age, or flees it and must be implored to return: "O goat-foot god of Arcady! This modern world hath need of thee!" as Wilde put it. Walter de la Mare's "They Told Me" (1906) catches the richest mood of such poems in its concluding line, "Tears of an antique bitterness." John Cowper Powys defines "escape" more subtly than is usual: his poet flees from "The restless soul, the human mind / . . . These intellectual searchings blind" to the "moss-covered ancient tree" that he may behold "The deathless ever-worshipped Pan." [50]

If Plutarch is especially in evidence, it is either to explain the wasting and melancholy of the dying god, so that he may have some of the claim upon our feelings that a human hero might have, or to provide a touch of conflict: Pan must often conquer death, or conquer those who allege his death, in order to continue piping. The sad and lonely Pan noted earlier returns frequently, both as an unsuccessful lover and as a dying, exiled god. Most Arcadiac poets denied the death of Pan on the Emersonian grounds that he was All Nature, in whatever specific manifestations the poet wished to describe. Changes were rung from time to time on the traditional Arcadian landscape, which in this period was likelier to be made up of woods and glades than the grots and bowers of the picturesque eighteenth-century pastoral. Winter landscapes made a pleasant change and, like urban scenes, provided a piquant contrast with received impressions of Pan's habitat. The North Americans could find Pan among the junipers or the Sequoias or the maples (as, most notably, in Bliss Carman's *The Pipes of Pan*, 1903). Robert Frost's "Pan With Us" (1913) and Rudyard Kipling's "Pan in Vermont" (1893) are the most successful of these transplanted Pans. The timing of cultural migrations is interesting. Pan "left imitation goat-tracks all over New Zealand poetry" not from 1890 to 1910, but from 1914 to 1924; New Zealand acquired the "Pans and dryads" of "fake-pagan Australian art" at two removes from the source.[51]

It goes without saying that the genre was highly imitative. Mrs. Browning (both "The Dead Pan" and "A Musical Instrument"), Stevenson ("Pan's Pipes"), Swinburne (not his terrifying Pan but rather his pagan settings and sentiments), and Emerson (a special sensitivity was often required to hear the pipes through which the Nature Spirit spoke to the poet) are perhaps most frequently laid under contribution. Wilde manages some very close echoes of Keats; W. E. Henley of Milton as well as Emerson. But to a great extent the genre was self-perpetuating; the Arcadiac poets imitated each other.

Among the most successful of these poems are the most frankly academic, those that play (as Landor had done) upon the kind of nostalgia that Theocritus was capable of rousing in his readers. Andrew Lang, a translator of Theocritus, wrote "Ballade to Theocritus, in Winter" (1879):

Ah! leave the smoke, the wealth, the roar
Of London, and the bustling street,
For still, by the Sicilian shore,
The murmur of the Muse is sweet . . .
What though they worship Pan no more,
That guarded once the shepherd's seat . . .
Where whispers pine to cypress tree;
They count the waves that idly beat
Where breaks the blue Sicilian sea.
Theocritus! thou canst restore
The pleasant years, and over-fleet;
With thee we live as men of yore,
We rest where running waters meet:
And then we turn unwilling feet
And seek the world — so must it be —
We may not linger in the heat
Where breaks the blue Sicilian sea!

In his poem "Theocritus" (1885) Edmund Gosse paid tribute
to Lang's translation, which, he says, makes possible the reminiscent recapture of "those ancient, innocent ecstasies": "Hither
to-day the nymphs shall flee, / And Pan forsake for our delight
/ The tomb of Helice." James Elroy Flecker's "Oak and Olive"
(1916) is a more buoyant version of this theme:

Though I was born a Londoner
    And bred in Gloucestershire,
I walked in Hellas years ago
    With friends in white attire . . .

    When those cold flutes and clear
Pipe with such fury down the street,
    My hands grow moist with fear . . .

And [then] our poets chanted Pan
    Back to his pipes and power . . .

When I go down the Gloucester lanes
    My friends are deaf and blind:

Fast as they turn their foolish eyes
    The Maenads leap behind,
And when I hear the fire-winged feet,
    They only hear the wind.

Have I not chased the fluting Pan
    Through Cranham's sober trees?

> Have I not sat on Painswick Hill
>   With a nymph upon my knees,
> And she as rosy as the dawn,
>   And naked as the breeze?

Let these stand for the hundred Arcadiac poems that I have omitted; very few had sentiments or ideas any deeper than these, and fewer still had as much grace.

Not all the minor poetry fits into this Arcadiac pattern, although it seems to be by far the most popular lyric mode. The Syrinx story brought forth some fairly insipid love poetry;[52] it also yielded a more darkly amorous Pan than Flecker's nymph or the "innocent ecstasies" of Gosse would lead one to believe possible. A group of women poets expressed the desire for erotic subjection to Pan: "Blow, Pan, blow! I am thy pipe, / Let me thy music be," said Amelia J. Burr in 1915. Teresa Hooley (?1921) put it more strongly: "Stamp, burn and pipe in me, Great Pan!"[53] Somerset Maugham commented on this literary phenomenon: "Poets saw him lurking in the twilight on London commons, and literary ladies in Surrey and New England, nymphs of an industrial age, mysteriously surrendered their virginity to his rough embrace. Spiritually they were never the same again."[54]

The only masculine equivalent is found in the poetry of Aleister Crowley; his "Orpheus" provides a link between the Orphic terror of Swinburne's Pan and the more concretely sexual "Dionysian" terror of later authors:

> For Pan is the world above
> And the world that is hidden beneath . . .
> What boots it a maiden to gird her?
> Her rape ere the aeons began
> Was sure; in one roar of red murder
> She breaks: He is Pan.

Crowley's "Hymn to Pan" (1913) is said to have been written for the sincerest Pan worship of modern times, a conglomeration of horrid mysteries more suited to the sinister Pan than to the innocent Arcadian on whose altars so many poets were laying lyric wreaths. But of the "Pan-Society at Cambridge"

(ca. 1907) and the Thelemite "temple to The Beast — Pan . . .
amid the Palomar mountains," the only literary remnant is this
hymn, chanted at Crowley's funeral: [55]

> Io Pan! Io Pan! Come over the sea
> From Sicily and from Arcady! . . .
> And wash thy white thigh beautiful God . . .
> Devil or god, to me, to me . . .
> Come with flute and come with pipe!
> Am I not ripe? . . .
> With the lonely lust of devildom
> Thrust thy sword through the galling fetter
> All-devourer, all-begetter:
> Give me the sign of the Open Eye
> And the token erect of thorny thigh
> And the word of madness and mystery,
> O Pan, Io Pan! . . .
> Do as thou wilt, as a great god can . . .
> The great beasts come, Io Pan! I am borne
> To death on the horn
> Of the Unicorn . . .
> Goat of thy flock, I am gold, I am god,
> Flesh to thy bone, flower to thy rod.
> With hoofs of steel I race on the rocks . . .
> Io Pan! Io Pan Pan! Pan! Io Pan! [56]

This poem has many drawbacks, including the dullest refrain
since Mrs. Browning's "Dead Pan," but the conception of Pan
which it embodies is closely paralleled in a much more respectable work of literature, D. H. Lawrence's *The Plumed Serpent*.

The savage and erotic Pans were distinctly unusual in poetry;
the vast majority of lyric Pans were much more like the benevolent Pans of prose. The sort of Pan who gave poetic exercise to
the literary young and entertainment to the reading public on
a scale which no Greek god has attained before or since, was, at
his best, the sort that E. M. Forster's Rickie might have written
in his "Pan Pipes" stage. Scott Fitzgerald's Amory Blaine might
have turned out some average specimens, when he was sixteen
or seventeen, just before the First World War: "In the Spring
[Amory Blaine] read 'L'Allegro,' by request, and was inspired
to lyrical outpourings on the subject of Arcady and the pipes

of Pan . . . a fairy-land of piping satyrs and nymphs with the faces of fair haired girls he passed in the streets of Eastchester . . . Arcady really lay just over the brow of a certain hill." [57] Neither Amory Blaine nor Rickie Elliot but William Faulkner wrote *The Marble Faun* (Boston, 1924), where in a dozen places in a slim volume romantic Pan's "faint far mystic tone" sounds again, perhaps for the last time, to a largely unheeding modern world:

> Pan —
> As he sat since the world began —
> Stays and broods upon the scene . . .
> And clearly simple does he blow
> A single thin clear melody . . .
> So alone I follow on
> Where slowly piping Pan has gone.[58]

RECAPITULATION: PROSE ALLUSIONS, 1840–1914

The one monotonous note fluted in the minor verse gives way to a most varied set of presumably self-explanatory associations with the concept or image of Pan in the prose of the period — prose of every sort, except, not unexpectedly, the realistic novel. The most casual and possibly obscure reference in these works generally has an analogue, source, or explication in some more extended treatment of the theme, and authors not only knew themselves, but could expect their readers to know, the series of recondite possibilities the image might hold, in a way impossible to post-Edwardian authors (always excepting Lawrence).

John Ruskin, for instance, in defining the music of Pan's pipes as "degraded in its passion" in contrast with the "inspired" music of Apollo gives a nonsatiric version of something like Antony Fisgrave's distinction between Apollo's intellectual and Pan's brutally meaningless music.[59] This form of allegorical interpretation was a trifle out of fashion even when Ruskin wrote; it appears very erudite and baffling indeed in Ezra Pound's "Midas lacking a Pan" in Canto XXI. Carlyle's extremely ingenious and satisfying allegory of Boswell (or Man) in terms of Pan looks back to the scholastic allegories of Bacon, as well as forward to a more fruitful concern with the mysterious and terrifying Irrational which is part of man's makeup ("mysterious Fear and half-mad *panic* Awe") — an early glimpse of the truly sinister Pan lurking within. Robert Louis Stevenson caught this superficially in the easy symmetrical antitheses of "wizard strains / Divine yet brutal," the "music which is itself the charm and terror of things." The image is less superficial in his response to the "shivering reeds" of "The Oise in Flood." There a near escape from drowning makes the Pan-like personification of the river as "cruel . . . strong and cold" and "the hollow notes of Pan's music" much less a merely picturesque abstraction of fear.[60]

But terror is far more likely to be muted into a pervasive melancholy. George Eliot showed how Pre-Raphaelite overtones could be added to a Theocritean base in her letter to Burne-Jones (March 20, 1873): the "special sadness" of his art "can no more be found fault with than the sadness of mid-day, when Pan is touchy like the rest of us." Burne-Jones' painting of Pan and Psyche, on which he was working at about this time, gives ample warrant for "sadness," if no evidence of the classically authenticated touchiness.

This melancholy may be the quality "vitally in sympathy with modern thought" which John Addington Symonds found in the work of Burne-Jones;[61] it is found, even more strikingly, in Walter Pater's "Study of Dionysus" (1876): "But the best spirits have found in them [Pan and the satyrs] also a certain human pathos, as in displaced beings, coming even nearer to most men, in their very roughness, than the noble and delicate person of the vine; dubious creatures, half-way between the animal and human kinds, speculating wistfully on their being, because not wholly understanding themselves and their place in nature." The whole of this passage is of great interest. Pan was "but a presence; the spiritual form" and "the reflexion, in sacred image or ideal" of an Arcadian life[62] only slightly more realistic than that of a Jacobean drama, with Pan playing much the same role. Both Pater and Symonds see it through a veil of wistfulness and muted yearning typical of Victorian and Edwardian pastoral. But Symonds emphasizes, in addition to the

Pan who is the spirit of pseudo-Theocritean idealized peasant life ("the simple natural earth"), the Pan who is the spirit of wild, solitary, picturesque natural scenes. His views on the nature of myth are consonant with the teachings of the Romantic poets: "satyrs and Pan, Narcissus, Hyacinth, and Clytia, are but forms found for uttering man's sense of his affinity to woods and flowers and waters"; "for a while, I entered into spiritual union with nature, and felt as though . . . Pan [might] appear"; "the reed by the river-margin had to be a girl pursued by Pan"; "PAN, the sense of an all-pervasive spirit in wild places." [63]

In Symonds, the scenic descriptions matter more than the mythic figure or the ideas. Pan adds "atmosphere" to scenes of two different types. The first is highly reminiscent of late eighteenth-century "picturesque" verse; Symonds makes the specific pictorial associations with Poussin and Salvator Rosa. "The hushed stillness of the hanging woods, the dells in which Pan cools himself in noontide heat among rank ferns and dripping mosses." The second type of scene is specifically classical. In "The Cornice" (1874), Symonds creates a palimpsest of the "real Christian present" and the pagan past that his imagination calls up before him as he travels. He dreams of finding "Priapus or pastoral Pan" still worshiped by the nineteenth-century Italian peasant; he comes across a crucifix. "Glad nature worship" is no longer possible, to be sure ("nothing can take us back to Phoebus or to Pan"), but Symonds' view of Italy would be very different had it never existed.[64]

In the prose equivalents of Arcadiac verse, Pan is likewise used to provide scenic "atmosphere," and no doubt every shade of nostalgia known to the poets could be found somewhere in prose as well.[65] But the nostalgia is likelier to be for the vanishing countryside of the present than for the vanished life of Symonds' idealized classical countryside; the landscapes are usually specifically English ones, without particular classical associations. In Kipling's "On the Great Wall," in *Puck of Pook's Hill* (1906), the "little altar . . . to the Sylvan Pan . . . with the line from Xenophon" contributes to the atmosphere of the Roman occupation of Britain. Pan can be, if anything, more "alive" on Flecker's Painswick Hill, or in Kenneth Grahame's and Rupert Brooke's Thames Valley, than in Symonds' Roman Campagna. Brooke, for instance, in a passage where he has been paraphrasing Pater's description of the gods in exile, can find no suitable task for a Pan in exile (neither Pater nor Heine supplied one) and has to fall back on a simple Arcadiac definition: "I myself have heard Pan piping among the reeds, down in Surrey." [66] Pan can get from Greece to England, but, in Brooke's opinion, he cannot get to America: "the maple and the birch conceal no dryads, and Pan has never been heard amongst these reed-beds . . . a godless place." The few dozen American poets who shared Brooke's view of Pan's function as a spirit of the landscape could scarcely be expected to agree with this restriction on it.

Richard Middleton, in his book *The Day Before Yesterday*, gives a different and more sentimental emphasis to the literary Pan-cult by an unusual combination with the cult of the saintly child, to produce a Pan rather more like Peter Pan: "Children, roused from their sleep, would hear Pan piping to his moonlit flocks, and would believe that they were still in the pleasant country of dreams." [67]

Forrest Reid, in his book *The Garden God*, wants the atmosphere of sentimentally recollected childhood and a setting of rural beauty, both with a classical gloss. The childhood recollected *is* somehow in the classical past, when "you played on the flute of Pan; and you bathed in the streams," and this past is reached through a mystical reverie, when "real and ideal . . . melted into a single dreamy haze . . . the voice of water . . . seemed to have the power to speak to him directly . . . when Pan and his followers had been in every thicket by the way!" [68]

Three of Lord Dunsany's short prose pieces (virtually prose poems) have the Arcadiac moral that Nature (in the form of Pan), though to all appearances dead and in its tomb, will eventually triumph over civilization. In one piece, flowers threatened by advancing factories cry out, and "the voice of Pan reproving them from Arcady" assures them that "these things are not for long." In the others, Pan "saw his tomb and laughed," or "leaped up." I assume that Dunsany derived the form of his prose poems from Turgenev's *Poems in Prose* (1878), of a similar length (about 250 words), and imbued with a similar elliptical melancholy. Turgenev's "The Nymphs" is more Heinesque and less Arcadiac than Dunsany's similar "Prayer of the Flowers": nymphs invoked by the poet's cry "Great Pan is arisen!" vanish as they see the golden cross at the top of a distant church.[69]

Dunsany's tales are graphic elaborations of the formula "Pan is (not) dead," far less frequent in prose than in poetry. Maurice Hewlett's Pan in *Pan and the Young Shepherd* (1898) replies to the charge that he is dead with a claim of his living power over men: "I am Pan still . . . and the Earth is mine" (pp. 99–100).

The dialectic of Pan and Christ was familiar enough to be mentioned allusively in this period. Max Beerbohm's Enoch Soames wrote a "dialogue between Pan and St. Ursula," of which we can know no more than that allusion conveys; its loss is much to be regretted, even though Beerbohm, that most percipient of Pan critics, felt that it lacked "snap." Edmund Gosse turned the conflict into a metaphor for his own intellectual development:

> I was at one moment devoutly pious, at the next haunted by visions of material beauty and longing for sensuous impressions. In my hot and silly brain, Jesus and Pan held sway together, as in a wayside chapel discordantly and impishly consecrated to Pagan and to Christian rites. But for the present, as in the great chorus [from Shelley's "Hellas"] which so marvelously portrays our double nature, "the folding-star of Bethlehem" was still dominant.[70]

Two authors saw the possibility of resolving the conflict. Michael Fairless used a method which is almost a throwback to the medieval. Her *Roadmender* (written ca. 1900) combines natural description with sentiment, piety, and reflective melancholy. Early in life she herself was "a shy lover of the fields and woods," but she learned, in time, "that man was no mere dweller in the woods to follow the footsteps of the piping god, but an integral part of an organized whole, in which Pan too has his fulfilment." "We can never be too Pagan when we are truly Christian, and the old myths are eternal truths held fast in the Church's net." But, like Wordsworth, Mrs. Browning, and James Russell Lowell, she finds that "there is more truth in the believing cry, 'Come from thy white cliffs, O Pan!' than in the religion that measures a man's life by the letter of the Ten Commandments." [71]

Havelock Ellis found a different and more sophisticated method of reconciliation: "Pan and the satyrs were divinities of Nature, as was Jesus on another plane. The wild being of the woods who knelt in adoration before the secret beauty of sleeping nymphs was one at heart with the Prophet who could see no more than a passing stain of sin in the wanton woman kissing his feet." As it happens, Ellis was commenting on his curious distinction (which he shares with D. H. Lawrence) of being compared with both Pan and Christ.[72] Ellis had to reconcile the apparent contradiction into something congruous with his own view of himself; the curious equation of Pan and Christ on the basis of their (misinterpreted) attitude toward women was a characteristic solution, but not one likely to be widely adopted.

Though to be compared to both Pan and Christ was unusual, there was nothing unusual about the comparison of a literary man with Pan. In fact, by far the most common of the minor allusions to Pan are of precisely this nature: this "modern ceremonial" usage resembles the Renaissance ceremonial in that poets (though not, as in Renaissance usage, monarchs as well) are considered, by virtue of their function, to be deserving of the epithet "Pan." [73] As the notion of "Pan" brought rather different things to mind in 1900 than it did in 1600, the reference is not as uniformly flattering as it had once been.

It is, however, much more specific. A strong degree of physical resemblance is postulated — a shaggy beard, for instance, is almost a *sine qua non* — and such resemblance of character as is conveyed by unorthodox sexual theories (in the cases of Ellis, Whitman, and Lawrence), as well as by a love of wild nature. The first and third of these themes, not without a hint of the second, are finely illustrated in the *Punch* cartoon by A. W. Lloyd (October 16, 1929; p. 438): "The Pan-Shavian Movement. Mr. Bernard Shaw has been vehemently denouncing the spoliation of the Malvern Hills."

Emerson's designation of Thoreau in 1842 as "young Pan under another name" seems to intend no reference either to appearance or to moral character; Thoreau is an artist in close communion with wild nature.[74] In the same literary circle, some years later, the epithet is applied to Walt Whitman (oddly enough, on the occasion of his meeting Thoreau), to whom it seems to refer in the more characteristically "modern" fashion: "Walt the satyr, the Bacchus, the very god Pan." [75]

Swinburne's rather obscure reference to an unnamed publisher as "a new PAN" is memorable for its tone of contemptuous derogation: after quoting, in Greek, two of the lines of Theocritus (I, 17–18) so important in his own poetry, he concludes resoundingly: "Arcadian virtue and Boeotian brain, under the presidency of such a stertorous and splenetic goat-god, given to be sleepy in broadest noonday, are not the best crucibles for art to be tried in." [76] This image opens up a whole new range of characteristics on the basis of which a ceremonial comparison could be made, but it was perhaps too erudite for what was becoming a casual and colloquial form of reference.

Biographies and memoirs of D. H. Lawrence are perhaps the most fertile field for such identifications; for his own psychological and literary reasons, he positively encouraged the comparison. Unlike the many other versions of Pan which find their last resting place in his works, the identification of artist and Pan still flourishes and is still expected to convey a meaning to the general reading public: *Time Magazine*, in 1961, put the caption "Always Pan" under a picture of Picasso.[77]

The Pan of sex adumbrated in the modern ceremonial appears more clearly in the orgiastic country dance that precedes the seduction of Tess of the D'Urbervilles (chapter x): "satyrs clasping nymphs — a multiplicity of Pans whirling a multiplicity of Syrinxes, Lotis attempting to elude Priapus, and always failing," and again in Bennett's *The Old Wives' Tale* (Bk. II, section 4), where Daniel Povey's frank interest in sex and procreation makes him "too fanatical a worshipper of the god Pan." But such usage, so common and indeed inevitable in twentieth-century literature, was still relatively rare in the nineteenth century.

Likewise the Pan of terror finds his way into the personal essay. Richard Le Gallienne, in an essay called "The Profession of Poet," elaborates clues found in Robert Louis Stevenson: Pan is "the father of poets," which should explain the wild and shaggy elements in the poetic character so displeasing, and even frightening, to the bourgeois.[78] Maurice Hewlett enlarges upon the terrifying aspects of Pan's disposition. In *The Lore of Proserpine*, Hewlett speaks of "that sudden gripe of fear which palsies limbs and freezes blood, which the ancients called the Stroke of Pan." [79] In his prose pastoral drama *Pan and the Young Shepherd*, we see this stroke being used: "I [Pan] blew upon his eyes. Very quiet and very deep, a shudder ran down all his limbs; he grew white, and in his eyes swam the glaze of death, and of panic-fear in the face of death . . . Pan is a terrible God." This play, one of very few post-Renaissance dramatic handlings of a Pan theme, combines a pastoral love story with a plot of evil enchantment, in the manner of folk or fairy tale. Pan is a shaggy folk devil with a "gnarly tree-bole of a face"; the countryfolk are Christians, and Pan, like Satan, is "gentleman-born." Hewlett's own analysis of the play in terms of "Pantheism" and "the oneness of creation" is perhaps clearer in intention than in execution, at least as far as the Pan figure is concerned. But Pan's importance to us is less in his personification of the natural forces of "Wind and Weather . . . Death, Fear" than in his more concrete character as a sinisterly vengeful god who is, at the same time (and ultimately, as far as the plot is concerned), a grotesque country godlet, assigned his place in the comedy romance as the husband of a shrew.[80]

The period that begins with Carlyle's ingenious twist to the allegorical Pan ends with casual allusions to a Pan of terror, as if it were the most obvious and familiar interpretation imaginable. A brief quotation from R. H. Benson's *The Sentimen-talists* (1906) combines an allegorical interpretation rather different from Carlyle's with the chief event of "The Man Who Went Too Far," a horror story by his brother E. F. Benson. "Pan was a charming god to adore in dreams, but he was rank and wet and loathsome in reality; he trampled his devotees instead of caressing them." [81]

But for Sinister Pan unalloyed by allegory and unsoftened by pastoral, we must return to Aleister Crowley, who did his best to play the part in real life. When Somerset Maugham drew freely on Crowley's appearance, character, and reputation (if not his actual deeds, which were loathsome on a much smaller scale than he would have liked the world to believe) for his book *The Magician* (1908), he included the following inci-dental description of "a great ruined tree."

> And in a moment she grew sick with fear, for a change came into the tree, and the tremulousness of life was in it; the rough bark was changed into brutish flesh and the twisted branches into human arms. It became a monstrous, goat-legged thing, more vast than the creatures of nightmare. She saw the horns and the long beard, the great hairy legs with their hoofs, and the man's rapacious hands. The face was horrible with lust and cruelty, and yet it was divine. It was Pan, play-ing on his pipes, and the lecherous eyes caressed her with a hideous tenderness . . . Then came all legendary monsters and foul beasts of a madman's fancy . . . creeping animals begotten of the slime . . . She took part in some festival of hideous lust, and the wickedness of the world was patent to her eyes . . . It was a scene of indescribable horror.[82]

This passage contains in (luckily) brief compass and in all its crudity the main characteristics of the Sinister (or Gothic) Pan as developed by Arthur Machen. Like Machen, Maugham is explicit about the sexual nature of the terror Pan inspires, but he omits the coating of philosophy which distracted Machen and several other horror-story writers from their main business of supplying melodrama.

The contributions made to Pan fiction by Maugham, and later by John Buchan,[83] on Crowley's behalf are more significant than Crowley's own contribution. In *The Diary of a Drug*

Fiend (1923), the addicts play at satanism in an old country house:

> You keep on saying, over and over: —
>   "Io Pan Pan! . . ."
> You go on till something comes.[84]

In the details of Crowley's worship, Life imitated Art. Crowley, the God of his own religion, must disguise himself (as Crowley) to protect the onlookers: "he may not appear in this true form; the Vision of Pan would drive men mad with fear." Though the nomenclature was largely Egyptian, the ritual eclectic, and the main impetus sexual and satanic, the great god Pan crops up from time to time in Crowley's liturgies.[85]

Liturgies pose one sort of literary problem, and prose fiction poses another. The problem of plausibility has scarcely arisen up to now, because Pan was seldom taken out of a mythical or symbolic context, but in Maugham's paragraph he is left to shift for himself in a quasi-realistic context. Maugham solves the problem here by making the Pan scene partly hallucination, partly the projection of the heroine's own fear, which turns the tree (mentioned again on page 178 in its rightful form) into a manifestation of the magician's sinister power. Other fiction writers would seek other solutions, often less successfully. This is not the last time that I shall apply Max Beerbohm's criteria to a piece of prose fiction: Maugham's Pan "even now, seems to me an admirable specimen of his class — wild and weird, earthy, goat-like, almost convincing."[86]

Chapter IV

THE BENEVOLENT PAN IN PROSE FICTION

In the early modern period, which is our chief concern, special problems are raised by the entry of Pan into prose fiction, rapidly becoming the dominant genre for the development of mythic motifs. We have seen in the last chapter how, after Swinburne and Meredith, Pan became the poetaster's cliché with which nothing new could be said; the old song of escape could only be hymned ever more thinly. Stevenson had, superficially but usefully, divided Pan's aspects into the beneficent and the terrifying. The poets concentrated on the former, and arrived quickly at a dead end. Prose writers chose one or the other. They reached the terrifying Pan by complex routes, involving unsuspected influences and strange rediscoveries, which will be outlined in the next chapter. The benevolent Pan in prose fiction was simply the logical development of the whole pastoral, Arcadian tradition in English literature — its final, if not its finest, fruit.

This tradition produced two minor classics of prose fiction; in each of them there is a Pan episode which must be discussed in detail. One, Kenneth Grahame's *The Wind in the Willows* (1908), keeps intrusions from the nonpastoral world to a minimum. It is highly successful, but offers no aid to later writers. The other, James Stephens' *The Crock of Gold* (1912), devises a comic Eden with room for a serpent in it; though not in itself the height of realism, the book is oddly full of clues as to how myth and realism may be brought into happy coexistence. Both authors solve the double problem of investing the Pan myth with a meaning valuable to the modern reader and of giving to the Pan figure worshipers congruous both with his own nature and with the demands — however slight — of realism. Grahame's brilliant solution led nowhere; Stephens' foreshadows the best myth-making of the twentieth century.

A full and admirable discussion of Grahame's place in the development of the Pan motif, and of the sociological, literary, biographical, and psychological implications of his Pan figures, may be found in Peter Green's biography of Grahame.[1] Green's chapter "The Rural Pan" is almost the only satisfying critical work on Pan in the early modern period. Other critics tend to mention Pan merely allusively, or to use the figure metaphorically instead of analyzing the actual motif in the texts (for examples see my comments in later chapters on criticisms of Lawrence and Forster). Green avoids critical metaphors and analyzes what Grahame and others have actually done with Pan (though a remark like "the Goat-foot peeped out in Brooke and 'Saki' and E. M. Forster's early short stories" — p. 140 — does combine in one category three Pans of distinctly different import).

Green finds the Pans in Grahame's own writing to be valid symbols for one half of Grahame's own divided nature, in which the lure of the "natural" and irresponsible life warred with the demands of respectability and human society. Green equates this split with a similar split in the Victorian consciousness as a whole, which he attributes to the rise of urban ugliness and the puritanical demands of commerce. The way to Pan's world of country walks, solitude, and peace is another of the "escape-routes from an intolerable everyday reality," with which we become so familiar in the works of the Victorian essayists, particularly, of course, in Stevenson, whose style, mood, and subject matter had a good deal of influence on Grahame's early essays.

The "natural" life never meant, for Grahame, either the crude and uncivilized life or the sophisticated and decadent life. The "rural Pan" (originally Arnold's phrase, with much the same connotation) of Grahame's early essay with that title represents an idealized country existence; he is a sort of Scholar Gypsy, milder even than Arnold's, with, as Green points out, strong elements of identification with Grahame himself; he is clearly a townsman on holiday, "*in* the country, but not *of* it." A good many aspects of Pan's nature are left out of such a Pan figure. He remains the god of animals, but their animality is idealized; it bears the same sort of relation to "nature red in tooth and claw" as the lives of Arcadian shepherds do to reality. Grahame repressed the "fierce unrestrained lechery" of Pan's nature; "the subtle emasculation he performed invalidated the entire concept," says Green, with some truth (p. 143). I think Green exaggerates the "unrestrained lechery" in the other Pan figures of the era. The only instance he gives — a very good one — is Browning's "Pan and Luna" (1880). He alludes to Machen's "The Great God Pan," where lechery is sublimated into terror, and, among Edwardians, Aleister Crowley, whose supreme example of satanic decadence was his hymn of worship to the phallic Pan. But many (if not most) other authors shared Grahame's fallaciously limited view; thus a sociological explanation might be more useful to us than a psychological one for Grahame's allying himself with the "benevolent" tradition in his conception of Pan. After all, it was the Alexandrians who first performed the "subtle emasculation" of the country goat-god for the benefit of the more squeamish city dweller. Likewise Grahame repressed the elements of death and horror, in Pan as in the rest of his allegorically pastoral world; we could never guess from anything Grahame wrote that the natural forces of terror and cruelty, under the name of Pan, could return to take their revenge upon man, as they do in works by Arthur Machen and Saki.

Green's definition of the classical Pan (p. 142) is largely a summary of the findings of archaeologists and anthropologists, as collected under "Pan" in Roscher's *Lexicon der Mythologie*, and perhaps he stresses insufficiently the extent to which authors were still dependent upon the more familiar literary sources, classical and postclassical, in which little or no mention is made of "Pan's history in the ancient world . . . a primitive mountain daemon, half-beast, half-man: ithyphallic, sender of epilepsy and bad dreams, protector of herds, saviour from plague, an ambivalent demi-god, whose image was whipped magically with squills in time of dearth. Nowhere did his cult touch the higher life of the society or the higher religion of the state." It seems to me, not that Grahame emasculated such a Pan, but simply that if it had ever crossed his path, he quickly dismissed it, as most other authors of the time would also have done, in favor of the Pan of the *Georgics* (which he certainly knew) or perhaps of Longus and Apuleius (whose Pans Grahame's much resembles). A fairer comparison would be not with the scholar's Pan, nor yet with the Pan of the terror stories, but with another Benevolent Pan, in whom the just claims of earthy sexuality are acknowledged: the Pan of *The Crock of Gold*.

The Pans in Grahame's earlier essays show a steady gain in concreteness of description and a slow withdrawal from the more conventional "literary" devices; both tendencies augur well for his culminating version of Pan in "The Piper at the Gates of Dawn" (chapter 7 of *The Wind in the Willows*). An undated manuscript fragment of Grahame's presents the most abstract Pan of all: "The mountain air of dreamland is always recuperating, and there Apollo and all the Muses, or at least Pan and his attendant Fauna [sic], await you."[2] The phrase "at least" is the most interesting part of this statement; in Grahame's earliest dated reference ("A Bohemian in Exile," 1890), no distinction of status is drawn between Pan and Apollo, whereas here a clear subordination is implied. Pan is once more a second-class god. Perhaps there is a gentle self-deprecation here, of the sort consonant with Green's suggestion of Grahame's identification of himself with the rural Pan. Grahame never got very close to the sort of poetry that Apollo might be expected to patronize (and, as we know from a different connection, had a distrust of "Olympians" anyway), but his dreamland is seldom one unsuited to Pan.

In "A Bohemian in Exile" Grahame says nothing more novel than "when old Pan was dead and Apollo's bow broken," the formula of all the Victorian laments for lost myth, which themselves scarcely differed from their Romantic ancestors. Grahame counts himself among the "faithful pagans" who continued the old worship, for "it was the life itself that we loved . . . one's blood danced to imagined pipings of Pan from happy fields far distant."[3] The latter clause strongly resembles the Arcadian formulas of the minor poets, except, perhaps, in the superfluous "imagined."

What Grahame means by "the life itself" is elucidated in "The Rural Pan" (1891), where he develops the theme of a solitary Pan piping among the familiar scenes of Surrey "for his foster-brothers the dab-chick and water-rat." "The hushed recesses of Hurley backwater" [4] where Pan pipes for "a chosen few" will become the little island where Rat and Mole "were called and chosen" to find Pan. Pan is already the "brother" of the little animals; the crucial step that Grahame takes next shifts the emphasis from brother to deity.

"The Lost Centaur" (1892) strengthens Pan's animal allegiance, but in a negative way. The nonhuman is here the Brute, the Goat-Foot, "linked to us by little but his love of melody; but for which saving grace, the hair would soon creep up from thigh to horn of him." His relationship to mankind is equivocal; he may help us at times, but he represents the worst in us. Although at the end of the essay Grahame establishes the claims of the beast in us, he never seeks to establish their dominance. In the passage that most resembles "The Piper at the Gates," Pan's relationship to the beasts is seen as negating the possibility of his relationship to us, and the "beast" is still our inferior. The words are almost the same as in "The Piper," but the context shows an important difference in the author's point of view. Pan's "sympathies are first for the beast: to which his horns are never horrific, but, with his hairy pelt, ever natural and familiar, and his voice (with its talk of help and healing) not harsh nor dissonant, but voice of very brother, as well as very god" (p. 179). Pan's song in "The Piper at the Gates" — "Helper and healer, I cheer — Small waifs in the woodland wet" — also reminds us of Pan's shaggy animal nature at the same time as his divinity. Yet Pan is no longer a god for men, but a god for animals, and the way is clear for Grahame's unique contribution to the history of the Pan figure.

In "The Piper at the Gates," the words used to describe Pan have more of the overtones of fatherhood than of brotherhood and are to that extent more congruous with the usual Christian

view of divinity. The next step is to turn his animals into creatures in whom, as Green puts it, "animal, human, and symbolic
traits co-exist, without any sense of incongruity, in the same
character" (p. 279). This done, Pan becomes, in a richer sense
than before, a god fit for human worship again; the concept of
the Arcadian Pan, though still pastoral, still idealized, has been
strengthened by touching earth with goat hoofs once more.
Among the various elements which make up the scene of the
coming of Pan in "The Piper at the Gates," not the least important is a genuine religious feeling; even though it is "distanced"
from Grahame's own experience by its translation to the world
of animals, it is stronger, in its way, than any previous literary
Pan worship. So intense is the vision of Pan that it cannot be
lived with, but it is typical of Grahame that his solution for this
is not death, as in the Sinister visions of Pan, but "forgetfulness"
(a gift "which he never had in antiquity, and which seems to be
a creation of Grahame's own").[5]

Grahame derives immense advantage from his use of animal
personae in "The Piper at the Gates." The pastoral Pan, the god
of shepherds, was never a very sophisticated god, and to make
him an object of reverence to sophisticated men involved many
a violation of his original nature; or else it involved a distinct and
unfortunate incongruity between the god and his worshipers;[6]
or, as in the Renaissance pastorals, it required a sense of make-
believe that reduced reverence to the plane of the trivial. Perhaps
only Keats and Longus have dealt more successfully with a
serious pastoral Pan than has Grahame. Keats made a mythic
world where the demands of realism could be ignored. Longus'
solution was very like Grahame's; his Daphnis and Chloe have
a sweet naiveté that makes belief in the shepherds' god plausible,
and are yet too dignified to be patronized by the reader. But if
Grahame himself, or Stevenson, or Brooke, or Flecker, go out
into the countryside to hear Pan piping, the result is either to
intellectualize or to sentimentalize a god whose essence is concretely bound up with lives lived in the countryside on the terms
the countryside offers. The pastoral of the personal essayist or
the lyricist is all too likely to be the weekend pastoral of the city

dweller, as indeed Longus' would probably have been, had he spoken for himself. And it is difficult to impute an articulated worship of Pan to a modern countryman; he may love the soil and its fruits as deeply as Daphnis did, but to revere a goat-god in consequence would be, in any postclassical time (as Forster points out in *The Longest Journey*), affectation or anachronism.

Grahame's solution is as admirable in its way as Longus'. His animals are, as animals, more idealized by far than Longus' people are, as people. But the demands of realism in an animal fable are correspondingly less great to begin with (as Orwell, for instance, discovered). A loving eye for the detail of landscape combined with a sensitivity to "its" mood (meaning the mood of the person observing it) was a gift that Grahame shared with innumerable Victorian and Edwardian authors; it was a gift bequeathed by the Romantics, of course, and it is now in relatively short supply. To find characters congruous with such a landscape, and thus able to worship a god of landscape without having to "escape" from a major part of their existence to do so, was less easy. The more formidable country folk of Emily Brontë or Thomas Hardy would have had to worship a sterner god of landscape than Pan, and T. H. White's acknowledged a far crueler one. White, himself a considerable fantasist, explicitly contradicts Grahame's gentle vision of Pan the Helper; with horrid irony he becomes Pan the Keeper, or Preserver: "he preserved us, like the pheasants at Euston." We are reminded that "the ancients worshipped Pan, but not like Mr. Kenneth Graham" [*sic*]; he was a god of joyful hunting and indeed of "nature red in tooth and claw," of the suffering and pain in the natural order.[7]

So the landscapes were either empty, as in the "purple patches" of many a novelist, or inhabited only by the special sensitivity of the poet or essayist. Grahame's unpretentious little animals fit into a gentle landscape, which they are presumed to observe on a smaller scale than is the normal custom of humans. Thus much reverent description that could only be a "purple patch" in the normal novel can be an integral part of the action in this one.

Grahame could have left this reverence implicit, as it is in the action of the rest of the novel; he chose to make it explicit in this one chapter. Just as the animals were suited to the scale of the landscape, so is the Pan of this chapter a god suited to the scale of the animals. And he is still recognizably the pastoral Pan who claimed the simple piety of Daphnis and Chloe.

There has been an infusion of Christian gentleness into the concept; Green compares this Pan to the Father-God of Arnold. Unlike Longus' Pan, this one could not have torn Echo to pieces or terrified a gang of pirates. He releases his animals from traps like a Good Shepherd; he protects the lost baby otter until it is rescued. And he grants a beatific vision of himself to "those who were called and chosen" (p. 126). Rat and Mole, like many a fictional human being before and after them, are summoned to this vision by "the thin, clear, happy call of the distant piping . . . and the call in it is stronger even than the music is sweet . . . the clear imperious summons that marched hand-in-hand with the intoxicating melody" (p. 124).

Grahame builds up to his climax carefully: the two small animals, Rat and Mole, are rowing their boat up the river in search of the baby otter when "the liquid run of that glad piping" comes first to one, then to both. The meaning of the summons is clear, though ineffable; they know when they arrive at the island that this is the "holy place" where they can find "Him." This pronoun has no antecedent, but it is clearly Pan, who, of course, has no special name to these animals. "And still there was utter silence in the populous bird-haunted branches around them; and still the light grew and grew." The nearness of the "august Presence" brings a feeling of awe; it is not "panic terror," yet when He is actually seen, Rat's "unutterable love" is somehow combined with fear. "Were Death himself waiting to strike him instantly, once he had looked with mortal eye on things rightly kept hidden" (p. 127), Mole must still obey the call to look at the God. "Death himself" or madness does await the mortals who look on Pan in most stories of such visions, but Grahame's is a gentler creed, and the penalty for seeing such a lovely vision is simply that they must lose it. We will encounter many more such fictional visions in the Theocritean silence of

noon hiding a significance "behind a veil" (p. 126); from none
have death and terror (and sex as well) been so completely removed as from this one. The loss of the vision is terrible enough,
but the mercy of the god mitigates the punishment by sending
them forgetfulness. They are gently lowered into their real lives
again. The last tangible signs of Pan's presence are (as in many
other Pan stories) "certain hoof-marks deep in the sward." All
Rat now knows from seeing them is that "some — great —
animal — has been here" (p. 130). The piping summons turns
into "far-away music" and that into the "reeds' soft thin whispering" (p. 132), which lulls them asleep.

Most fictional visions of Pan are not only nastier in their effect
than this one, but vaguer in their cause. Grahame has been unusually courageous in giving a finely concrete description of the
goat-god that his characters see:

He looked in the very eyes of the Friend and Helper; saw the back-
ward sweep of the curved horns, gleaming in the growing daylight;
saw the stern, hooked nose between the kindly eyes that were looking
down on them humorously, while the bearded mouth broke into a
half-smile at the corners; saw the rippling muscles on the arm that
lay across the broad chest, the long supple hand still holding the
pan-pipes only just fallen away from the parted lips; saw the splendid
curves of the shaggy limbs disposed in majestic ease on the sward;
saw, last of all, nestling between his very hooves, sleeping soundly in
entire peace and contentment, the little, round, podgy, childish form
of the baby otter. (p. 127)

The story gains great strength from the realism of the vision, as
will be seen by comparison with the ineffabilities of subsequent
authors. Yet they are not to be blamed altogether, for it is clearly
better to be vague than preposterous; it seems unlikely that an
author could devise, outside a completely mythic world, characters who could see a Pan like this and feel any combination of
fear and reverence without becoming mawkishly absurd.

So Grahame's animals say something for human beings that
human beings could not say for themselves: if we were as good
and simple as they, we too could worship such a god. One part
of our complex natures yearns for a life so innocent and lovely,

Grahame implies; by transferring his own reverence to these personae, Grahame can tell us of this aspect in ourselves without offending any but the most cynical. As the goat-god is to these animals, so some deity bound in with nature is to us. Such a deity had often been called "Pan" by Romantics and Transcendentalists (though oftener simply "Nature"). As many poets discovered, it is hard to imagine and harder to describe what such a god might be. The God Pan is much more at home with Rat and Mole on an island which is both in the Thames and at the Gates of Dawn than he is with twentieth-century heroes and heroines who can only believe in abstractions and spend rather too much time in London.

The Pan of James Stephens' more ironic fable *The Crock of Gold* (1912) has many of the same merits as Grahame's Piper at the Gates. Chief among these is a sense of propriety; Stephens, too, creates a world, though one very different from Grahame's, where Pan may appear in his own shaggy shape without apology. The goat-god moves so easily among Stephens' other characters because, whether human or superhuman, they are all allegorical grotesques from a comic fairyland, with a truly Irish capacity for reciprocal belief in one another's existence. It is an eclectic fairyland, to be sure, but only a purist like the Philosopher (Stephens' personification of Intellect) would protest the untraditional nature of Pan's visit to Ireland.

Unlike Grahame's Pan, or indeed, most nondramatic Pans, this one is not only a cause of action in others, but a performer of actions as well. His allegorical functions are not left to the author to define; they are illustrated in his deeds and explained by his own highly philosophical dialogue. The burden of abstraction, although comic in intention, becomes heavy at times; it is lightened by touches of "humanity," by Pan's melancholy, irritability, humor, and occasional sheer inconsequence. This is one of the few occasions when it is proper to speak of a Pan character as well as a Pan figure.

The plot of the episode in which Pan appears deals with the awakening of a young girl, Caitilin, into sensuous womanhood.

She is first summoned by Pan's music; then terrified by his hairy legs; then won, partly because of his "wonderful, sad, grotesque face" (I, 57), chiefly because he was "naked and unashamed" (p. 62), and not at all by his complex arguments, which are largely for the reader's benefit. The Philosopher comes to rescue her, and another debate ensues. Such maxims as "Virtue . . . is the performance of pleasant actions" (II, 102), or "the beginning of wisdom . . . is carelessness" (I, 93), elicit from the Philosopher the grossest accusations in his vocabulary, "materialism" and "animalism" (II, 103). Pan's demonstration of the power of instinct easily defeats the academic and moralistic claims of Intellect. He cures the Philosopher of his desire to think by smothering his lucubrations with the ecstasy of newly awakened perceptions, and changes his notions of good and evil so completely that the Philosopher becomes capable of uttering such a Pan-like precept as "dancing is the first and last duty of man" (V, 235).

But there is a far stronger competitor for the soul of Caitilin than Intellect. Angus Óg, the native Irish god of growth and fertility, perhaps also a sun god, is summoned to the rescue. ("The devil you know is better than the devil you don't know," says her father—I, 71.) Both gods present their arguments; Caitilin chooses Angus, but again she has a more finely feminine reason for her choice: "his need of her was very great" (III, 157). She has learned what Instinct and Desire have to teach her; she is therefore able to respond to the higher claims of the Divine Imagination, of Óg's "tenderness" (p. 147). She "withdrew herself from the arms of her desires," yet "her body bore the marks of [Pan's] grip [for] many days" (p. 156).

Stephens' dialectic is clearly Nietzschean, or perhaps mock-Nietzschean, which may help explain in terms of a common ancestry the numerous parallels with Lawrence's arguments: "I sing of the beast and the descent . . . the thought that is not born in the measure or the ice or the head, but in the feet and the hot blood and the pulse of fury," says Pan (I, 61). But Caitilin finds that Pan's offer of happiness yields only "unrest and fever and a longing which could not be satisfied" (III, 146). Angus Óg

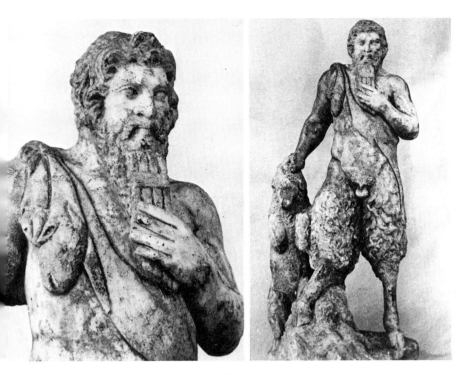

1. Pan, the Arcadian goat-god. Statue found in Crete, 1967

2. "A lurking, rustic god." Silver, ca. 300 B.C.

3. The "foolish judgment" of Midas in the contest between Apollo
and Pan, 1501

4. "The Mad Merry Pranks of Robin Goodfellow,"
   looking very much like Pan. Blackletter ballad,
   seventeenth century

5. "To the bearer of all things." *Le Songe de Poliphile*, 1561

Pana fugit Syrinx ripam Ladonis ad vdam,
Damq; fugit// numen fluminis orat opem.

Vertitur in calamum refonantis arundinis, hunc Pan
Clangentem dulci flamine femper amat.

6. Pan and Syrinx, Hendrik Goltzius, 1589. "Thy hot eyes reach and revel on the maid"

7. Syrinx seeks refuge in the arms of the river-god Ladon; "Fear'd, or seem'd to fear." Nicolas Poussin.

8. The victory of Apollo's classical harmonies over Pan's vulgar pipings. *Musicalisches Theatrum*, by Johann Christoph Weigel, 1714

9. "The Great God Pan." Frederick Leighton's illustration
for the first printing of Mrs. Browning's "A Musical
Instrument," 1860

10. Pan and Psyche. Sir Edward Burne-Jones, 1874

11. Nymphs trying to teach Pan to dance. A. W. Bouguereau, 1873

12. Pan in *The Yellow Book*. "The Reflected Faun," by
Laurence Housman, 1894

13. Pan in *The Dial*. "Pan Mountain," by T. Sturge Moore, 1894

14. "The Offering of Pan," by Althea Gyles, 1896. The Christ-child
wins a sentimental victory

15. Crucifixion Scene by Dorothy Brett. D. H. Lawrence as both Pan and Christ

THE PAN-SHAVIAN MOVEMENT.
MR. BERNARD SHAW HAS BEEN VEHEMENTLY DENOUNC-
ING THE SPOLIATION OF THE MALVERN HILLS.

16. The Modern Ceremonial: George Bernard
Shaw as Pan, 1929

17. "Faune musicien," by Pablo Picasso, 1948

confirms her feelings in stronger terms: "Singer of the Vine . . . I know your names — they are Desire and Fever and Lust and Death" (p. 149). Happiness, which is to her the greatest thing in the world, is not to be found in her Dionysian instinct to love "the shaggy beast that goes down" (I, 61), but in her Apollonian aspiration toward "Infinite Joy, Infinite Love," in the person of Angus. The perfect synthesis is found, as Angus points out, in the wedding of "Thought" and "Instinct," of which his wedding with Caitilin, the wedding of "Divine Imagination" and humanity, may be taken as a prototype. These dichotomies are sex-linked, in the Nietzschean (or Lawrentian) fashion: Emotion, Intuition, Happiness are female, while Thought and "Common-sense" are male. Both gods are masculine, but Caitilin, as part of her developing womanhood, takes over from Pan the duty of representing Instinct. Pan, though defeated, is no straw man in the dialectic; his need of Caitilin was almost as great as Angus'; neither god had found worshipers in Ireland.

Both Pan and Angus oppose the domination of Thought: Pan, because he is pressing the claims of the "depths," of "Hunger"; Angus, because the Divine Imagination is trapped by thought and can only be freed by its union with Instinct. Both gods express their view of Thought in aphorisms that have a Nietzschean ring to them. "The Crown of Life is not lodged in the sun: the wise gods have buried it deeply where the thoughtful will not find it, nor the good: but the Gay Ones, the Adventurous Ones, the Careless Plungers, they will bring it to the wise and astonish them," says Pan (I, 61). And Angus: "Thought has snared my birds in his nets and sold them in the market-places. Who will deliver me from Thought . . . the maker of chains and traps" (III, 154). The author's own comment similarly equates Logic with "automatic ideas" and "Mechanism" (words which sound particularly Lawrentian), "for life may not be consecutive, but explosive and variable, else it is a shackled and timorous slave" (IV, 162).

Stephens' commitment to a Dionysian Pan makes impossible any consistent use of the traditional allegorical interpretation (as in Bacon and Carlyle) whereby Pan, the Beast-God, represents the uneasy coupling of the divine and the animal in man himself. Pan hints at this possibility when he says that "Man is a god and a brute. He aspires to the stars with his head but his feet are contented in the grasses of the field" (I, 60). But Pan himself is only concerned with the latter aspect, for Angus will come to represent the former when Stephens' allegory requires it.

The argument outlined above gives "meaning" to the plot; another, less conspicuous level of allegory gives it "plausibility." Thought is not only the "maker of chains and traps"; it is also creative. "The Divine Imagination may only be known through the thoughts of His creatures" (III, 151). The episode of Pan and Angus Óg is a psychomachy of adolescent development; Caitilin's "unborn thought strangely audible" (I, 55) was Pan's music, for which she listened "not with her ears, but with her blood." Such a thought cannot be comprehended, says Stephens quite explicitly, until "we at last fashion for it those symbols which are its protection and its banner" (p. 52). Both Pan and Angus Óg are parts of the young heroine's "unborn thought" externalized and clothed in symbol, so that they may do battle for her. Caitilin has just reached the "sensual age" when Pan begins to have power over human beings; Angus Óg, her own wisdom and maturity, must be sent to rescue Caitilin from an aspect of herself. Stephens is not the only author to make the Pan outside a symbol for the Pan within (as in Browning's "Bishop," or, more recently, in Lawrence Durrell), but he is the only one so medievally up-to-date as to make his Pan a living character in a living allegory, as if the *Romaunt of the Rose* were concerned with a psychological development instead of warring aspects of a basically unchanging personality.

In emphasis and sheer length, the philosophical allegory far outweighs the psychological allegory; Pan, as spokesman for the Dionysian in Stephens' dialectic, articulates far more ideas than could possibly be expected to reside in Caitilin's subconscious. The gain in "meaning" would scarcely offset the loss in "plausibility" if the impact of the fable were to depend on its explicit allegorical significances.[8]

In fact a third technique, one much more obvious and orthodox, underlies the aspects of the fable that linger in the reader's
mind. Like Longus and Grahame, Stephens, for all the apparent
(and real) inconsequence of his fable, has provided believers
congruous with the gods believed in. Caitilin's innocent vision
of fearful shaggy legs and sad, kindly face, and Pan's straight-
forward injunction "know that they are indeed the legs of a
beast and then you will not be afraid any more," tie together the
persons, the fable, and the moral far more successfully than the
"printer's devil's personifications" of the mock-dialectic.

The Apuleian Pan, the chief classical model for the Benevolent
Pan of kindly counsel, is present of course in Grahame and
Stephens. The Philosopher's children, not having reached the
"sensual age" as yet, see Pan in his avuncular aspect; he responds
with kindliness to their simple wonder. But Stephens is franker
and less sentimental about the Beast in man than are his successors in this genre. There is a sharp drop in literary power to
the Pans of whimsy and fantasy found in Eden Phillpotts, Lord
Dunsany, Richard Garnett, and others, whose Pans, even when
allegedly enriching the instinctual lives of his worshipers, are
"emasculated" in the decorous pastoral way and lack the genuine
earthy relevance to human life found in Stephens and Grahame.

Stephens has the clue to what will prove one of the two best
ways of making Pan plausible, or indeed of relating any mythical figure to an undistorted modern sensibility. A thought can
be externalized into a Pan figure in his fashion, whereby his
characters become the witnesses or the mental creators of Pan,
or else the Pan figure can be internalized, and become all or part
of the character himself, in the fashion of D. H. Lawrence.

Stephens does have this in common with his successors: he
does not make his Pan more "modern," but his worshipers less
so. Phillpotts' children, Dunsany's childlike villagers, Garnett's
nymph, all have the naiveté and capacity for innocent wonder
of Grahame's animals or Stephens' Caitilin.

Richard Garnett's symbolic fantasy "Pan's Wand"[9] shows
Pan in the typical "Apuleian" situation of counseling a young
girl, though the subject upon which Iridion seeks advice is not

love, but Death; for her life depended upon her enchanted lily, and it had been accidentally broken. "The honest god was on excellent terms with the simple people" (p. 225); to Iridion he shows courtesy and compassion in endeavoring to reconcile her to the idea of death by demonstrating the superiority of thought to feeling (although the argument, and the thought it requires, goes somewhat against the grain of his own temperament). Pan, though kindly and ingenious, is not omnipotent. Twice, with the aid of his wand, he turns Death away. When Death, defrauded of Iridion, whom Pan had metamorphosed into a lily, returns to claim the plant, Pan declares, "with more decision than dignity," in a variation of the Apuleian formula, "I am a poor country god, but I know the law" (p. 230). Law or no law, Death turns Pan's wand into a worm of dissolution and takes the nymph. In a splendid turn of symbolism, the worm becomes a Psyche butterfly. Death comes a third time, "but Pan heeded him not" (p. 231).

Eden Phillpotts' cheerful fable *The Girl and the Faun* (London, 1916) deploys these Apuleian characteristics more powerfully; his Pan is not just a simple "country god," but, in the Romantic fashion, the god of all nature. The Faun, Coix, gentlemanly, sentimentally amorous, and not very bright, is in a filial relationship with Pan, the god and the "good father" of fauns. Coix combines the goat-feet of the usual Pan figure with the amoral impulsiveness of Hawthorne's Donatello. His actions, as a worshiper of nymphs and as Pan's servant, are analogous to those of the Satyr in Fletcher's *The Faithful Shepherdess*, of whom he appears to be a less shaggy, more domesticated descendant. We are not told what Pan himself looks like, but in temperament he is the opposite of the eternally naive and youthful Faun, being benevolent, venerable, and philosophically inclined — in short, Apuleian. The idea he stands for, however, is much more like that of the Emersonian invisible and universal Pan, a spirit infused in and speaking through all aspects of physical nature, audible only to those who are especially receptive: "As Spring said to the dryad, you must cultivate your cosmic sympathies, or Pan will not attend to you . . . one of his myriad voices will fall upon your ear. It may be the sound of the wind in the hair of an ancient forest . . . or the murmur of waterfalls; it may be in the distant cry of birds that fly by night." [10]

Another benevolent, amiable Pan of a philosophical turn of mind appears in Phillpotts' historical novel for children, *Pan and the Twins* (New York, 1922). It is set at the time of the victory of Christianity over paganism, early in Valentinian's reign, when the last temple to Pan was built. Pan himself is a "tolerant" god (p. 169 — this curious epithet is later used by Lawrence in *The Man Who Died*, 1928), a "restful, a kindly, a wise deity" (p. 196), who regrets his coincidental resemblance to the "swarthy, sinister" Satan of Christian literature (p. 218). He teaches one twin to understand the speech of "pad and hoof and wing" (p. 10), and warns him of the growing intolerance and the bloody future of Christianity; he converts the other twin, an excessively ascetic Christian, to an appreciation of sex and love, to a Christianity no longer ascetic and negative, but active and alive. But the twin who is actually Pan's worshiper, like Pan himself, is only a "loved ghost . . . a picturesque and harmless survival of a happier age." It is a pleasant, humane, and slightly melancholy paganism that Pan represents, probably more typical of the fin-de-siècle than of its alleged historical context. The book resembles, in both mood and setting, Dmitri Merejkowski's *Christ and Anti-Christ* (*The Death of the Gods*, I; London, 1901), in which Julian, later the Apostate, is brought up under the spell of "that pleasant melancholy, that golden faery twilight" of pagan ceremonies. Paganism is more often typified by Dionysus or Astarte in this book; but, in more childlike or pastoral contexts, little statues of Pan appear frequently. Surely Phillpotts' book must have seemed very old fashioned in 1922. Or are the adult fashions of one generation watered down for the children of the next?

One more historical setting for Pan deserves to be mentioned; it is the unexpected blend of a Theocritean pastoral world and the "real" world at the time of the Crusades. In Margaret Sherwood's "Pan and the Crusader" (1910),[11] a knight escapes briefly from the call of Christian action to the fairylike enchantments of a Greek island. Pan, as in Phillpotts, is said to be a god of peace, life, and joy, with "the wise smile of one who understands all of life, down to the tail and hoofs," in contrast to the Christian "cruel god of war" and suffering. The Crusader comes closer and closer to a vision of Pan, but realizes just in time that Pan (unlike Christ) cannot answer the problem of death. The Crusaders' fleet rescues him, and returns him to "the joy and pain of the quest." This is the Christian answer to such a benevolently hedonistic Pan as Phillpotts'.

Lord Dunsany, in *The Blessing of Pan* (New York, 1928), turns from the idea of a twilit Pan defeated by Christianity at the beginning of our era to the converse idea of Christianity, enfeebled, being defeated by Pan at the present day. Anwrel, the conscientious vicar of Wolding, has no defense against Pan, whose strange piping lures his parishioners one by one back to a worship which speaks to them from a deeper past than that of Christianity. The vicar, throughout most of the book, thinks of this Pan as the sinister enemy of Good. Pan's piping is produced for him by a simple country lad subject to some "pre-natal influence from a perfectly shocking source" (p. 73; compare Machen). The sexual nature of Pan's attraction is hinted at, for the young women are the first to follow the piping, but it is not stressed. Sheer loneliness drives Anwrel toward what is now the religion of his parishioners, and when his last supporter contradicts his assumption of Pan's malevolence — "Why, Pan was always friendly to Man . . . there are worse than Pan in the woods of the night" (p. 172) — his defenses crumble. With the vicar's inevitable capitulation the book must end, for "man . . . turning back from the path that steam and steel had shown him, to ways that were more of the Earth than the foxes knew" (p. 204) has restored Arcadia at last.

The happy glow that permeates the book is that of the escapist dream of an Arcadian oasis, summarized in so much minor verse at the turn of the century. A more modern flavor is given by emphasizing not the Alexandrian idyll, but a primitive idyll with anthropological touches. There is much talk of racial memory welling up from the past, in an almost Jungian fashion; a man is hunted (though not killed); a living sacrifice is made to Pan (but it is only a very old bull "kept back for this," p. 260); the vicar becomes the priest and wields the flint axe: he had "queer memories of how the old axe liked to be carried" (p. 250). It is a delineation of a small society's return to primitive ritual, rather different from, for instance, William Golding's. The story is an uneasy mixture of serious fantasy, clerical whimsy (faintly reminiscent of scenes in *Barchester Towers*), and village whimsy of the sort found, with weightier undertones, in T. F. Powys; the style is that of Mary Webb halfway down the road to Cold Comfort Farm.

It is not the only story apparently written to Beerbohm's recipe in "Maltby and Braxton," of fauns "coming suddenly out of woods to wean quiet English villages from respectability." A pale imitation of Dunsany's book, suffering from the same vicar and village whimsy, appeared in an anthology in 1947.[12] Margery Lawrence makes her case less subtle than Dunsany's; her clergyman is crudely Puritanical instead of merely well-meaning. His reform is achieved by a mocking, youthful Pan figure who, disguised as the vicar himself, preaches a sermon on the joys of pagan worship (the highly bowdlerized list includes joy, youth, laughter, sun, and blue sky: "ecstasies" even more "innocent" than Gosse's). The vicar is at last able to fall in love and marry; he pours a yearly libation to the "old God who taught him wisdom . . . the great god Pan, who, in a whimsy moment, came and played parson to save a parson's soul" (p. 176).

Even feebler than these prose equivalents of Arcadiac poetry is the slender genre of Pan in modern dress, whose only respectable practitioner is Aldous Huxley ("Cynthia," in *Limbo*, 1920). James Huneker wrote a story called "Pan" (1905), in which a personification of Pan appears in the form of a Hungarian gypsy who plays the dulcimer. A girl listening to his music has a vision of satyrs, fauns, and "a monster with a black goat-face . . . and most melancholy were the eyes of the defeated Pan."[13] The notion of a Pan without worshipers, "a thin and saddened god" forced to seek employment among humans, is taken over by

Lester del Rey (1941), whose Pan becomes a clarinetist and finds his worshipers again in the wild ecstasy of the jazz age dancers. Both of these stories, Huneker's more subtly, remind one of the nineteenth-century fashion for delineating the lives of the Olympians when reduced to the condition of humans.[14] After exploring Pan in modern dress, it was something of a relief to come across Dorothy Sayers' inimitable episode of modern man in Pan dress: Lord Peter Wimsey adopts the guise of Pan to terrify a wrongdoer by his uncanny appearances in a darkened grove. The Pan is more sinister than benevolent, in theory, but the effect of the scene is comic.[15]

The most famous Pan in modern English literature deserves at least a parenthetical comment here. As I have eliminated a great many Pan-like figures from the discussion because they were not called Pan, it seems only just to include a figure who borrows his name but not his attributes. James Barrie's *Peter Pan* owes much more, I suspect, to some archetypal figure like Sidney's "shepherd who piped as if he never would be old," or Blake's "Piper," than he does to any version of Pan. As a little boy with human feet he resembles a faun more than a Pan, and an "elf-child," to use Barrie's own word, more than either. Yet Barrie hoped to gain some aura of "Pan-ness," however imprecise, and there are signs scattered through *The Little White Bird* and *Peter Pan* that the name was not chosen at random: Peter "skipped up and down the room, playing on his heartless pipes";[16] "Gentlemen . . . write to say they heard a nightingale" in Kensington Gardens, which turns out to be Peter, riding a goat, and playing on "a pipe of reeds" that he made on a little island there.[17] In *Peter and Wendy* he becomes even more Pan-like when he clothes himself in "skeleton leaves and the juices that ooze out of trees" and is worshiped by the redskins, who perhaps appreciate the pagan implications of his friendships with birds and his cry "I'm youth, I'm joy."

The Arcadian tradition lies behind all stories of the benevolent Pan. If Pan is melancholy, it is because he is exiled from Arcadia and needs his worshipers; if he issues powerful summonses, it is because he is calling men back toward Arcadia; if he is wise, protective, kindly, it is largely because Apuleius gave particular force to that view of the shepherd god: "He is oftener friendly to man / And ever to beasts and their brood." Stephens enriched the meaning of his final Arcadian vision by being franker about the causes and consequences of its natural joys; there is still room in the "country of the gods" for a Pan whose largely sexual significance reminds us more of Lawrence and his successors than of Stephens' own more decorous contemporaries.

The problem of "plausibility," in the sense of a believable relationship between Pan and some representative of humanity, arises whenever the myth is adapted to fiction, a process which involves inevitably some concession, however slight, to the demands of realism. Even Phillpotts' Faun is human, all too human. A pure fantasy or fairy tale, such as Garnett's, can avoid the problem by keeping all its creatures on the same level of improbability, but, in fiction, only Stephens and Grahame solved satisfactorily a problem which engulfed so many lesser authors.

Of the numerous authors who have used the Pan myth for fiction in the modern period, Grahame is the only one, apart from D. H. Lawrence, who paid the god the compliment of taking the myth seriously. Some fine and interesting work has been done with tongue in cheek (by Stephens and Saki, for example), but this is not the way to achieve what Graham Hough calls "the reality of a myth"; and it was all too easy for most authors to exploit the Pan story merely for sensation or sentiment. Grahame could make the myth of the Golden Age into the modern pastoral by shifting his focus to animals; Lawrence made plausible a Pan of sex and terror by shifting Pan from the outer world to the inner. These two remarkably different authors [18] are alike in expressing a belief about the nature of the world through the symbol of Pan, and in claiming a degree of reverence for what the Pan figure represented.

Chapter V

THE SINISTER PAN IN PROSE FICTION

Only two really good new Pan stories have been devised since the times of the first myth makers. One is Plutarch's story of the Death of Pan, the history of which we have followed in some detail. The other, the theme of the sinister or terrifying Pan, is the most satisfying one yet found for modern fiction, wherever Pan, visible or invisible, is the main driving force behind the action. The benevolent Pans which were the dominant type up to the time of Swinburne are always with us, but in fiction they do better in minor roles: when called upon to support an entire action, they tended, as we have seen, to lapse into the whimsical.

The upsurge of the terrifying Pan in fiction between 1890 and 1930, but especially from 1904 to 1912, is not easy to account for. The poems of Swinburne give him his first home; I incline to credit Swinburne with some originality (at any rate of tone and emphasis), whatever terror may have been latent or subsidiary in Pans from the time of Theocritus. The genre of the Victorian and Edwardian horror story turned the Swinburnian Pan to the purposes of prose. The horror story flourished from 1880 to 1914, overlapping with the early tales of mystery and detection; it has some enfeebled descendants in certain branches of fantasy and science fiction. It is not quite the same thing as a ghost story.

PAN IN THE HORROR STORY

The ancestry of the horror story, as far as we need to trace it, is in the Gothic novel of the Romantics, which flourished from about 1790 (*The Mysteries of Udolpho*, 1794) to 1820 (*Melmoth the Wanderer*). I know of no trace of Pan in the half-dozen better-known Gothic novels, and would be agreeably surprised to find him well represented in the others. But Thomas Hood sets Pan in a Gothic background in his poem "The Elm Tree: A Dream in the Woods" (1842). After an orthodox romantic opening ("The Sylvan Nymph is dumb") in which Pan is conspicuously absent, the forest setting becomes macabre; the spirits that do still remain in the woods are malignant ones.

> And many a gnarlèd trunk was there,
> That ages long had stood,
> Till Time had wrought them into shapes
> Like Pan's fantastic brood;
> Or still more foul and hideous forms
> That Pagans carve in wood!
> A crouching Satyr lurking here —
>   And there a Goblin grim —
> As staring full of demon life
>   As Gothic sculptor's whim.

It seems to be generally agreed that Gothic elements have been employed in a much more enduring literary form by later American authors than by earlier English ones. The Gothicism of Faulkner will concern us shortly, but we must begin with that of Hawthorne, for Pan's first ambiguous brush with the Gothic is in *The Marble Faun* (1860).

Hawthorne's Pan figure appears briefly in the Arcadian country scenes of the first third of the book, which counterpoint with sunny radiance the gloom of the city catacombs and the complex, terrifying events that occur there. Pan thus plays his normal pastoral role; he is part of the prelapsarian state of the Faun.

Hawthorne, as is his wont, is perfectly clear and specific about the symbolic contrast that he has in mind:

> It was a glimpse far backward into Arcadian life, or, further still, into the Golden Age, before mankind was burdened with sin and sorrow, and before pleasure had been darkened with those shadows that bring it into high relief, and make it happiness.
>
> "Hark! . . . there is music somewhere in the grove!"
>
> "It is your kinsman, Pan, most likely," said Miriam, "playing on his pipe. Let us go seek him, and make him puff out his rough cheeks and pipe his merriest air!" (chapter ix)

But it is not possible for the other characters to stay long in Arcadia; only for the Donatello of the beginning is it anything like a permanent way of being.

In Miriam's remembrance the scene had a character of fantasy. It was as if a company of satyrs, fauns, and nymphs, with Pan in the midst of them, had been disporting themselves in these venerable woods only a moment ago; and now in another moment, because some profane eye had looked at them too closely, or some intruder [Miriam's sinister persecutor] had cast a shadow on their mirth, the sylvan pageant had utterly disappeared.

The glade, briefly Arcadian, has become again a "tract where the crimes and calamities of ages . . . have corrupted all the soil" (chapter x).

As the novel progresses, the same symbol is brought in to demonstrate, more allusively, the degeneration of both Donatello's Arcadian qualities and his powers over nature; this loss, in itself a source of pathos, is yet necessary to the Faun's spiritual development. The walls of Donatello's "antique saloon" are covered with frescoes "of a festive and joyous character, representing Arcadian scenes, where nymphs, fauns and satyrs disported themselves among mortal youths and maidens; and Pan, and the god of wine, and he of sunshine and music, disdained not to brighten some sylvan merrymaking with the scarcely veiled glory of their presence." But they are suffering the effects of time: "the joyousness had quite vanished out of them all" (chapter xxv). Donatello's forefathers, Arcadians in a more literal sense, and also faunlike (chapter xxvi), might have been " 'gladdening the hearts of men and women, with their wine of Sunshine, even in the Iron Age, as Pan and Bacchus, whom we see yonder, did in the Golden one!' . . . [Donatello replies] 'But, methinks, they have all faded since I saw them last' " (chapter xxv). And indeeed, this passage, halfway through the book, is the last we hear of Pan.

I must reject firmly any attempt to see the Faun himself as a Pan figure.[1] There are several reasons for distinguishing Pan types from faun types. A careless, joyful amorality, "not incapable of being touched by pathos" (chapter i), of a type emphatically characteristic of youth, or of an immortal state analogous with human youth,[2] has never been typical of any significant Pan figure. Although the Faun of Praxiteles, and therefore Donatello himself, might well possess "a certain caudal appendage" as well as "pointed and furry ears" (chapter i), neither of them is alleged to have the feet or legs of a goat; they lack the crucial degree of physical resemblance to the goat-god. More important is the simple presence of a character, however minor, who is a Pan figure, and who, with "goatskin breeches," pipe, and shaggy, dancing rusticity, plays the part much better than Donatello could (chapter x). When Donatello is, for rhetorical purposes, compared to a specific deity, it is, as it happens (for the subject under discussion is the marvelous wine of Monte Beni), Bacchus rather than Pan (chapter xxvi).

Furthermore, neither the Faun of Praxiteles nor Donatello could possibly be extrapolated to include the manifold specifically Pan-like possibilities. Hawthorne shows himself to be aware of at least one of the "actions" that distinguish Pan from every other sylvan deity. Hilda makes an almost serious suggestion that Donatello really is "one of that strange, wild, happy race of creatures, that used to laugh and sport in the woods, in the old, old times." To this Kenyon's reply is "A Faun! A Faun! Great Pan is not dead, then, after all! The whole tribe of mythical creatures yet live in the moonlit seclusion of a young girl's fancy, and find it a lovelier abode and play-place, I doubt not, than their Arcadian haunts of yore" (chapter xii). But lest we think that this, the sentimentally romantic answer to Mrs. Browning's "The Dead Pan," even with its kindly jesting reservation, in "a young girl's fancy," is Hawthorne's considered opinion, the author makes his own comment three chapters later in a much harsher tone.

Of a certain sculptor (who does not figure otherwise in the plot) it is said that "gifted with a more delicate power than any other man alive, he had forgone to be a Christian reality [sic], and perverted himself into a Pagan idealist, whose business or efficacy, in our present world, it would be exceedingly difficult to define" (chapter xv). In short, he creates the sculptor's equivalent of Arcadiac poetry, or of the monotonously unvaried "dead mythology" (chapter xxxvii) of the picture galleries, of which Hawthorne complains: "Venuses, Cupids, Bacchuses, and a vast deal of other marble progeny of dreamwork" (chapter xv). The author of "The Dead Pan" herself could put it no better:

> O ye vain false gods of Hellas,
> Ye are silent evermore!
> What is true and just and honest . . .
> These are themes for poets' uses,
> Stirring nobler than the Muses
> > Ere Pan was dead.

I have said that the Pan figure is contrasted with Gothic terrors, yet forms no part of them himself. Donatello, the Faun, passes from the Arcadian world to the Gothic world of sin, fear, and retribution in the course of his "Transformation," but Pan, not a character but a fixed symbol of the Arcadian, cannot follow him to "the black depths [where] the Faun had found a soul" (chapter xxix).

The same Gothic world in the hands of a horror writer, such as Arthur Machen, has need of a Pan of a different sort. Machen, E. F. Benson, Saki, Stephen McKenna, Nelson Bond, D. H. Lawrence, and William Faulkner have written stories of this general type: a human being affronts or trifles with the Pan demon who, like other demons in other horror stories, takes a swift, nasty, and inevitable revenge. Although, as in the early Gothic novels, moral psychology has given way to melodrama, a crude pattern of sin, fear, and retribution may still be discerned. Satan was the prototypical monster of the earlier Gothic novels, generally appearing in approximately human form; vampires (like Dracula) and werewolves gained favor later, as theology gave way to folklore. In the periods we are discussing, Pan is only one among a great many different exemplars of evil, some dredged up from excessively occult sources.

There is another, more flexible way of using a terrifying Pan in fiction, offering greater scope for characterization, which will prove more significant in the long run. E. M. Forster and Algernon Blackwood have written stories where Pan motivates the action in a double fashion, being benevolent to some characters and terrifying to others. In Forster's novels we shall see the transition from a Pan who is an actor or a causer of action to a Pan with a purely symbolic function, in works where the motivations are entirely human; a transition, in short, from fantasy to fiction, looking back to Hawthorne and forward to D. H. Lawrence in its use of the Pan motif.

Arthur Machen's "The Great God Pan,"[3] a novella written in 1890–91 and published in 1894, is Gothic in its atmosphere of supernatural horror and in its narrative technique as well. The reviewers noticed with acerbity, and Machen himself admits, the excessive influence of Robert Louis Stevenson on the style and technique of his principal works.[4] The criticism applies with particular force to "The Great God Pan," which is a *Rahmenerzählung* gone mad. "Dr. Jekyll and Mr. Hyde" (1886) was clearly the model at hand, but a structure of story within story, of flashbacks via documents, of chance encounters and coincidences providing necessary narrative links — for which modern taste prefers at least a pretense of cause and effect — can be found highly developed in such Gothic novels as *Melmoth the Wanderer* (1820), and is as old as the form of the prose romance itself.

At the beginning of Machen's story Pan is equated with "the real world" which lies beyond the "veil" of material things: lifting the veil is called "seeing the god Pan" (p. 62). A mad scientist, or at the least an insanely obsessed one, seeks to lift the veil from the eyes of another person whose "life is mine, to use as I see fit" (p. 64). It is clear from the last phrase that a sin is being committed, though its nature lies not in the immoral exploitation of others — a Kantian sin, as it were — but (to quote "The White People," another of the several Machen stories of which this is the moral basis) in "the taking of heaven by storm . . . an attempt to penetrate into another and higher sphere in a forbidden manner" (p. 119). Machen continues the parallel by saying that such action "repeats the Fall," though we might think, too, of Faust or, more likely in the context of "The Great God Pan," of Frankenstein.

The punishment for the experiment is visited on its innocent victim, Mary. At first she sees something wonderful, but then she sees something terrifying, so terrifying that she is reduced to hopeless idiocy. And again the doctor calls this nameless horror by the name of "The Great God Pan" (p. 68). Clarke, the neutral observer from whose point of view this episode is told, has a reverie during the experiment: perhaps when "an infinite silence seemed to fall on all things, and the wood was hushed" she too saw "a presence, that was neither man nor beast, neither the living nor the dead, but all things mingled, the form of all things but devoid of all form" (p. 66). Thus the first chapter ends; its real horror may not be where the author intended, but it is effective enough.[5]

In Chapter two, the "Chinese boxes" (Machen's own phrase, p. 79), the narratives within narratives, begin, and there is complexity and mystery to spare. The relevant episode is that of a small boy driven mad by the sight of a girl, Helen, playing with a "strange naked man" in a forest near an old Roman road (p. 72). We eventually deduce the "man" to be Pan, because the boy is later terrified by the sight of a satyr's head carved in stone. Helen is involved in another episode, again told in hints. A local girl disappears after recounting a wild story of an adventure "too incredible, too monstrous" for the author to share with us. The words "Et Diabolus incarnatus est" (And the Devil was made incarnate) and "awful, unspeakable elements enthroned as it were, and triumphant in human flesh" (p. 75) may help to explain. In any event, the adventure will be elucidated later in the story.

Chapter five details another mysterious death, and again evidence of Helen's connection with it is supplied in graphic form. The dead artist has left a picture of a "frightful Walpurgis-night of evil . . . The figures of fauns and satyrs and Aegipans danced before his eyes," and the last picture in the portfolio is of Helen Vaughan. The portfolio is documented by a Latin quotation which describes some Bacchic orgy on the seashore near Mt. Atlas: "Silet per diem universus, nec sine horrore secretus est; lucet nocturnis ignibus, chorus Aegipanum undique personatur: audiuntur et cantus tibiarum, et tinnitus cymbalor-

um per oram maritimam." [6] (The whole place is silent throughout the day, nor is its remoteness without horror; it glows with
nocturnal fires, the chorus of the Aegipans rings through everywhere: both the sounds of the pipes and the clanging of the
cymbals are heard along the seashore.)

In the seventh chapter the narrator finds "an account of the
entertainment Mrs. Beaumont [Helen] provided for her choicer
guests" (p. 106), but this, again, is too horrible to give us directly. We are told that it is "an old mystery played in our day, and
in dim London streets instead of amidst the vineyards and the
olive gardens" (p. 107), but we must deduce the visual details
as best we can from the decorous Latin of the portfolio. However, there is further explanation. "We know what happened
to those who chanced to meet the Great God Pan . . . an ex-
quisite symbol beneath which men long ago veiled their knowledge of the most awful, most secret forces which lie at the heart
of all things; forces before which the souls of men must wither
and die and blacken . . . Such forces cannot be named, cannot be spoken, cannot be imagined except under a veil and a
symbol" (p. 107).

The last chapter begins with "the papers" of yet another
character, who describes the death of Helen thus: "I saw the
body descend to the beasts whence it ascended . . . The principle of life . . . always remained, while the outward form
changed . . . a Form, shaped in dimness before me, which I
will not farther describe. But the symbol of this form may be
seen in ancient sculptures, and in paintings which survived
beneath the lava, too foul to be spoken of [7] . . . as a horrible
and unspeakable shape, neither man nor beast, was changed
into human form, there came finally death" (pp. 110–111).

All that is needed now to tie the last threads of the story together is the link between Helen and the "Mary" of the original
experiment. A letter from the obsessed scientist, now somewhat
chastened, reveals the vital clue: Helen was Mary's child, "born
nine months after that night" when Mary saw the god Pan (p.
114).

Stripped of its two dozen supernumerary characters, and with the mystery pursued through eight chapters at last elucidated, the story is simply of the conception, birth, life, and death of a female creature who is the daughter of the God Pan and is his embodiment upon earth. The activities of her life, and thus the events of the story, consist largely of leading others to their death of terror, by forcing or persuading them to look upon Pan; at last her own death restores the normal balance of life.

The plot depends for its horror upon two basic themes. One is that the sight of Pan is so terrifying that it must result in death, or, at best, insanity. Machen's reading was wide and often obscure, but an obvious source is, again, Eusebius:

[Porphyry] affirms that [Pan] being one of the good daemons appeared once upon a time to those who were working in the fields . . . those to whom this blessed sight was vouchsafed all died at once . . . For nine persons were found dead; and when the inhabitants of the country district inquired the cause, the god made answer:

> Lo! where the golden-hornèd Pan
> In sturdy Dionysos' train
> Leaps o'er the mountains' wooded slopes!
> His right hand holds a shepherd's staff,
> His left a smooth shrill-breathing pipe
> That charms the gentle wood-nymph's soul.
> But at the sound of that strange song
> Each startled woodsman dropp'd his axe,
> And all in frozen terror gaz'd
> Upon the Daemon's frantic course. (189 c-d)

The other theme is that of an unholy rape: "I was shown a small square pillar of white stone, which had been recently discovered in the wood [where Helen's childhood had been spent] . . . The inscription is as follows: 'To the great god Nodens (the god of the Great Deep or Abyss) Flavius Senilis has erected this pillar on account of the marriage which he saw beneath the shade'" (p. 114). The "marriage," it is implied, is the unholy and enforced union of the goat-god and a human woman, which took place in Roman Britain even as in modern Wales.

Now, this is of a completely different order of imaginary

experience from the stories of Pan and Luna, or Pan and Syrinx, where the beings in question are of the same level of reality and no question of ritual worship is involved. It finds a much closer analogue in Herodotus' account of "the worship of Pan, called Mendes, by the Egyptians": "One he-goat is the most sacred of all . . . Mendes is the name both for the he-goat and for Pan. In my lifetime a monstrous thing happened in this province, a woman having open intercourse with a he-goat" [8] (II, 46). Nearer still to the spirit of Machen's unholy rape is Payne Knight's *Account of the Remains of the Worship of Priapus*. He refers to the ritual copulation of a goat and a woman as "the reciprocal incarnation of man with the deity," and then goes on to discuss Pan in terms of Orphic literature as "the principle of universal order" and "the origin and source of all things." [9] Machen obligingly provides evidence of having read Payne Knight in "The Novel of the White Powder," where Knight is mentioned (p. 58) to lend authority to an account of the Witches' Sabbath: "if you care to read the appendix to Payne Knight's monograph, you will find that the true Sabbath was something very different, though the writer has very nicely refrained from printing all he knew" (a typical Machen innuendo, calculated to increase suspense without increasing any real justification for it). Machen, because of his predilection for the theme of unholy rape, which is repeated in all of his "Stevensonian" stories,[10] made ample use of Payne Knight's evidence.

This "morbidity," if such it be, drew heavy criticism from the reviewers, although "an incoherent nightmare of sex and the supposed horrible mysteries behind it" (*Westminster Gazette*) is perhaps putting it a bit strongly. The *Saturday Review* is more precise and less worried: "his particular obsession is a kind of infernal matrimonial agency, and the begetting of human-diabolical mules." Some reviewers felt a disgust more emotional than critical: "these awful stories strongly suggest the half-mad imaginings of a degenerate mind steeped in morbidity" (*Birmingham Gazette and Express*). *The Lady's Pictorial* was one of the journals forced to express its "utter disgust," but, unlike the other reviewers, this one tells us what sort of Pan she (?)

prefers: "I bethought me of the curious old legend, so exquisitely told in verse by Mrs. Browning, of the death of 'The Great God Pan.' It was a waste of time for Mr. Machen to bring him to life again." [11]

But the criticisms made most frequently are less tied to the literary conventions of the time. The usual reason given for dissatisfaction, and given quite pungently by many critics, is that Machen's terrors are too intangible; we are shown them only at second hand in the reactions of people too weakly characterized to matter to us. Of Pan, nominally the central motif, all they have to say is that for the present age (1894 or 1906 as the case may be) "this mythical monstrosity" is too absurd to be frightening.

Machen, in his own accounts of the genesis of the story, says nothing of the origin of the Pan figure. He claims simply to have translated a landscape into a tale as Stevenson would have done, and, though with more dignity than his critics, he puts his own flaw down in writing: "I saw the lonely house between the dark forest and the silver river, and years after I wrote 'The Great God Pan,' an endeavour to pass on the *vague, indefinable sense of awe and mystery and terror* that I had received." [12] The inspiration came from visions of "the late' sixties" of countryside near his boyhood home; the hill, the house, and the woods had a mystic beauty for him, which is not recorded in direct scenic descriptions in the tale, but in the "awe, mystery and terror" of which Pan and his embodiment ought to be the vehicles. The description given here comes closer to connecting the emotion with its "objective correlative" than does anything in the story itself, largely because Machen is better at introspection and description of landscape than at characterization and action.

The story consists of quasi-scientific bits of material evidence, as in a detective story, held together by vague emotive hints of unspeakable horror. So cumbersome is the paraphernalia of "Chinese boxes" that the theme, which was not very solid to begin with, is smothered. Pan appears at the beginning and is mentioned at the end, and from time to time he hovers briefly over the plot in touches like the satyr head or the Aegipans of

Solinus' narration. For the most part, his human incarnation, Helen, has to take the brunt of the theme, and she is no more specifically Pan-like than are any of the diabolical Fatal Women of the nineteenth-century's Romantic Agonies.

Vaguely described as are Pan's two "actions" of rape and murder (Machen's probable sources give more concrete details than he does), Machen is vaguer yet about Pan's physical attributes, leaving the reader to supply them from his own knowledge. There is, however, a felicitous contrast of habitat in which Pan may be worshiped: "the vineyards and the olive gardens," and the "dim London streets"; and the Welsh countryside blurs into a Greek landscape for Clarke's vision of Pan: "The beech alley was transformed to a path beneath ilex-trees."

Like several later writers, Machen is determined that Pan should not only "be but mean," and Pan means "all things mingled, the form of all things but devoid of all form" (p. 67). Machen may well have had available many more occultly neo-Platonic sources [13] than the works of Emerson for this Pan, but the "eternal Pan / Who . . . Halteth never in one shape" of "Woodnotes II" provides one possible analogue, and "The Natural History of Intellect" provides another: "he was only seen under disguises, and was not represented by any outward image." Machen invites the comparison by calling the branch of science that makes possible Mary's vision "transcendental medicine" (p. 61).[14]

A visible world which is only "dreams and shadows," hiding the real world somewhere beyond, does not lend itself to the description of a solid and visualized Pan; like Emerson's, Machen's Pan is too Protean, and the effect of terror is diminished accordingly. When "Human flesh may become the veil of a horror one dare not express" (p. 115), the inexpressible is likely to remain the unconveyed; when "that which is without form [takes] to itself a form" (p. 107), its incarnation should be more memorably appropriate than is "Helen."

We have seen that the consequences of such a mystic vision are disastrous to the mortal soul and frame, and whatever the moral status of the "real world" may be, the vision of it is purely evil. If Machen's notion of Pan as transcendental resembles Emerson's, his notion of the horror of Pan is more like Swinburne's in "A Nympholept": "If I live, and the life that may look on him drop not dead . . . / Yet man should fear lest he see what of old men saw / And withered." He was, like Machen, shudderingly vague, though more succinct, about what happened when one saw Pan. Machen's answer, or that of his characters, to Swinburne's question "Is it rapture or terror that circles me round?" is that first there is rapture, which is swiftly glossed over, and then there is terror, which matters far more. Swinburne is concerned with the paradox of apparently contradictory emotions, the rapture *of* terror; Machen uses the other emotions simply to counterpoint terror.

The result of Machen's "ransack[ing] the whole British Museum" (*Standard* review) to dig up Solinus, and Payne Knight, and Roman artifacts of a "peculiarly horrid" nature was to bring back to the Pan motif possibilities that had lain buried for centuries, to counteract the pretty sterilities of the minor poets and provide the first major example of a Pan in modern prose fiction. If Machen did not make the best of the material himself, he at least made fruitful the dry data of his relatively obscure sources, to give the Pan motif a different meaning and a new lease on life.

The Great God Pan is finding himself extremely popular among the novelists just now. It was Mr. Benson who began it, earlier in the year, and since that time the number of novels in which we are vouchsafed manifestations of the goat-god—complete even to the hoofs, and with an attendant murky odour thrown in—increases almost daily. Of course it is natural enough, for nobody, not even a novelist, knows much about Pan, whence unlimited possibilities of mystery and thrills . . . None of us can take the great God Pan, nor witches, nor warlocks, very seriously nowadays—even if surgeons with alarming surgical instruments are introduced into the same story to keep them in countenance by their up-to-date associations . . . Pan was killed by the Game Laws, if not before.

This passage from the *Tribune's* review of Machen's "The Great God Pan" (*Precious Balms*) is misleading in two respects. In the first place, Benson did not "begin" the fashion;

that honor is Machen's, for "The Great God Pan" first appeared eleven years earlier (a fact of which no mention is made in the review), and was thus the first representative, as it remains the best known, of this small subdivision of the horror story. Furthermore, Machen makes precisely the mistake of leaving out the hoofs and the murky odour; it was Benson who improved the genre immeasurably by putting them back in.

The novel the critic refers to is E. F. Benson's *The Angel of Pain*, and the year is 1906. Its subplot, which is the part that concerns us, is a reworking of a story called "The Man Who Went Too Far." The two versions are identical in essentials, although it could be argued that the novel version is made less intense and less credible by being split up into installments sandwiched between episodes in a main plot, allegedly realistic, of social, sentimental melodrama. The novel's structure further necessitates a great deal of repetition from one section to another. The links between the two plots are highly artificial; there is no necessity in terms of the action for them to be in the same book at all, although the author clearly intended a close network of thematic parallels, in the manner of, say, *King Lear*. Unfortunately the conjunction emphasizes the emotional implausibility of the one plot and the realistic implausibility of the other. However, as the volume of short stories is somewhat the scarcer of two very scarce publications, I shall quote normally from the novel.

The title of the short story, "The Man Who Went Too Far," [15] reveals the contents of the Pan plot much better than does the novel title; it emphasizes the tale's resemblance to the part of Machen's plot that I have characterized as "Faustian," dealing with "overreaching" and its penalties.

The hero of the novel, Tom Merivale, has discovered seemingly perfect content and a renewal of the simple happiness of youth, in a way of life involving exile from society, a diet of home-grown vegetables and a physical communion, which becomes more and more intimate, with the English countryside. "He was not more himself than was the stream, the stream was not more itself than it was he" (p. 76). From time to time he hears the Pipes of Pan, "unending, eternal . . . universal" (p. 45), though somehow fearful, too. They are at first a great distance off, but come ever closer as his goal and his doom, becoming "one with nature," approaches. There is an air of foreboding in even the most graceful lyric descriptions of the piping, for a friend has said, almost in the words of Machen, "Some day . . . he will see Pan. And I shall then have to attend a funeral" (p. 18).

Tom has gone to great lengths to avoid all suffering in his life, but as the climax approaches he grows willing to face it, to "see Pan, the god of all Nature, of the suffering and sorrow of Nature as well as the illimitable life and joy of her" (p. 235), and hopes only that "the blinding, dreadful flash of revelation" (p. 238) will be quickly over. His friend thinks of Pan only as "the incarnation of all the terror and fear and sorrow of the world" (p. 239), but Tom corrects him: "Pan means 'everything,' and to see everything would be clearly more than one could stand. And so to see Pan means death" (p. 240; compare Stevenson: "the fear of him was the most terrible, since it embraces all"). This is virtually Machen's point; it gains forcefulness here from the simple clarity of the statement, freed of Machen's superfluous mystifications.

Just before the end, Tom realizes that Pan comes to certain people, not to certain places, and could find him anywhere. He hears "a tap as of some hoofed thing," sees "a frightful big goat," and smells "a sort of goaty smell" (p. 299). The Pan pipes, which promise to make him one with the eternal harmony, are "never silent now." Tom praises this harmony still, but we see the final events through the eyes of the skeptical friend. "The rain ceased altogether and there was a dead silence." The friend hears Tom's Faustian cry "Oh, my God! . . . Oh, Christ!" (although this is in modern idiom, I think we are meant to give the phrase its more emphatic and literal meaning); he sees a "strange irregular blot . . . that black thing . . . [giving] dreadful frolicsome leaps and bounds," and he finds his friend's body "as if a monstrous goat had leaped and danced on him" (p. 304). In the short story "a little mocking, bleating laugh" (p. 237) counterpoints the cry; his face is at first "a mask of horrible contorted terror," but finally, in death, it is like that of "a boy tired with play . . . smiling . . . [as] to the music of the unheard melody of Pan's pipes" (p. 239).

The title of the novel, *The Angel of Pain*, links the main plot and the subplot; Pan himself, in the subplot, represents "the angel of pain" who, in the main plot, redressed an imbalance of joy and suffering in purely human terms, without recourse to the supernatural. There is a marked resemblance between Benson's idea of the necessity of suffering — which he uses to make plausible a terrifying Pan in a story of the joys of pantheism — and the idea of Nietzsche in *The Birth of Tragedy* that pain (*Unheil*) is "implicit in the very structure of things — which the contemplative Aryan is not disposed to explain away." [16] Tom explains it away at first, and as he is drawn ever closer to the heart of nature and reality, he has more than his share of joy. He comes to realize that he "has a long bill to settle" (p. 236). Yet he still imagines the possibility of "immortal life, lived here and now" (p. 300), though he is on the point of an agonizing death. Then, as he dies, all the suffering he had failed to acknowledge "came to him in a flash, making him perfect" (p. 307).

Benson's Pan pipes cause an "awe and terror" like the "Dionysian strains" of Nietzsche, in which "all of nature's excess in joy, sorrow and knowledge become audible even in piercing shrieks" (section iv), and "ecstasy may wring sounds of agony from us . . . a cry of horror" (section ii). The Dionysian feels "as if the veil of Maya had been torn aside . . . before the mysterious Primordial Unity" (section i); Tom senses that "at one end of the antechamber there is a curtain drawn, and behind that is the Presence. Soon I think it will be drawn back" (p. 300). Nietzsche expresses these ideas in various places throughout his work, but one passage summarizes the chief points of resemblance:

Dionysian art, too, wishes to convince us of the eternal joy of existence: only we are to seek this joy not in phenomena, but behind them. We are to recognize that all that comes into being must be ready for a sorrowful end . . . We are really for a brief moment Primordial Being itself, feeling its raging desire for existence and joy in existence; the struggle, the pain, the destruction of phenomena, now appear to us as a necessary thing . . . in view of the exuberant fertility of the universal will. We are pierced by the maddening sting of these pains just when we have become, as it were, one with the infinite primordial joy in existence, and when we anticipate, in Dionysian ecstasy, the indestructibility and eternity of this joy. (section xvii)

So far Nietzsche and Benson follow a similar track, but of course Benson veers sharply away in deducing a Christian conclusion from Nietzsche's postulates: "for if suffering is necessary it is certainly sacred . . . I should . . . take not only my share of it, but the share of anybody else" (p. 237). Furthermore Benson paints a very mild picture of the animal vitality and sexuality that Nietzsche counted among the Dionysian virtues; he might have agreed that the satyr "is the offspring of longing for the primitive and natural" (section viii), but he does not choose to take advantage of Nietzsche's corollary that he is also the "emblem of the sexual omnipotence of nature." Tom defends "nature" against "Puritanism," of course, but to comply with Benson's taste and that of his audience, he denies any possibility of sensuality in his mystical ecstasy. The British reader cannot yet be expected to take the Dionysian at full strength, although D. H. Lawrence will shortly ask him to do so.[17]

Although these ideas are brought in [18] to account for Pan's function in the plot, they do not alter fundamentally the Machen-like nature of the main action, nor do they influence the characteristics of the Pan who acts, as distinguished from the "Pan" who provides the subject of extensive conversation. The undoubted superiority of Benson's final scene to anything in Machen is not owing to any improvement in ideas, but simply to a more solid narrative structure — which builds suspense up to one climax instead of diffusing it in a tangle of episodes — and to a respect for physical detail, which makes more palpable both the cause of horror and its effect.

Saki's "The Music on the Hill" (1911) is almost a parody of the Pan horror story,[19] being a happy combination of all its necessary elements with some of the materials and methods of social satire. The story has a moral, to be sure, and a sound one, very similar to the moral of "The Great God Pan": one should not meddle frivolously with matters too mysteriously important for one's limited understanding. But Saki's story does without the dead weight of overt philosophizing that other writers felt obliged to plaster on to their story line; it shows by pointed contrast the artistic discipline of well-chosen omissions.

Saki, too, employs forebodings, but they are subtly ironic hints rather than flaming signposts. His heroine at first "looked on the country as something excellent and wholesome in its way, which was apt to become troublesome if you encouraged it overmuch." In words which almost summarize Benson's method, Sylvia sees in the landscape "a stealthy linking of the joy of life with the terror of unseen things." Her husband, who understands "unseen things" better than she does, assures her that "the worship of Pan never has died out . . . Other newer gods have drawn aside his votaries from time to time, but he is the Nature-God to whom all must come back at last." "And if you're wise you won't disbelieve in him too boastfully."

The animals know her for an alien and show their disapproval. The "echo of a boy's laughter, golden and equivocal" —the boy, to all appearances, does not exist—"was added to her other impressions of a furtive sinister 'something' that hung around Yessney." She is slow to learn; she removes a bunch of grapes left as an offering at "a small bronze figure of a youthful Pan" in the woods. The punishment for her sin of skepticism and folly, of meddlesomeness rather than true curiosity, begins at once: "a boy's face was scowling at her, brown and beautiful, with unutterably evil eyes." "Unutterably evil eyes," like "furtive sinister 'something'" and even "the horror of something she saw," are phrases that manage both to parody gently the clichés of Machen's "nameless horrors" and, in their context, to convey something of the effect Machen hoped for. Her husband's warnings become more specific: "I've heard it said that the Wood Gods are rather horrible to those who molest them . . . I should avoid the woods and orchards if I were you, and give a wide berth to the horned beasts on the farm." For all her skepticism, Sylvia cannot help uneasiness. Her husband threatens, as impersonally as he had previously warned: "I don't think you will ever go back to Town."

On her next walk, she escapes "the low, fitful piping, as of some reedy flute," only to find herself in the area of a stag hunt. Here I can do no better than quote the final scene, for Saki achieves the effect so earnestly sought by Machen, Benson, and others, and he does it in very few words.

But the music of the pack seemed to have died away for a moment, and in its place she heard again that wild piping, which rose now on this side, now on that, as though urging the failing stag to a final effort . . . The pipe music shrilled suddenly around her, seeming to come from the bushes at her very feet, and at the same moment the great beast slewed round and bore directly down upon her. In an instant her pity for the hunted animal was changed to wild terror at her own danger; the thick heather roots mocked her scrambling efforts at flight, and she looked frantically downward for a glimpse of oncoming hounds. The huge antler spikes were within a few yards of her, and in a flash of numbing fear she remembered Mortimer's warning, to beware of horned beasts on the farm. And then with a quick throb of joy she saw that she was not alone; a human figure stood a few paces aside, knee-deep in the whortle bushes.

"Drive it off!" she shrieked. But the figure made no answering movement.

The antlers drove straight at her breast, the acrid smell of the hunted animal was in her nostrils, but her eyes were filled with the horror of something she saw other than her oncoming death. And in her ears rang the echo of a boy's laughter, golden and equivocal.

An eerie piping is one of the most characteristic manifestations of Pan's power; it is found in some form in virtually every piece of prose fiction in which he appears. (Machen's is an exception.) The classical warranty for its use in tales of terror may well be in Longus' *Daphnis and Chloe*: "Chloe's goats and sheep were led by the most ravishing music of the pipe, and none could see the piper. Sheep and goats moved forward, grazing as they went, entranced by the melody" (p. 52). Saki, in his emphasis on the pipes as a control over animals, is closer to the spirit of Longus than are those authors who use it as a summons to mystic experience. Longus is similarly practical in accounting for the terror of the pipes: "From the top of the cliff which towered sheer over the headland there was heard the sound of a pipe, producing, however, not the pleasant notes a pipe yields, but terrifying hearers with a trumpet blast." The pipes warn of the approach of an invisible, nonexistent enemy; no modern author would sacrifice the indefinably mysterious fearfulness for so prosaic an explanation, but the phenomenon itself they are happy to adopt.

Saki similarly feels under no greater obligation than Longus to account for the existence of Pan; and the action that he cites as provoking Pan's revenge is one that Longus, too, would have found acceptable: "To all who could think reasonably," such as Sylvia's husband, "it was obvious that all that had transpired, the appearances and the sounds, were the work of Pan, who had some cause for anger against the sailors. But the cause they could not conjecture, *for they had ravaged no sanctuary of Pan*" (Longus, p. 50, italics mine).

Saki's only major break with classical precedent is in making his Pan figure youthful; they are most often middle-aged or ageless. This makes Pan or his representative, however, a typical Saki hero, a beautiful, cruel boy whose chief amusement, and indeed occupation, is the arrangement of heartless practical jokes. His victims have usually done something to deserve their fate, even as Sylvia has, but, to most tastes, the punishment is disproportionate to the crime. Both Reginald and Clovis are such; even Comus Bassington, who has another dimension to his character as well, looks at times like "some wickedly laughing faun." The "boy's laughter, golden and equivocal" which serves here as a refrain echoes through many another Saki story. "A bronze statue of a youthful Pan" would be a fitting emblem for all of these heroes, for they are the Superbeasts who use ordinary Beasts as the agents of their revenge.

Saki's virtues are not just the negative ones of knowing what to leave out, though we are glad to hear no more of Pan's mystical and meaningful qualities than might be implied by the bare definition of "the Nature-God to whom all must come back at last." His story has the horrid plausibility necessary to an effect of terror; we are led to the improbable by way of the perfectly possible.[20] Simply to provide a rational explanation by the side of the irrational one will not do: Benson, for instance, mentioned the possibility of a "real" goat to cheer up a hypothetical coroner's jury. Saki does much better to keep beast and superbeast in a delicate and ironically equivocal suspense.

There is room for a sinister Pan, of a sort, even in the eclectic mock-mythologies of James Branch Cabell's *Jurgen* (1919). The Brown Man with Queer Feet (chapter xix) is said to be based on Machen's Pan,[21] and allowing for the transmutation effected by Cabell's style and point of view, this is certainly plausible. But no reading of Machen, of all people, could possibly have given rise to the opening scene, where Jurgen "presently observed a sun-browned brawny fellow, who sat upon the bank of a stream, dabbling his feet in the water, and making music with a pipe constructed of seven reeds of irregular lengths . . . Jurgen saw that this man's feet were unusual" (p. 136). It is as if Candide had come across a Pan designed by Elizabeth Barrett Browning. This is the clearest way of describing a Pan who is to be recognizable but anonymous; Machen would have named him but left him no physical attribute by which to be recognized. Jurgen's enquiries elicit the following satisfactorily abstract self-characterization: "'I am everything that was and that is to be. I am the Prince of this world. Never has any mortal been able to discover what I am' ["and live" Machen might have added] . . . 'What are you about to show me?' 'All'."

The result of Jurgen's mystic vision, which Cabell sensibly refrains from describing further, is a parody of Machen's awful experience. "The brown man was smiling, and Jurgen was in a flutter. 'It is not true,' Jurgen protested. 'What you have shown me is . . . sorcery and pure childishness and abominable blasphemy.' 'But Merlin would have died, and Merlin would have died without regret, if Merlin had seen what you have seen, because Merlin receives facts reasonably'" (p. 137). Cabell soon tires of abstractions, however. The brown man is metamorphosed into something closer to tangible nature and far more terrifying: "This noise seemed to come multitudinously from every side [a common feature of Pan's horrid appearances] . . . The earth moved under Jurgen's feet very much as a beast twitches its skin. [Trees] had bended, much as candles bend in very hot weather, to lay their topmost foliage at the feet of the brown man [cf. Meredith]. 'How if I slew you now? . . . Have you not just seen that which you may not ever quite forget?'" (p. 138). And Cabell concludes with a triumphant understatement of Machen's supreme horror: "The brown man had left him physically unharmed. But the state of Jurgen's nervous system was deplorable" (p. 140).

Cabell and Saki share two happy secrets, unfortunately kept from Benson, Machen, and Algernon Blackwood: one is the value of brevity, and the other is that the sinister Pan cannot be taken with total seriousness all the time. Yet the joke is itself largely a literary one; had those authors been less serious, Cabell and Saki would have lacked a whetstone on which to hone their scalpels.

Like Machen, Blackwood, and Benson, Stephen McKenna, in his novel *The Oldest God* (Boston, 1926), sets up an intellectual position which can be conveniently symbolized by "Pan," and then manipulates a rather weakly characterized set of people so as to work out the consequences of that position. Machen, Blackwood, and Benson share roughly similar assumptions, which are based on the identification of Pan with a universal nature spirit and which vary mainly in the relative proportions of the Swinburnian ingredients of ecstasy and terror. McKenna has an entirely different initial assumption; his book is based on a virtually complete equivalence of Pan and the Devil.

He presents the case for this equivalence early in the book, so thoroughly that one wonders why no one had made full use of it before. The possibility occurred, of course, to Forster's Mr. Sandbach ("The Story of a Panic"), but he spoke only for himself; Forster's Rickie rejects it. Those with a stake in the Orphic Pan could not afford to take it too seriously, unless, like Machen, they were prepared to risk a moral ambiguity by considering the vision of "all" nature to be an evil vision. Pan and the Devil perform analogous functions in Machen's fiction, but he does not identify them; for if he did, his stories would resemble one another even more than they do already. Meredith and H. W. Nevinson, like Eden Phillpotts, admitted the similarity, but avoided or denied the identification.[22] Eugene O'Neill, in *The Great God Brown* (1925), used a mask of Pan to denote an early stage of degeneration which although it easily developed into the Mephistophelean was not precisely synonymous with it.

McKenna uses the pagan and the Christian schemes of reference almost interchangeably. Pan appears more prominently than the Devil in the theoretical discussions, and his name is used more often in speaking of the figure in question; but in the action itself there are at least as many clues from Devil literature as from Pan literature.

Some members of a houseparty on a country estate near the old Roman wall[23] express a wish, seen to be rash by soberer persons present, to follow their natural instincts, to return to Arcady and Pan. It seems that they have invoked him, for a latecomer (who resembles Silenus) brings an unknown friend with him, a man called Stranger, who had not, until the last moment, felt certain of a welcome there. Like the Devil, he must be invited willingly; yet this can also be described as "Pan answering an invocation" (p. 260). The majority of the guests have their wish granted and do indeed begin to live "naturally," or, as an opponent puts it, as if they had "slipped back into some earlier, wilder belief" (p. 140). The results are a rash of adulteries, a fight over a woman by two men behaving like stags, shamelessness conquering the pagan party, and shock overcoming the ascetics. The ascetics, for whom the narrator is spokesman, have refused to welcome Pan; they have voted for "civilization."

As in the Pan stories, signs of horror include "an animal smell" (p. 190) and several references to hoofmarks. But, like the Devil, who must keep one cloven hoof in his human form, Stranger leaves tracks half shoe and half hoof. He is the Pan-

Devil in modern dress; he explains, when rather shaky enquiries are made, that one foot was shot off in the War. (The time is 1924). There is a personal attachment between Stranger and the Silenus figure, which is much more like Satan's long-term contracts than like Pan's swift revenges. And it is specified that for "a time, at least, their souls had been stolen from them" (p. 325); the god Pan was not really interested in souls, as such. Pan comes to the fore for a moment when the narrator reflects that Stranger "was in his own kingdom here" and if menaced "had only to stampede the highland cattle [like Saki's "horned beasts on the farm"] and leave me a gored and trampled corpse" (p. 286). When shoeless, Stranger can "run like a man or bound like a goat" (p. 196).

This Pan figure has to do double duty as an ordinary human character as well; indeed he is at his most frightening when the narrator senses him shifting unexpectedly from one role to another. There is very little precedent for a Pan in modern dress (Machen's "Helen" could scarcely be any help), but it seems reasonable to suppose that the characteristics of a Pan worshiper, like Benson's Tom Merivale, might be useful guides. And indeed Stranger does like country walks in any weather, and says of his self-imposed solitude: "in the country I could not be lonely if I tried" (p. 132). He has, like Merivale and Donatello, a strange influence over birds. He can be mildly wistful, romantically melancholy in appearance, like "a dog that has been left behind"; in this he resembles H. W. Nevinson's Pan, among others, the only survivor of the gods, once a "god-of-all-work" for Demeter, now full of "a kind of melancholy, too, as though he were a little tired with all he had seen." [24]

In some other respects he is more like any other gentlemanly "man or god or devil" (p. 286). He claims to live "*semper, omnibus, ubique,* like the Catholic Church" (p. 289); he is reticent, well-mannered, but capable of triumphant mockery and a rather melodramatic laugh. In the end, having proved McKenna's point about the consequences of "natural" behavior, he simply retires from the field, by the curious route of a Christian chapel on the estate. He is in fact as much in control of events as ever, although it is supposed that he has once more submitted himself "to the pale Galilean" (p. 352). Presumably he will return again whenever invited.

There are two other Pans in McKenna's fiction. One, in *Lilith*, is very similar, in capsule form, to *The Oldest God*. "The spirit of Pan is abroad," it is said, as one member after another of a postwar "fast set" succumbs to an epidemic madness of scandalous behavior and breaches of decorum. The other reference is in a slight story about the sinister attraction that an Italian peasant girl exerts over a gentlemanly artist. "The pure animal in the guise of woman . . . led him to christen her a daughter of Pan." [25] The narrator, obtusely disapproving of passion, like McKenna's other spokesmen, feels "a panic fear" at the sight of the girl, but, as in the case of a heroine who was more literally "the daughter of Pan," the parallel cannot be taken very far.

The final effect of the Pan figure in *The Oldest God* is that of a reply (which indeed McKenna may have intended) to authors like Blackwood and Benson, and even D. H. Lawrence, as if to say "Look at the consequences in actual society of the conduct you advocate, by your preference for the 'natural' at the expense of the 'civilized' and inhibited. You hint that you know your Pan to be the Devil: so indeed he is, and you are 'of the Devil's party.' "

Whether or not McKenna's readers agree with his position, they are likely to wonder if he has really grasped the essence of sinfulness, or if he is merely playing with some of its social manifestations in the year 1924. Machen, for all his Baudelairean posturing, at least feels strongly about evil, though he may find it too ineffable to express. McKenna's sins are tied down to the milieu of the houseparty. They would do as well as any others, of course (Henry James would not have needed a tenth of the actions performed in *The Oldest God* to fill several novels with the spirit of evil), to express the unutterable evil that lurks in every human heart, repressed only by society and the Christian ethic, if only McKenna showed the slightest hint of ever having sensed the presence of anything profounder than "naughtiness" or "good behavior." For this reason, although McKenna's Pan figure is strongly delineated and represents facts and ideas that should terrify us more than any Orphic Pan could do, he is not really fearful; the glimpse he gives us into ourselves is but a shallow one.

Perhaps William Faulkner's early short story "Black Music" (*Doctor Martino*, 1934) permits a somewhat deeper look. It is, among other things, Saki in upstate New York, transmuted into Faulkner's language and social idiom. An insensitive society woman plans to "grub up the grape vines" to build a summer house "like the Coliseum," although the men (as in Saki and Landor) "know [better] what to leave be." Pan has to turn a meek draftsman into a maniacal Faun tooting on a tin flute, and employ him, as well as a wild bull, to frighten off the trespassers upon his grape-vined sanctuary. Mr. Midgleston does a fairly good job of explaining what it feels like to have a vision of Pan explode inside his head, and to become a "farn" for a day — and what happens to his domestic and professional life as a result. The scene of the naked Midgleston's pursuit of Mrs. Van Dyming through the underbrush, while she mistakes his penny whistle for a murderous knife, is one of the better things in Pan horror fiction.

One example of the sinister Pan taken from the realm of pulp horror fiction will suffice to show the *reductio ad absurdum* of the convention imaginatively begun by Machen and masterfully handled by Saki. As Nelson Bond's "The Master of Cotswold" [26] is a debased pastiche of the genre down to the smallest detail, a brief summary of the plot, with a partial list of analogues, will serve as a recapitulation of some of the narrative elements suited to the Pan who terrifies.

The narrator, whose notebook we are reading, has decided to escape the machine age by buying a demesne in the Cotswolds. He has a prescience of some frightful horror; he is warned not to investigate a strange hoofmark. But of course he does (compare Machen, Saki, Benson, for the usual theme of the revenge of the god upon a man who goes too far). The god begins to manifest himself in "gypsy" pipes, beckoning and yet repelling, which grow ever louder. A servant girl is found dead in the quarry, her face "a mask of frozen horror"; she had been lured over the edge by a strange "hooman" (compare Machen), and (compare Blackwood) flowers have grown in great abundance where she fell. The gateway has been opened (compare Machen) to "other gods, less kindly." The accursed piping, productive of "anguish and ecstasy," drives the girl's mother mad. She dies under similar circumstances. The father dies, too, but in more manly fashion, "beaten to death . . . under horrendous hoofs" (compare Benson). The narrator then reads an earlier journal (compare Machen's "Chinese Boxes") supplied by a priest. He kills the priest, taking his cross to protect himself, which implies, of course, that the Devil (compare McKenna) is at work. The narrator, in words almost quoted from Benson, realizes that he has "been companion of the grasses, friend and confidant of the trees . . . There is a price to pay." In comparing the dead girl to Syrinx in her immortality he does, however, prove a wider knowledge of Pan's doings than the reading of horror stories alone could have provided. He then smells the hairy scent of the goat (compare Benson, Saki, McKenna) and dies crying (compare Benson) "My master — Pan! Pan! Oh, *culpe mea*" (sic). At this point the only unplagiarized touch to the story, its title, is elucidated, and, indeed, "The Master of Cotswold" is a happy irony deserving of a better vehicle.

The story is largely taken from "The Man Who Went Too Far," although Blackwood, Machen, and possibly Saki have been laid under contribution as well. As a piece of fiction, it is beneath criticism; though Bond is not the first author to labor under the misapprehension that if one Pan-caused death is frightening, several such deaths must be more so.

In "The Master of Cotswold," in short, this subdivision of the horror story — which was born in the powerful though imprecise imaginings of Arthur Machen, reached a peak of craftsmanship, at least, in "Music on the Hill," and had been of some use to two major writers — has come to an inglorious end.

"TERROR AND ECSTASY": THE DUAL VISION

In E. M. Forster's "The Story of a Panic" (1904),[27] Pan is once more, as in Benson and Machen, the guide into a profound mystical experience, which has as concomitants the emotions of terror and ecstasy. But the attributes of malevolence are combined with the essence of benevolence. The approach of Pan reveals the inner world to those capable of perceiving it, while the representatives of ordinary insensitive humanity are forced to flee in terror, like a herd of animals seized by what the Greeks had called Panic. Just so do the Philistine English plunge down the hill to escape they know not what. The chief among them, the narrator, Tytler, almost escapes from his Philistinism when he perceives that "I was afraid not as a man, but as a beast."[28]

The boy Eustace, freed of the encumbering presence of the others, sees whatever it is that the goat-god has to show him, something that perfects his humanity by bringing him into intimacy with nature, which spoils him for the Anglo-Saxons and makes him a brother of the Italians. The earth is found to be imprinted with goats' hoofs, the same simple representation that Benson used of the incarnation of joy and terror in the god Pan. Forster is more interested in the joy than in the terror, but "to see Pan" still means "to die." Forster's characters die, it is true, not from the vision, but from the consequences of a civilization that denies the vision. Gennaro and Caterina are killed by the civilized, who cannot bear to let them escape, and they nearly kill Eustace as well. The often abstract conflict of the Arcadian and the civilized is made concrete in these characters.

The narrators of the stories discussed earlier have scarcely any character traits at all beyond a slight skepticism designed, by a very common device in such stories, to give an air of reality to the improbable: if *they*, sturdy, normal, sane, unimaginative Britons, were convinced of the existence of Pan as seen in his effect on their oversensitive and recently deceased friends, and it takes little more than hoofprints and the goaty smell to convince them, why should we not be? Forster improves upon this same narrative formula. Tytler, who betrays himself as not only insensitive but actually hostile to the life of the spirit, has himself felt inexplicable terror and seen the hoofprints. How can we not believe him?

Forster lets events carry their own suggestion of deeper meanings, when such are required. The lizard that runs out of Eustace's cuff and the hare that perches on his arm tell us that he is now closer to Nature. Tom Merivale swam in the river and asked a nightingale to perch on his finger and sing, but then found it necessary to explain at repetitive length what these actions symbolized.[29]

Like Saki, Forster has cut out the superfluous; unlike Saki he has added the essential — the dimension of real concern with human nature, which he chooses to define in terms of its relationship with supernature. Saki, insofar as he characterizes at all — and here, too, he exercises classic restraint — uses the same principle. There are those who revere the unknowable, and those who mock and are punished, but in "Music on the Hill" both exist only for the sake of the plot.

Two "literary" views of the nature of Pan are presented by two of the minor characters, at the beginning of "The Story of a Panic," and both views are found wanting in terms of the action. Leyland, the artist, knows what the romantic poets said about Pan. "All the poetry is going from Nature . . . Everywhere we see the vulgarity of desolation spreading . . . We are all hopelessly steeped in vulgarity," he says, referring to the selling of trees for cash. "It is through us, and to our shame, that the Nereids have left the waters and the Oreads the mountains, that the woods no longer give shelter to Pan" (p. 8). One might suppose that the holder of such a Coleridgean (or Schilleresque) view might be the very one to understand a boy who has been possessed by the veritable Pan. But even the narrator sees clearly the "mock misery" of his sentiment. It is further apparent from his comments on the landscape that, like the poet Gray, who asked for a little more art to make a landscape satisfyingly picturesque, Leyland wishes to improve what nature provides. He is the first to feel panic. He cuts in two the whistle which, however excruciatingly discordant it may sound to the civilized, represents the pipes of Pan in this story. He disapproves (in his effeteness, it is implied) of Eustace's displays of primitive energy, finds the boy's raptures over the beauties of nature to be a "diabolical caricature" (p. 29), and aids eagerly

to recapture him. So much for the Arcadian Pan. Leyland may
mourn his death, but he is the last person to want him revived
in actuality.[30]

Sandbach knows his Eusebius, or some derivative thereof. He
uses the Plutarchan story of the death of Pan to explain Leyland's remark about Pan's disappearance, ties Pan's death in
with Christ's birth, and subsequently associates Pan's effect on
Eustace with the doings of Satan. Forster scarcely bothers to
refute this view, which the whole story refutes by implication.
It is simply the explanation which would occur to a man of
religious training and superstitious outlook.[31]

The narrator is more complex. His usual stand is based on a
strong desire to discipline Eustace by force into conformity with
"English" standards, but he has moments almost of compunc-
tion as he betrays Eustace and is not unmoved by the boy's
crude verbal expression of the rapture he feels. Unlike the others,
the narrator can appreciate at least the resurgence of energy —
"like a real boy" (p. 19) — that typifies the new Eustace.

The women in this story are not strong-minded enough to
think of any explanation for Eustace's conduct. Rose, the young-
est, however, has some strange affinity with Eustace. She almost
stays to face Pan with him: "I somehow felt that if I could stop
on it would be quite different, that I shouldn't be frightened at
all, so to speak." But she fled because she saw "mamma" go (p.
14). She has one intuition that tells her that Gennaro could recapture the boy, and another that prompts her to betray Eustace
by suggesting this to her father. She has a foot in both camps,
but as she grows up, she is growing toward "civilized" standards
with great rapidity.

Gennaro is really on Eustace's side; he has no explanation for
Pan, but he has "been in the woods and understood things too"
(p. 35). Even he can be tempted by civilization's temptation,
money.

Only Eustace has a true and consistent vision of Pan, and he
cannot articulate it. He knows when he is captured that "I
nearly saw everything, and now I can see nothing at all" (p. 34),
and when he is free "the trees, hills, stars, water, I can see all"

(p. 33); but "the shouts and the laughter of the escaping boy" (p. 38) express the vision better than words can.

Although characterization and narrative technique make "The Story of a Panic" vastly superior to its predecessors and contemporaries in this area of fantasy, it is the same sort of story, with the same sort of Pan in it. He is still the representative of the ineffable "beyond the veil," be it joy or terror, and to see him is death and/or fulfillment. He cannot be defined in terms of ordinary human nature, for he is something outside of it. The mental or spiritual quality in the characters that enables them to respond to Pan may be treated as an element of characterization, of course, but this is easier to do in the negative. Eustace is inevitably something of a wraith; it is the narrator who, albeit disagreeably, comes to life.

"The trees, hills, stars, water, I can see all. But isn't it odd! I can't make out men a bit." This is the trouble with visions of Pan. They don't help a bit at making out men. Even in the hands of a master like Forster, this defines their limitations in the field of fiction. Forster would never rely on Pan so heavily again; and Lawrence, who wanted to "make out men" with the aid of a Pan potentially terrifying, had to use a radically different approach.

Several critics of Forster use Pan as a convenient shorthand symbol, not only for the ruling spirit of the short stories, but for major elements and ideas in his novels as well, a device which may be helpful for understanding Forster, but is most unhelpful for understanding Pan. There are no other Pan figures in the short stories.[32] "The Curate's Friend," mentioned by Lionel Trilling[33] as well as by W. R. Irwin, comes the closest, but he is an altogether less powerful and awe-inspiring teacher of eternal verities, and only claims ears and a tail, which, though dismaying, is scarcely cause for Panic. The other stories are indeed about man's possible closeness to nature, but that is a theme for which Greek mythology, and mythologies of Forster's own devising as well, have a rich variety of symbols.

R. A. Scott-James, at least, does not claim to be using Pan other than as a figure of speech, whether for an aspect of Forster's writing or of his life as a whole. He equates the Pan spirit with "belief in the natural, the spontaneous, the unashamed," from which it follows that Forster "believes in the genius of place. Every hillside in his mythology has its Pan, every wood its dryad, and every natural man has his proper abode," of which *Howards End* is cited as the clearest example. Forster himself has been silent for forty years; "why should he write something else, of a world in which his Pan is dead?"[34]

For my purposes F. R. Leavis conveys much the same thing, while keeping the Pan metaphor in its place with enviable precision: "Italy, in those novels, represents the bent of interest that Pan and the other symbols represent in the tales," and that is "a radical dissatisfaction with civilization."[35]

I prefer to begin, not with a "spirit of Pan" in Forster's work that might have innumerable manifestations, definable only in terms of his entire literary outlook, but with the actual references that Forster makes to Pan in his novels. They touch upon narrower ideas and a smaller number of characters than the pervasive "Pan-genius." In fact I shall be discussing only a very small motif, which may, of course, encapsulate larger ideas.

Where Angels Fear to Tread and *Passage to India* make no mention of Pan. *Howards End* mentions him only to reject him as a viable symbol. The one reference in *A Room with a View* is an arch parenthesis supplied by the author *in propria persona*. Only in *The Longest Journey* is Pan anything other than parenthetical. He is one of the more important of the many classical images that give the book its "rhythm," but Forster ironically uses the symbol most often to exploit its artificial and literary quality, to counterpoint it against the actualities it is meant to represent.

The Pan of *A Room with a View* (1908) is the closest in spirit to the Pan of "The Story of a Panic."[36] The novel, like the short story, includes a picnic scene on an Italian hillside — a remarkably similar hillside — where a few see a vision of beauty, but the majority see only wrongdoing or confusion. "Some complicated game had been playing up and down the hillside all the afternoon . . . There was a general sense of groping and bewilderment. Pan had been amongst them — not the great god Pan, who has been buried these two thousand years, but the little god Pan, who presides over social contretemps and unsuccessful picnics" (chapter vii). Forster refuses to define Lucy's kiss in terms of Pan.[37] Had he done so, it would probably have been "the great god Pan," who though "buried," lived again for Eustace. The Pan of *A Room with a View* is "the little god Pan," of "unsuccessful picnics." He is a comic version of the Pan who terrified the insensitive members of the earlier picnic party; he sends "groping and bewilderment" instead of stark panic. Forster allowed for both contingencies in his own definition of fantasy:

> on behalf of fantasy let us now invoke all beings who inhabit the lower air, the shallow water, and the smaller hills, all Fauns and Dryads and slips of the memory, all verbal coincidences, Pans and puns, all that is medieval this side of the grave . . . The stuff of daily life will be tugged and strained in various directions, the earth will be given little tilts mischievous or pensive, spot-lights will fall on objects that have no reason to anticipate or welcome them, and tragedy herself, though not excluded, will have a fortuitous air as if a word would disarm her.[38]

"The Story of a Panic" is almost tragic fantasy; Eustace escapes, Gennaro dies — it could have been the other way round. In *A Room with a View*, Pan is a minor manifestation, a specialized agent, so to speak, of the "Comic Muse" (inherited from Meredith) who "though able to look after her own interests, did not disdain [human] assistance" in organizing the supreme "muddles" of the story (p. 183).

The Virgilian phrase "Pan ovium custos" (Pan the guardian of the sheep; *Georgics* I, 16) appears in two different contexts in *The Longest Journey* (1907), linking two incidents — one in Stephen's boyhood, the other in Rickie's adulthood — which might otherwise seem unrelated. When Stephen Wonham, as a child, was frightened by the advance of a flock of sheep upon him in a wood, scholarly Mr. Failing quotes the phrase in explanation. Soon after, Stephen, an undisciplined schoolboy, is thrashed for mistranslating that same phrase. He has known

Panic terror in actuality; he rejects what is to him an artificial label for it.

He was trespassing in those woods, when he met in a narrow glade a flock of sheep. They had neither dog nor shepherd, and advanced towards him silently . . . He retired, slowly at first, then fast; and the flock, in a dense mass, pressed after him. His terror increased. He turned and screamed at their long white faces; and still they came on, all stuck together, like some horrible jelly. If once he got into them! Bellowing and screeching, he rushed into the undergrowth, tore himself all over, and reached home in convulsions. Mr. Failing, his only grown-up friend, was sympathetic, but quite stupid. "Pan ovium custos," he remarked as he pulled out the thorns.[39]

Later Rickie, an all-too-well-disciplined schoolmaster, gives this same phrase to his form, with the difference that he completes the invocation, "tua si tibi Maenala curae / Adsis, O Tegaee, favens" (If you care for your own Maenalus, / Come, Tegean god, and befriend us). It has no special application in his mind. "He was not required to provide it with an atmosphere. The scheme of work was already mapped out, and he started gaily upon familiar words" (p. 181). It is almost as if the invocation has been successful; shortly thereafter the boys turn into a mob and bully a terrified victim: "There arose at Dunwood House one of those waves of hostility of which no boy knows the origin nor any master can calculate the course . . . One evening nearly the whole house set on him . . . [Pembroke] would not admit that if you herd together human beings before they can understand each other the great god Pan is angry, and will in the end evade your regulations and drive them mad. That night the victim was screaming with pain" (p. 209).

The Virgilian lines link Stephen and Rickie, the one as a herder of sheep, the other as a herder of schoolboys, and the only realistic atmosphere for such quotation, that of the schoolroom, hangs over both episodes. These lines thus underscore the falsity of Rickie's school-mastering, for they are at that moment all he knows of Pan; yet his favorite poet had once been Theocritus (p. 10), and his own book was called *Pan Pipes*.

Stephen, who cannot construe the lines, has felt the touch of Pan. Rickie, who has the words to hand — "Pan ovium custos" — is being turned to stony ineffectualness by "Medusa in Arcady," his wife. He is able neither to prevent the disaster, nor to connect the words and the violence which they foreshadow. The implication must be drawn by the reader.

Neither Rickie nor Ansell, who is the same sort of man as Rickie, but uncorrupted, can quite face the realities that their poetry represents. Rickie is shocked by a village scandal, even though it is paralleled in "a beautiful idyll of Theocritus" (p. 130). Ansell passes by "the monuments of our more reticent beliefs . . . the statue of the Cnidian Demeter. Honest, he knew that here were powers he could not cope with, nor, as yet, understand" (p. 206), yet her "immortal features and the shattered knees" (p. 318) link symbolically Stephen's youth, over which she had pictorially presided, Rickie's emotional insufficiencies, and his eventual fulfillment, dying, returning to the earth, to save his brother's life. Like Jackson and Failing of the older generation, Ansell and Rickie know that "the Greeks looked very straight at things, and Demeter or Aphrodite are thinner veils than . . . modern journalese." Rickie senses that "poetry, not prose, lies at the core" (p. 197), and Forster is clearly on his side, while showing that a failure to "connect" the poetry with the prose, Pan with panic, will break him in the end. Rickie realizes that the dead pagans to whom Mrs. Failing mockingly compares Stephen are soldiers and shepherds who worshiped, not the devil, as Mrs. Failing alleges, but "Mars or Pan — Erda perhaps." Yet he can never really love the man, his brother, who is "a shepherd if ever there was" (p. 149). Mrs. Failing brings out the contrast by throwing the terms of Rickie's belief at Stephen's head: "Is there no one, in all these downs, who warbles with eager thought the Doric lay?" Like Coleridge's schoolmaster at the beginning of the *Biographia Literaria*, Stephen translates that into what he really knows: "Chaps sing to themselves at times, if you mean that" (p. 103). When she remarks of her "thoroughbred pagan" that he has "gone to worship Nature" (p. 142), it is on one level mockery, on another, sober earnest.

Perhaps Stephen's father, Robert, had best defined what the worship of Pan might be in practice (though like his son he would have scorned the literary term), when he described the earth as a creature with a living skin, defying the researches of the scientists, which must in the last resort be understood through instinct and a love not without reverence.

How much autobiography, whether of fact or of mood, there is in Forster's account of the anthology *Pan Pipes*, I do not know,[40] but the general theme of "this ridiculous idea of getting into touch with Nature" (p. 84), and the particular story, which made so little sense to Stephen, of the girl who became a Dryad, make inevitable a comparison with the anthology *The Celestial Omnibus*, and the story "Other Kingdom." *Pan Pipes* would be an appropriate title for either volume, for Pan is the god of nature, as even Pembroke knows, in a pedantic sort of way, and his pipe music is a message that some men may hear. In the time of Emerson, who was very nearly the last man to write profound poetry about the music of Pan's pipes, this would have seemed a very good title indeed. On the other hand, Stephen makes a shrewd literary comment: "Are you sure 'Pan Pipes' haven't been used up already?" By 1907 they had;[41] they were a literary cliché, beginning to go out of fashion, which would have labeled Rickie's stories as those of a very youthful idealist in the mode of Arcadian sentiment. His vision is doubtless truer and more real than that of the minor poets of the time, but the words are the same, and "as a whole," they fail to convince (p. 165).

So in this book there are two approaches, Stephen's and Rickie's, to the great god Pan, the benevolent Pan, the Pan of Eustace's vision. One is the result of a time when Rickie "believed, actually believed, that Fauns lived in a certain double hedgerow near the Gog Magogs" (p. 84). Such a belief is good and true, Forster seems to say; and he implies that such was the fabric of his own youthful beliefs. Yet the use of the name "Pan" suggests a separation from the reality it represents, which can be only partially atoned for by a nostalgia for it. If Stephen were parted from the earth he loved, he might "stretch out his hands with a pagan's yearning" (p. 269), and *then* he might learn to use Rickie's words for such things.

But Forster does not neglect the little god Pan, the god, not of the instinctive knowledge of earth, who is "most places, as name implies [sic]" ("Other Kingdom"), but the god of specific attributes and actions, a disembodied spirit whose presence is to be perceived through his effect on sheep and schoolboys. Pan is merely mischievous in *A Room with a View*; in *The Longest Journey* he is malevolent. But in both cases, he represents a multiple and social evil, where fear is closely allied to madness (compare Longus, p. 70). The "little god Pan" is a god of groups, whereas the great god Pan speaks to individuals.[42]

The two Pans represent aspects of life that recur constantly in Forster's work. In *Howards End* "panic and emptiness" go with the life of "telegrams and anger." In *Passage to India* there is panic in the Marabar Caves and panic among the Anglo-Indians, mob-madness with an individual victim. Mrs. Moore has a vision of oneness with nature and Adela Quested a vision of truth which can almost cancel out the hallucination of panic. But I do not take these examples, or the endless others which might be chosen, as warranting the division of all Forster's work into pervasive little Pans and pervasive great Pans any more than I would agree to seeing a Pan spirit in every example of a union of self and nature, or of primal energy.

Forster's chief concerns remain very much the same, but he weans himself rapidly from the Pan symbol as a means of expressing them. We can see the process in *The Longest Journey*, which is in part an ironic exploration of the limitations of the poetic ideal in the world of "prose," or, to make an analogy in literary terms, of the limited possibilities of pure fantasy in the novel. The relationship between the mythic symbols (including Pan) which represent the possibly truer truth of poetry and the fictional representation of reality in life is more complicated than appears at first sight.

In *Howards End*, the struggle, as far as Pan is concerned, is over. Forster himself wryly renounces Pan as a played-out literary motif:

To speak against London is no longer fashionable. The Earth as an artistic cult has had its day, and the literature of the near future will probably ignore the country and seek inspiration from the town. One can understand the reaction. Of Pan and the elemental forces, the public has heard a little too much — they seem Victorian, while London is Georgian — and those who care for the earth with sincerity may wait long ere the pendulum swings back to her again. (chapter xiii)

Unfortunately, there is no "native English Pan," and Forster must make do with a wych elm as a guardian spirit of the landscape.[43] "Why has not England a great mythology? Our folklore has never advanced beyond daintiness, and the greater melodies about our country-side have all issued through the pipes of Greece . . . It cannot vivify one fraction of a summer field" (chapter xxxiii). That is the end of the Pan symbol in Forster's fiction. When he returns to mythology, it is to the very different mythology of modern India.

Algernon Blackwood's "A Touch of Pan"[44] is of interest chiefly because it attempts the same division of human types according to their relationship with Pan that Forster makes in "The Story of a Panic." There is a sensitive and receptive minority, but for most Pan is still sinister, still the cause of panic.

One couple possesses "the secret of some instinctual knowledge that was not only joy, but a kind of sheer natural joy" (p. 289), and Pan, in a merry Bacchic revel, which blurs into a quasi-religious vision, blesses their lovemaking in the woods. The hero has, or acquires, two small horns; Pan comes; they feel "the panic of reverent awe . . . there rose the shrill, faint piping of a little reed . . . With the stupendous Presence there was joy" (pp. 303–304).

Preferring a "happy, natural, vagabond life," seeking the "natural, wild, untamed" (p. 296), this couple had fled a dreadful houseparty — "not natural" — where "women smoked their cigarettes with an air of invitation [of which] they feigned a guilty ignorance" (p. 305). They are followed into the woods by another couple, more sophisticated, who properly belong to the world of the houseparty where "shamelessness . . aped emancipation" (p. 297). The two sophisticates are seeking furtive pleasures, however, and Pan puts them to flight in guilty terror (pp. 305–310).

Whether Pan is to be benevolent or malevolent depends on some state of inner grace, or possibly of conscience. The author clearly dislikes the contemporary atmosphere of libertinism and approves another pattern of conduct which is natural and innocent; the god Pan is dragged in to ratify the moral judgments of which the characterization alone could not convince us.[45] Whatever the distinction between the two sorts of sexuality may be, Pan is established overtly now as a suitable patron deity for whichever is to be glorified. Blackwood's trivial story will find better formulated parallels in some of Lawrence's fiction.

Blackwood's novel *The Centaur* (London, 1911) is strongly reminiscent of Benson's Pan story; although Pan is replaced as chief actor by the very similar figure of the Centaur, he still retains two wearily familiar functions. He is the universal god who is represented in this world by the beauty of landscape, the patron deity of a "beyond" more concrete than usual, an Arcadia populated by fauns, satyrs, and especially centaurs. He is also the piper whose flutings summon the hero to enter this world, to fuse with nature, to accept the mystic vision fully, and to die. The dramatic conflict is minimal because nothing holds the hero to life, and there is nothing evil in this death. Death is a release and an escape, since civilized life, in the manner of oversimplified romanticism, is the only source of pain and evil.

To the ignorant who surround the hero, this process is terrifying; the peasants say truthfully, without understanding the glory of merging with the infinite, that the centaurs are "old as the stones . . . to see them is — to die!" (p. 222). Even to the hero himself the summons causes an instinctive fear which he must learn to overcome. But in the story as a whole, terror plays a small and unconvincing role, as rapture does in "The Great God Pan"; Blackwood has the same difficulty as Machen in dealing with one incomprehensibly great emotion. Blackwood describes ineffable joy by claiming its existence, giving facial expressions, symbolizing it in the vague language of natural beauty, and then repeating himself a great many times.[46]

Blackwood's collection of short stories that came out a year later was much more successful. The title was *Pan's Garden*, meaning Earth; yet none of the stories is about Pan. However, in the sense in which Blackwood has defined Pan in *The Centaur*, they are all about Pan, for each one describes the merging of its hero into some aspect of physical nature: desert sand, Alpine snow, or grotesquely healthy and prolific flowers. Ecstasy is muted and horror is developed, to the great gain of the story line, for this union is not an escape, but a capture.[47]

Success with a Pan figure, whether sinister or benevolent, or both at once, comes largely from keeping a balance between the goat and the god, between concreteness and mystery. Bond, who has no sense of wonder, and Machen, who has no head for detail, both fail to realize the possibilities of the sinister Pan: being trampled to death by a goat is crudely grotesque; being trampled to death by the spirit of evil in the universe is implausible and hard to visualize. Saki and Benson, on the other hand, preserve the tension between the two elements of Pan's paradoxical nature. They do justice to both goat and god, and thereby achieve some measure of literary terror.

The Centaur shows glaringly the limitations of a Pan who is both benevolent and universal.[48] Such a Pan can hardly avoid impalpability, unless, as in Forster, his meanings in the human mind and manifestations in human actions are vividly recorded; even then his malevolence may prove more rewarding. One acknowledges the limitations of the dual Pan, and the fictional superiority of his evil side, by writing, not the novel of a vision, but "The Story of a Panic."

Chapter VI

CULMINATIONS: D. H. LAWRENCE

"Of Pan and the elemental forces, the public has heard a little too much — they seem Victorian," Forster had said in 1910. Though the popularity of the Pan figure, so largely empty and banal at the time he wrote, ebbed not with the death of the old Queen, but more nearly with the coming of the Great War, he was in essence right. How curious that D. H. Lawrence, writing when the Pan motif, so luxuriant in the period 1890–1914, had been out of fashion for ten years, began afresh to study all the traditional possibilities of the myth. He considered in his work every important aspect, the Pan-Christ dialectic, the death of Pan, the romantic-transcendental Pan, and especially the Gothic-visionary Pan of Machen and his successors, and infused them all with his own mythic conceptions, his own Gothic visions of the ecstasy and terror of the cosmos. As both critic and exponent of the Pan tradition, he has no serious competitors in modern literature.

At first Lawrence used Pan, and other classical images, in a schematic fashion not unlike Forster's; each individual reference is logically explicable in terms of commonly accepted classical or traditional connotations. This is true of the scattered, relatively trivial, references in the early works, from *The White Peacock* in 1911 through *Sea and Sardinia* in 1921, as well as in the two last works, *Lady Chatterley's Lover* and *The Man Who Died* (1928); they range over eighteen of Lawrence's twenty productive years, but chiefly between 1911 and 1915. There are ten years (1915–1924), in which Lawrence almost forgets about Pan altogether.

The second group of references, which I shall call the "Pan cluster," is made up of images from virtually every work Lawrence wrote between 1924 and 1926, from "Pan in America" to

The Plumed Serpent.[1] They are not only more frequent, more emphatic, more closely interwoven one with another, and more important to the central meanings of the works in which they are found; they are also much less susceptible to logical analysis. If the earlier, more formal images correspond to Lawrence's definition of "allegory [which] can always be explained: and explained away," the images of the Pan cluster correspond to "the true symbol [which, like "the true myth"] defies all explanation." Once set in motion by the poet, the "true symbol" achieves a "certain course of circuit of its own," and, like the Greek myths themselves, follows "the logic of action rather than of reason."[2]

Lawrence's earliest Pan, the comparison of Annable, the gamekeeper of *The White Peacock* (1911), to "some malicious Pan" (II, i), contains only in embryo, if at all, the complex meanings to be attributed to Pan as a symbol of the Lawrentian "Dark Hero" (for example, Cipriano in *The Plumed Serpent*; Lewis in *St. Mawr*). The simile has the same sort of casual appropriateness as another mythological simile later in the same book: George "laughed like a sardonic Jove" (II, vi) while feeding the pigs, to whom he has the same godlike relation that Annable has with his woodland kingdom. Still, it is of interest that where Lawrence might have found only a tame pastoral Pan, suitable for inclusion in the mock-idyll of a later chapter (II, ix), he has already found a quasi-sinister one: "He stood in the rim of light, darkly; fine, powerful form, menacing us. He did not move, but like some malicious Pan looked down on us" (II, i).

"Pan" is one classical simile among the many that form an element of the novel's structure, used either as a sign of youthful romanticism (compare Forster) or as a symptom of anxious culture. It is much more frequent in the earlier part of the book; as the narrator matures he tends to use it only nostalgically: the "dryads" whom he had seen in his youth, "glancing wistfully, turned back like pale flowers falling" (III, vii), like those of Heine or Turgenev. Lawrence does not really believe that "the Greeks saw straighter"; not until he has invested classical images, and particularly the image of Pan, with his special Lawrentian meanings will they matter very much to him.

The symbolic structure of *The Rainbow* (1915), though more sophisticated, is of much the same sort. The heavy clustering of Christian imagery, in the parts of the book dealing with Ursula's early life, enlarges to include classical imagery at a later stage of her development. Pan appears at a point where the two modes overlap. The Christian mode is still dominant; but its classical antithesis has just entered, only to be rejected. "Jove . . . had begotten in her a giant, a hero. Very good, so he had, in Greece. For herself, she was no Grecian woman. Not Jove nor Pan nor any of those gods, not even Bacchus nor Apollo, could come to her. But the Sons of God who took to wife the daughters of men, these were such as should take her to wife" (chapter x). Figures from the Book of Genesis (6.1–4) are here developed, by way of Milton's *Paradise Regained* (II, 178–191), to symbolize the first stirrings in Ursula's mind of a wider point of view than she had had in her childhood. When Flood and Arcadian images mingle again, she no longer rejects the "dryads and fauns . . . Ursula wished she had been a nymph. She would have laughed through the window of the ark" (chapter xi). Furthermore, she sees that "religions were local and religion was universal" (chapter xii).

This last insight is very like Lawrence's own in his review of *Georgian Poetry*: 1911–1912: "I worship Christ, I worship Jehovah, I worship Pan, I worship Aphrodite. But I do not worship hands nailed and running with blood upon a cross, nor licentiousness, nor lust. I want them all, all the gods. They are all God." [3] Lawrence never ceases to "worship Pan" in one sense or another, but twelve years later he would explicate his worship rather differently: "No god, that men can conceive of, could possibly be absolute or absolutely right. All the gods that men ever discovered are still God: and they contradict one another and fly down one another's throats, marvellously. Yet they are *all* God: the incalculable Pan." [4] In 1913 Pan was still a "local" god, one member of the pantheon which makes up God; in 1925 Pan is himself the universal God.

Lawrence's earliest attempt to invest Pan with a meaning both wider and more personal ("The Crown," 1915) reduces the multiplicity of the pantheon to a dualism, highly Nietzschean, of a "Pagan, aristocratic, lordly, sensuous . . Eternity of the Origin," and a "Christian, humble, spiritual, unselfish, democratic . . . Eternity of the Issue, the End." Lawrence chooses "the pagan eternity, the eternity of Pan," [5] much as the Victorian essayists chose between Pan and Christ. In the terms of the Pan cluster, Pan is no longer one half of a duality; he is the "oldest Pan-mystery," or "the flame-life in all the universe." [6] As Henry Miller said of Lawrence's key images, they are "the resolution of two opposites in the form of a mystery." [7] Miller instances "Phoenix, Crown, Rainbow, Plumed Serpent" as resolving images: the Pan symbol, as used in the Pan cluster, would illustrate his point equally well.

In the next eleven years (1911–1922), Lawrence's only two Pan references are both fleeting and stereotyped. Pan is included in his traditional role as a member of the train of Dionysus in "David" (1919),[8] an essay which owes a great deal to Pater's "Study of Dionysus," and is in places a simple rewriting of it. Lawrence, however, is not at this point interested in Pater's elaborations of the role of Pan. In *Sea and Sardinia* (1921), Pan is a classical spirit in the Italian landscape, in the manner hallowed by innumerable writers of travel books: "One is conscious of the present, or of the medieval influences, or of the far, mysterious gods of the early Mediterranean. Wherever one is, the place has its conscious genus [sic] . . . The expression may be Proserpine, or Pan, or even the strange 'shrouded gods' of the Etruscans or the Sikels, none the less it is an expression. The land has been humanized" (chapter vi).[9]

For Lawrence "it was the greatest pity in the world, when philosophy and fiction [which had been united in ancient myth] got split"; the Pan cluster is one attempt to heal this split by creating a modern myth capable of arousing "the deep emotional self" and re-establishing "the living organic connections with the cosmos," by way of "a whole human experience, of which the purpose is too deep, going too deep in the blood and soul, for mental explanation or description." [10] Image clus-

ters are a primary technique of Lawrence's myth-making; yet,
according to a paraphrase of Lawrence's conversation, "What
was wrong with all the religions was that they had always
'plucked the lily,' had found one or another symbol and had
clung to it, refusing to relinquish it as its vitality was exhausted.
Yet a symbol, he had found, lasted only about twenty minutes
— he didn't know why; then it had to be replaced by another." [11]
The Pan image enjoyed a most vigorous "twenty minutes" of
life, from 1924 to 1926. The essay "Pan in America" is more
"philosophical"; the Pan figures of the novels are more "fictional." The overlaps between the preacher's arguments and the
novelist's characterizations are at their best a mythical triumph
and at their worst muddled, but still, in Lawrence's sense,
mythical.

"Pan in America" is the manifesto of this period, the first
splash of a single wave of enthusiasm for Pan as a symbol for
key Lawrentian concepts, explained by other symbols before
1924 and after 1926. It should not be considered in relation to
Lawrence's work alone; just as "The Last Laugh" fits into the
tradition of horror stories, so "Pan in America" fits into the
prose essay tradition.

Lawrence begins his essay with the story of the death of Pan,
finding, as have so many authors before and after him, that
this strange story is the surest way to catch attention. Like
Clemenceau, who began in the same fashion, Lawrence is far
more interested in Pan's rebirth than in his death; both give a
capsule history of the motif, and choose to emphasize a Pan
descended from the Romantic and transcendental Pans. Like
Stevenson, though less superficially, Lawrence mingles the
beauty and terror of nature in the unifying figure of Pan and
demands that man, for his own health (or, one might say,
salvation), leave "fact" or "machine" and return to "Pan," or
"mystery." Terror is itself beautiful for Lawrence; for Stevenson
it was only picturesque.

The novelty in the structure of the opening section is in Lawrence's literary criticisms of other Pan interpretations, which
are no less pungently effective because they support his own

interpretation of Pan. Lawrence asks for a definition of Pan: "But who was he, really?" The first answer is given in terms of classical literature, liberally interlarded with his own interpretation: "a lurking rustic god" is precise enough; "a goat's white lightning in his eyes" adds a stylistic twist; "laughing with the uncanny derision of one who feels himself defeated by something lesser than himself" is pure Lawrence. "Till at last the old Pan died, and was turned into the devil of the Christians," [12] and that accounts for him until the Renaissance, and after. To say that Pan gave rise to an eighteenth-century "ism," meaning pantheism, is an oversimplification, but a shaft aimed at Wordsworth's whole interpretation of nature hits Wordsworth's actual Pan figure en route: "Lucy Gray, alas, was the form that William Wordsworth thought fit to give to the Great God Pan." Wordsworth's is too optimistic, too "sweet-and-pure" a Pan figure; Lawrence, rightly, misses the bite of malevolence that he found in the classical Pan and would put into his own.

"All Walt is Pan, but all Pan is not Walt," declares "the old goat-legged gentleman from Greece" (Lawrence's closest approach to a whimsical Pan); "the new American pantheism collapses" under this triumph of logic.[13] Post-transcendental poetry gets equally short shrift: "the poets dress up a few fauns and nymphs . . . But, alas, these tame guinea-pigs soon became boring." Lawrence's Pan, like the classical one, expresses a whole life experience; the "private 'grounds'" of the minor poets exclude too much. Lawrence had been struck by the paradox of the Orphic Pan: "That which is everything has goat's feet and a tail!" Yet for all his air of surprise, he establishes and adheres to this same criterion of concreteness for himself. Measured thereby, Romantic, transcendental, and Arcadiac Pans are all found wanting: "Alas, poor Pan! Is this what you've come to? Legless, hornless, faceless, even smileless [this last word is part of Lawrence's special definition], you are less than everything or anything, except a lie." [14]

Lawrence, in establishing the "true" Pan, encounters at once the difficulty with which Forster had wrestled: to name Pan is to deny him, for the label involves a separation from the thing itself. "Speech is the death of Pan, who can but laugh and sound the reed-flute" (p. 27); Stephen can *know* Pan, while Rickie can only label him. For the writer this poses a contradiction in terms; he must name things so that we may know what things he means and must use his brain to describe what instead blood should experience. The only solution is metaphor. "Pan" is the primary metaphor here, but "Pan" cannot be used as part of his own definition, particularly since the god has already been defined in the incorrect or limited ways which Lawrence has just criticized. Lawrence requires a secondary metaphor with which to refresh the primary one, and he chooses the pine tree as a special case, in which the effects he needs can be concentrated. (He wisely avoids Stevenson's mistake of trying to cover the great variety of objects that might, just as suitably, represent Pan.) Lawrence describes first his own relationship "within the allness of Pan" to its "powerful mystery": "It vibrates its presence into my soul, and I am with Pan." He becomes more like the pine tree and (logically, but unusual in an account of communion with nature) the pine tree becomes a little more like him as well.

The pine tree, "fierce and bristling" and "turpentiney," supplies some of the power, the "oldest Pan," that man must receive from other living things. The primitive knew this, Lawrence has discovered it, and the rest of us need to learn it. And it is not to be learned from a Wordsworthian tree with the turpentine left out. "Vivid relatedness between the man and the living universe" is the basic prose meaning of the Pan symbol here. At this point, Lawrence shifts his attention from the pine tree to the Indian who, as a primitive, has a relatedness less intellectual, less thought-out and therefore deeper than Lawrence's own. The Indian, being part of Pan, too, has an "inscrutable Pan-smile" (an almost invariable attribute of any Lawrentian Dark Hero), and speaks in a "Pan-voice" to the tree, the fire, the rock, the deer, and to his woman (all in much the same tone). What he is alleged to say is much less successful than what Lawrence says with his own voice, and Lawrence realizes the difficulty. The Romantic poets faced the same problem, and "the Pan silence, that is so full of unutterable things" and of "soundless sounds" seems to me to be a romantic way of stating it.

We had "life-contact" as savages; we have lost it because we have learned to use ideas, abstractions, and machines. The opening metaphor of the death of Pan is worked into the argument here; Pan died when this connection was severed, when mystery was replaced with fact. It is a perfect romantic case. Indeed, for all its pungent criticism of Romantic Pans, the essay is an extension of the Romantic definition, rather than a denial of it.[15]

The primitive life and the nobility of the savage, as described in the essay, belong, of course, to an inaccessible golden age, even though the American Indians Lawrence saw might remind him of it.[16] He is realistic enough to see that a flight to Taos in 1924 does not in itself restore the "Pan relationship." Indeed, as so often with romantic tracts, the problem remains in this essay clearer than the solution, which is presumably some version of salvation through faith. We are left only with the assertion that even the city dweller can reject the "mechanical conquered universe" in favor of "the living universe of Pan." But there is no more place in urban life for Lawrence's Pan than there was for the "universal Pan" of Leigh Hunt, a century earlier.

The Indian in "Pan in America" is more obviously a mere rhetorical device, illustrating the argument, than are the Pan figures of the novels, who are (in theory, if not always in practice) individual characters, replacing the argument. But of course the association of a character with Pan power and Pan mystery makes him a spokesman for primitive elemental forces which are (by definition) greater than either the individual ego or the individual reasoning power. In the Dark Heroes Pan power has welled up; however realistic the characterization may be in other parts of the novels in which they appear, at the moment the Dark Heroes are linked with Pan they become vehicles for the argument.

Lawrence first develops a Pan figure in *Twilight in Italy* (1912). Il Duro, apparently a real person (like many of the characters in the novels), becomes archetypal, like the Indian, as Lawrence interprets what he observes. Throughout the whole description, the terms "god," "devil," and "goat," with various appropriate characteristics, mingle with the realistic description, spreading the Pan identification far beyond the explicit statements of identity. Il Duro's eyes are "sinister . . . like a god's pale-gleaming eyes," as well as "half-diabolic, half-tortured . . . like a goat's." [17] "Bestial, and yet godlike crouching before the plant as if he were the god of lower life"; when the comparison is so explicit, the mention of Pan himself comes as no surprise. As Il Duro performs his godlike task of grafting the vines, he is, like the Indian, "a creature in intimate communion with the sensible world." So far it is a finely vivid description of a Pan figure, whom Browning might have appreciated for his strong earthy qualities and Wordsworth disapproved of for the same reason.

Lawrence takes full advantage of the duality of god and goat, though goat predominates. Whereas the Indian continues to be like an Indian at the very moment that he speaks with the voice of Pan, Il Duro is like Pan himself, as he has been traditionally visualized in concrete terms. The curious eyes are characteristic of Lawrence's special interpretation; even more idiosyncratic is the repeated emphasis on Il Duro's isolation and refusal to marry. "Pan and the ministers of Pan do not marry, the sylvan gods." Marriage is of the spirit, and Il Duro "belonged to the god Pan, to the absolute of the senses." However, Lawrence is not yet expounding his own myth, as we find it in the Pan cluster. Il Duro is a "minister of Pan," belonging to the god, rather than a man in whom a portion of the Pan mystery has welled up. The Pan he serves is still a finite individual god, rather than the universal principle which contains all gods: Il Duro bears the same relation to the later Pan figures as the Pan of the *Georgian Poetry* review does to the "universal Pan" of 1925.

Virtually everything that Lawrence wrote between *Twilight in Italy* and "Pan in America" has a Dark Hero of the characteristically Lawrentian type, of whom Annable is a recognizable forerunner and Il Duro a representative specimen. Yet none of the gamekeepers, peasants, and savages noted by every reader in the works of that twelve-year period is explicitly related to Pan, though critics have often identified them as Pan figures.[18] It seems to me more useful to consider Pan figures as a subdivision of the Dark Hero rather than the other way round. If a prototype must be found, I prefer to derive them all (as has often been done) from an original father-miner figure, coming up from an underground kingdom; this allows a wider choice of biographical-psychological or literary interpretations and is chronologically tidier.

Count Dionys, in "The Ladybird" (1922), has a good many of the attributes of the Pan figures; that he derives his divine powers from Dionysus, or rather from Pluto, god of the underworld, and not from Pan, seems to be chance rather than fundamental necessity. The Dark Hero himself is fully developed, but the "twenty minutes" during which Pan will be the dominant symbol for him have not yet begun.

In *St. Mawr* (1925), Lawrence delineates in novelistic terms some of the distinctions drawn in "Pan in America." The astrologer-artist Cartwright both expounds and represents the wrong sort of Pan, the "fallen Pan." Unlike most fallen Pans (and most men are only fallen Pans, if Pans at all), Cartwright at least realizes intellectually, if not instinctively, that his Panness has been defeated by man's Fall into consciousness. He is equated with the "goaty old satyrs" and "the fallen Pan," just as in the essay Pan is called "the father of fauns and nymphs, satyrs and dryads . . . [whose] passion was degraded with the lust of senility." Like the other fallen Pans of the short stories, Cartwright looks more like the goat-god than the actual Pan figures do; he has "yellow-grey twinkling eyes . . . [a] face curiously like Pan's" and "the tilted eyebrows, the twinkling goaty look, and the pointed ears of a goat-Pan" (p. 53). Lawrence does not develop the interesting possibilities of Cartwright's state; he is only a lay figure necessary for explication.[19] Lawrence is more concerned with the evidences of "unfallen Pan" in the horse St. Mawr, and in Lewis.

One of Lawrence's most successful complex symbols, St. Mawr

has some features in common with Il Duro. He is demonic; he is like a god; he has fearsome eyes; like Il Duro, he rejects intimacy and sex: "no good as a stud." He is, by definition, animal, but his horseness has more essential life or "flame" in it than most men's humanness. In essence St. Mawr is more like the Indian or even the pine tree of "Pan in America"; he is not a minister of Pan, but a creature who carries within him the power and mystery of the unfallen Pan.

Lewis, the groom, knows of Pan in much the same way as Forster's Gennaro does. He has heard and felt something in the woods at night, which he associates with fairies and moon boys, and he knows that "the world has its own life, the sky has a life of its own." The term "Pan" is not within his frame of reference, but Lawrence supplies it for him: when Mrs. Witt asks Lewis about God, he is "walking his horse alongside in the shadow of the wood's edge, the darkness of the old Pan" (p. 102). In the terms of the essay, Lewis is one who has "dimly" seen Pan at night, and ever after had a "Pan-power . . . particularly on women," of which his power over Mrs. Witt is ample proof. Like Il Duro and St. Mawr, he combines this power with a complete detachment from women. Phoenix, who will exchange his sex-power for white woman's cash, is nowhere related to Pan, but he clearly corresponds to the "bored savage, for whom Pan is dead," who "will kill Pan with his own hands, for the sake of a motor-car." Neither of the Pan figures provides an answer for Lou's quest. In the end, she comes closest to Pan in the way Lawrence himself does in "Pan in America." She feels herself welcomed by the spirit of the New Mexican landscape, in which Pan (by analogy with the essay) may be said to dwell.[20]

Where Lou had to find Pan, if at all, manifested in landscape and animals, Kate, in *The Plumed Serpent* (1926), is lucky enough to find a real, unfallen Pan-male. Cipriano resembles the other Pan figures in many respects, but his characteristic isolation and detachment do not prevent him being both a leader of men and a sexual partner. Yet these do make his sex life, and Kate's, of an unusual sort. The sexual act is basically a religious act; Kate must submerge her ego as she acknowl-

edges the divine Pan in Cipriano.[21] The religious sanction given
to a masochistic sexual submission has a curiously perverted
effect, which I can only compare to the mingling of sex and
terror at which Machen aims in "The Great God Pan." As far
as the Pan elements of *The Plumed Serpent* are concerned,
Lawrence achieves, not a new religious text, but a new horror
story, in which Cipriano plays the part of the sinister Pan with
an "inhuman [and indecent] assurance" (chapter xx).

The Plumed Serpent is far from being the only work in
which Lawrence builds a "new Gothic" on the foundations of
the "old Gothic" of the horror stories.[22] All Lawrence's Pan
figures are uncanny, and most are fierce and demonic as well.
In "Pan in America," the Romantic, universal Pan is the chief
prototype, but Lawrence restores the terror Pan in the "fierce,
bristling" pine tree, as well as in its acknowledged historical
context: "Lurking among the leafy recesses, he was almost more
demon than god. To be feared, not loved or approached. A
man who should see Pan by daylight fell dead, as if blasted by
lightning" (p. 22). Similarly, in *St. Mawr*, Cartwright admits
that "if you ever saw the God instead of the thing, you died"
(p. 54). Terror becomes a necessary characteristic of Pan's universality, as in the horror stories: the horse, St. Mawr, terrifies
the fallen Pan-men, who are incapable of dealing with him, and
even Lou sees a "vision of evil" (p. 68) when St. Mawr is betrayed "by something lesser than himself," his rider. The New
Mexican landscape aims "some mysterious malevolence" (p.
144) at those who are inimical to it; the pine tree, so similar to
the secondary Pan metaphor of "Pan in America," is "a bristling,
almost demonish guardian" conveying "the power and the slight
horror of the pre-sexual primeval world" (p. 146). As in the
horror stories, the vision of the "real" world beyond the veil of
matter is, for the wrong people, a fatal vision (p. 153).

This fatal vision may be caused by evoking the past. "The re-
evoked past is frightening, and if it be re-evoked to overwhelm
the present, it is fiendish" (*Plumed Serpent*, xxi, p. 366). We are
reminded of "the old savage England" and of "that old fighting
stock that worshipped devils among these stones" (*St. Mawr*,

pp. 63–64) as a prelude to Lou's vision of "dark-grey waves of evil" (p. 69), when St. Mawr's "pale-gold, inverted bulk seemed to fill the universe" (p. 67). Only for a moment does this scene alter the scale of the novel; in *The Plumed Serpent*, on the other hand, the ritual of Huitzilopochtli's revenge, along with the equally ritualistic love-making of the god-demon Pan, dwarf —as they are meant to do—the human scale of events.

> Once you entered his mystery the scale of all things changed, and he became a living male power, undefined and unconfined . . . that little natural tuft of black goats' beard hanging light from his chin, the tilt of his brows . . . were like symbols to her, of another mystery, the bygone mystery of the twilit, primitive world, where shapes that are small suddenly loom up huge, gigantic on the shadow, and a face like Cipriano's is the face at once of a god and a devil, the undying Pan face. (chapter xx, p. 341)

The horse looms as the pine tree looms (and the image is foreshadowed as early as Annable, dark, and looking down). In the case of Cipriano, the imagery is more explicitly phallic: "like a rearing serpent or a rising tree"; the woman, "submitting, succumbing," is "swooned prone beneath." [23]

But *The Plumed Serpent* is not entirely successful as a horror story. The savage Huitzilopochtli (the Pan-demon in his political aspect, exercising power over other males), who might have been as "shaggy as the pine-trees, and horrible as the lightning," [24] is simply a public executioner in fancy dress. Kate's own deathlike and fearful surrender to the "twilit Pan" conveys much better than does the sadistic public ritual the sensations of an individual surrendering to the myth and becoming part of it. Lawrence had strong views on the supernatural: "being a witch is a much more serious and strenous matter." [25] Kate's thoughts as she submits to her "Master, The everlasting Pan" (chapter xx) transmit the seriousness and strenuousness, if nothing else, of being a mate of the God-demon Pan (Machen's Mary can hardly be said to have made the best of her opportunity). The sinister Pan was not, however, Lawrence's most completely successful image for conveying this Gothic blend of sex and terror. The emotion of a religious yet sexual horror is more concentrated and effective in the ritual death of the woman who rode away, for instance, than in Kate's very similar sacrificial consummation.

"It would seem that for Lawrence any spiritual force was good, and evil resided only in the absence of spirituality"[26] says T. S. Eliot, a statement corroborated by the curious ambiguities of *The Plumed Serpent*. In this novel the road to salvation passes by all the landmarks of what an "old" Gothic writer would take to be the road to Hell. Lawrence explicates this ambiguity, though not, I think (as regards the effect of the scenes discussed), very satisfactorily. The moral view, according to Lawrence, is Kate's western, unconverted point of view; she must emphasize the moral nature of her vision because of her training and her habit of logical thinking, and she must therefore disapprove of what she has seen. Cipriano himself, who is at first "sinister, almost repellent" to Kate, has one counterargument: "Horror is real. Why not a bit of horror, as you say, among all the rest?" (chapter xvi). Ramon has another: "The oldest Pan is in us, and he will not be denied." Pan is "the vision of the living cosmos" (chapter xx); the morally loaded concept of horror is replaced by a morally neutral sense of necessity. Pan is not really sinister: he is that part of Ramon or Cipriano which is at one with the power of the whole "living cosmos." But in practice, the "demonic" has a sinister surface which clashes with its morally neutral meaning. Lawrence combines the sinister Pan and the universal Pan (facing, but not resolving the problem that Machen burked), using much the same armory of attributes and actions as the writers of melodramatic horror fiction, and just failing to convey, in Heilman's phrase, the "integrity of feeling that greatly deepens the convention."

Still, there is much clearer evidence of Lawrence's indebtedness to the Pan horror story than is provided even in the Machen-like ecstasies of *The Plumed Serpent*. Lawrence's obscure little short story "The Last Laugh" is the last significant member of that very genre. The explication of the story would be much simpler if one could leave it at that, if the tale merely showed "the swift retribution visited upon the man who penetrates the mystery of the god's existence." [27] But the biographical elements in the story are as important as the literary, for one thing; for another, the "laugh" of the title is a key to the story's structure that cannot be accounted for in the terms of the "sinister" tradition alone.

Two letters, both written at Hampstead on January 9, 1924, provide considerable evidence of Lawrence's special concern with a "laughing Pan," at the very time when the story must have been germinating.

In the letter to Mabel Dodge Luhan, Lawrence advises her against taking herself too seriously; he recommends "common horse-sense [which] is the centaur's way of knowledge . . . sensible, a bit fierce, and amused." Mabel is not the only culprit; John Middleton Murry, the group at Taos the previous year, the whole of present-day society — they all take themselves too seriously.[28] Lawrence claims to follow his own advice: the hatred that he senses the English feel for him "only makes me laugh. My gods, like the Great God Pan, have a bit of a natural grin on their face." Pan "grins a bit, and when he gets driven too hard, goes fierce." The "uncanny derision" of Pan, so much more prominent in the Pan heroes than a "natural grin," is presumably the result of adversity; Lawrence in London may well have laughed at his enemies with the "uncanny derision of one who feels himself defeated by something lesser than himself."

The letter to Willard Johnson, written the same day, gives, not intimate advice, but general impersonal counsel. What was meant for mankind is focused gently upon Johnson. The image of the centaur recurs;[29] the "pale Galilean" has killed the horse in Europe, but in America he survives; "it's a turquoise centaur who laughs, who laughs longest and laughs last." [30] "When Jesus was born, the spirits wailed round the Mediterranean: *Pan is dead*," and the Centaur died at the Renaissance (compare "David").

"The Last Laugh" is one of a group of short stories ("The Border Line," "Jimmy and the Desperate Woman," and "Smile" are the others), written at much the same time, all of which center upon a kind of inverted Dark Hero, an ineffectual man, negated and hollow. These heroes have a strong resemblance to each other, and an equally strong resemblance, though it is the resemblance of caricature, to Lawrence's erstwhile friend John Middleton Murry. Lawrence and Murry had been having rather complicated disagreements on literary matters for some time, but the point at issue in these stories is a much less open one: an unspoken rivalry for Frieda.[31]

Jimmy, the hero of "Jimmy and the Desperate Woman," is a mock Pan figure; the comparisons with Pan at the beginning of the story are ironic heightenings of his insufficiency. In the kinder and more philosophical idiom of *St. Mawr*, he would be called, like Cartwright, a "fallen" Pan, one of those who look more like Pan than a true Pan figure does: "Like the face of the laughing faun . . . In his mocking moments when he seemed most himself, it was a pure Pan face, with thick black eyebrows cocked up, and grey eyes with a sardonic goaty gleam . . . In the opinion of his men friends, he was, or should be, a consistently grinning faun, satyr or Pan-person. In his own opinion, he was a Martyred Saint Sebastian." Where the true Pan dominated women and is aloof from them, Jimmy is pathetically dependent and at their mercy.[32]

In "The Last Laugh" Pan, turned "fierce," serves the function of a brutal Comic Muse, punishing, with a final and fatal laughter, not a man who goes "too far," but a man who takes himself too seriously — Murry again. The chief flaw in the story (and here it differs from the far more successful "The Border Line") is that the revenge appears irrational; its motive is explicable only in terms of Lawrence's personal pique.

On the first page, we are introduced to Lawrence's own wish-fulfilling self-projection, the red-beared Lorenzo, resident in Hampstead. It is a snowy evening — probably the very same evening mentioned in Dorothy Brett's reminiscences (when she and Murry left Lawrence's house together) and in Lawrence's letter. Lorenzo is never mentioned again, but he hovers over the action in a curiously antecedentless pronoun, "he," the active agent of the plot. This "he" is on one level Lorenzo, and on another, Pan (a role Lawrence himself seems to have enjoyed). The omission of Pan's name (or Lorenzo's) is meant, presumably, to heighten the mystery; in fact, it only heightens the confusion.

"Grinning like a satyr," Lorenzo bids goodbye to his two guests, the weary, sardonic Marchbanks, who has the negated-Pan face of Jimmy or Cartwright, and the nymphlike Miss James, deaf, the daughter of a peer. (Lawrence has gone to even less trouble than usual to hide his borrowings from real life.) Supernatural effects begin as the two start their walk home through the snow. Marchbanks hears laughing, but when the deaf woman turns on her machine to listen, Marchbanks himself "gave the weirdest, slightly neighing laugh . . . [compare the Centaur of the letters] watching her with queer, gleaming, goat-like eyes." Some spell appears to be intensifying his pannishness. A young policeman also hears Marchbanks' laughter; yet Marchbanks continues to claim that there is some other laughter going on, "the most marvellous sound in the world." Miss James's archetypal qualities are accentuated, too; she accepts with "nymph-like voluptuousness" the casually helpful touch of the policeman — she who, like the other, better-known representation of Dorothy Brett in "The Princess," had always stayed aloof from physical contact.

Then Lawrence, rather crudely, removes Marchbanks from the scene; he is not to return until the end of the story. The supernatural agency (which I shall henceforth call "Pan," although at this stage of the discussion it may be begging the question) arranges that he shall go into the house of a woman he has never seen before, for an assignation, unpremeditated by either of them, to which he went "hastening like a hound" (a phrase of moral condemnation, similar to Lawrence's use of the word "doggy" for modern, meaningless promiscuity).

Like Lewis, or the Pan-seer at the beginning of "Pan in America," Miss James sees Pan dimly in the night, "the dark face among the holly bushes, with the brilliant, mocking eyes." She hears whirling voices among the thunder and lightning of a storm saying, from a nearby church, "he's come back!" as if in answer to the voices crying of Pan's death which Lawrence mentions in the letter to Johnson. "Pan's" effect on Miss James is quite as strong as his effect on Marchbanks, though it is finer and more natural, and more subtly manifested: "ancient fear" and "a blithe unaccustomed sense of power . . . throbbing sensation beneath her breasts . . . a sort of flame." While the policeman cowers in her living room, trying to get warm, Miss James laughs over her own paintings upstairs, seeing their absurdity at last, like someone who has absorbed the lessons of Lawrence's letters to Johnson and Mrs. Luhan. She is no longer deaf; she sees a "new blue heaven" and thinks "but how wonderful of him [Pan-Lorenzo?] to come back and alter all the world immediately . . . What a wonderful being!" She realizes that "he certainly will have the last laugh." She hints at the beginnings of a willingness to surrender virginity: "if that man kept on laughing something would happen to me . . . Wouldn't it be wonderful if he just touched her?" This is her Pan vision; now she can live more abundantly and see more clearly.[33]

In the meanwhile the Pan effect has spread to the young policeman, who hears the voices and the laughter and feels a "tame-animal" fear that soon becomes mortal terror. This contrasts strikingly with the exultation that the woman feels; the two divide between them the traditional reactions of terror and ecstasy. Pan's final joke on the policeman is to make him lame; one foot becomes a hoof.[34] As Pan manifests himself in Marchbanks' voice and in Miss James's ears, so this is his touch upon this well-meaning, innocent young man.

Marchbanks returns. Still sardonic, he laughs maliciously, implies improprieties between Miss James and the policeman, and tells her that she has no soul (neither, incidentally, had Il Duro). But Miss James has realized by this time that she took Marchbanks too seriously, that he takes himself much too seriously and that both their previous relationship and his present view of her are a pure joke.

The climax comes suddenly and almost randomly. There is yet another low, eternal laugh, and without warning Marchbanks is struck down "like a shot animal."

His white face was drawn, distorted in a curious grin, that was chiefly agony but partly wild recognition. He was staring with fixed eyes at something. And in the rolling agony of his eyes was the horrible grin of a man who realises that he has made a final, and this time a fatal, fool of himself.

"Why," he yelped in a high voice, "I knew it was he!" And with a queer shuddering laugh he pitched forward on the carpet and lay writhing for a moment on the floor. Then he lay still, in a weird, distorted position, like a man struck by lightning.

This climax need only be compared with any account in the horror stories of Pan's ultimate revenge. For instance, Saki: "her eyes were filled with the horror of something she saw other than her oncoming death"; or Benson: his hero's face is "a mask of horrible contorted terror." [35] Some touches are Lawrence's own. The image of lightning, prepared for earlier in the story, is a great improvement on Machen's less concrete "forces before which the souls of men must wither and die and blacken." Compare "Pan in America": "a man who should see Pan by daylight fell dead, as if blasted by lightning," and both *St. Mawr* and "Pan in America" for pine trees scarred by lightning.

It is very common in the horror story to provide Pan with a mocking or bleating laugh, heard once (in Saki, twice) as he consummates his revenge. It is equally common to punctuate a whole story with the sinister enchantment of his fluting. Lawrence has neatly reversed the relative importance of these two motifs: at one point the wind "runs over the organ-pipes like pan-pipes" (the only explicit reference to Pan in the whole story), but the story is punctuated throughout, monotonously and repetitively, by the obsessive refrain of laughter.

The refusal of any sympathy to the victim because he has, in the comic manner, made a "fatal fool of himself" clashes oddly with the traditional elements of the horror story. Lawrence's cynical detachment from the victim does not matter in itself (compare Saki's attitude toward his heroine); what does matter is that Lawrence undercuts our identification with the hero to such an extent that we cannot even share his terror — only, and in a different sense, his surprise.

The chief weakness of the story lies not so much in its melo-dramatic antecedents as in their uneasy combination with bio-graphical elements to form a *conte à clef*. The initial encounters with Pan are plausible enough in themselves, but the story re-mains disjointed because the mainspring of the action, Lorenzo's savage practical joke on the other characters, remains a private joke. Miss James holds together as a character,[36] but Marchbanks is incomprehensible without an acquaintance with Murry as seen through Lawrence's eyes at the time of writing. There is something of Lawrence in all the Pan figures; there is too much of him in the Pan who wreaks the author's fantasy revenge upon the trespassing Murry: one should not have to disinter private piques to elucidate a fictional revenge. For these reasons, I am regretfully forced to concur with Graham Hough's judgment of the story: "one of those embarrassing visitations of Pan to Hampstead that illustrates emphatically the way not to evoke the chthonic powers."

Another short story of the same year, "The Overtone," like-wise requires explication in terms of the Pan tradition. The heart of the story is a quasi-philosophical dialogue in which, for the first time in Lawrence's work, there is a direct confronta-tion between the figures of Pan and Christ. Lawrence, like a bullfighter luring a bull, has been narrowly avoiding this cliché for many years: the *Georgian Poetry* review, "The Crown," *The Rainbow*, all provide some evidence for Graham Hough's dictum that "A paganism haunted by Christianity is something inevitably different from a paganism that has never known it. And Lawrence is haunted by Christianity."[37] But for most of the Pan cluster, Pan has a clear field. Jimmy and Marchbanks are merely lesser children of Pan with ruinous admixtures of the Christian: "a Martyred Saint Sebastian," and "a sort of faun on the Cross, with all the malice of the complication." "Pan in America" postulated Pan's death in the Plutarchan way, and at the "beginning of the Christian era," but it cannot draw the usual conclusion, because it was not the advent of Christianity that killed Pan, but man's own psychic evolution into the "vanity of ideas."[38]

"The Overtone" also shares with "The Last Laugh" an apparent uneasiness with the problems of plot and structure. There is a very slender realistic plot, with three characters, but the bulk of the story consists of one meditation by each of the three, unheard by the others, which is the "overtone" that adds the richness of another dimension to the action. The husband's "overtone" is an emotionally heightened narrative flashback; the wife's is a more lyrical flashback; the girl's contains, not retrospection, because her life is ahead of her, but an argument and a theory.

The two flashbacks explain the unsatisfactory sex life of the middle-aged married couple: love died between them because the husband was once denied his wife's favors on a romantically moonlit hilltop and was too hurt ever to try effectively again; ironically, all this time the wife was waiting, patiently, like a flower for rain. The combination of an overblown lyricism with a case history of the sort that appears in "Can This Marriage Be Saved?" columns of the ladies' magazines seems to be leading Lawrence nowhere. So halfway through the story he shifts into a dialogue, which conveys the plot: the girl tries to see if there are any traces of Pan left in the husband, concludes that there are not, and leaves the couple to their own destiny. In the dialogue the dichotomy of Pan and Christ is employed to turn the special case into a general principle. "Pan is dead," says the husband, Renshaw, meaning that the girl has nothing to fear from him sexually. She grasps his meaning, but his wife fights off the significance with a defensive literary judgment, "Isn't that rather trite?" [39] The three agree with the "they say" of received tradition (and Arcadiac poetry) that Christ killed Pan; the couple turns this into a statement of their own condition (and of a common problem in Lawrence's fiction): Christ, as a woman, killed Pan by mocking his maleness. The girl also applies the statement to herself: if (all) Pan is dead, she, as a nymph, ought to die too. However, it has not been made clear that Pan is dead in all individual males; we only know that he is dead in Renshaw. In this story Pan is clearly an element of personality, in the usual novelistic sense (like the "Pan" in

Browning's Bishop), rather than a metaphysical principle. Pan in Renshaw is very different from Pan in Ramon or Cipriano.

Lawrence employs a classical myth for almost the only time when he uses Pan and Luna to point up the idealized virility which is Pan's meaning in this context. Having failed to unclothe his wife at the crucial moment, all the broken Renshaw could do in the situation of Pan and Luna is "fetch a wrap, probably." The same imagery of clothing and nakedness continues in the girl's lyrical monologue, which concludes the story. It is in effect a prose hymn, which seems in places like an experimental sketch for the hymns of *The Plumed Serpent*, done in the manner of *The Song of Songs*. Her solution to the problem is to look into a man's eyes for the faun within (as she has done, unsuccessfully, in the case of Renshaw). Having found the faun, the two of them will leave their daytime clothing outside Pan's wood. She will serve both Christ and Pan, rather in the manner of Lady Daphne in "The Ladybird": Christ as husband, for the sake of justice, in the daytime; Pan as man, for the sake of passion, at night.[40] For Christ she will be a woman, and for Pan she will be a nymph. The daytime love gets, for the sake of symmetry, a much fairer hearing in this story than it did in "The Ladybird," but her feelings are clearly with Pan.

Her solution is a highly artificial, symmetrical polarity, which is no real answer to the problem that is posed, at first, in terms of fairly realistic characters. Presumably the import of the tale is that she will not make the same mistake, but as life has not yet tested her lyrical construct, we may well wonder.

"The Overtone" presents Pan and Christ in an uneasy balance of separate but equal symbolic functions, like the quasi-philosophic dualities of Victorian poetry. No real reconciliation is possible, "for how can a nymph cling at the crucifix?" There cannot even be contact, let alone identity between Pan and Christ. "If once His faun, the faun of the young Jesus had run free, seen one white nymph's brief breast, He would not have been content to die on a Cross."

In *The Man Who Died*, Lawrence investigates that very possibility: Christ once reborn into a more Pan-like way of life, experiencing desire and fulfillment in and of the flesh, is not content to die on the cross again. But Lawrence identifies him, not with Pan, but with the risen Osiris.[41] Pan is referred to once in this story: "The sun was curving down to the sea, in grand winter splendour. It fell on the twinkling, naked bodies of the slaves, with their ruddy broad hams and their small black heads, as they ran spreading the nets on the pebble beach. The all-tolerant Pan watched over them. All-tolerant Pan should be their god for ever." I take this to mean that Pan is not the god of the risen Christ, nor of his priestess, of the aristocratically aloof with whom Lawrence would identify himself to the end, but of slaves, the frisky, naked group-men whom the priestess found "a little repulsive" (p. 193), and whom the risen Christ had largely ignored.

A comparison with the very similar passage in *Lady Chatterley's Lover* reinforces my view that, in Lawrence's last two works, Pan has been demoted from his lofty position as a key symbol for divine beauty and horror. At the end of the book, Mellors confides his theories on the treatment of the masses to Connie, in a way that is, for him, unusually ratiocinative. One can hear the voice of Lawrence speaking:

> They ought to learn to be naked and handsome, and to sing in a mass and dance the old group dances, and carve the stools they sit on, and embroider their own emblems. Then they wouldn't need money . . . the mass of people oughtn't even to try to think, because they *can't*! They should be alive and frisky, and acknowledge the great god Pan. He's the only god for the masses, forever. The few can go in for higher cults if they like. But let the mass be forever pagan.[42]

The "higher cults" doubtless include the religion of tenderness that Christ and the Priestess, Connie and Mellors, act out in their own lives. Like Kate's and Cipriano's, it is based on the sexual relation. But the Pan of *The Plumed Serpent* was the least tender of gods: "the god-demon Pan preceded kindness"; the desert landscape of *St. Mawr* was "a world before and after the God of Love." The crucial element of tenderness has been added to Lawrence's philosophy of sex, and it was apparently easier to omit Pan than to turn him into a god of "this tender touch of life." It could have been done, just as Dionys, the almost-Pan of "The Ladybird," could have been a Pan figure. But by 1928 Pan's "vitality was exhausted," and Lawrence willingly relinquished the image. Pan was not conquered by Christ, nor identified with Christ, but replaced by him.

Pan is still god of the nonthinking people and of their animal sexuality; in keeping with Lawrence's new mood his epithet is "all-tolerant." He had once been the "Pan-mystery," of which "whichever flame flames in your manhood" was a part; Mellors now guards his "little forked flame" without any help from Pan. Pan has almost returned to his classical role as a lesser god of the common people, one especially associated with song, dances, and country festivals.

Just as it is possible to consider Pan as the prototype of the Dark Hero, so it is possible to see a battle between the Christ principle and the Pan principle running through Lawrence's life and works. The evidence of his works will support neither metaphor,[43] but the remarks of his friends and the argument of one eminent biographer show how tempting these metaphors are. Piero Nardi's *Vita di D. H. Lawrence* includes the most sensible and systematic study of Lawrence's Pan images that I have yet encountered,[44] marred only (from a thematic point of view) by defining Pan (and Christ) too broadly. Nardi's method works very well when he comes to analyze the biographical implications of Dorothy Brett's recurrent references to Lawrence as Pan. Nardi is not imposing the metaphor upon her when he comments that Brett rather enjoyed the safe but distinctly sexual pleasure of seeing Lawrence as Pan, and it seems likely that Lawrence encouraged the identification. The chief period of their friendship was in fact the time of the Pan cluster; at one point, for instance, she was typing the manuscript of *St. Mawr*, in which many a pretty Pan figure is to be found. Osbert Sitwell, Cecil Grey, Achsah Brewster, even Middleton Murry, all reported that Lawrence looked (or wanted to look) like Pan, but no one else made the identification with Brett's banal fervor: "A leopard skin, a mass of flowers and leaves . . . Out of your thick hair, two small horns poke their sharp points; the slender, cloven hoofs lie entangled in weeds. The flute slips from your hand." [45] These lines are perhaps the high point of one of the most popular (in both senses) of modern Pan usages, the artist seen as Pan.

We have seen that the answer to my implied question — "What can a knowledge of the Pan tradition do for the study of Lawrence?" — is that it helps to explicate sections of one of his worst novels and is an essential tool in understanding two of his least successful short stories. More important, the Pan cluster is a fine example of a Lawrentian image cluster, from which interesting conclusions about Lawrence's use of imagery might be drawn. The Pan tradition does not help much in interpreting the meanings of the Pan figures, which are more closely related to Lawrence's other figures (other types of the Dark Hero, for instance) than to previous Pans. Yet he follows the traditions with great care, while developing and adapting them; he seldom falls below his own critical standard of vividness and concreteness proclaimed in "Pan in America." The short stories fail for technical, chiefly structural, reasons; even the passages in *The Plumed Serpent*, with all their faults, are the ablest recognition in English of the chief import of the sinister Pan (as developed by Machen, Maugham, and Crowley): sex is one of the two terrifying facts in life; the other is death. The "new" Gothic is an improvement, in both sincerity and skill, upon the "old."

The English literary tradition had at least four different types of Pan figure in a high state of development by the time Lawrence began to write. Lawrence ignored the whimsical, benevolent, emasculated Pans of the Edwardians; later writers have taken no interest in the Pan–Christ dialectic, or the closely related theme of the death of Pan, or the Romantic transcendental Pan, but that post-Lawrentian authors think of Pan (if they think of him at all) in largely sexual terms is, I think, partly to be attributed to Lawrence's addition of beauty to the Pan of sex and terror.

Lawrence, the myth-maker, created his Pan myth by respecting the Pan paradox, the mysterious synthesis of goat and god, and by taking it to one possible logical conclusion: he sees the goat in man — the demonically and often sinisterly sexual — as synonymous with the divine in man. A satisfying meaning for the Pan image has at last been fused with its essential form, and that is a better reason than even chronology provides for treating Lawrence's Pans as the culmination of the Pan tradition in English literature.

Chapter VII

AFTERMATH

"Thirty years ago in literary circles God was all the fashion . . . then God went out (oddly enough with cricket and beer) and Pan came in. In a hundred novels his cloven hoof left its imprint on the sward; poets saw him lurking in the twilight . . . But Pan went out and now beauty has taken his place." Thus Somerset Maugham, in 1930, looked back upon the Edwardian Pan cult;[1] "a hundred novels" is hyperbolic, but it is undeniable that Pan "came in" and "went out." He did not go out entirely; a glance at the handful of serious versions in recent literature and a brief survey of Pan's descent into an underworld of pulp fiction and "popular" nonliterary art forms will perhaps define more closely the boundaries of the strange fashion which has been my central topic.

The shadows of Nietzsche's concept of the Dionysian and Freud's concept of the Unconscious hover over the descendants of the Gothic Pan. Eugene O'Neill's *The Great God Brown* (1925) uses the mask of Pan as a powerful metaphor for a state of soul. The false god Brown's frustration of "the creative pagan acceptance of life"[2] in Dion Anthony turns Dion's mask from Pan to Mephistopheles: "When Pan was forbidden the light and warmth of the sun he grew sensitive and self-conscious and proud and revengeful — and became Prince of Darkness" (II, iii). Like Nietzsche's "Apollonian masks," the masks of O'Neill's characters are "the necessary productions of a deep look into the horror of nature."[3] But Pan himself represents a positive vision: "Live! Dissolve into dew . . . into peace . . . into joy — into God — into the Great God Pan!" (Prologue). It follows that when "Great Pan is dead" it is time to "be ashamed." Twenty years later, when O'Neill considers the two types of visionary experience again, his association of Pan with the negative vision seems a deliberate anachronism, designed to fit the literary matrix of the nineties (Dowson, Swinburne, Wilde, among others) that characterizes much of Edmund's imagery: "Who wants to see life as it is, if they can help it? It's the three Gorgons in one. You look in their faces and turn to stone. Or it's Pan. You see him and you die — that is, inside you — and have to go on living as a ghost" (act IV).[4]

On the other hand writers of more conservative views betrayed a distinct distaste for anything "Dionysian" that is not kept firmly controlled by the principles of decency and order. Stephen McKenna, in the twenties, took Pan as the symbol of postwar license; Osbert Sitwell, although capable of such Lawrentian turns of phrase as "a pure white goat that was like a flame in its proud, white maleness," allegorizes the outbreak of war in August 1914: "Pan and Mars had broken loose together and had set out to conquer" the man who wound and set the clocks that regulated civilized living. This local god (the title of the story, "Death of a God," involves a slight play on the Plutarchan formula) dies just as "beyond the sea, as here, the primeval, brutish world was breaking out."[5]

More characteristic of contemporary fiction than this overt symbolism is the allusive imagery of Lawrence Durrell's "Alexandria" novels. "Pan," whether as a name or as an actual artifact (the influence of archaeology is strong), carries sexual or religious overtones: the intaglio of "a Pan raping a goat, his hands grasping its horns, his head thrown back in ecstasy," caught in a headlight, illuminates the chaotic sexuality of the Alexandrian Carnival. The recurrent Pan image thus links an ancient hillock in Alexandria, once sacred to Pan, with the Pan-bearded Balthazar, a "goat-like apparition from the underworld," a Mephistophelean seeker after a new religious truth of ascetic libertinism. "Weber's *Pan* played *every day*" on a piano is a musical motif that brings Durrell's Nessim some curious occult "message from the powers of good and evil."[6]

The allusive technique is not new, of course. The title of Knut Hamsun's *Pan* (1894; English translation, 1921) carries a suggestion of his presence, as the spirit of the irrational, through a book where he is seldom mentioned. The hero's "powder horn with the little figure of Pan on it"[7] focuses attention on his Pan-like characteristics: this gauche, wild hunter who excites women with his animal look, who rejoices in his closeness to the pervasive, living spirit of nature, is more like a Lawrentian Pan figure than Lawrence's scornful depreciation of Hamsun's book as a "wearisome sickening little personal novel"[8] might lead one to suppose.

In broad outline, Continental authors have followed the same historical pattern in their use of Pan as have the British and Americans, though at no time as intensively. Even before Nietzsche, the Germans, for instance, seem to have preferred the weightier figure of Dionysus (the Bacchic nightmare of Mann's *Death in Venice* is the logical outcome of this preference); there is no clear equivalent to the Anglo-American Pan cult. In spite of — or perhaps because of — this, some Europeans have explored characteristically modern channels that the British and Americans have barely entered. A group of twentieth-century tales celebrate a demonically powerful Dionysian goat-god, in Mediterreanean landscapes as primitive as the passions they engender. Gerhart Hauptmann's idyllic hymn to fertility of the priest turned goatherd (*The Heretic of Soana*, 1918) has, in gentler, more optimistic form, some of this quality, as does the immensely sad and moving death of the last demi-god, the goatish Beast who summons his worshipers to a final Sabbath of the animals, in Joseph d'Arbaud's *Beast of the Vaccarès* (1926). Franz Werfel's play *Goat-Song* (1921) has a more explicit moral about the resurgence of the "primeval, brutish world," which worships as a god the monstrous goat-idiot, who in turn begets his own monstrous child upon a woman in an "unholy marriage," as if to say that violent horror is never to be stamped out. A more complex parable is found in Pär Lagerkvist's *The Sybil* (1956), where the woman whom the goat-god raped is powerfully characterized in her strange painful love for the god's son, an idiot, but perhaps a divine one. The only explicit Pan figure in the group is Ernst Wiechert's outcast forest-dweller, Silvestris, mysteriously born and with strange musical power over animals and women ("Pan im Dorfe," 1930).

This group as a whole makes the pseudo-primitivism of much of the English fiction enhanced by a touch of Pan look very tame in comparison. The primitivism is so often expatriate exoticism, where the Anglo-American in Italy comes across some remains of the primitive religion cheek by jowl with Christianity among the modern peasantry — we are back with John Addington Symonds' topological palimpsest of past and present — where "Priapus or Pan" provides a *frisson* of strange and preferably phallic mysteries, and a dash of local color.[9] Morris West's *The Devil's Advocate* (New York, 1959), though not unmarred by the preciousness of the expatriate conventions, is by far the best example. "Was there yet in these mountain folk a half-conscious hope that Pan might do what the new god had not done: make the raped land virgin again and fruitful with grass and trees? . . . the crude stone symbol and its active survival not half a mile from the Bishop's domain . . . Was this the real explanation of the death of Giacomo Nerone [an Englishman, being considered for sainthood], that he had been trampled under the hoofs of the goat-god?" (p. 125). West's tale invites comparison, at least, with Cesare Pavese's myth of "Il Dio-Caprone" (1933), the evocation of the primitive sexuality of that same countryside, or with Jean Giono's cosmic lyricism of the "Panic" terror felt in cold and solitary places.[10]

This sort of thing does not export well. The savage ritual murder in Robert Bolt's play *Gentle Jack* (New York, 1965) is blurred by the affectations of country-house mythologizing (the country house is a variant of the expatriate pattern; someone has come into the country who does not really belong there), which are not redeemed by intimations of a study of folklore. "*Pan? . . . Here? . . .* Not by the very name of Pan. Jack-in-the Green, an English variant," is to be elected, and then killed, in "a very ancient ceremony" (Act I, p. 23; italics Bolt's).

So far post-Frazerian anthropology and mythography have, for the purposes of literature, scarcely improved upon the savage sexual ritual that has been the staple of the Gothic Pan for sixty years. The interpretations, for instance, of the most notable heir of the mythographers, Robert Graves, in terms of history, ritual, and natural phenomena, represent, for poetic purposes, little advance upon Sir William Jones (1808), comparing Pan to the Indian wind god Pavan and the shepherd god Crishna, or upon George Cox (1881), defining him as "the gentle or intermittent breeze . . . the lover of Pitys, the pine-tree." [11]

But Ezra Pound can turn the data of mythography to good use; he gives a twist to the poetic cliché we grew so familiar with ("Pan megas tethnéké" or "the great Pan is dead") to bring us back to Reinach's anthropological interpretation, now a most abstruse allusion in both form and content:

> And that was when Troy was down, all right,
>   superbo Ilion . . .
> And they were sailing along
> Sitting in the stern-sheets,
> Under the lee of an island
> And the wind drifting off from the island.
> "Tet, tet . . .
>   what is it?" said Anchises.
> "Tethnéké," said the helmsman, "I think they
> Are howling because Adonis died virgin." (Canto XXIII, 1933)

And Lawrence Durrell can play on the limitations of Frazerian anthropological myth, using another of his finely allusive artifacts:

> Chapters of clay and whitewash. Others here
> Find only a jar of red clay, a Pan
> The superstitious whipped and overturned.
> Yet nothing of ourselves can equal it. ("The Parthenon") [12]

It is not surprising that modern poetry, still consciously in rebellion against the false imagery of Edwardian and Georgian verse, should have little room for Pan. It is Durrell, again, who articulates the chief poetic role that remains: in "the bestiary of [the] heart" dwells "the little hairy sexer, Pan" ("Letters in Darkness, III"). Ramon Guthrie, likewise, sees Pan as the wild, shaggy daydream of that self-pitying, repressed academic Prufrock, "Professor Greywood as Pan," who, from the bestiary of his heart, pursues unavailingly the unwitting Syrinxes of the college scene. [13]

Pan is clearly still valuable as an allusive image in prose and poetry, but as a character or major theme in fiction, he shows two symptoms of having long outlived his usefulness. On the one hand Pan is often kept deliberately anonymous, as if the mental effort of filling out a crossword puzzle were needed to give extra spice to a jaded motif. Pan's characteristics are of course so familiar by this time that authors need not be wary of mystifying their readers. Aldous Huxley's short story "Cynthia" (1920), a modern-dress comic version of "Pan and Luna," depends for its effect on the reader's anticipating the narrator in identifying the hero, or at least in catching the allusion when the narrator finally "looked up the matter in Lemprière." Louis Bromfield's *The Strange Case of Miss Annie Spragg* (especially pages 142–146) tells of a woman and a goat participating in strange rituals. The man who kills the goat is in turn killed by a strange sharp instrument, and his murderer is never found. Again the sense of solving a mystery story makes more palatable what would otherwise be one more story of Pan's revenge upon someone who flouts his power — a literary game quite different from the anonymity of the demonic forces in Werfel and Lagerkvist, too great and mysterious to label.

As we descend further into the regions of pulp fiction, a more central characteristic of any worn-out motif, extreme unoriginality, becomes very apparent. Modern Pan stories, as we have seen in earlier chapters, tend to be third-rate imitations of what were, at best, only second-rate originals.[14]

Charles Beaumont's short story "Dark Music" (1956; note the Faulknerian title and touches of the Faulknerian plot) is a crude Freudian parable, using the baleful ecstasies of a Machen-like plot sequence to show that repression is evil in its consequences for self and society. Pan, anonymous again, but readily identifiable by his "high-pitched, dancing pipes" and "goaty animal smell," punishes an old-maid schoolteacher by showing her the terrifying joys of sexuality that she had denied in herself and others, and leaving her pregnant.[15]

Pan's place in the popular imagination of the present day is that of an archetypal sex symbol, veering from the beastly and lecherous Pans of the modern Gothic (as in Beaumont) to the "dear amorous jolly old Pan"[16] of cartoon and film, representative of the Arcadiac tradition as adapted to modern needs. Jean Renoir's film *Le Déjeuner sur l'herbe* (*Picnic on the Grass*), with its goat led by a filthy, jolly tramp, whose piping turns a prim picnic into a cross between an orgy and an idyll, catches this mood to perfection.[17]

"What does the union of god and goat . . . really mean?" asked Nietzsche. Part of the answer is that, since the first World War, it has meant more or less what Nietzsche said it meant. "Pan" is an especially English equivalent for what Nietzsche defines as the "satyr," as "the Dionysiac reveler — primary man,"[18] the intoxicated worshiper of the life-affirming Antichrist; by extension, "Pan" may mean the (primarily sexual) life force itself. To the conservatives such a Pan is "brutal" and "primitive"; to the more characteristically modern writers it is a welcome symbol for the repudiation of "Apollonian" authority.[19] To both it is primarily sexual, and the closer it gets to the level of popular folklore the more exclusively sexual it becomes.

But this unchanging form, the paradoxical "union of god and goat," which has been the stable focal point of my investigation, has only very recently taken sexuality, whether cheerful or terrifying, as his central literary characteristic. For most of Pan's history in English literature, the benevolent, pastoral, often rustic descendants of the goat-god of the Arcadian shepherds have been dominant. Nineteenth-century authors began to exploit the two philological accidents that had, in classical times, enlarged the possibilities of the motif. Emerson and the Romantics found the "Orphic" Pan a convenient symbol for their concept of Nature as an all-pervading universal spirit. The early Victorians, led by Mrs. Browning, found Plutarch's story of the Death of Pan admirably suited to the requirements of debate; what began as a symbol for a point of view gradually became merely a decorative allusion. The Romantic Pan culminated in the joyous visionary experience of Forster's Eustace and Grahame's animals; Plutarchan Pan lasted until Lawrence and the *Cantos*. Charles Williams perhaps rightly felt that he was closing a chapter of literary history with the end of the lesser myths when, in 1935, he said: "In general, in public, they were done, and it was time. Hector and Solomon, Helios and Odin, had had a long day, and it may be that still some poet may find them necessary; if so, it will be private compulsion rather than public habit. Pan is dead." Ronald Knox in 1930 was closing a chapter of more than literary history: "The great Pan is dead, *and the world of which he is the symbol*," the world of Victorian-Edwardian classical humanism, which had been so hospitable to its own somewhat muted vision of the goat-god. "We can never recapture it." [20]

An undercurrent of interpretation, far less clearly justified in classical literary sources, made eddies from time to time in the calmer pastoral surface. Ronsard, Reginald Scot, and Henry More showed that the Pan–devil equivalence was still alive in popular belief. Browning added sexuality to the Pan motif; Stevenson and Swinburne added the possibilities of malevolence and terror. Even so, the Gothic Pan is still largely the creation of Arthur Machen, who rediscovered the "horrid mysteries" of Priapic worship and included them in a vision of evil that, meretricious though it is, gains some power as a dim reflection of the negative visionary experience behind the original concept of "Panic" terror. Gothic Pan overlaps with the more sophisti-cated Dionysian Pan used to symbolize Nietzschean concepts in their English guises. The Dionysian found a timid admirer in E. F. Benson, an artfully comic theorist in James Stephens, and a "hot-gospeller" in Aleister Crowley, but it would scarcely justify the interest I have shown in it, had it not inspired the core of the Pan motif in Lawrence and O'Neill. If the Pan of contemporary folklore seems an undignified inheritor of this long tradition, such seems to be the course of literary history: the rustically pastoral Pan of the Renaissance deteriorated into eighteenth-century burlesque; Romantic pastoral Pan shed its last pallid glow in Arcadiac verse.

Pan was once a comic-grotesque little country god, kept under control by the laughter of the more "civilized" Olympian gods. But, equated with Satan, he became most mightily malignant;

equated with sex, most basic and irresistible and, in some contexts, terrifying; equated with Greek civilization and its culture, most humanistically lofty or paganly vigorous, depending on one's view of Greece. Pan can represent the countryside as opposed to the city, a contrast not without intrinsic power even at its most trivial, for men have always wanted an escape from the world they have made for themselves. Such a Pan can be merely the touch of local color in an Arcadiac description, or he can be the universal, transcendental Nature in which man ought to acknowledge his membership. If Pan is simply All there is, he becomes the subject of mystery cult, of philosophical rather than literary contemplation. Yet a central role for Pan in modern literature is as the object of mystic visions, Satanic or beatific, which pay feeble tribute to "the dark presence of the otherness that lies beyond the boundaries of man's conscious mind." [21]

Thus "Pan" has generally meant "nature" (outside of man) or the "natural" (within man); I have avoided these terms as far as possible up to this point, partly because they require redefinition at every use, and partly because although "All Walt is Pan, all Pan is not Walt." The Pan motif has never at any time represented more than a tiny fraction of the possible ways of defining or considering "nature," a term which yet forces its way into any attempt to summarize the motif. In early modern literature (1890–1914), he provided a powerful and necessary expression of the nonrational, at a time when the mainstream of literature was realistic, socially oriented, and, in some matters, inhibited. Although Pan is unlikely to become a literary fashion or a "public myth" again — as such, he "died" in 1914 — we may yet concur with D. H. Lawrence, perhaps the only English author to create a compelling "private" myth of Pan, that Pan keeps on being reborn, in all kinds of strange ways.

Appendix / Selected Bibliography / Notes / Index

APPENDIX

THE HOMERIC HYMN TO PAN

Translated by George Chapman

Sing, Muse, this chiefe of Hermes' love-got Joies,
Goate-footed, Two-horn'd, amorous of noise,
That through the faire-Greenes, al adorn'd with Trees,
Together goes with Nymphs, whose nimble knees
Can every Dance foot, that affect to scale   5
The most inaccessible Tops of all
Uprightest rocks, and ever use to call
On Pan, the bright-hayr'd God of Pastorall—
Who yet is leane and lovelesse, and doth owe
By lot all loftiest Mountaines crown'd with snowe;   10
All Tops of Hills and cliffie Highnesses,
All Silvan Copses, and the Fortresses
Of Thorniest Queaches, here and there doth rove,
And sometimes (by allurement of his love)
Will wade the watrie softnesses. Sometimes   15
(In quite oppos'de Capriccios) he climes
The hardest Rocks and highest, every way
Running their Ridges. Often will convaie
Himselfe up to a watch-Towr's Top, where sheepe
Have their Observance; oft through Hills as steepe   20
His Gotes he runns upon, and never rests.
Then turns he head, and flies on savage Beasts,
Mad of their slaughters—so most sharpe an eye
Setting upon them as his Beames let flie
Through all their thickest Tapistries. And then   25
(When Hesp'rus calls to folde the flocks of Men)
From the greene Clossets of his loftiest Reedes
He rushes forth, and Joy with Song he feedes—
When (under shadow of their motions set)
He plaies a verse forth so profoundly sweet   30
As not the Bird that in the flowrie Spring
(Amidds the leaves set) makes the Thickets ring
Of her sowre sorrowes, sweetened with her song,
Runns her divisions varied so and strong.
And then the sweete-voic't Nymphs that crowne his
      mountaines   35

(Flockt round about the deepe-black-watred fountaines)
Fall in with their Contention of song,
To which the Echoes all the Hills along
Their repercussions add. Then here and there
(Plac't in the midd'st) the God the Guide doth beare   40
Of all their Dances, winding in and out,
A Lynce's Hide (besprinckled round about
With blood) cast on his shoulders. And thus He
With well-made songs maintaines th'alacritie
Of his free minde, in silken Meddows crownde   45
With Hyacynths and Saffrons, that abound
In sweete-breath'd Odors, that th'unnumber'd grasse
(Besides their sents) give as through all they passe.
And these, in all their pleasures, ever raise
The blessed Gods' and long Olympus' praise;   50
Like zealous Hermes, who (of all) I said
Most Profits up to all the Gods convaide.
Who, likewise, came into th'Arcadian state
(That's rich in Fountaines, and all celebrate
For Nurse of flocks) where he had vowd a Grove   55
(Surnam'd Cyllenius) to his God-head's love.
Yet even himselfe (although a God he were),
Clad in a squallid sheepskinn governd there
A Mortall's sheepe. For soft Love, entring him,
Conformd his state to his conceipted Trimm,   60
And made him long in an extreame degree
T'enjoy the fayre-hayrd Virgine Dryope.
Which, ere he could, she made him consummate
The florishing Rites of Hymen's honord State,
And brought him such a peece of Progenie   65
As showd (at first sight) monstrous to the eye,
Gote-footed, Two-horn'd, full of noise even then,
And (opposite quite to other children)
Told (in sweete laughter) he ought death no Teare.
Yet strait his Mother start, and fled in feare   70
The sight of so unsatisfying a Thing,
In whose face put forth such a bristled spring.
Yet the most usefull Mercurie embrac't,
And tooke into his armes, his homely-fac't,
Beyond all measure joyfull with his sight;   75
And up to heaven with him made instant flight,
Wrapt in the warme skinne of a Mountaine Hare,
Set him by Jove, and made most merrie fare

To all the Deities else with his Sonne's sight,
Which most of all fill'd Bacchus with delight;   80
And Pan they call'd him, since he brought to All
Of Mirth so rare and full a Festivall.
    And thus, all honor to the shepherds' King!
    For Sacrifice to Thee my Muse shall sing!

THE ORPHIC HYMN TO PAN
Translated by Thomas Taylor

TO PAN

The Fumigation from Various Odours

I call strong Pan, the substance of the whole,
Etherial, marine, earthly, general soul,
Immortal fire; for all the world is thine,
And all are parts of thee, O pow'r divine.
Come, blessed Pan, whom rural haunts delight,   5
Come, leaping, agile, wand'ring, starry light;
The Hours and Seasons, wait thy high command,
And round thy throne in graceful order stand.
Goat-footed, horned, Bacchanalian Pan,
Fanatic pow'r, from whom the world began,   10
Whose various parts by thee inspir'd, combine
In endless dance and melody divine.
In thee a refuge from our fears we find,
Those fears peculiar to the human kind.
Thee shepherds, streams of water, goats rejoice,   15
Thou lov'st the chace, and Echo's secret voice:
The sportive nymphs, thy ev'ry step attend,
And all thy works fulfill their destin'd end.
O all-producing pow'r, much-fam'd, divine,
The world's great ruler, rich increase is thine.   20
All fertile Paean, heav'nly splendor pure,
In fruits rejoicing, and in caves obscure.
True serpent-horned Jove, whose dreadful rage
When rous'd, 'tis hard for mortals to asswage.
By thee the earth wide-bosom'd deep and long,   25
Stands on a basis permanent and strong.
Th' unwearied waters of the rolling sea,
Profoundly spreading, yield to thy decree.
Old Ocean too reveres thy high command,

Whose liquid arms begirt the solid land,   30
The spacious air, whose nutrimental fire,
And vivid blasts, the heat of life inspire;
The lighter frame of fire, whose sparkling eye
Shines on the summit of the azure sky,
Submit alike to thee, whose general sway   35
All parts of matter, various form'd, obey.
All nature's change thro' thy protecting care,
And all mankind thy lib'ral bounties share:
For these where'er dispers'd thro' boundless space,
Still find thy providence support their race.   40
Come, Bacchanalian, blessed power draw near,
Fanatic Pan, thy humble suppliant hear,
Propitious to these holy rites attend,
And grant my life may meet a prosp'rous end;
Drive panic Fury too, wherever found,
From human kind, to earth's remotest bound.   45

SELECTED BIBLIOGRAPHY OF SECONDARY SOURCES

The titles asterisked are particularly useful sources of further references.

Boccaccio, Giovanni. *Genealogie Deorum Gentilium Libri*, ed. Vincenzo Romano. Bari, 1951. 2 vols.

* Bush, Douglas. *Mythology and the Renaissance Tradition in English Poetry*. New York, 1957.

* —— *Mythology and the Romantic Tradition in English Poetry*. New York, 1957.

Campbell, F. Leota. "The God Pan in Greek and Latin Literature." Unpublished M.A. thesis. University of Southern California, 1918.

Carman, Barbara E. "A Study of Natalis Comes' Theory of Mythology and of Its Influence in England." Unpublished Ph.D. thesis, University of London, 1966.

Gale, Thomas, ed. *Opuscula Mythologica*. Amsterdam, 1688.

Garello, Luigi. *La Morte di Pàn: psicologia morale del mito*. Rome, 1908.

* Gerhard, G. A. "Der Tod des grossen Pan," *Heidelberger Akademie der Wissenschaften, Sitzungsberichte Philos.-Hist. Klasse*, 6 (1915): 3–52.

* —— "Nochmals zum Tod des grossen Pan," *Wiener Studien*, 38.2 (1916): 343–376.

* —— "Zum Tod des grossen Pan," *Wiener Studien*, 37.2 (1915): 323–352.

* Green, Peter. *Kenneth Grahame: A Biography*. Cleveland, 1959.

Hedelin, François. (Abbé d'Aubignac). *Des Satyres, Brutes, Monstres, et Demons*. Paris, 1888.

* Herbig, Reinhard. *Pan der griechische Bocksgott: Versuch einer Monographie*. Frankfurt am Main, 1949.

* Irwin, W. R. "The Survival of Pan," *PMLA*, 76 (June 1961): 159–167.

* Kerlin, R. T. *Theocritus in English Literature*. Lynchburg, Va., 1910.

* Law, Helen H. *Bibliography of Greek Myth in English Poetry*. American Classical League Bulletin XXVII. Oxford, Ohio, 1955.

Lemprière, John. *Bibliotheca Classica: or, a Classical Dictionary*. London, 1788.

Osma, José de. Introduction. Pedro Calderón de la Barca. *El Verdadero Dios Pan*. University of Kansas Humanistic Studies, no. 28. Lawrence, Kansas, 1949.

* Patrides, C. A. "The Cessation of the Oracles: The History of a Legend," *Modern Language Review*, 60.4 (October 1965): 500–507.

Philadelpheus, Alexander. *Der Pan in der antiken Kunst*. Athens, 1899.

Poggioli, Renato. "The Oaten Flute," *Harvard Library Bulletin*, 11.2 (Spring 1957): 147–184.

* Reinach, Salomon. "La Mort du grand Pan," *Bulletin de Correspondance hellénique*, 31 (1907): 5–19.

* Roscher, W. H. "Pan als Allgott," in *Festschrift für Johannes Overbeck*. Leipzig, 1893. Pages 56–72.

—— ed. "Epitheta Deorum quae apud poetas graecos leguntur," *Ausführliches Lexicon der griechischen und römischen Mythologie*. Supp. III (1893).

—— ed. "Epitheta Deorum quae apud poetas latinos leguntur." *Ausführliches Lexicon.* Supp. II (1902).

Ross, Alexander. *Mystagogus Poeticus.* London, 1648.

* Schoff, Wilfred H. "Tammuz, Pan and Christ," *The Open Court,* 26 (September 1912): 513–531 and 27 (August 1913): 449–460.

* Screech, M. A. "The Death of Pan and the Death of Heroes in the Fourth Book of Rabelais: A Study in Syncretism," *Bibliothèque d'Humanisme et Renaissance,* 18 (1955): 36–55.

Spence, Joseph. *A Guide to Classical Learning or Polymetis Abridged.* London, 1765.

—— *Polymetis: or, An Enquiry Concerning the Agreement between the Works of the Roman Poets, and the Remains of the Antient Artists.* London, 1747.

Spevack-Husmann, Helga. *The Mighty Pan: Miltons Mythologische Vergleiche.* Münster, 1963.

Tooke, Andrew. *Pantheon.* London, 1781.

* Weinreich, Otto. "Zum Tod des grossen Pan," *Archiv der Religionswissenschaft,* 13 (1910), 467–473.

* Wernicke, Konrad. "Pan," *Ausführliches Lexicon,* ed. W. R. Roscher, vol. III (Leipzig, 1897–1900), cols. 1347–1481.

NOTES

CHAPTER I. FROM THE ARCADIAN TO THE AUGUSTAN

1. Two sources, Reinhard Herbig's *Pan: Der griechische Bocksgott* (Frankfurt am Main, 1949), primarily art history, and Konrad Wernicke's article, "Pan," in Roscher's *Ausführliches Lexicon*, which has a strong anthropological bias, have been drawn on heavily for this introductory section. See also Frank Brommer, *Satyroi* (Würzburg, 1937), for a discussion of the categories, for the purposes of classical art, of fauns, satyrs, and Pans.

2. T. W. Allen and W. E. Sikes, *The Homeric Hymns* (London, 1904), p. 262. The editors date the Hymn to Pan, on linguistic grounds, as fifth-century, no earlier than Pindar (pp. lxxii, 261).

3. Pindar associates Pan with the worship of the Great Mother in *Pyth.* III, 77–79, and Frag. 95. But biographical legend involves them further: see "Pindar," in the *Imagines* of Philostratus the Elder and the scholium on *Pyth.* III, 77, given in Norwood's edition of Pindar. See also Aelius Aristides, *Vita Ambrosiana* (Geneva, 1604), I, 53, 71, and III, 285; *Greek Anthology* XVI, 305, and, for a more modern version, Politian's *Nutricia*, as quoted in J. A. Symonds' *Renaissance in Italy* (London, 1906), II, 330. See Joan A. Haldane, "Pindar and Pan," *Phoenix*, 21.1 (Spring 1968): 18–31.

4. Aeschylus: *Agamemnon* 54–58; *Persians* 449; Sophocles: *Ajax* 694–700; and especially Euripides: *Hippolytus* 141–144; *Medea* 1171–1172; *Rhesus* 36–37; *Helena* 179–191 (and also *Electra* 703; *Bacchae* 951; and *Ion* 492). The *Agamemnon* and the first four citations from Euripides present Pan as the inspirer of fear and madness. These fleeting references are among the very rare literary comments on these well-known powers of Pan.

5. *Lysistrata* 2, 721, 912, 998; *Frogs* 229; and *Thesmophor.* 977. *Lysistrata*, as might be expected, gives jesting clues to the sexual nature of Pan, plentifully corroborated in art and archaeology (see Herbig, *Pan*), but much less emphasized in literary sources. For Pan in New Comedy, see Menander's *Dyskolos*.

6. *Phaedrus* 263; *Cratylus* 408B.

7. This and all subsequent translations from Herodotus are by A. D. Godley, in the Loeb Classical Library (London, 1921).

8. Tr. W. R. Paton (Loeb: London, 1960), VI, 32. Among the many repetitious dedications other themes are to be found — Pan unhappy in love, whether for the nymph Echo or the youth Daphnis: "No longer do I, goat-footed Pan, desire to dwell among the goats . . . Daphnis is dead . . . Here in the city will I dwell; let some one else set forth to hunt the wild beasts" (an amusing foreshadowing of late nineteenth-century "Arcadiac" verse in its retreat to the city when the representative of country joys — later Pan himself — has died); Pan aggressive in love (attributed to Theocritus): "But Pan hunts thee [Daphnis], Pan and Priapus . . . dispel the gathering drowsiness of sleep and fly" (Priapus and Pan are more frequently linked in decorous agricultural tasks); Pan the warrior of Marathon (VII, 535; IX, 338; XVI, 232–233).

9. I, 15–18. *The Idylls of Theocritus Literally Translated into English Prose,* by the Reverend J. Banks (London, 1878), p. 2.

10. Tr. Robert Graves (Penguin, 1950), chap. VIII, pp. 135–136.

11. See also the military Pan of Valerius Flaccus, fl. A.D. 70–93 (*Argonautica*

III, 46–57), and the prose romance of Achilles Tatius (*Leucippe and Cleitophon*, ca. A.D. 290), where Pan is used for mildly sexual symbolism, much in the manner of Aristophanes.

12. Lucretius is the only other classical author to deny Pan myths in this manner (*De Rerum Natura* IV, 589f); he subscribes to the naturalistic explanation of myth, and his skepticism is unmixed with satire.

13. Compare "Dionysus" (I, 51) with Hyginus' *Fabulae* CXCVI. See also "Icaromenippus" II, 313, for "Pan and the Corybantes and Attis and Sabazius, those alien gods of doubtful status" (cf. V, 423). For the funniest Lucianic Pan (a skit on the genealogy given in the Homeric Hymn and elsewhere), see *Dialogues of the Gods* xxii, "Mercury Against His Will Is Persuaded by Pan that He Is His Father," which concludes, in William Tooke's translation, "Embrace me! But be sure never to call me father, when anybody is within hearing" (p. 115).

14. See also *Georg.* I, 16–18; III, 391–393 (Pan and Luna); *Ecl.* IV, 53–59; V, 58–59; VIII, 22–24; X, 26–30.

15. Lines 855–887 of Arthur Golding's translation, 1567.

16. As translated by Croxall in the Garth edition, 1717.

17. "Incerti ad Panem," xxix, *Poetae Latini Minores*, ed. Emil Baehrens (Leipzig, 1881), III, 170.

18. See Cyril Bailey, *Religion in Virgil* (Oxford, 1935), p. 145, though I think the author perhaps overestimates the extent to which Pan and Faunus were interchangeable.

19. "A literary abstraction." Herbig, *Pan*, p. 64. Pages 63–69 contain a useful discussion of this whole question.

20. Nor have they stopped yet. See Margaret Murray, *The God of the Witches* (New York, 1933), p. 20: "His universality is shown by his name, which points to a time when he was the only deity in his own locality."

21. I am relying heavily on his "Pan als Allgott," *Festschrift für Johannes Overbeck* (Leipzig, 1893), pp. 56–72.

22. In Roscher's view, the more important factor was the identification of Pan with Chnum-Mendes, the Egyptian goat- or ram-god, also a pantheistic deity. But this point is controversial and, in any case, matters less for our purposes than an explanation that could have occurred to each encyclopedist in turn. See Herodotus, II, 46.

23. The first allegorical interpretation of Pan actually occurs in Plato's *Cratylus* (408C). It may have influenced the more familiar one, but its import is rather different: "speech signifies all things, and is always turning them round and round, and has two forms, true and false . . . Is not the truth that is in him the smooth or sacred form which dwell above among the Gods, whereas falsehood dwells among men below, and is rough like the goat of tragedy?" Tr. Jowett (Oxford, 1924), p. 351.

24. "De Pane" (sec. 27), *Phurnuti Liber de Natura Deorum*, in *Opuscula Mythologica* (Amsterdam, 1688), p. 203.

25. Commentary on Virgil, *Ecl.* II, 31. The key phrase "totius naturae deus est" is his.

26. "De Deis Gentium" (Ch. XI, sec. I.d), *Originum*, VIII, in *Isidori Hispalensis Episcopi Opera Omnia* (Paris, 1601), p. 113.

27. *Works* (Philadelphia, 1857), I, 289–292. First published in Latin, 1609; in English, 1619. See C. W. Lemmi, *The Classic Deities in Bacon* (Baltimore, 1933), pp. 61–74, for an account of Bacon's probable indebtedness to Natalis Comes, Macrobius, and Boccaccio, among others.

28. Lilius Gyraldus, *De Deis gentium* (Lyons, 1565), p. 383; Macrobius (ca. A.D. 400), *Saturnalia* I, 22, iii. But allegory, of a different kind, is among Macrobius' methods for proving Pan to be the Sun as God (ii–vii).

29. Natalis Comes, "De Pane," V, vi, *Mythologiae, sive Explicationum fabularum* of 1551 (Frankfurt, 1631), p. 458. See also Vincenzo Cartari's *Imagini delli Dei de gl'Antichi* of 1556 (Venice, 1647, repr. Graz, 1963), pp. 72–78, 268–269; Giacomo Zucchi, *Discorso sopra li dei de Gentili*; and especially Giovanni Boccaccio, *Genealogie Deorum Gentilium Libri*, from the late fourteenth century. Renaissance dictionaries, such as those of Perottus, Calepine, the Stephani, and others, give very brief accounts, often derived (or quoted) from Servius.

30. Herbig, *Pan*, plate X. See page 77 for a discussion of this painting and page 64 for comments on the difficulty of turning the Orphic Pan into viable art forms. Compare Emerson's development of a "Protean" Pan.

31. Tr. Frank Cole Babbitt. Loeb Classical Library (Cambridge, Mass. 1957).

32. *Praep. Ev.* 208a. Ed. E. H. Gifford (Oxford, 1903).

33. I have relied heavily on the invaluable discussion of Rabelais' Pan by M. A. Screech, "The Death of Pan in the Fourth Book of Rabelais," *Bibliothèque d'Humanisme et Renaissance* 17 (1955): 36–55. Screech suggests the works of Bigot and Postel as possible intermediaries between Paulus Marsus and Rabelais, and Postel as a possible (though not essential) anticipator of Rabelais in the expansion of the Plutarchan formula. He also comments on the "longstanding misconception" by which, even in recent and scholarly editions, the Rabelaisian interpretation has been identified with the Eusebian and "grand Servateur" has been glossed accordingly. The mistake is not confined to French criticism. Screech's discussion is continued and developed by A. J. Krailsheimer, *Rabelais and the Franciscans* (Oxford, 1963), chapter 11.

34. Scot, *Discoverie of Witchcraft* (1584), VIII, 3, "That Oracles are Ceased." He gives Plutarch, Eusebius, and Paulus Marsus as his sources. Abbé Antoine Banier, *The Mythology and Fables of the Ancients, Explain'd from History* (London, 1739), I, 541. The first note of skepticism was supplied as early as 1559, in the *Historia Ecclesiastica* of the Centuriatores Magdeburgici (Basel, 1624), part I, bk. ii, chap. xv, col. 523b. "Eusebius . . . ubi et de Pane, sub Tiberio, mortuo, ridicula narrat" (where Eusebius also tells ridiculous things about Pan, dead in the reign of Tiberius).

35. Salomon Reinach, "La Mort du grand Pan," *Bulletin de correspondance héllenique*, 31 (1907): 5–19, and reprinted in his *Cultes, mythes et religions*, III (1908), 1–15. Frazer (in his commentary on Ovid's *Fasti*) and Roscher approach this position as well, and anthropological controversy flourishes still on such minor aspects of the problem as "northern parallels" to the death of Pan.

36. Bibliographies in studies published between 1910 and 1916 by Wilfred H. Schoff, G. A. Gerhard, and Otto Weinreich (see the Selected Bibliography above) supply upwards of sixty complete examples of such scholarly interpretations, along with more allusive examples and some literary references. Gerhard is perhaps the most precise in scholarship and judgment. C. A. Patrides brings the argument up to date in "The Cessation of Oracles: The History of a Legend," *Modern Language Review*, 60.4 (October 1965): 500–507; however the Cessation of Oracles is a tradition overlapping but not identical with the Death of Pan.

Curiously enough, the mythographers and encyclopedists alluded to earlier, who were repeating and developing the pastoral, Orphic, and allegorical Pans of Servius and others, tended not to mention the Death of Pan, although the story was readily available. (There is a brief and rather uninterested note in Gyraldus.) Conversely, the commentators listed in the Schoff, Gerhard, and Weinreich bibliographies, who were likely to be using the story as a counter in religious debate, seldom discussed Pan's other actions and attributes. In non-literary sources, the Death of Pan was virtually a separate tradition from the main stream of mythological interpretation.

37. Ludwig Lavater's Pan–Christ interpretation in *Of Ghostes and Spirites Walking by Night* (London, 1572), perhaps the most familiar and important of these sources because of its appearance in E. K.'s notes to the *Shepheardes Calender*, is such an example: the story has very little connection with the argument that enfolds it. The two best samples of prose writing that I encountered in my explorations of the bibliographies were Remigius' suspense-filled retelling of the story in his *Daemonolatria* (Hamburg, 1693), and Antony Van Dale's tightly knit polemic argument in his *Dissertationes Duae de oraculis veterum ethnicorum* (Amsterdam, 1683), on behalf of the skeptical party.

38. *An Apologie for Poetrie* (Cambridge, 1951), p. 46; *Pseudodoxia* VII, 12.

39. *Book of the Duchesse* (1369), l. 512. See F. N. Robinson's note on this line in *The Works of Geoffrey Chaucer* (Boston, 1957), p. 775.

40. *Confessio Amantis* (ca. 1386–1390), VIII, lines 2239–2240. See also V, 1005–1044, for a passage emphasizing Pan's role as the teacher of shepherds, "every crafte for mannes helpe," including the art of the "double pipes" (not the seven-reed Syrinx of classical tradition). Lines 1038–1042, when juxtaposed with lines 116–117 of the Prologue, are seen to mean something not unlike Milton's "And thank the gods amiss":

> "And thus the nyce reverence
> Of foles, whan that he was ded,
> The fot hath torned to the hed,
> And clepen him god of nature
> For so thei maden his figure."

(*The English Works*, ed. G. C. Macaulay, London, 1900, I, 430.) See also the *Assembly of Gods* (formerly attributed to John Lydgate), lines 323–324: "And by her [Fortune] sate though he unworthy were/ The rewde god Pan of sheperdys the gyde."

41. "Perversa Iudicia," *Whitney's Choice of Emblemes* (London, 1866), p. 218. (The accompanying woodcut shows Pan playing a bagpipe: cf. Kane O'Hara's *Midas*, 1764, for this curious choice of instrument.) The basis for the emblem is perhaps found in Erasmus' *Praise of Folly* (1511): "the ears which, in the old days, our friend Midas inclined to the god Pan" are those with which to listen to clowns and jesters; "stupid Pan moves the laughter of all by some ballad, which the gods prefer above hearing the Muses themselves"; "Ignorance, Pan's daughter" (1, 7, 4).

There are other ways of allegorizing the story: a lyric allusion antedating Whitney is Thomas Wyatt's hyperbolic example of flattery ("Myn Own John Poynz"):

> "I cannot flatter as courtiers must . . .
> I am not he, such eloquence to boast
> . . . and say that Pan
> Passeth Apollo in music manifold."

This appears to be Wyatt's own addition to his close abridgment of the tenth

Satire of Alamanni. See the Earl of Oxford's similar rhetorical exemplification of the fickleness of women: "How oft from Phoebus they do flee to Pan" in "Renunciation"; Spenser's *Shepheardes Calender*, "June," 65–70; Fletcher's *Faithful Shepherdess* (IV, 1); the first Hymn in Jonson's *Pan's Anniversarie*. The *Ovide Moralisé en Prose* (a fifteenth-century prose resumé of an earlier poetic allegorization of Ovid) defines Midas as piety feigned for the sake of vanity, and bears no relation to the "perversum iudicium," perverse judgment, and its descendants. Pan (in a comment on a minor allusion in *Met*. XIV, 638) "signifie vaine gloire, vantance, orgeuil, arrogance, faulx semblant et ypocrisie" (stands for vainglory, boasting, pride, arrogance, false seeming and hypocrisy), none of which are qualities commonly associated with him (Ed. Cornelis de Boer, Amsterdam, 1954, p. 369).

42. Sandys' religious allegory (*Ovid's Metamorphosis*, Oxford, 1632, p. 390), by which Human Reason fails to appreciate and acknowledge the superior claims of Divine Providence (cf. Bacon), has parallels in some of the lesser ingredients of Heywood's allegory: Midas, by his decision, shows that he is "all earthie, Nothing Caelestiall" (V, 133); similarly in Lyly: "Pan wilt thou contend with Apollo, who tunes the heavens, and makes them all hang by harmony? . . . Pan . . . excluded from heaven and in earth not honoured" (IV, 1). Although political satire (with Philip of Spain as Midas — cf. Sandys' political allegory of "Midas a suspitious prince") is clearly the dominating element in the play as a whole (see C. W. Dilke, ed., *Old English Plays*, London, 1814, I, 292, and Albert Feuillerat's *Lyly*, Cambridge, Eng., 1910, p. 200, and elsewhere), I find the internal evidence inadequate to support Feuillerat's interpretation, for this particular scene, of Pan as the Catholic Church and Apollo as Protestantism. Analogous to the question of political satire in *Midas* is that of personal satire in *Love's Mistris*. There are strong suggestions that Heywood is settling scores in some dramatists' controversy; F. G. Fleay identifies Apollo and Pan with Heywood and Shirley, while A. M. Clark, disagreeing with Fleay (*Thomas Heywood, Playwright and Miscellanist*, Oxford, 1931, p. 162), gives no specific correspondence for Pan himself. Clark also mentions the Dekker, Day, and Chettle play (p. 134) *The Golden Ass & Cupid and Psiches* (1600), not extant.

43. A vestige of the Apuleian role of serious and kindly counselor may perhaps be found in the comic counsel that Pan gives Venus in matters of love (I, 1). Heywood's familiarity with Lucian's Pans, as shown in his translations of "Jupiter and Ganimede" and "The Man-Hater," raises the possibility of some Lucianic influence. Only Shakerly Marmion, in his *Cupid and Psyche* of 1637, puts a genuine Apuleian Pan on the stage:

> "Though I a rustick, and a shepheard be
> Scorn not for that my counsell, and advice."

I, iv, 64–65; Philadelphia, 1944, p. 132. See Alice J. Nearing's introduction to this edition for an excellent survey of English versions of Cupid and Psyche, none of which seem to delineate Pan as effectively as Apuleius himself does.

44. James Shirley, *Love's Tricks, or the Schoole of Compliments* (1625), especially the song on Pan's Holiday. With these dramatic examples compare Michael Drayton's *The Man in the Moone* and, in a lighter vein, William Warner's *Albion's England*, VI, xxxi. See Joshua Sylvester's version of Du Bartas' *La Semaine*, II, iv, 2 ("Magnificence") for an entertainment at the court of Solomon visualized, apologetically, in terms of a Renaissance masque:

> "Heer, many a horned *Satyre*, many a *Pan* . . .

With lustie frisks and lively bounds bring in
Th'Antike . . .
For even Gods Servants (God knowes how) have supt
The sugred baen of *Pagan* Rites corrupt."

Divine Weeks and Works (London, 1611), p. 574.

45. Renato Poggioli, "The Oaten Flute," *Harvard Library Bulletin*, 11.2 (Spring 1957): 169.

46. European intermediaries for all these Theocritean techniques can probably be found. Even the most specific, the reference to Pan asleep (I, i), resembles the First Eclogue of Alamanni, lines 16–20.

47. Compare the more crudely topical identification with James I that Jonson made seventeen years earlier in *The Satyr* (1603):

"This is Cyparissus' face,
And the dame hath Syrinx' grace
O that Pan were now in place!"

48. When "we find that Pan is at various times Henry VIII, the pope, and Christ, we may be disconcerted." Douglas Bush, *Mythology and the Renaissance Tradition in English Poetry* (New York, 1957), p. 95. My more general debts to Bush's work will be obvious through the whole of this chapter.

49. Eclogue III, *Oeuvres Lyriques*, ed. C. A. Mayer (London, 1964), p. 350. In a way this detailed allegory is more like the hymns to Pan in Jonson's *Pan's Anniversarie* than like Spenser's "Pan" for "Henry VIII" without elaborations or explanation. (But compare Jonson and Spenser for Pan and Syrinx as a royal couple, as if Ovid's Pan had actually caught up with his prey). In one passage Marot depicts Pan in a deliberately antiquarian manner, linking the royal identification, empty of concrete details, with the more vivid allegorical images of the encyclopedists:

"De dur cormier houlette riche & forte:
Et l'autre tient chalemelle fournye
De sept tuyaulx, faictz selon l'armonye
Des cieulx, où sont les sept dieux clers & haulx,
Et denotans les sept artz liberaulx,
Qui sont escriptz dedans ta teste saincte
Toute de Pin bien couronnée & ceincte."

[One hand holds] a fine, strong sheephook of tough sorb-wood:
And the other holds a syrinx provided
With seven pipes, fashioned according to the harmony
Of the heavens, where the seven bright and lofty gods are,
And betokening the seven liberal arts,
Which are inscribed upon your sacred head
All crowned and well-girded with Pine.

See also Eclogue I, "Sur ma Dame Loyse de Savoye," pp. 321–337, and "Ballade XV" in *Oeuvres Diverses* (London, 1966). An earlier royal identification than Marot's is found in Petrarch's Ecloga Duodecima ("Conflictatio") of 1356, in which John II is identified as Pan, a warring shepherd-king defending his sheepfold. The allegory is not taken very far.

50. M. Y. Hughes (*Virgil and Spenser*, Berkeley, 1929, p. 301) uses this phrase in assessing Spenser's debt to Boccaccio, XIV, 23 ("Pastorum venerande Deus, Pan, deprecor, assis" — O Pan, God revered by the shepherds, I pray you

to be of aid) and XIV, 77 ("Quas, Pan, tibi laudes / Quas, Silvane, canam?" — What praises shall I sing to you, Pan, and what, Sylvanus, to you?) from the *Bucolicum Carmen*. Hughes' phrase seems to me to define the relationship with more precision than Lotspeich's listing of the Boccaccio lines, the Marot "Complaincte" (no longer attributed to him with certainty; see Mayer on the canon) and Mantuan's fourth Eclogue, line 184, as precedents for the Spenser Pan–Christ identification. I could find no reference to Pan at all in the last source cited; lines 184–187 read in Latin:

> "et noster Deus, unde salus et vita resurgit.
> haec sunt, pastores, haec sunt mysteria vobis
> advertenda: animi fugiunt obscena viriles,
> femineas loca delectant infamia mentes."

> and our God, from whom arise our life and well-being.
> these are, O shepherds, mysteries that you ought to notice:
> manly souls flee filthy things,
> disgusting places delight womanly minds.

Eclogues, ed. Wilfred P. Mustard (Baltimore, 1911), p. 82. Line 186 appears in Turbervile's English translation (1567) as "By nature Man and kinde is bent / all filthie things t'eschue," giving "Man" a heavy Gothic capital that might be read "Pan." (See the facsimile edition, ed. Douglas Bush, New York, 1937, p. 37, side 2.) But a later reference contrasts "Pan" (printed, like all the proper names in this text, in clear, thin-line italics), with the Virgin Mary: "Now needlesse is to follow *Pan* / or any rusticke Saint" (Eclogue VIII, 114, p. 77, side 2). See H. G. Lotspeich, *Classical Mythology in Spenser's Poetry* (Princeton, 1932), p. 96.

A. S. Cook, "Notes on Milton's Nativity Ode," *Transactions of the Connecticut Academy*, 15 (1909): 336, cites Rabelais and Marot. He also cites Marguerite of Navarre's charming "Comédie sur le Trespas du Roi" (1547). This is probably the first poem to use the Pan–monarch identification (Francis I, as earlier in Marot) in an elegiac sense. But though Pan was "ravy aux cieulx . . . Puisque la mort faict de sy cruelz to[u]rs" (snatched off to the heavens . . . Since death plays such cruel tricks), there is no suggestion whatever of Plutarchan influence, and Pan (Francis I) is very clearly distinguished from Christ, "le grand Pasteur du troupeau," the great Shepherd of the flock. As is common in the pastoral elegy, the poet claims immortality for the deceased; here it is done in an amusing coincidental anticipation of the nineteenth-century "Arcadiac" cry, "Pan is *not* dead" (the reverse or negation of the Plutarchan formula). Marguerite of Navarre says

> "Pan n'est poinct mort mais plus que jamais vit
> Avec Moïse et Jacob et David,
> Et sont aux cieulx parlans de bergerie."

> Pan is not dead at all but lives more than ever
> With Moses and Jacob and David,
> And they are up in heaven talking about the sheep-fold.

Comédie sur le Trespas du Roy, Dernières Poésies (Paris, 1896), p. 59.

51. This is Reissert's interpretation, variorum edition of *The Shepheardes Calender* (Baltimore, 1932), p. 333.

52. J. A. Symonds, in chapter 8 of his *Renaissance in Italy: The Revival of Learning* (London, 1906), p. 361–362, gives two examples of a Pan–Pope ident-

ification: Navagero on Julius II and Fracastoro on Julius III ("Hoc in Monte Dei pecudes pascentur et agni" — There on the Mountain of God the flocks and the lambs are being pastured).

53. "Pitie the paines, that thou thy selfe didst prove" ("Jan." 18). Here it is important to remember that Pan failed to catch Syrinx, while in April it was necessary to pretend lightly that he had.

There are other examples of Pan as a Petrarchan lover in the poems of Browne. Watson (1582) has two lines showing the earthy, matter-of-fact interpretation of the Syrinx story being turned into Petrarchan convention before our eyes, to justify the sonneteer's own amours:

> "If cuntrie Pan might folowe Nymphes in chase
> And yet through love remain devoyd of blame."

Hekatompathia or Passionate Centurie of Love, XXXVII. See also Sidney's *Arcadia* (London, 1590), as quoted in that treasury of minor pastoral references, E. K. Chambers' *English Pastorals* (Glasgow, 1895), p. 33.

54. *Faerie Queene* II, ii, 7–8, and VII, vi, 42–53. Horace's "Faune nympharum fugientem amator" (O Faunus, lover of the fleeing nymphs) may have been the guiding example behind this definition of Faunus. The latter episode from the Mutabilitie Cantos has affinities of mood with Ovid's *Fasti* II, 303f: in both Faunus plays the comic-erotic role of a lover presuming beyond his station, and is mocked for his pains. See *Faerie Queene* II, ix, 40 for the only Spenserian Pan outside *The Shepheardes Calender*, a brief and obscure allusion to the story of Pan and Iynx.

55. Spenser, with his genius for conflation, ascribes two former loves to Sylvanus (who, insofar as he is weak and old, is not Pan-like); one of them, Dryope, is properly Faunus', and the other, Pholoe, is properly Pan's.

Two other examples of Elizabethan satyr poetry are perhaps worth noting (I have made no attempt to be exhaustive). Faunus, in John Weever's *Faunus and Melliflora* (1599), is simply the beautiful young hero of countless erotic epyllia, even to his finely shaped ivory feet (the clearest possible indication that he cannot be identified with a goat-god). But the half-humorous, half-grotesque birth of his satyr-son, toward the end of the poem (lines 1031–1042) bears a strong resemblance to the birth of Pan as narrated in the Homeric Hymn to Pan. The best characterization of an ugly, terrifying satyr figure is perhaps that in Drayton's tenth "Nymphall," in *Muses Elizium*, where the satyr's own feelings are allowed some expression. But compare the Pan of a speech to the Queen at Bisham (1592), "an eie-sore to chast Nymphes; yet still importunate." He defines his own character, using the chestnut as an emblem: "as the huske was thornye and tough, yet the meate sweete, so though my hyde were rough and hateful, yet my heart was smooth and loving." *Progresses of Queen Elizabeth*, ed. John Nichols (London, 1823), III, 131–133.

56. This translation appears in Sandys' *Ovid*, p. 484, in the commentary on Book XIV. The commentator in the Lyons, 1574, edition of Alciati, p. 110, remarks "Proinde hominem in sua mixta natura" (Exactly like man in his conjoint nature). In two cases Alciati uses "Faunus" where "Pan" would have been legitimate: "Luxuria" (Lechery), p. 84 ("salacis hirci natura" — with the nature of a lustful he-goat — is the comment), and "In subitum terrorem" (On sudden terror), p. 140 (glossed "subitos terrores antiqui Panicos dicebant"; the ancients used to call sudden terrors Panics); the illustrator made no visible distinction between Faunus and Pan. This sort of emblematic interpretation is perhaps echoed in the speech at Bisham: "As he hath two shapes, so hath he two harts;

the one of a man wherewith his tongue is tipped, dissembling; the other of a beast, wherewith his thoughts are poysoned, lust," p. 133.

57. "Nico and Dorus," *Arcadia* (1590), as quoted in Chambers, *English Pastorals*, p. 33. Other Pans which may be of interest, for the most part fleeting, nonsatiric pastoral references: Luigi Alamanni, *Ecl.* 1, and 2; J.-A. Baïf, *Ecl.* 2; Pietro Bembo, "Galatea"; Castiglione, "Alcon"; Drayton, *Endimion and Phoebe*, lines 15, 180, and in Eclogues from *The Shepherd's Garland*; William Drummond of Hawthornden, "Damon's Lament"; Thomas Heywood, *Gynaikeion* (London, 1624), I, p. 42, and "Mercurie's Song" in *Pleasant Dialogues and Dramas*; Ben Jonson, "To Penshurst"; George Peele, "The Handiwork of Flora"; Giovanni Pontano, "De Quercu Diis Sacra," *Carmina* no. 9; Francis Sabie, *Pan's Pipe* (three pastoral eclogues); Sidney, *Arcadia* (London, 1907), pp. 14, 94, 99, 101, 506–507, 672, and (prose) 95, 98, 494 (Pan, Hercules and Iole [sic, for "Omphale"?]) — cf. *The Lady of May*, final song; Torquato Tasso, *Aminta*, I, i, and IV, ii; William Warner, *Albion's England*, VI, chap. 30; Thomas Watson, "A Lament for Meliboeus," *Poems*, pp. 163, 173; Geoffrey Whitney, "In Curiosos," p. 145; George Wither, "A Shepherd's Swain," in *Fair-Virtue*; Anon., "Phillida's Love-Call," in *England's Helicon* (1600).

58. C. G. Osgood, under "Pan" in his *Classical Mythology of Milton's English Poems* (New York, 1900), points out that the places mentioned in this song are all associated with Pan or with Hermes, his father.

59. Compare neo-Platonist usage, as for instance Politian:

> "O King of all things, deathless God, Thou Pan
> supreme, celestial!
> That seest all, and movest all, and all with might
> sustainest."

J. A. Symonds trans., as quoted by Cook, "Notes on Milton's Nativity Ode," p. 337. See also "Uranus and Psyche," an unpublished allegorical pastoral of ca. 1630 (BM Addl. 40,145), from which a feeble poem is quoted in Norman Ault's *Seventeenth Century Lyrics* (London, 1928), p. 66. Like Politian, the author is much indebted to the *Orphic Hymn to Pan*. A basically Christian notion ("For Pan ascended is on high") is here loosely garbed in pagan phrases (sometimes with a Herbertian ring); a basically Christian allegory of "Pancrates" as God Almighty and Psyche as the soul is put in the frame of a Jonsonian pastoral with lyric interludes.

60. George Sandys' interpretation of the Plutarch story, "which declared the death of Christ (the great Shepheard,) and subjection of Sathan," in *A Relation of a Journey begun An: Dom: 1610* (London, 1627), p. 11, and George Hakewill's *Apologie* (London, 1630), p. 208 (both cited, along with Giles Fletcher's *Christ's Victorie and Triumph*, in Thomas Warton's notes on line 181 of the Nativity Ode), are thus interpretations of the more usual sort, as are the numerous biblical commentaries that gloss the account of the Crucifixion (*Matt.* 27.51) with a reference to Plutarch.

61. For example, Milton himself, in *Paradise Regained* I, 455–460. See Chapter II, note 35, for other examples.

62. Bush, *Renaissance Tradition*, p. 261. See also Bush, pp. 271–272, 274, 285; A. W. Verity's comments, *Paradise Lost* (Cambridge, Eng., 1929), II, 672–674; and R. H. West, *Milton and the Angels* (Athens, Ga., 1955), pp. 130, 169–170, 176–177. The clearest Elizabethan authority appears to be Richard Hooker, *Of the Laws of Ecclesiastical Polity* (1594), I, 4, 3: "These wicked spirits [the fallen angels] the heathens honoured instead of gods . . . some in oracles, some

as household gods, some as nymphs" (London, 1907, p. 164). Sir Walter Raleigh, in his summary of the defeat of the pagan devils (at the time of Julian) gives "the great God *Pan* hath broken his Pipes" as one metaphor for this defeat. *History of the World*, I, 6, 8 (London, 1614), p. 75.

63. Cook ("Notes on Milton's Nativity Ode," p. 360) quotes these lines (*Dionysii Areopagite*, I, 296–297, 305–307, in the Paris, 1513, edition of the *Opera*, I, 197a), in a note on lines 224–225 of Milton's *Nativity*, but in a discussion of Pan they seem more appropriate here: whatever other gods may have fallen in the *Nativity*, there are good and sufficient reasons for Pan not being among them.

64. *Hymne des Daimons*, ed. Albert-Marie Schmidt (Paris, 1939), pp. 59–61. The juxtaposition of encyclopedic imagery ("marqueté comme Fans") and Virgilian imagery ("la face vermeille") is interesting; the editor makes, I think, too general a note on the latter. Commenting on Ronsard's "connaissance en archéologie mythologique" (knowledge of mythical archaeology), he points out that "les anciens coloraient de vermillon la figure des Dieux" (the ancients colored the faces of the Gods with vermilion). But cf. *Ecl*. x, 26–27:

> "Pan deus Arcadiae venit, quem vidimus ipsi
> sanguineis ebuli bacis minioque rubentem."

(Pan, the god of Arcadia, came, whom we ourselves saw crimsoned with vermilion and blood-red elderberries.)

65. *The Complete Poems*, ed. A. B. Grosart (Edinburgh, 1878), pp. 119, 124, and 18. See also the obscure allegorical poem *Cupid's Conflict* (p. 174), where Pan is equated with the joys of "this living clay" in contrast with the soul, which, neglected, protests "For Pan, is dead but I am still alive." Whatever Wordsworth's other debts to *The Praexistency of the Soul* may be (see stanzas 5 and 6 of *Intimations of Immortality*), his Pan figures owe nothing whatsoever to More's.

Clearly the connection between Pan and the Satan of medieval and Renaissance diabolism could be traced, despite the infrequency of its literary manifestations: see, for example, *Carmina Burana* no. 54, ed. Hilka and Schumann (Heidelberg, 1930), p. 110, "Omne genus demoniorum . . . vos exorcizo . . . Fauni . . . Nymphe . . . Satyri" (I exorcize you . . . Fauns . . . Nymphs . . . Satyrs . . . all species of demons); a seventeenth-century woodcut of a priapic "Robin Goodfellow" at a witches' sabbath, who looks more like Pan than like Satan (reproduced, among other places, in Margaret Murray's *The God of the Witches*, fig. 5, p. 62); *Hypnerotomachie ou Discours du Songe de Poliphile* (Paris, 1561; from the Italian) for a Pan described as the younger brother of Priapus, a relationship which the illustrations amply confirm. *Des Satyres, Brutes, Monstres et Demons*, by François Hedelin, Abbé d'Aubignac (1627), is the most thorough contemporary discussion I know of the (non-Plutarchan) Pan–demon equivalence. Hedelin cites Ronsard and Porphyry, attributes Panic terrors to demons, identifies the pastoral Pan asleep at noon with the Psalmist's "demon de midy" (demon of noon), and equates Bacchanals with witches' sabbaths (Paris, 1888, esp. pp. 109–114, 119–120, 124). Reginald Scot, *The Discoverie of Witchcraft*, VII, xv, specifically includes "satyrs, pans, faunes" in a long list of "bugs," which nursemaids teach children to fear. Thomas Nashe, in his *Terrors of the Night* (1594), *Works*, ed. McKerrow (Oxford, 1958), I, 347, reminds us of "Robbin-good-fellowes. . . which idolatrous former daies and the fantasticall world of Greece ycleaped *Fawnes, Satyres*." Also quoted in Cook's "Notes on Milton's Nativity Ode," p. 366. For Nashe's own view of Pan, the typical Elizabethan critic's metaphor of Pan, Midas, and Apollo, see the allusions in "The Anatomie of Absurditie" (I, 44) and in the "Preface to *Astrophel and Stella*" (III, 329).

66. See also the less concise Latin version, lines 47–48.

"Capripes & peteret quod *Pan Syringa* fugacem,
Hoc erat ut *Calamum* posset reperire Sonorum."

And thus the goatfooted Pan pursued the fleeing Syrinx,
This was in order to invent the sounding reed.

67. *A Collection of Miscellanies* (London, 1706), pp. 54–58. Corollary to this is Robert Herrick's more graceful wish that Pan might pipe to Charles at his birth (1640): *A Pastorall Upon the Birth of Prince Charles*, in *Poetical Works* (Oxford, 1956), p. 86. See also Herrick, pp. 159, 184.

68. This "Lobrede," by Daniel Casper von Lohenstein, unpaginated, is bound in with Hoffmanwaldau's *Poemata et Orationes* (Leipzig, 1696). Also published in *Deutsche Übersetzungen und Gedichte* (Breslau, 1679). More recently Paul Heyse used the same conceit for the death of Goethe:

"Rings durch die Welt, als sei sie selbst bedroht
Von Todesnacht, und durch die Lüfte zittern
Hört man den Klageruf: der grosse Pan ist todt!"

Right round the world, as if the world itself were threatened
By the night of death, and quivering in the winds
One heard the lamentation: the great Pan is dead!

Das Goethe-Haus in Weimar, Gedichte (Berlin, 1889), p. 222. Alfred Jarry's "Nécrologie" for Stéphane Mallarmé (*Almanach du Père Ubu*, Paris, 1899) is more oblique: "la voix horrifique informant par trois fois Thamoun de la mort de celui dont aussi écrit . . . Herodote, et Cicéron" (the horrifying voice informing Thamus three times of the death of him of whom . . . Herodotus and Cicero have also written). *Tout Ubu* (Paris, 1962), p. 385. Here Jarry is mimicking Rabelais (IV, 28).

69. Bush, *Renaissance Tradition*, p. 296.

70. London, 1671, p. 59. See also "The Hunting of the Gods," ibid., and *The Covent Garden Drollery* (London, 1672), p. 93.

71. Cf. Longus' *Daphnis and Chloe* for a less blandly superficial acknowledgment of Pan's unsuitability as a patron of allegedly monogamous rustic love affairs.

72. Compare Dryden's translation of Ovid's Pan-Syrinx story. The only other aspect of Pan's relation to love that interests Pope is his quasi-Virgilian role as a consoler of rustic loves: "Pan came and ask'd, what magic caused my smart, / Or what ill eyes malignant glances dart?" (*Pastorals*, III, 81–82). Cf. Baron Lyttelton ("An Irregular Ode Writ at Wickham in 1746") for another attempt to naturalize Pan in England; Pan and the Graces dance on Norwood Hill.

73. *The Story of Cephisa*, ll. 68–70. Compare Dryden's patriotic verses:

"Fair *Britain* all the World outvyes;
And *Pan*, as in *Arcadia* Reigns,
Where Pleasure mixt with Profit lies."

King Arthur, or the British Worthy (1691), V, 1.

74. In Ault, *Treasury of Unfamiliar Lyrics* (London, 1938), p. 375.

75. "For His Majesty's Birthday," quoted in R. T. Kerlin's very helpful *Theocritus in English Literature* (Lynchburg, Va., 1910), p. 71.

76. Bowles, "On a Landscape of Rubens," *Sonnets and Other Poems*, 1802. Kerlin, p. 85. "The Visionary Boy," *Sonnets*, 1789. Kerlin, p. 84. Compare Keats's "realm of Flora and old Pan" in "Sleep and Poetry," and the picturesque settings for Pan in *Endymion* and *Hyperion*. A direct influence seems perfectly possible.

77. Compare Herrick's "A Pastorall Sung to the King," Jonson's "Hymn to Pan," Dryden's versions of the fourth Satire of Persius and of the eighth book of the *Metamorphoses* (it does not occur in the originals), for the formula "Pan and Pales"; Pope's *Windsor Forest*, line 37, for "Pan and Pomona"; James Thomson's *Castle of Indolence* (II, xxviii) for both formulas at once — "Pan, Pales, Flora and Pomona play'd" — and William Diaper, "Dryades" (744–745), for "Pan and the Shepherd-youth."

For Pan as the deity of a radically different picturesque landscape, see Carolus Linnaeus' account of the rigorous and impenetrable Lapland forest (a region much associated with witchcraft at that time), as "the residence of Pan himself." "June 1" 1732, *Lachesis Lapponica, or a Tour in Lapland*, London, 1811.

78. The series includes Henry VIII (Spenser), James I (Jonson), Oliver Cromwell (Marvell), Charles II (Norris), James II and William of Orange (Dryden). The reference in *King Arthur* (see note 73 above), whether originally intended for William or not, could not in 1691 have been otherwise interpreted. I do not know of any comparable identification with Charles I, but there may well be one.

79. See R. P. Bond's *English Burlesque Poetry, 1700–1750* (Cambridge, Mass., 1932), pp. 302, 416.

80. See Frank E. Manuel, *The Eighteenth Century Confronts the Gods* (Cambridge, Mass., 1959), for a complex and valuable discusssion of the evolution of aims and methods in eighteenth-century mythography (with no special bearing on the Pan motif).

81. John Lemprière, *Bibliotheca Classica* (1788); Karl von Knoblauch, *Über den Pan und sein Verhältnis zum Sylvanus: Eine antiquarisch-philosophische Abhandlung* (1794), esp. p. 41; Richard Payne Knight, *Some Remains of the Worship of Priapus* (1786); Spence, *Polymetis*, 254–255; C. F. Dupuis, *Origine de tous les Cultes* (1794), esp. IV, ix. This would be a fascinating subject to pursue in detail, but, as I have indicated, its relevance to the literary motif is limited to certain special cases.

82. Not, Charles Morgan speculates, because he did not know the correct meaning, but because horns were easier to carve and equally honored by (albeit erroneous) biblical tradition. See his *Life of Michelangelo* (New York, 1960), p. 109.

83. Proposition IV, chap. viii, secs. i (p. 151) and iv (pp. 157–158) and Prop. IX, chap. xxxvi, sec. iv (p. 931).

84. Number xii in *Fables* (London, 1796), II, 64 (first ed., 1738). In Gay, of course, the balance of interest has been shifted from the picture to the poem.

85. Cf. Mark Schorer's comment in *William Blake: The Politics of Vision* (New York, 1946), p. 409.

86. Compare Lyly and Heywood for the association of Pan's non-Apollonian verse with Ignorance (Pan) and the Love of Folly (Midas). The Pan–Phoebus clash could also (as in the Renaissance) be made into a superficial rhetorical device, the background of which the poet could expect his audience to grasp

at once. See, for instance, Lyttelton's "Progress of Love," Eclogue II (1732), quoted in Kerlin, *Theocritus in English Literature*, p. 65.

"Nor Pan, nor Phoebus, tunes our artless reeds:
From love alone their melody proceeds."

87. O'Hara's burlesque (the text of which can be found in *The British Drama*, London, 1864, I, 148–155) has parallels in continental operas. A. E. M. Grétry's *Partition du Jugement de Midas* (Paris, 1778), rather more elevated in tone, lacks even the mild satirical touches of the burletta. J. S. Bach's pastoral opera *Der Streit zwischen Phoebus und Pan* (1731), Cantata no. 201 (Leipzig, 1930), is the only Pan opera which has not sunk into apparently well-deserved obscurity. Bach makes the same satirical point as Heywood (and Antony Fisgrave): Pan's songs either defend "popular" art or criticize, ignorantly, Phoebus' genuine art; Midas, the critic who supports Pan, deserves his fate. The popular art in question is the Italian opera of the time; Apollo's is Bach's own. M. A. Charpentier's pastorale *Le Jugement de Pan* (ca. 1690) is presumably similar; Georg Bronner's *Der Todt des grossen Pan* (1702) and J. E. Galliard's *Pan et Syrinx* (1717) employ other aspects of Pan less familiar to the musicians of the time. (See Grove's *Dictionary of Music and Musicians*, 1954, for the last three listed.) *Pan et Doris*, a heroic pastoral in one act (Paris, 1737), by J. B. de M. Aigueberre, brings on stage Pan, the pastoral lover, "déguisé en berger." See also H. J. Byron's pastoral extravaganza *Pan* (1865) for a late example: Lewis Carroll attended a performance, April 17, 1865. *Diaries* (New York, 1954), I, 229.

88. The suggestion that "Fisgrave" is a pseudonym is found in the Library of Congress copy (N75 F5).

89. Although the Midas story made no very strong appeal to the nonsatiric ages which followed, it did not die out entirely. Mary Shelley (*Midas*, a playlet memorable only as the context for her husband's "Hymn of Pan") and John Ruskin made references to the contest of Pan and Apollo without any of the comic-satiric overtones discussed here. Barry Cornwall makes a pair of fleeting references in his *Dramatic Scenes* (1820).

CHAPTER II. ROMANTIC PAN

1. *Works* (London, 1930), VI, 192. The last phrase is quoted again by Hazlitt in "English Students at Rome" (XVII, 139) less relevantly: "I did not consider that Nature is always the great thing, or that 'Pan is a God, Apollo is no more!'" The phrase is slightly ambiguous taken out of context; it states the equality of Pan and Apollo in the original, not the superiority of Pan.

2. See VI, 201, "On Lyly, Marlow [sic], Heywood," for Hazlitt's comments on Lyly's *Midas*; and p. 249 for "On Beaumont and Fletcher," where he misquotes Milton in order to turn a critical tag, changing the Pan symbol of Comus from a morally undesirable pagan deity to an essence of Nature. Beaumont and Fletcher are criticized for their haste and prodigality: "In the economy of nature's gifts, they 'misuse the bounteous Pan, and thank the Gods amiss.'" For Caliban, see "On the Tempest," II, 239; for Rembrandt, see "Table Talk. On the Picturesque and Ideal," VIII, 319. Hazlitt quotes (or misquotes) *Paradise Lost* IV, 266–268, "Universal *Pan* / Knit with the *Graces* and the *Hours* in dance," no less than four times, in each case to describe a painting by Claude

Lorrain (VI, 178; X, 13; XVI, 308; XVIII, 28). For Coleridge, see *Spirit of the Age* (1825), XI, 33.

3. This notion of a darker, infusing power is one Coleridge expressed more commonly in the figure of Bacchus. If the junction of Moses and Pan did not reach him directly from Huetius, it might have reached him indirectly through Andrew Tooke (VIII, v, pp. 71–73), who elaborates Huetius' very similar parallel of Moses and Bacchus. See J. B. Beer, *Coleridge the Visionary* (London, 1959), pp. 95–96, for a discussion of the "visionary" nature of Moses and of a Bacchus whom Coleridge considers to be "representative of the organic energies of the Universe, that work by passion and joy without apparent distinct consciousness . . . deity of all the vehement and awful passions." *Coleridge's Shakespearian Criticism*, I, 184–185.

4. "Clitumnus" is from the *Georgics*, IV, 126; the rest of the passage is based on Horace's *Odes*, I, 17.

> "Velox amoenum saepe Lucretilem
> Mutat Lycaeo Faunus et igneam
>   Defendit aestatem capellis
>   Usque meis pluviosque ventos"

and "utcumque dulci fistula . . . levia personuere saxa."

> Fleet Faunus often leaves his Lycaean hill
> To visit fair Lucretilis now and then;
>   And from my she-goats wards off fiery
>   Heat, and protects them from rainy windstorms.
>   . . . when from Faunus' pipe,
> His joyous pipe, O Tyndaris, echo sounds
>   From valleys and the smooth-worn rocks.

From *The Odes of Horace*, translated by Helen Rowe Henze. Copyright 1961 by the University of Oklahoma Press.

5. Published 1819. "Poems Dedicated to National Independence and Liberty," II, 5.

6. "It was not, however, pagan enough for Landor, who declared in his Landorian way that 'after eight most noble Pindaric verses on Pan and the Fawns and Satyrs, he lays hold on a coffin and a convict.'" Douglas Bush, *Mythology and the Romantic Tradition in English Poetry* (New York, 1957), p. 69.

7. London, 1781, p. 199. William King, in *An Historical Account of the Heathen Gods and Heroes* (1710), chapter xxix, does the same thing, more elaborately. He tells the story of Mercury turning into a goat to father Pan upon Penelope, and, like Tooke, transfers the story of the shepherd disguise (a variant version of the Mercury-Penelope story) to Pan's courtship of Dryope. See Alex Zwerdling's valuable discussion, "Wordsworth and Greek Myth," *University of Toronto Quarterly*, 33.4 (July 1964): 344, for evidence that Wordsworth owned and probably used Tooke.

8. Phurnutus (Cornutus) quoted in Tooke, p. 197.

9. Lucretius, *De Rerum Natura*, iv, 589f, supplies the earliest poetic version of the rationalistic explanation; it is, of course, more genuinely skeptical than those discussed here, since he was concerned to destroy the harmful effects of superstition rather than to preserve the beneficial effects of myth.

10. The effect is a little like the "visions and sudden terrors" of the Orphic Hymn, in which, however, as in Keats, Pan is on the whole benevolent. Cf.

Edward Baldwin's (William Godwin's) *Pantheon* (London, 1806), p. 104: "All the strange, mysterious and unaccountable sounds which were heard in solitary places, were attributed to Pan, the God of rural scenery." For a fuller account of the sources of the "Hymn to Pan," see Claude Lee Finney, *The Evolution of Keats's Poetry* (Cambridge, Mass., 1936), I, 261–266. In addition to the sources I mentioned, he stresses Sandys' version of the Syrinx story (*Ovid*, book I) and of Alciatus' emblem (*Ovid*, book XIV); Browne's version of Syrinx and of Pan's Palace in *Britannia's Pastorals* (book 2, song 4); Lemprière, Spence, and Diodorus Siculus for Pan's relation to the naiads and satyrs; and Lemprière, Tooke's *Pantheon*, and Sandys (*Ovid*, book XIV) for the universal Pan of the last stanza. (Though the changes needed to turn the schematic allegories of those three sources into Keats's more Orphic conception — emphasizing the infusing spirit rather than the external emblem — are greater and different in kind from the relatively simple assimilations of information in the earlier stanzas.)

11. *The Mystical Initiations: or, Hymns of Orpheus* (London, 1787), p. 130. The Hymn was also translated by Thomas Blackwell (1748).

12. Cf. Huetius' farfetched comparison of Pan and Moses, based, *inter alia*, on this characteristic, and the "solitary thinkings" of the "Hymn to Pan," which Finney (*Evolution of Keats's Poetry*, p. 267) connects with Sandys' "Pan is said to live solitarily, in that there is but one world."

13. *Proserpine and Midas: Two Unpublished Mythological Dramas*, ed. A. Koszul (London, 1922), esp. p. 53.

14. The references to Tmolus seated in judgment take us back to the original Ovidian version (*Met.* XI) in which Tmolus was in fact the judge and Midas an onlooker who disputed his decision; the Renaissance and eighteenth-century versions, whether for simplicity in staging or from fidelity to the original "emblematic" version in Whitney's *Emblems*, simply omit Tmolus.

15. *Notebooks*, November–December 1805, 2739.

16. Shelley makes another, passing, reference to Syrinx in "Orpheus":

> ". . . an endless spring of gloom
> Upon whose edge hovers the tender light,
> Trembling to mingle with its paramour, —
> But as Syrinx fled Pan, so night flies day."

For a more light-hearted version of Pan, Syrinx, and the problem of Art see Jules Laforgue's ironic fable "Pan et la Syrinx: ou l'Invention de la flûte à sept tuyaux" (1887), in his collection *Moralités légendaires*.

Wordsworth's phrase "Pan, invisible God" occurs in a part of the *Prelude* (VIII, 183) to which Shelley would not have had access in 1820. There is probably a common mythographical source for the deduction of Pan's invisibility from his Orphic universality (cf. Emerson), for example, Taylor, as summarized in Grabo's appendix (p. 132), "the deities of the pagan mythology personify, then, or symbolize, powers of the invisible God, the One," which "one" god is, of course, equated with Pan in interpretations of Orphic material (as in Taylor himself, and Cudworth). Carl Grabo, *The Meaning of the Witch of Atlas* (Chapel Hill, 1935), pp. 124–129. See the next note.

17. Ralph Cudworth, *The True Intellectual System of the Universe* (New York, 1837–1838), I, 458–459, (first ed. 1678). "God as displaying himself in the world [Pan] nor as endued with a plastic nature only . . . but as proceeding from a rational and intellectual principle, diffusing itself through all."

Cudworth was also fully aware of the concrete, schematic allegory of Pan, which the Romantic poets neglected.

18. See Spenser for a similar substitution of Faunus for Pan, but for (as I have hazarded) a different reason than mere congruousness.

19. Bush, *Romantic Tradition*, p. 54, describes it as a "very free adaptation." (*Die Piccolomini* is the second play in Schiller's trilogy *Wallenstein*.) Shelley had another view of the relationship of Christ and Pan, which he expressed in his early and unpublished "Essay on Christianity" (*The Prose of Shelley*, Albuquerque, 1954, p. 197): the death of Christ was "accompanied by an accumulation of tremendous prodigies . . . a visitation of that Universal Pan"; later in the same essay, somewhat confusingly, God "is neither the Proteus nor the Pan of the material world . . . [but the] interfused and overruling Spirit of all the energy and wisdom included within the circle of existing things" (p. 201). In Shelley's "Essay on the Devil and Devils" (p. 274), he blames the Christians for turning such "poetical personages" and "innocent beings" as the "ancient Gods of the woods . . . with their leader, the great Pan . . . to purposes of deformity and falsehood."

20. Letter to Thomas Jefferson Hogg, January 22, 1818, in W. S. Scott, *The Athenians* (London: Golden Cockerel Press, 1943), pp. 43–44.

21. W. S. Scott, ed., *Shelley at Oxford* (London, 1944), p. 61.

22. November 29, 1818. *Works*, VIII, 207. All Peacock quotations are from the New York, 1931, edition of the *Works*.

23. [Percy Bysshe Shelley], *Shelley and Mary* (London, 1882), p. 641. The Homeric epithets "Far-darting" and "Smynthian" (referring to a town in the Troad sacred to Apollo) are also used of Apollo in Taylor's translation of the Orphic Hymn to Apollo, *Mystical Initiations*, no. 33, p. 161.

24. *Shelley at Oxford*, pp. 64–65. The parenthetical phrase, like ΣΜΙΝΘΕΕΙ in the previous letter, is written in Greek characters in the text. The epithet "oreibateis" comes from an epigram "On a Statue of Pan" by Alcaeus of Messene, *Greek Anthology*, XVI, no. 226. "O Pan, who walkest on the mountains, breathe music with thy sweet lips."

25. See J. A. Notopoulos' discussion in *The Platonism of Shelley* (Durham, N. C., 1949), pp. 68–70, esp. note 177.

26. "Pan in Town," *Paper Money Lyrics* (written, 1825; published, 1837). *Poems and Plays*, in *Works*, VII, 101. The notion that Peacock pretends to attribute to Hunt, of Pan in town as a "fashionable arrival for the season," is very much in the manner of Lucian's "non-resident taxpayer" in a grotto under the Acropolis. There are similar Lucianic touches in Peacock's other satiric Pans.

27. Innumerable satires have been written on this basis, satirizing with one thrust both the notion of the gods and the conditions of earthly society. Heinrich Heine, Walter Pater, and Edmund Gosse provide later examples of the afterlife of the gods, but Gosse's *Hypolympia* is the only one of the three to include a Pan figure. *Calidore* is included under Unfinished Tales and Novels, *Works*, VIII, 303–341.

28. II, 66. Taylor is also guyed, and much less kindly, in chapters 26 and 27 of Isaac Disraeli's *Vaurien* (London, 1797), for ideas on the humanity of animals similar to those expressed here, and for "chaunting a noon-day hymn to Apollo" (p. 188). See Carl Van Doren's *Life of Thomas Love Peacock* (London, 1911), pp. 129–130, for details of Peacock's acquaintance with Taylor, and for the comment by a friend on Peacock's combination of skepticism with a generalized paganism: "if he had worshipped anything, Peacock would have been inclined to worship Jupiter, as it was said that Taylor did." See Van Doren, p. 245.

29. He actually resembles not Pan so much as Pan's messenger, the Satyr of *The Faithful Shepherdess* (to whom he is compared — p. 453 — as a shaggy admirer and servant of womanly loveliness).

30. *Works*, VII, pp. 29–30. *Rhododaphne* was finished in November 1817 and published in February 1818 (p. 439). Peacock's notes relate "Birds . . . to soothe old Pan's meridian rest" to Theocritus' first Idyll, as we might expect, but "Arcadian Daemogorgon, the father of Pan" is taken, we are told in a fine display of erudition, from "Natalis Comes," "Pronapides in his Protocosmus," and "Boccaccio . . . on the *Genealogy of the Gods*" (p. 94). (Some of these sources are also cited in Blackwell's *Letters Concerning Mythology*, London, 1748, p. 168).

31. The passage was written at least two months before Hunt's letter and six years before Byron's unpublished fragment "Aristomenes," either or both of which might well be extensions of Peacock's thought. (See Van Doren, *Life*, pp. 105–106, for evidence of Byron's interest in the poem.) See also the much later and more famous passage, in *Gryll Grange* (1861), *Works*, V, 79. "There can be no intellectual power resident in a wood, where the only inscription is not '*Genio loci*,' but 'Trespassers will be prosecuted' . . . No; the intellectual life of the material world is dead. Imagination cannot replace it."

32. *Works*, ed. Buxton Forman, II (London, 1880), 17–23. Also quoted in Peacock, VII, 441.

33. Virtually all of the critics mentioned in Bush's very helpful footnote on the question of the Romantic debt to Schiller (*Romantic Tradition*, p. 61) quote part of this passage. The specific verbal parallels they suggest, especially those with Wordsworth, are not very convincing; a really minor poet, like Felicia Hemans, provides much more convincing "echoes" of the sources imitated. See her *Modern Greece*, stanzas xxiii, lxiv, xc, and above all, xxvi and xxvii.

34. "Syrinx' Klage tönt' aus jenem Schilfe" (The cry of Syrinx sounds from every reed bank; stanza iv) and "Faun und Satyr taumeln ihm voran" (Faun and Satyr come reeling in before him; stanza viii, said of Bacchus) are the closest approaches to a Pan reference in the lyric *Die Götter Griechenlands*.

35. As, for instance, John Beaumont's *Gleanings of Antiquities* (London, 1724), of which part II is entitled "A Discourse of Oracles . . . To which is Added . . . an Account . . . of the Rise and Cessation of Oracles." More interestingly, John Potter, whose *Archaeologica Graeca* Mrs. Hemans cites in her own notes, also discusses it, mentioning Plutarch and Antony Van Dale (the latter the author of one of the best-known skeptical interpretations of the Death of Pan, the one upon which Fontenelle's *Histoire des Oracles*, 1687, was based), again without alluding to the Death of Pan. Thomas de Quincey's "The Pagan Oracles" (1842), in *Memorials and Other Papers* (1856), is a turgid reply to Fontenelle, with no Pan allusion. Cf. *Paradise Regained* I, 455–460. See *Modern Greece*, stanzas xxii, xxv, lxii, lxv, and lxxi, for Mrs. Hemans' evocations of nostalgia from "the voice of oracles gone by."

36. *Works of Lord Byron*, ed. Ernest Hartley Coleridge (London and New York, 1901), I, 566. The "autograph MS . . . now for the first time printed" is headed "Canto First. I." and signed "Cephalonia, Septr. 10th 1823." The editor suggests Coleridge's *Piccolomini* as a possible source for lines 5–11. Frederic Ewen's remark that Byron "approached Schiller as one who had not read Coleridge very attentively" (*Prestige of Schiller in England, 1788–1859*, New York, 1932, p. 122) and Bush's "halting imitation of Coleridge's regrets" (*Romantic Tradition*, p. 77) both confirm E. H. Coleridge's views on lines 5–11, but none of the three accounts for lines 1–4.

37. Mrs. Hemans uses a similar expression (stanza xxx), "how much hath perished there." We know that Byron commented ferociously upon her poem, finding it "good for nothing," partly because Mrs. Hemans had never been in Greece. This is not conclusive proof that he read the whole of the poem, which is rather long and moves slowly; he may never have reached stanza xxx.

38. Other Romantic Pans can be found in Barry Cornwall's *The Worship of Dian. A Sicilian Story* (2nd ed., 1820) and "A Vision" and "Michelangelo" from the same; "For a Fountain," in *The Oxford Book of English Verse* (1957). I have not discussed the Romantic versions of the legend of Cupid and Psyche; none that I have seen add anything to the interpretation of the Apuleian Pan.

Thomas Lovell Beddoes has a cryptic reference to Pan in *Death's Jest Book* (1825–1828), I, I: "O world, world! The gods and fairies left thee, for thou wert too wise; and now, thou Socratic star, thy demon, the great Pan, Folly, is parting from thee. The oracles still talked in their sleep, shall our grand-children say, till Master Merriman's kingdom was broken up: now is every man his own fool, and the world's cheerless." This appears to combine an oblique Plutarchan reference with something like the Pans of Erasmus' *Praise of Folly*.

The finest gathering of Pan pastiche is surely Horace Smith's *Amarynthus, the Nympholept: A Pastoral Drama* (London, 1821); directly in nearly two hundred lines and implicitly throughout the play, Fletcher (including the chaste and Christian emphases) has been brought up to date à la Keats and Wordsworth, with a dash of Theocritus and Herodotus to taste, an extensive versifying of encyclopedic allegory, and a rational interpretation as well. Crabb Robinson was not amused and expressed his discontent in almost Johnsonian terms: "an ill-chosen subject. Who will give himself the trouble to understand a fable involving the refinements of the Greek mythology? A pastoral poem encumbered with nymphs of the air and wood, priests and priestesses of Pan, etc. is hardly readable." *Books and Their Writers*, I, 409 (September 13, 1832).

CHAPTER III. VICTORIAN PAN

1. *Complete Works* (London, 1933), XIV, 319, 323. All Landor quotations are from this edition. Each of these idyls appeared in three versions. In 1815 and 1820 Latin versions were published. The versions cited here appeared in 1847, translated from the Latin; Landor made another translation which appeared in 1859 (printed by Wheeler in an appendix, p. 386 and p. 389). R. H. Super, in *Walter Savage Landor: A Biography* (New York, 1954), p. 451, gives the impression that the retranslation in 1857 owed nothing to the earlier English version, which Landor did not, apparently, remember making. For my purposes, there is no significant difference in any of the versions, although the earlier and longer translation is less elliptical and in some cases clearer. "Pitys" (1815) is of course earlier than most Romantic Pans (1817–1820), and the quarter-century gap between Latin and English versions corresponds roughly to the long barren interlude in English literature between the Romantic Pans and the rediscovery of Pan by the Brownings.

2. The earliest version seems to be Servius' (on *Ecl.* II, 31): Pan "a poetis fingitur cum Amore luctatus et ab eo victus, quia, ut legimus, omnia vincit Amor" (is depicted by the poets as wrestling with Love and defeated by him, since, as we read, Love conquers all). Cf. Natalis Comes, Giraldus, and Gower.

See Anthony Blunt, *Nicolas Poussin* (New York, 1967), I, fig. 108, for Matham's emblematic illustration of this theme, and for Poussin's own adaptations of it.

3. Libanius, *Orationes et Declamationes*, ed. J. Reiske (Altenburg, 1797), p. 1108, gives both versions. *Les XX Livres de Constantin César*, tr. Anthoine Pierre (Poitiers, 1545), cxxxv verso (more commonly known as the *Geoponica*, XI, 10), says Boreas "iecta la pucelle contre les pierres, dont elle mourut" (threw the maid against the stones, as a result of which she died); Earth changes her to a pine, but she continues to express her preference for Pan over Boreas: "car Pan est couronné de son germe mais il pleure et iecte larmes, quand Boreas vient à souffler" (for Pan is crowned with her wreath, but it weeps and sheds tears when Boreas comes to blow).

4. See also "Theron and Zoe," XIV, 306: "By Pan! / Who punishes with restless nights [nightmares; cf. Menander's *The Dyskolos*] the false"; "Hath Pan done this? Pan, who doth such strange things." "Corythos," XIII, 372: "While that bold wanton [Helen], fearing neither Pan / Nor Zeus." Compare *Hippolytus* 141–142, *Rhesus* 36–37, and especially *Agamemnon* (Chorus) 54–58. The two Pitys allusions not discussed in the text are at the end of "Cupid and Pan" (1859) where "a wreath less soft and fragrant shalt thou wear," and in "Crysaor" (XIII, 57): "No pine surrender'd by retreating Pan." For the Theocritean concluding "turn" in the poem "Pan," cf. Theocritus, XIV, 70, or Virgil, *Ecl*. III, 111. Other minor allusions in Landor are XV, 194, and XII, 6.

5. See Lionel Stevenson, "The Pertinacious Victorian Poets," in *Victorian Literature*, ed. Austin Wright (London: Oxford University Press, 1961), p. 26, for this formulation of the psychological aspects of Victorian myth.

6. Arthur J. Carr, "Tennyson as a Modern Poet," ibid., p. 320.

7. *Letters of Elizabeth Barrett Browning*, ed. F. G. Kenyon (New York, 1897), I, 3. See *Poetical Works* (Oxford, 1932) for the texts of the poems quoted.

8. *Letters*, I, 127. Compare James Russell Lowell's "The Foot-Path" (1868).

9. If T. J. Wise's holograph MS (facsimile) of the first sixteen stanzas is to be trusted, she did make the refrain less repetitious as she revised the poem. Only two of the refrains vary in form from the majority, "Pan, Pan is dead," as compared with seven variations, or nearly half, in the revised version of these stanzas. *A Browning Library: A Catalogue* (London, 1929), p. 79.

See also Mrs. Browning's minor allusions in "Wine of Cyprus" (p. 271; published in 1844), which includes a light-hearted hyperbole of a Pan who could drink deeper from that wine than the poetess herself could do, who "might dip his head so deep in / That his ears alone pricked out"; in the fragment of a projected drama, "Psyche Apocalypte" (published for private circulation; London, 1871); and in her paraphrases of Apuleius, "Psyche and Pan," *Works*, p. 586, and (briefly) "Marriage of Psyche and Cupid," p. 589, and of Nonnus, "How Bacchus Finds Ariadne Sleeping," p. 590.

10. "Lines Written in Kensington Gardens," *Poems* (Oxford University Press, 1940), p. 182. This stanza was included in Arnold's 1852 version (printed in 1867), but omitted from the final version (printed in 1877). Had the phrase by then become too much of a cliché? For an imitation of both Arnold and Tennyson, see John Buchan's "Through tributary hamlets ran / The piping of the rustic Pan," in "Oxford Prologizes," *Poems, Scots and English* (London, 1936). Arnold is very Keatsian in "Cromwell" (1843): "Sounds—such as erst the lone wayfaring man / Caught, as he journey'd, from the lips of Pan," but so, at about the same time, is Lowell: "Or heard . . . Mysterious tones from the lone pipe of Pan," "Sonnet — to Keats," 1842 (*Uncollected Poems*: Philadelphia, 1950, p. 14). The luxuriantly pictorial Bacchic procession of Arnold's

"The Strayed Reveller" (1849) includes but does not describe Pan, though the "sweet fumes [of Circe's wine are] . . . more soft, ah me! / More subtle-winding / Than Pan's flute music." In *Empedocles on Etna* (Act II) "jealous Pan with Marsyas did conspire," but Pan's own semiludicrous competition with Apollo lacks the tragic intensity Arnold wished.

11. Bush, *Romantic Tradition*, p. 377. He cites Browning's *Letters* (ed. Hood), pp. 246, 298, 373. See Robert Spindler, *Robert Browning und die Antike* (Leipzig, 1930), II, 52, for a discussion of Browning's sources in Lucian and Herodotus.

12. *Ausserlösenes Schönes Werck* (Augsburg, n.d.), 11, 89, and compare *Songe du Poliphile* (Paris, 1561), p. 23. Lairesse's "feigned story" is from his *Art of Painting*, tr. J. F. Fritsch (London, 1778), p. 247. The story Browning uses in the poem is from Moschus' "Pan, Echo and the Satyr"; compare Browning's free adaptation with Shelley's fairly close translation.

13. See, to name a few of many examples, Poussin's "Pan and Syrinx" and several "Bacchanals"; Rubens' "Diana"; Boucher's "Pan and Syrinx"; and, in a more modern vein, Arnold Böcklin's "Syrinx flieht vor Pan" (1859). The distinction between "Pan" and "satyr," fairly important in literature, is both harder to maintain and less important in painting. The "Nymphs and Satyr" of A. W. Bouguereau (1873) is almost certainly a painting of the Pan story from Philostratus' *Imagines*, available, for instance, in Goethe's translation of 1818. Perhaps paintings of Apuleius' "Pan and Psyche" scene could be found, showing a kindly Pan as vigorous as Browning's. But Browning's description is unlikely to owe anything to the sentimental and softly youthful Pan of Burne-Jones' illustration for "Pan and Psyche" in Morris' *The Earthly Paradise*. The Pre-Raphaelite style of Burne-Jones is very nearly as unfair to Morris as it is to Apuleius.

14. H. C. Goddard, *Studies in New England Transcendentalism* (New York, 1908), p. 74, describes the effect on Emerson of Wordsworth's "description of the influence of nature upon the mind of a boy." Compare Emerson's essay "The Poet": "For poetry was all written before time was, and whenever we . . . can penetrate into that region where the air is music, we hear those primal warblings and attempt to write them down . . . The men of more delicate ear write down these cadences more faithfully, and these transcripts, though imperfect, become the songs of the nations." *Works* (Boston, 1893), III, 15. All quotations from Emerson's prose are from this edition.

15. Emerson had been dipping into Beaumont and Fletcher around 1835, according to Goddard, *New England Transcendentalism*, p. 78.

16. Yvor Winters' comment on "Emerson and his contemporaries," in "The Significance of *The Bridge*," *In Defense of Reason* (Denver, 1943), p. 587. "He could speak of . . . impulse as if it were conscience," and, of course, vice versa.

17. Emerson could have dipped into the allegorical tradition at many points, but for the sake of simplicity I shall assume that his chief sources were Bacon's *The Wisdom of the Ancients* and Cudworth's *True Intellectual System of the Universe*, since the parallels are close and both are authors he is known to have valued. In his introduction to Plutarch's *Moralia* (Boston, 1883), I, he couples these authors in the same sentence (linked, less usefully for our purposes, by a third, Dryden) as instances of the great influence of the *Moralia* upon English literature. It is amusing that the one influence that it might have had upon Emerson's Pans was one that he (like Bacon but unlike Cudworth) stoutly resisted; the *Moralia* contains, of course, the story of the Death of Pan — the one major story almost impossible to mesh with an Orphic Pan, though

Cudworth (I, 461) and Peacock attempt it. In minor poetry it is usually done by way of a strained negation — "Pan is Nature and therefore cannot die." See Goddard, *New England Transcendentalism*, pp. 68, 70, for other evidence of Emerson's extensive and early reading of Bacon and Cudworth.

18. "Boswell's Life of Johnson," *Critical and Miscellaneous Essays* (New York, 1899), III, 75. This essay was first printed in 1832, and Emerson is very likely to have read it.

19. Pico, *Conclusiones*, no. 28. See Edgar Wind, *Pagan Mysteries of the Renaissance* (New Haven, 1958), p. 164. Compare also Cudworth, *True Intellectual System*, "Which matter of the universe is always substantially the same, and neither more nor less, but only Proteanly transformed into different shapes" (I, 94).

20. Page 297. See Emerson's "Nature" (1846) for his one long reference to Proteus: "*Natura naturans*, the quick cause before which all forms flee as the driven snows; itself secret, its works driven before it in flocks and multitudes, (as the ancients represented nature by Proteus, a shepherd,) and in undescribable variety" (III, 146). He makes several other very brief allusions to Proteus, of a conventional nature, that do not affect the argument one way or the other. There is an obscure reference to Pan in "Alphonso of Castile" (1847): "Puny man and scentless rose / Tormenting Pan to double the dose" (p. 28), which presents Pan as a spirit at the heart of nature, yet somewhat less powerful than the supreme Pan of the other poems.

21. Theocritean imitations in English neglect the possibility of terror, such as it is (and Theocritus' homespun realism as well), in favor of nostalgia, lament, or simply pastoral background and atmosphere. R. T. Kerlin's *Theocritus in English Literature* tends to confirm my own impression of the extreme scarcity of the terror motif, finding it only in Swinburne's "Pan and Thalassius" among his innumerable examples of Theocritean influence. There is, of course, no necessary connection between such influence and an interest in Pan; consider Tennyson — whom Kerlin finds among the most "Theocritean" of English poets — who scarcely mentions Pan.

22. Unless otherwise stated quotations from Swinburne's poems are from the six-volume edition published in London in 1906. For "A Nympholept" see VI, 127–134.

23. *Praep. Ev.* 189c–d, 190b.

24. *The French Revolution* (London, 1837), vol. III, bk. 1, chap. 1. Compare Baudelaire's skit on the Revolutionary Pan in "L'Ecole païenne" (1852):

"Dans un banquet commémoratif de la révolution de Février, un toast a été porté au dieu Pan . . .

—— Mais, lui disais-je, qu'est-ce que le dieu Pan a de commun avec la révolution?

—— Comment donc? répondait-il; mais c'est le dieu Pan qui fait la révolution. Il est la révolution.

—— D'ailleurs, n'est-il pas mort depuis longtemps? [Plutarch's story follows]

—— C'est un bruit qu'on fait courir. Ce sont de mauvaises langues . . . Il va revenir.

—— Il parlait du dieu Pan comme du prisonnier de Sainte-Hélène."

"At a banquet commemorating the February revolution, a toast was proposed to the god Pan . . .

'But,' I said to him, 'what has the god Pan in common with the revolution?'

'How can you ask?' he replied; 'it's the god Pan who made the revolution, of course. He is the revolution.'

'Besides, hasn't he been dead for a long time?'

'That's a rumor that people spread around. Nasty gossip . . . He's going to come back.'

He spoke of the god Pan as if he were the prisoner of St. Helena."

25. See the Chorus from *Atalanta in Calydon* for Swinburne's earliest and best-known allusion: "Pan by noon and Bacchus by night" inspire an erotic terror rather different from the type discussed here (and more usual in English poetry), in the objects of their amorous pursuit. Compare Meredith's light hearted triptych on the pursuit of nymphs, "Daphne," "The Rape of Aurora" (both 1851), and "The Teaching of the Nude" (1892), where Pan (or the Satyr) is partly Peeping Tom, partly active ally of Apollo's rough wooings:

> "But all nature is against her!
> Pan, with all his sylvan troop,
> Thro' the vista'd woodland valleys
> Blocks her course with cry and whoop!"

And, as in Swinburne's "Ripe grasses trammel a travelling foot," normally passive nature is made malignantly active; Daphne's sense of panic is personified in the vines and plants. But Meredith is more like Browning in his concern with character:

> "Musing on the fate of Daphne,
> Many feelings urged my breast,
> For the God so keen desiring,
> And the nymph so deep distrest."

26. Written before September 1842, at which point it had been in her possession for some time (*Letters*, I, p. 109); published in *A Day at Tivoli, With Other Verses* (London, 1849), pp. 109–115. In a note on p. 244, Kenyon admits that the "paraphrase has been made through the medium of a literal English translation; the writer himself not knowing German." See *Letters*, I, 130, for her further comment on "The Dead Pan."

27. *Poetical Works*, p. 597. In section III of this essay, p. 616, she makes her only other reference to the death of Pan: "When he [John Damascenus] writes out of his heart . . . he is another man, and almost a strong man; for the heart being sufficient to speak we want no Delphic oracle — 'Pan is NOT dead.' " As this was first printed in March 1842 (the *Athenaeum*, March 12), it may have been written before she saw Kenyon's paraphrase. The possible distinction in Spenser's passage between Pan as Christ and Pan as the Christian divinity (discussed in chapter I) is not relevant in this context.

28. Pierre Albouy, *La Création mythologique chez Victor Hugo* (Paris, 1963), chapter one, has an excellent discussion of this debate, which seems to have resulted in more than one vaguely Miltonic "théogonie chrétienne."

29. Book II of *Heinrich Heine über Ludwig Börne* (Hamburg, 1840) consisted of selections from Heine's Heligoland Journal (the rest of which is unpublished) for the period July 1 to August 19, 1830. It does not seem to have been translated at that time, and I do not know whether Mrs. Browning's German was as good then as it was in 1860, when she translated some poems of Heine. She makes an inconclusive reference to Heine in a letter of 1846 (*Letters*, I, 301); in a letter of 1854 (II, 175) she pities Heine's "living death" and rejoices in his "change of opinion" of 1848. Sol Liptzin (*English Legend of Heinrich Heine*, New York, 1959, p. 56) claims, not surprisingly, that "English

readers" had been "revolted by [Heine's] earlier cynicism and bitter irony" and quotes this letter of 1854 to illustrate a shift in feeling.

30. This refrain ends three consecutive entries: August 1, in interrogative form (p. 116); August 6 (p. 124) and August 10 (p. 132), in exclamatory form. It occurs a fourth time in the text (p. 104) of Heine's German translation of Plutarch's story. On p. 104 and p. 116, Heine uses the adjective "grosse" in the phrase.

31. *Kasidah of Hâjî Abdû el-Yezdî* (New York, 1929), p. 30, section IV, lines 24–31. The poem was written in 1853 and first published in 1880. Cf. Heine, p. 109, for a discussion of the Trinity.

32. "The Death of Pan," *Ballads and Lyrics* (London, 1859), p. 52.

33. *A Modern Faust and Other Poems* (London, 1888), pp. 49–58. "Pan" (in Book III, canto ii, of the title poem) is introduced as an "ode . . . responsive to the songs / A German, and an English poet made" (p. 48). Such Pans did not have to be solemn ones. See Dean Mansel's *Phrontisterion* (1852), in *Three Oxford Ironies* (London, 1927), p. 92, for a "Hymn to the Infinite" by a chorus of German professors who equate Pan with the "Absolute-Infinite, / The Universe-Ego, the Plenary-Void," and much else, and rejoice that "the great God Pan is alive again."

34. London, 1891, 58 pp. I know of two rather muddled twentieth-century versions of this general type. Geoffrey Dearmer's "The Death of Pan," in *The Day's Delight* (London, 1923), p. 39, shows Pan dying because Nature has deserted him for a new allegiance to Christ. His enemy, the Child, mercifully nurses the dying god, and digs his grave. Laurence Whistler's "The Death of Pan: A Fragment," in *The World's Room* (London, 1949), p. 10 (also printed in 1932), postulates, in ninety-nine blank verse lines, Pan's survival into the Christian era, sad, ill, and frightened, taken by passing Christians for Satan himself. It is not long before an "awful voice arose, / Wailing upon the darkness — PAN IS DEAD!" (p. 13).

35. "A hundred lesser spirits panted 'Pan!' " is somewhat below his usual standard. *Complete Poetical Works* in two volumes (London, 1901), I, 30.

36. *La Légende des siècles*, XXII, i, iv.

37. I, 34. Somewhat of a sentimentalizing of Hugo's evolutionary revelation of godhood. Buchanan ends this poem in a Tennysonian vein, with Pan's

> ". . . . wondrous music dying afar away
> Upon the fringes of the setting sun."

Compare "Pan, or the Myth of Eubulus," in *The King's Sacrifice and Other Poems* (London, 1876), pp. 213–225, which employs a very similar myth of "Pan empire bent, with Zeus dethroned." The anonymous author uses Hugo's "Je suis Pan; Jupiter, à genoux!" (so punctuated) as an epigraph. Like the fallen giant of Hugo's "Le Titan," Pan is at first imprisoned in the rocks.

38. Hugo, "Le Satyre," iv.

39. "Pan and Apollo and great Zeus are dead / And Jesus Christ hangs cold upon the Cross" (II, 366; cf. II, 11). Balder and Gautama (cf. Roden Noel) are among the many other gods whose death is of interest. For other references to Pan in Buchanan's poetry, see I: 35, 66, 161; II: 5, 19–21, 43, 101, 105, 113, 125, 149, 218, 225, 260, 396, 407. For the Death of the Gods, see also I, 287; II: 104, 119f, 309, 312, 342, 376, 428. Compare also, of course, Keats's "forlorn divinity / The pale Omega of a withered race" (*Fall of Hyperion*, I, 297–298) and his "wandering in vain about bewildered shores" (*Hyperion*, III, 9). Buchanan often

associates fallen godhood with drowning and marshy lakes; "Behung with weary weeds and mosses dark" (II, 113) gives a faintly Keatsian effect.

40. Other Pans in Lowell include two pseudo-Keatsian ones: the "Sonnet to Keats," quoted above in connection with Arnold, and "The Pregnant Comment" (1888), where

> "Like Poussin's nymphs my pulses dance
> And whirl my fancy where it sees
> Pan piping 'neath Arcadian trees,
> Whose leaves no winter-scenes rehearse
> Still *young* and glad as Homer's verse."

(Italics mine.) Keats's "old" ("Sleep and Poetry," l. 102), I find preferable on iconological grounds. A detailed comparison of Lowell's "Invita Minerva" (1855) and Mrs. Browning's "A Musical Instrument" (1859) might prove illuminating. "The double pipes of Life and Death" are, in context, weakly Emersonian. Strongly Emersonian, with a touch of Carlyle, is Lowell's "Essay on Wordsworth" of 1875: Wordsworth's "appropriate instrument, the pastoral reed . . . that which Pan endowed with every melody of the visible universe, — the same in which the soul of the despairing nymph took refuge and gifted with her dual nature, — so that ever and anon, amid the notes of human joy or sorrow, there comes suddenly a deeper and almost awful tone, thrilling us into dim consciousness of a forgotten divinity." *Among My Books*, in *Works* (Cambridge, Mass. 1904), III, 228.

41. "Hymn to Physical Beauty" (1896), *Lyrics* (London, 1935), p. 51. This is the first association of Pan with homosexuality since the time of the Greek Anthology (for example, Loeb II, p. 289, no. 535; Loeb III, p. 183, no. 338), so far as I am aware.

42. The rest of the book to which the essay "Le Grand Pan" forms the eighty-four page introduction is taken up with questions of social, economic, and political reform in contemporary France. Quotations are taken from the edition published in Paris, 1919.

43. Perhaps the Dutch socialist Herman Gorter is an "unusual romantic." His Universal Pan (*Pan: een Gedicht*, Amsterdam, 1908) seems to be closely linked with "the soul of man under Socialism." See also his earlier poem *Mei*.

44. Clemenceau refers to this poem on page 27 of the essay. See André Dumas' note on page 366 of the Garnier edition for a concise statement of Hugo's rationalist position, and Albouy, *Création mythologique*, esp. pp. 234–236, 260, for Hugo and the "myth of humanity."

Edgar Quinet's Pan-filled *Merlin l'Enchanteur* (ca. 1877) is another fictional version of this intellectual-mythological scheme (see I, 475; II, 417), which perhaps owes something to Jules Michelet: "On avait follement dit: Le grand Pan est mort. Puis voyant qu'il vivait, on l'avait fait un dieu du mal; à travers le chaos, on pouvait s'y tromper. Mais voici qu'il vit harmonique dans la sublime fixité des lois qui dirigent l'étoile et qui non moins dirigent le mystère profond de la vie." (Foolishly they said: The great Pan is dead. Then seeing that he was still living, they made him into a god of evil; in the midst of chaos, it was possible to make a mistake. But here he is, living harmoniously in the sublime firmness of the laws which direct the stars and which, no less, direct the profound mystery of life.) The epigraph to Act II of Charles van Lerberghe's *Pan: Comédie satirique*, 1906; no further attribution given.

Michelet's comment on "La Mort des dieux," *La Sorcière*, I, 17, takes a slightly different tack, giving Pan a symbolic place in the mythology of nihilism:

" 'Le grand Pan est mort.' L'antique Dieu universel de la Nature était fini. Grande joie. On se figurait que, la Nature étant morte, morte était la tentation. Troublée si longtemps de l'orage, l'âme humaine va donc reposer . . . La Nature va disparaître, la vie s'éteindre, qu'enfin on touche à la fin du monde . . . Tout tombe, s'écroule, s'abîme. Le Tout devient le Néant: 'Le grand Pan est mort!' " ("The great Pan is dead." The ancient universal god of Nature was finished. Jubilation. They imagined that, Nature being dead, temptation was dead. The human soul, troubled so long by the storm, is now going to rest . . . Nature is going to disappear, life to be extinguished, at last the end of the world is near . . . Everything falls, crumbles, is engulfed. The All becomes Nothingness: "The great Pan is dead!")

45. Since he cites works by Milton, Shelley, Swinburne, Leopardi, and Schiller, as well as Heine's "Gods of Greece" and other works of Heine, not including *Ludwig Börne* — in none of which the death of Pan is emphasized — along with Mrs. Browning's "The Dead Pan," he is clearly considering the death of Pan as the most vivid special case of the death of pagan myth. *Satires and Profanities* (London, 1884), pp. 105–109.

The most eccentric fruit of the prose tradition appeared in 1913: Leonard Stuart's *The Great God Pan: An All-Time Story* (Tudor Society: New York, 1913). It consists largely of a popularized but fairly well-informed account of Pan's mythical and legendary life; its purpose is to aid the growth of an ethical Christian "Gospel of Humanity" by dispelling such legends.

46. IV, 187. See also *Clarel*, I, 74, 161; II, 190, 260; III, 141; and *Collected Poems*, pp. 219, 238–239, 249, 261 (an Arcadiac variant), and 325.

47. Up to this point, I have given at least a footnote to any English Pan reference that has come to my attention. But about a hundred and forty minor poems, the great majority of which were written between 1880 and 1914, will be discussed here generically. An ample bibliography of such poems can be assembled simply by conflating the relevant references in Bush's bibliography (*Romantic Tradition*, pp. 560f), which is an indispensable aid in this area of research, and Helen H. Law's *Bibliography* (1955), pp. 28–30. My own searchings turned up many others, and there are certainly many more scattered about in the periodicals and slim volumes of the period. (I came across about fifty items for the first time in each of the bibliographies named.)

48. This is obviously amusing and suggestive rather than conclusive. I am assuming that her investigation of Pan was not simply much more thorough than that for other deities, so that an exhaustive list, if such were possible, would, while increasing the totals, preserve roughly the same proportions. In my listings I have included many allusions of interest and have not adhered to her implied requirement that the poems be chiefly about Pan.

49. Bush, *Romantic Tradition*, pp. 295, 530, 461.

50. Oscar Wilde, "Pan: A Double Villanelle"; J. C. Powys, "The Faun," *Poems* (London, 1899), p. 76. Compare "Earth-Worship" (p. 10): "Let me grow part of thee, / Forgetting all the thoughts and ways of man, / Deep-region'd PAN."

51. Robert Chapman and Jonathan Bennett, introduction to the *Anthology of New Zealand Verse* (Oxford, 1956), xxi. For some pleasant examples of the "Austral Pan" and a discussion of the vitality of the earth-god as a poetic symbol of the Australian national spirit up to the Great Depression, which killed Pan, see T. Inglis Moore, "The Passing of Pan," *Australian Quarterly*, 17.1 (March 1945): 76–84.

52. James B. Kenyon's "Syrinx" — "Leave me, O Pan; thou hast been made

the fool / Of thy hot love" (*Songs in All Seasons*, Boston, 1885, p. 111) — and Lady Margaret Sackville's "Pan and the Maiden" (*Poems*, London, 1901, p. 1) are more sensitive and interesting than the majority of versions. Aleister Crowley's sonnet "Syrinx and Pan" is more temperately Browningesque than his other Pan poems. *Works* (London, 1907), III, 119.

53. Amelia J. Burr, "Syrinx," *Life and Living* (New York, 1916), p. 77. Teresa Hooley, "Prayer to Pan," *Selected Poems* (Oxford, 1947), p. 116. See Lady Margaret Sackville's "Syrinx" (1911–1912) in *Selected Poems* (London, 1919), p. 40–45, for a more intelligent version of this theme; Leonora Speyer's "A Note from the Pipes" (1919) in *A Canopic Jar* (New York, 1921), p. 67, is a less overtly masochistic version.

54. *Cakes and Ale* (1930), chap. 11.

55. John Symonds, *The Great Beast: The Life of Aleister Crowley* (New York, 1952), pp. 293, 297. See also the *Sunday Express* (November 26, 1922): "In 1910 Crowley . . . cultivated an immoral society for the worship of the god Pan; and he organized every kind of evil rite." Quoted in P. R. Stephensen, *The Legend of Aleister Crowley* (London, 1930), p. 138. More explicit detail about the "evil rites" (homosexual acts) and the Pan symbols of Crowley's paintings and liturgy can be found in Symonds' later book *The Magic of Aleister Crowley* (London, 1958).

56. Crowley, *Magick in Theory and Practice* (Paris, 1929), pp. vii–xiv; also quoted by Symonds, *The Great Beast*, p. 141. It was first published in *Equinox* III (Detroit, 1919). Crowley gives lines 693–698 of Sophocles' *Ajax*, in Greek, as an epigraph: "I thrill with rapture, I soar on wings of sudden joy! O Pan, O Pan, appear to us, O Pan, roving o'er the sea, from the craggy ridge of snow-beaten Cyllene, king who makest dances for the gods." (Tr. R. C. Jebb, Cambridge, 1896.) Crowley can hardly be said to have improved on the original. Burco Partridge, in *A History of Orgies* (New York, 1960), p. 215, describes it as "one of his most successful poems and a fair statement of his faith," which seems a gloomy prospect on both counts.

See Victor B. Neuburg's *Triumph of Pan* (Equinox: London, 1910) for sadistic Swinburnian eroticism in a less coherent version of the Crowley manner (esp. pp. 6–7, 9, 19, 50, 145, 166). Neuburg was closely associated with Crowley for some years and had been a leading light of the "Pan-Society." See Symonds, *The Great Beast*, p. 216, and Jean Overton Fuller, *The Magical Dilemma of Victor Neuburg* (London, 1965).

57. *This Side of Paradise* (New York, 1948), p. 36 (first published in 1920).

58. Pages 16, 20. See also pp. 13–15, 17, 22, 26, 33, 35, 37, 49.

The small number of Pan poems written in the idiom of modern poetry will be discussed later. Another class of minor poetry which I am omitting is made up of the very respectable reworkings of classical themes by very respectable poets: versions of "Cupid and Psyche" by Mrs. Browning (1845), Robert Bridges (1885, the year of Pater's prose version in *Marius the Epicurean*), Sturge Moore (1904), and William Morris (in *The Earthly Paradise*, 1868–1870). I found Morris' the liveliest. In 1874, Burne-Jones, overlooking the epithet "old" in Morris' text, painted a youthful sentimental Pan looking down upon a yearning Psyche, as an illustration to the poem. The picture is in the Fogg Museum at Harvard, and details are given in the Fogg Museum Catalogue *Paintings and Drawings of the Pre-Raphaelites*, 1946, p. 35. Sophie Jewett, seeing the painting, and apparently not having read the poem, wrote a poem of her own ("Pan and Psyche: A Painting by Sir Edward Burne-Jones," *The*

Pilgrim and Other Poems, New York and London, 1896, p. 62), which makes Pan into Psyche's wistfully unsuccessful lover, rather than her counselor. There were pitfalls in the path of the Pre-Raphaelite marriage of the arts. Sturge Moore's "Hercules and Omphale" leaves out Ovid's comedy of Pan and the transvestites (*Fasti* II, 352), and reduces Pan's role to that of a vague fear in the woods. See also T. I. M. Forster's tedious extended pastiche of the "Nativity Ode" (*Pan, a Pastoral of the First Age*, 1840), William Aytoun's "universal Pan" in *Firmilian* (1854), and especially a marvelous late development of some Keatsian and Meredithian possibilities, Lord de Tabley's "Ode to Pan" (1893): "To Pan the bud-expander, who awakes / Nature, and is a god in nature's core."

59. Ruskin, "Athena Chalinitis" (1869), *Works* (London, 1905), XIX, 343. In "Architecture and Painting IV: Pre-Raphaelitism" (1853), he applies the dichotomy of Pan and Christ to education much as Mrs. Browning applied it to poetry: "Ask yourselves what you expect your own children to be taught . . . Is it Christian history, or the histories of Pan and Silenus? Your present education, to all intents and purposes, denies Christ." *Works*, XII, 142. See also XXIX, 271, and XXVII, 579.

60. "Et Tu in Arcadia Vixisti," VIII, 126. *Pan's Pipes*, II, 201. "The Oise in Flood," from *An Inland Voyage* (1878), I, 70–71, 77. See his letter to Sidney Colvin (January or February 1878), à propos of the illustrations for *An Inland Voyage*, saying that the river should look "'cruel, lewd and kindly' all at once. There is more sense in that Greek myth of Pan than in any other that I recollect except the luminous Hebrew one of the Fall . . . religions are no more than representations of life" (*Works*, XX, 372). All quotations from Stevenson are from the *Works*, Vailima edition (London, 1922).

61. Symonds thought highly of Burne-Jones' pictorial treatment of myth: "tales so trite as that of Pan and Syrinx . . . evolving from their kernel something which is vitally in sympathy with modern thought." "Nature Myths and Allegories," *Essays Speculative and Suggestive*, II (London, 1890), p. 148. I have been unable to locate a Burne-Jones painting of Pan and Syrinx.

62. *Greek Studies*, 1895 (London, 1899), pp. 7–10, esp. p. 8.

63. Symonds, *Essays Speculative*, pp. 134, 128, 80. "Rimini," *Sketches and Studies in Italy and Greece*, second series (London, 1900), p. 22. Cf. "Landscape," *Essays Speculative*, pp. 79, 101; *Sketches*, third series, p. 277, and first series, p. 63.

64. *In the Key of Blue* (London, 1893), p. 184. *Sketches*, first series, pp. 88–89. See also third series, p. 180. These pages could be amusingly counterpointed by Payne Knight's account, a century earlier, of some veritable "remnants of glad Nature-worship."

The use of Pan to provide a specifically classical atmosphere in highly charged travel literature, making a "palimpsest" of present and past, to help in achieving mood, has lasted well into this century. See for example, D. H. Lawrence's *Twilight in Italy* and *Sea and Sardinia*; Axel Munthe's *Story of San Michele*, (New York, 1931), pp. 443–446, 496; Freya Stark's *Perseus in the Wind* (Boston, 1956), p. 172; and especially Gerhart Hauptmann's *Griechischer Frühling* (Berlin, 1908), pp. 164–165, where neopagan sentimentality about the Death of Pan is mingled with something like the Dionysian of Nietzsche and the primitivism of Knut Hamsun.

65. O. Henry, for instance, uses "Pan's pipe notes" to symbolize the lure of the farm for the boy who should never have gone to the city. "The Defeat of the City" (1908). See also "Roads of Destiny."

66. "Lecture on Modern Poetry" (1906) and "Letters from America" (1911) in *The Prose of Rupert Brooke* (London, 1956), pp. xii, 59.

67. London, 1912, p. 151, and see also pp. 83, 110, 116, 133–134, 218 for "Peter Pannish" references. *Poems and Songs* (1912), pp. 39, 65–66, 74, gives a more traditional Arcadiac view, but see *Poems and Songs*, Second Series, p. 45, for Middleton's most graceful Pan poem, with its sharp denial of the generally received tradition: "Not as a goat, but as a lovely child."

68. *The Garden God* (London, 1906), pp. 19, 50. The story resembles the visions of Pan told of by E. F. Benson, E. M. Forster, and Algernon Blackwood.

69. "The Death of Pan," "The Prayer of the Flowers," and "The Tomb of Pan," *Fifty-One Tales* (London, 1915), pp. 5, 25, 109. See Dunsany's autobiography, *Bright Patches of Sunlight* (London, 1938), p. 155, for his claim to have translated certain (unspecified) prose poems of Turgenev from the French. For "The Nymphs" see *Poems in Prose* (London, 1906), p. 298. See also Turgenev's "The Song of Triumphant Love," *Dream Tales* (London 1906), p. 178.

70. *Father and Son* (New York, 1907), p. 324. See also p. 280. Compare Maurice Egan's description of Maurice de Guérin:

> "A pagan heart, a Christian soul had he,
> He followed Christ, yet for dead Pan he sighed,
> Till earth and heaven met within his breast:
> As if Theocritus in Sicily
> Had come upon the Figure crucified
> And lost his gods in deep, Christ-given rest."

Preludes (Philadelphia, 1880), p. 21 (and see p. 22).

71. *The Roadmender* (London, 1931), pp. 59, 66, 108. Cf. *Ajax* (693–698) for "snowbound Cyllene." "Michael Fairless" is the pseudonym of Margaret Fairless Barber (d. 1901).

72. J. S. Collis, *Havelock Ellis: Artist of Life* (New York, 1959), p. 83; no source given. Edward Carpenter, *My Days and Dreams* (London, 1916), p. 225, describes Ellis' "fine free head and figure, as of some great god Pan." Also quoted by Collis, p. 83.

73. The Renaissance ceremonial on its last legs may be exemplified by J. H. Reynolds' doggerel ("Odes and Addresses to Great People," in collaboration with Thomas Hood, 1825) where "R. W. Elliston, Esquire" is identified as "Immortal Pan / Of all the pipes that play in Drury Lane!" Here the monarchical and artistic aspects of Pan are combined in the person of a theater manager. In *Poems of Thomas Hood* (Oxford, 1920), p. 725.

74. *Letters*, April 9, 1842 (New York, 1939), III, 44. Cf. Robert Louis Stevenson's remark that Thoreau was the original of Hawthorne's Donatello because of his friendship for animals. Part one of "Henry David Thoreau," *Familiar Studies of Men and Books*, in *Works*, IV, 149. See Thoreau's *A Week on the Concord and Merrimack Rivers* for his own account of his constancy at Pan's shrine.

75. Bronson Alcott, diary entry for November 10, 1856. As summarized, incorrectly, in Thoreau's *Familiar Letters* (Boston, 1906), VI, 298. Alcott himself (*Journals*, Boston, 1938) mentions Hercules, Bacchus, satyr, Silenus (p. 290), and Sylvanus and "the modern Pantheon," (p. 294), but not Pan.

Two modern authors shared (or perhaps inherited) Thoreau's version of Alcott's view of Whitman. Hart Crane's inaccurate pun "Panis angelicus" ("Cape Hatteras," *The Bridge*, IV, 1930, in *Complete Poems*, New York, 1958, pp. 40–42) means "angelic Pan," as can be seen in its context of "aureole" and "pasture-shine." Edwin Markham is even more explicit: "O shaggy god of the ground, barbaric Pan" (*New Poems: Eighty Songs at Eighty*, New York, 1932, p. 95).

76. *William Blake: A Critical Study* (London, 1868), p. 111.

77. March 3, 1961, p. 98. A number of similar comparisons are of interest. Tennyson commented on the poet De Tabley: "He is Faunus! He is a woodland creature!" (as quoted in Bush, *Romantic Tradition*, p. 426). Edith Cooper described Sturge Moore (in 1901) as "a primeval forest god — terrible — the source of panic and of the cruel laughter of simplicity"; to this Moore's biographer, F. L. Gwynn, added that Moore had "a Pan-like face, gentle and yet saturnine" (*Sturge Moore and the Life of Art*, Lawrence, Kansas, 1951, p. 72). Robert Payne's *The Great God Pan: A Biography of the Tramp Played by Charles Chaplin* (New York, 1952) identifies Chaplin with a Pan who is, among other things, "the spirit of license." And, last and least, Herb Caen, in his column "Down the Road — A Peace" in the *San Francisco Chronicle* (March 27, 1962), finds "bearded satyrs and the Pipes of Pan" in Big Sur; this is partly because of Big Sur's peaceful wildness — and partly because it was the residence of Henry Miller.

78. *Attitudes and Avowals* (New York, 1910), esp. pp. 19–21. He quotes Mrs. Browning's "A Musical Instrument" twice. For further parallels to Stevenson, including balanced antitheses, see his poem "Pan" in *The Junkman and Other Poems* (New York, 1920), p. 172.

79. New York, 1913. See also pp. 6, 58, 61, 232. Cf. Euripides, *Rhesus* 36–37.

80. *Pan and the Young Shepherd: A Pastoral Drama in Two Acts* (London, 1898), pp. 112, 114, 127. See Hewlett's *Letters* (London, 1926), p. 84, and the epigraph to the play itself, "And Universal Pan, 'tis said was there," from Shelley's "Witch of Atlas."

For a very similar combination of sinister power and comic grotesqueness, see C. van der Brugge's *Pan in Holland: Comedie in verzen* (Amsterdam, 1946), esp. pp. 10–13, 15. "Pan die sterreft niet / Hij leeft in 't vlakke veld" (Pan who does not die / He lives in the open field), says Pan, as did Hewlett's Pan; "een spook, de duivel zelf" (A spirit, the devil himself) is the view of the other characters. Hewlett's play had as its rivals in the field of early modern Pan drama only such school pantomimes as Otto Julius Bierbaum's *Pan im Busch: Ein Tanzspiel* (Berlin, 1900), Mary MacMillan's *Pan or Pierrot: A Masque* (New York, 1924), and Helen Simpson's *Pan in Pimlico: A Fantasy*, in *Twenty-five Short Plays*, ed. Frank Shay (New York, 1925), or *The Atonement of Pan: A Music Drama*, by Joseph D. Redding (San Francisco, 1912), which was "produced by members of the Bohemian Club in their grove, Sonoma County, California, on the evening of August the tenth nineteen hundred and twelve." Cf. also Charles van Lerberghe's *Pan* (Paris, 1906), a "comédie satirique" of clerical Puritans trying to repress the Pan worship that is part of the renewal of rural pagan joys.

81. London, 1906, p. 268. The Church rescues the hero from the bestial natural life represented by Pan.

82. London, 1956, pp. 104–105. See also page 43, and Maugham's preface, in which he tells of Crowley's reaction to the book upon its publication in 1908.

83. The sinister magician of a small Mediterranean island, the protagonist of Buchan's *The Dancing Floor* (London, 1926), is obviously another version of Crowley.

84. New York, 1923, p. 216. On page 214, there is a rude reference to the

plagiarisms that Maugham committed in writing *The Magician*. In the *Diary*, Pan represents false satanism in contrast to the true worship of the idyllic Crowleyite community shown in the last scenes.

85. *Magick in Theory and Practice* (Paris, 1929), pp. 36–37. See page 229 for a poem much more compact than the "Hymn to Pan" with the lines:

> "Do what thou wilt, for every man
> And every woman is a star
> Pan is not dead; he liveth, Pan!
> Break down the bar!"

See also pp. 69, 99, 279, 290, 312, 327, 333, 338, 354, 396. The bibliography (p. 212) contains references to Arthur Machen, Payne Knight, and Hewlett's *Lore of Proserpine*. The poem, "One Star in Sight," is reprinted in *Equinox* 3.3 (London, 1936), in the form of an additional pamphlet.

86. "Maltby and Braxton," *Seven Men* (London, 1919), p. 53. It is said of Stephen Braxton's novel *A Faun on the Cotswolds*.

Other minor prose references, too fleeting even for this section, can be found in Aubrey Beardsley's *Under the Hill*, ca. 1896 (Olympia Press, 1959), p. 40 (Beardsley's leering, curlicued satyrs and Termini in numerous drawings are a much more potent part of the tradition); Robert Louis Stevenson, "An Object of Pity," *Works*, VII, 466; Matthew Arnold's translations of de Guérin's "Centaur" (1865), *Essays in Criticism*, First Series; "Souvenirs of an Egoist," *Stories of Ernest Dowson* (New York, 1960), pp. 30–31 (with a reminiscence of Mrs. Browning); and Trollope's description of Pan as garden statuary, *Barchester Towers*, chapter xxii. Melville's *Redburn* (1849), chapter xlix, and *Moby Dick*, chapter cxi ("The Pacific"), are more intriguingly Transcendental allusions.

CHAPTER IV. THE BENEVOLENT PAN IN PROSE FICTION

1. *Kenneth Grahame: A Biography* (Cleveland, 1959), chapter six, especially pp. 139–147.

2. In Patrick R. Chalmers, *Kenneth Grahame: Life, Letters and Unpublished Work* (London, 1933), pp. 271–272.

3. *Pagan Papers* (London, 1904), pp. 139–140.

4. *Pagan Papers*, pp. 65–71. The river setting has been traditionally suitable to Pan, of course, from Ovid to Mrs. Browning or James Branch Cabell, and even in the *Notebooks* of Coleridge (October 1804.2212). Grahame does not stress the story of Syrinx, which provides Pan's usual reason for being "down in the reeds by the river." He mentions it here along with Marathon, but in "The Lost Centaur" (*Pagan Papers*, p. 179) he replaces it with an allusion to the Apuleian story of Pan's aid to Psyche. Even when turned into an allegory of artistic creativity (as by Marvell, Shelley, and Mrs. Browning) the implications of the Syrinx story are still heavily sexual. Green makes some interesting comments on the importance of the river setting in Grahame's life as well as his fiction.

5. Green, p. 253. Green calls the vision of Pan in this story "the supreme example of nineteenth-century neo-pagan mysticism" (p. 252), and considers the possibility of an actual "intense visionary experience of a semi-mystical nature" on Grahame's part (p. 84).

6. As in most modern Pan stories. Algernon Blackwood's "Touch of Pan" has a scene very similar to Grahame's, but the "reverent awe of the august presence" that Blackwood's vagabond lovers are said to feel fails dismally to impress. There are other reasons as well, but their all too obvious modernity is one major factor.

7. White, *Gone to Ground* (London, 1935), pp. 249–267.

8. Any number of other levels of allegory could be devised, without ever reaching the bedrock of Stephens' genuine but often contradictory convictions. Cornelius Weygandt suggests a political allegory: "Ireland's way to happiness lies through a frank recognition of earthly joys." "The Riddling of James Stephens," *Tuesdays at Ten* (Philadelphia, 1928), p. 124. The Pan of John Cowper Powys' *Atlantis* (London, 1954) is rather like Stephens'. Powys writes mytho-philosophical whimsy less successfully than Stephens; his Pan is even more lecherously amiable. See pp. 160–165, 215 (for a Caitilin-like relationship), 218, 226, 241, 380, 392, 448 (the withering away of the gods), 461.

9. *The Twilight of the Gods and Other Tales* (New York, 1926), pp. 224–231. First printed in "a Christmas number of *The Illustrated London News*" (see p. 304 of this edition); first collected, 1903.

10. Page 57. See Frank Brangwyn's illustrations to the story. This optimistic and superficial characterization of Pan was not Phillpotts' only view of his relationship to the world of nature, as can be seen in Phillpotts' poem "Litany to Pan" (1911), where the aspects of Nature in whose name Pan is summoned are of a savagery unmatched even in Meredith:

> "By the eternal waste of baffled lust . . .
> By the hot mouthful of a thing not dead,
> By all thy bleeding, struggling, shrieking red,
> Oh, hear!
> By all the agonies of all the past . . .
> By [earth's] return to the unconscious vast."

As the Wind Blows (London, 1920), p. 44.

11. *Atlantic Monthly*, August 1910, pp. 145–165.

12. "Mr. Minchin's Midsummer," in *The Night Side: Masterpieces of the Strange and Terrible* (New York, 1947), pp. 159–176. *Pan's Parish*, by Louise Redfield Peattie (London, 1932), is another tale of this same general type, with in addition some of the robustness of the Provençal myths of Pan's survival; but see Paul Arène, Jean Giono, Joseph d'Arbaud for the real thing. Compare also the theme of Forster's charming "The Curate's Friend," which, were the "friend" Pan rather than a Faun, would constitute the third great example of the Benevolent Pan.

13. *Visionaries* (New York, 1920), pp. 332–342.

14. "The Pipes of Pan," *Other Worlds*, ed. Phil Stong (New York, 1941), pp. 107–125. Peacock, Heine, Pater, and Gosse had intellectual and stylistic resources denied to Huneker and del Rey. Compare Stephens as well as the Victorian authors mentioned earlier for the sad grotesqueness in Pan.

15. *Murder Must Advertise* (New York, 1933), p. 148. In the interest of completeness, I should perhaps add the names of two other stories dealing with a benevolent Pan, neither of which I can recommend: Mary Austin, "Pan and the Pot-Hunter," *One-Smoke Stories* (Boston, 1934), pp. 250–262; M. Tracy, "Pan of Stony Brook," *Everybody's* (June, 1911), pp. 761–784.

16. *Peter Pan* (London, 1904), p. 143.

17. *Little White Bird* (London, 1902), p. 122.

18. This juxtaposition was suggested indirectly by Green's theory that adumbrations of Lawrence's "cult of the blood" were to be found in Grahame's, to my mind, singularly halfhearted acknowledgments of flesh and instinct in "The Lost Centaur" and "Orion" (Green, *Kenneth Grahame*, p. 122).

CHAPTER V. THE SINISTER PAN IN PROSE FICTION

1. "That Donatello is a Pan-figure, though not an embodiment of the god himself, scarcely needs to be proved." W. R. Irwin, "The Survival of Pan," *PMLA*, 76 (June 1961): 164.

2. Compare Eden Phillpotts, *The Girl and the Faun*, where such a faun is very carefully distinguished from the god Pan. The "faune" of Mallarmé, who is most Pan-like in general conduct, and does not have the disqualifying characteristics of evident youthfulness and smoothness of limb, might be an exception to my rigorous separation of fauns from Pans. At any rate, in that case there is no competing Pan figure, and the question could be left open.

3. Machen, *Tales of Horror and the Supernatural*, ed. Philip van Doren Stern (New York, 1948), pp. 61–115. All quotations from Machen's stories are from this edition.

4. Machen, *Things Near and Far* (London, 1923), p. 100. He claims to have soon wearied of this style, but, ironically, his development of a less derivative style (after 1896) led to nothing which competes with the "Stevensonian" stories for a share of what fame he possesses.

5. The reviewer for *The Academy Review*, in *Precious Balms* (London, 1924), p. 58, made a similar comment. *Precious Balms* is Machen's own collection of (predominantly bad) reviews, for which he seems to have had an almost masochistic affection.

6. Page 93. Machen used a similar pseudo-realistic device to lend a combination of mystery and authority to "The Novel of the Black Seal." There, however, the source of the quotation, which deals, likewise, with "foeda mysteria" in Libya, is given: "a fine old quarto printed by the Stephani, containing the three books of Pomponius Mela, *De Situ Orbis*, and other of the ancient geographers . . . my attention was caught by the heading of a chapter in Solinus" (p. 16). The quotation in "The Great God Pan" also turns out to be from Solinus, a third century Latin geographer. *Collectanea Rerum Memorabilium*, 24:10. See *Far Off Things* (London, 1923), p. 136, for Machen's actual encounter with this quarto.

7. Compare John Buchan, *The Dancing Floor* (London, 1926), for a similar, though more explicit and concrete description: "Pan and his satyrs were there, and a bevy of nymphs, and strange figures half animal, half human . . . a carnival of bestiality . . . darker gods even than Priapus" (xiv, p. 226). The scene also resembles the Pan-begotten hallucinations of Maugham's *The Magician*, quoted in chapter IV.

8. Machen, although he does not mention Eusebius' *De Praeparatio Evangelica* specifically, claims that the Fathers, in an English version made by the Tractarians, were among his boyhood reading. In *Far Off Things*, p. 18, he describes "strange relics — fragments of the temple of 'Nodens, god of the depths,'" which he saw as a boy in Caerwent, "also a Roman city," On p. 148 he notes that he was reading Herodotus on the "Mysteries of the Egyptian Religion," in about 1884.

9. Privately printed, London, 1786, pp. 35–38. See also Knight's *Symbolical Language of Ancient Art and Mythology* (New York, 1876), p. 142 (first published, 1818).

10. In "The Novel of the Black Seal," the Primeval, in the form of a Celtic fairy, mates forcibly with a woman to produce the idiot boy from whose body it comes forth again in the form of an awful Tentacle (Machen's version of the "ectoplasm" of the seances, as he admits in *Things Near and Far*, p. 107). In "The Novel of the White Powder," a demonological debauch destroys the hero, and its greatest horror, in intention at least, is the "nuptiae Sabbati . . . [where] the primal fall was repeated" (p. 59). "The White People" is even more suggestive in its hints of an obscene idol: "the queerest doll I had ever seen" (p. 140) and a stone which "in the Middle Ages the followers of a very old tradition had known how to use . . . for their own purposes. In fact it had been incorporated into the monstrous mythology of the Sabbath" (p. 154). This suggests a further reading of Payne Knight, on the survival of Priapic cults. The heroine dies "in time," but the heroine of "The Shining Pyramid" is less lucky: she is "no longer fit for earth" just before she dies (p. 207). The plot line of "The Inmost Light" is compressed: the devil becomes incarnate in a woman simply as a result of an operation on the brain which left a vacuum, as it were, into which he could come.

11. See *Precious Balms*, pp. 10, 23, 65, 12, and also the *Standard* review, p. 60. The modern critical consensus is perhaps expressed by Edmund Wilson: "a demonology of ancient cults driven underground by Christianity but persisting into our own day, and exploit[ing] the identification of the Devil with the pagan god Pan. Machen's story on this theme . . . seems to me to sum up in a fatal way everything that was most 'ham' in the aesthetic satanism of the *fin de siècle*." "A Treatise on Tales of Horror," *Classics and Commercials* (New York, 1950), p. 178.

12. *Far Off Things*, p. 18. Italics mine. The mood of a particular landscape likewise inspired E. M. Forster in the writing of his Pan story (see his introduction to the *Collected Tales*). Lord Dunsany was more specifically brought to think of Pan, and thence of his story *The Blessing of Pan*, by something in the landscape (it turned out to be a hare). *Bright Patches of Sunlight*, p. 9.

13. He himself mentions, for example, Oswaldus Crollius (1580–1604), whose gnomic saying "In every grain of wheat . . . there lies hidden the soul of a Star" Machen interprets as "all matter is one, manifested under many forms." *Things Near and Far*, p. 17. Nothing in Crollius apart from this one sentence was of much use to him.

14. Machen's mystic vision is even more Emersonian in "The Novel of the White Powder." "The whole universe . . . is a tremendous sacrament; a mystic, ineffable force and energy, veiled by an outward form of matter; and man, and the sun and the other stars, and the flower of the grass, and the crystal in the test-tube, are each and every one as spiritual, as material, and subject to an inner working" (p. 57).

15. First published, as far as I can find out, in *The Room in the Tower and Other Stories* (London, 1912), pp. 206–240. Benson remarks in a short preface (p. v) that "Some of those tales have appeared before in various magazines; the remainder are new. One, the story of 'The Man Who Went Too Far,' is the germ of what subsequently developed into a book called 'The Angel of Pain.'"

16. Section ix of *The Birth of Tragedy*, in *The Works of Nietzsche* (New York, 1931). With Tom's deliberate avoidance of suffering and pain, compare Part III, section xiv of *The Genealogy of Morals* (in the same edition): "The

sick are the great danger of man. It is above all essential that the healthy should remain separated from the sick."

17. Although *The Birth of Tragedy* was not available in English translation until 1909, there was a French translation in 1901. Probably more useful to Benson, however, was Havelock Ellis' interpretation of Nietzsche in *Affirmations* (London, 1898), also printed serially in the *Savoy* (1896). Ellis emphasizes, for instance, "the holiness of pain," and "the discipline of suffering," as essential to the development of a man's "own naked personality." This idea reappears as Ellis' own in several of his other works, notably, for the present context, in *My Confessional* (Boston and New York, 1934), p. 55, in a chapter called "The Discipline of Pain," where he uses the sentence "pain is the guardian angel of life." E. F. Benson's brother, R. H. Benson, used the same idea in a specifically Catholic context in his novel *Initiation* (London, 1914): suffering is necessary to balance an excess of joy. A "Pan-given ecstasy" (p. 155) signals the onset of the hero's phase of nature worship (seen as an unsatisfactory substitute for the true Catholic religion). There are numerous other parallels, irrelevant here, between the two novels.

18. Benson's one piece of rueful self-criticism, in an autobiography conspicuous for its lack of reference to his literary beliefs and practices, was that "I disliked thinking for myself." *Final Edition* (New York and London, 1940), p. 194.

19. H. H. Munro, *The Short Stories of Saki* (New York: Modern Library, 1951), pp. 179–185. First published in *The Chronicles of Clovis* (1911). Compare his "Gabriel-Ernest" as a parody of the werewolf story, for example. (*Short Stories*, p. 68).

20. Was not the German governess in "The Elk" gored to death by a horned beast in a story which has no touch of the supernatural in it? *Short Stories*, p. 401. First collected in *Beasts and Super-Beasts* (1914).

21. By J. P. Cover, *Notes on Jurgen* (New York, 1938), p. 45. See also W. F. Gekle, *Arthur Machen: Weaver of Fantasy* (Milbrook, N.Y., 1949), pp. 3 and 9, for comments on Cabell's admiration for Machen.

22. Meredith is quoted as saying, in a conversation with H. W. Nevinson, June 1904, "Pan . . . has always been very close to me. He is everywhere — so is the devil, who was framed on the model of him by our medieval instructors." *More Changes More Chances* (London, 1925), pp. 34–35. Nevinson himself makes the same point twice in his *Plea of Pan* (London, 1901). In the section "Verticordia," he stresses the ignorance of a canon who sees a cloven hoof on the sanctuary grass and attributes it to the Devil. In "A New Pheidippides," Pan himself says "I go to and fro upon the earth . . . like him who has long caused my form and attributes to be blasphemed." *Essays, Poems and Tales of H. W. Nevinson* (London, 1948), p. 150. Cf. also D. H. Lawrence's "Pan in America."

23. The geographical setting is obviously significant: compare Machen's Roman town and Roman relics and Kipling's altar to Pan on the "Great Wall." The narrator of John Buchan's "The Green Glen" (1912) is seized by a dreadful panic near the site of a Roman encampment, past which flows the river Fawn, named by a Roman for his woodland god. Even Forster mentions a possible Roman origin of the Wiltshire "Rings" in *The Longest Journey*. It is as if these authors felt an obligation to legitimize Pan's presence in an English setting by reminding us that he was once worshiped there under the Roman occupation.

24. "A New Pheidippides," *Essays*, p. 148, and *The Plea of Pan* (London,

1901). For all his weariness, Nevinson's Pan is still both strong-minded and talkative; he is one of the best benevolent Pan characterizations. Pan fled from civilization, and especially Puritanism; he "survived" to provide a shelter for those "souls in exile," out of key with society and "yearning for [they] know not what," who are able to find him. It is a more sophisticated, less lyrically contrived version of Stevenson's escape route from the man-made world, with the sense of horror eliminated and the association with the innocently, pleasurably natural stressed. Cf. Blackwood's *The Centaur*.

25. *Lilith* (New York, 1920), p. 58. (Chap. iii, "The Spirit of Pan.") See also McKenna's early autobiography, *While I Remember* (London, 1921), pp. 221, 242, for a very similar disapproval, minus the imagery, of the "resurgence of primitive man," and of "the mad orgy which broke out in 1918." "A Daughter of Pan," *Tales of Intrigue and Revenge* (Boston, 1925), p. 70.

26. *Mr. Mergenthwirker's Lobblies and Other Fantastic Tales* (New York, 1946), pp. 61–89. This anthology was first published in 1937; presumably its separate elements were published earlier in periodicals.

27. *The Collected Tales of E. M. Forster* (New York, 1952), pp. 3–38. "The Story of a Panic" was written in May 1902, first published in the *Independent Review*, 3 (1904): 453, and first collected in *The Celestial Omnibus* (1911). See Katherine Leeds's short story, "Pan: a Memory," *Pall Mall Magazine*, 14:444 (1898) for a sentimental analogue to the Forster tale.

28. Page 12. An uncanny silence preceding the moment of panic — "All sounds died away . . . everything was absolutely motionless and still" (p. 10) — derives ultimately from the silence observed by Theocritus' pipers for fear of disturbing Pan as he sleeps at noon. Like the pervasive music noted earlier, it is a common feature of Pan's appearances. "Summer, and noon, and a splendor of silence, felt," is Swinburne's vaguer, more mysterious formulation. Whether the silence is stressed, as in Machen and Forster, or alluded to, as by Saki and Benson, the logic of its origin is long forgotten.

29. One episode is curiously similar. Both the hero of "The Man Who Went Too Far" (written before 1906 but published in book form in 1912) and Eustace express their affirmation of life by kissing on the cheek an unknown old country woman, met quite by chance. Benson omits this episode from the novel (1906).

30. Yet Leyland's final actions are ambiguous: he knocks over the lamp and struggles with Sandbach in the dark, thus perhaps unconsciously aiding Eustace's escape. Even Forster's minor characterizations are not to be pinned down too easily. (Compare Miss Bartlett's action at the end of *A Room with a View*.)

31. Another noteworthy dialogue with multiple interpretations of Pan is found in chapter xiv of Chesterton's *The Man Who Was Thursday*, where Sunday is variously described as "An animal . . . a god . . . the universe itself . . . clashing his hoofs [like] Pan [who] means everything [and] also means Panic" (New York, 1908, pp. 256–258).

32. Yet Irwin finds that "the objectification of clarity in a Pan-figure [the Curate's friend] is both engaging and effective. The spirit of Pan is implicit in others of Forster's stories . . . Thus a Pan-genius pervades Forster's fiction even when Pan himself is not named" ("Survival of Pan," p. 166). The metaphor is sometimes less complimentary. Leonard Woolf, for instance, speaks slightingly of Forster's "early Pan-ridden short stories." *Sowing: An Autobiography* (New York, 1960), p. 187. More allusively, Frank Tuohy seems to deprecate "the Edwardian Hellenism which has printed its shy goat's hoof-

marks over some of the earlier stories." "The English Question," a review of J. B. Beer's *The Achievement of E. M. Forster*, in the *Spectator*, July 6, 1962, p. 30.

33. Lionel Trilling, *E. M. Forster* (Norfolk, Conn., 1943), p. 50. "Pan can bring about [the salvation of a] clergyman."

34. *Fifty Years of English Literature. 1900–1950* (London, 1951), pp. 69, 71.

35. "E. M. Forster," *The Importance of Scrutiny*, ed. Eric Bentley (New York, 1948), p. 296. See also Wilfred Stone, in *The Cave and the Mountain* (Stanford, 1966), p. 383: "Both writers [Lawrence and Forster] visit Pan on the residents of suburbia for the same reason — to awaken civilized society from its sleep of death."

36. This is less surprising if we take Trilling's statement that "Forster drafted a large part of it in 1903" (*E. M. Forster*, p. 97) to include the picnic scene and its aftermath.

37. Likewise it is through the human agency of Mr. Emerson that she comes to her final vision, to "see the whole of everything at once" (p. 311). And the whole refers not to the world of Nature, as such, but to those very truths of human relationships that Eustace could not "see" by way of Pan.

38. *Aspects of the Novel*, chapter vi, "Fantasy."

39. London, 1947, p. 136. Subsequent references are to this edition.

40. Forster reinforces the comparison by commenting that "Rickie more than any" is a character resembling himself. *Writers at Work*, ed. Malcolm Cowley (New York, 1958), p. 53. The stories of *The Celestial Omnibus*, including "The Story of a Panic," which was Forster's first story (see the introduction to the *Collected Tales*, p. v), bear roughly the same relation to Forster's later novels that the era of *Pan-Pipes* does to Rickie's later life.

41. For example, in Stevenson's "Pan's Pipes," *Virginibus Puerisque* (London, 1881), and frequently reprinted; in Bliss Carman's *Pipes of Pan*, 5 vols. (1902–1905); in James Whitcomb Riley's *Pipes o' Pan at Zekesbury* (1888); in Walter Crane's *Pan Pipes: A Book of Old Songs* (London, 1881). Cf. Max Beerbohm, "Maltby and Braxton": "Current literature did not suffer from any lack of fauns . . . We did tire [of them] later."

42. Forster does not separate the terms with the same consistency with which he separates the function: "great god Pan" is the expression used in the schoolboy scene. I have, for convenience, extended the terminology used in *A Room with a View*.

43. But see Irwin, "Survival of Pan," p. 166, for a different interpretation of this passage and of Forster's "native English Pan."

44. *Tales of the Uncanny and the Supernatural* (New York, 1950), pp. 289–310. First collected in *Day and Night Stories* (1917).

45. Compare McKenna's use of Pan to convey a social judgment; but McKenna is more consistent than Blackwood, for he would not dream of making a case for a "genuine" pagan passion as distinguished from sensual debauchery.

46. Blackwood has another device for spinning out a short story to the length of a novel, and that is documentation, both in prose and poetry. A stanza from "Adonais" points up by contrast the weaknesses of Blackwood's lyric style; a stanza from Mrs. Browning's "A Musical Instrument" fits in rather well. "Pan 'blew in power' across these Caucasian heights and valleys. 'Sweet, sweet, sweet, O Pan! Piercing sweet by the river'" (p. 233). His theme is stated in verse by W. E. Henley: "Here we but peak and dwindle/. . . The universal Pan/ Still wanders fluting — fluting — /. . . Come! let us go a-maying, /And pipe

with him our fill" (quoted on p. 259), and Blackwood rephrases it in prose (p. 243). He cites H. W. Nevinson's *The Plea of Pan* as a source for the character of the hero, a soul in exile struggling to return to the natural world. William James (especially on G. T. Fechner), F. H. Bradley, Henri Bergson, and the German poet Novalis, among others, are continually quoted or paraphrased *in extenso* to provide a philosophic basis for the fantasy.

47. *Pan's Garden: A Volume of Nature Stories* (London, 1912). In "The Sea Fit," p. 128, the Plutarchan Pan makes one of his very rare appearances in horror fiction, as an implied rhetorical comparison: "'All along the shore of the Aegean that ancient cry [no antecedent given] once rang. But it was a lie, a thumping and audacious lie. And He is not the only one. Another still lives — and, by Poseidon, He comes!' . . . That reference to the Aegean 'cry'! It was so wonderful. Every one, of course, except the soldier, seized the allusion." (The second "He" is the minor sea god Glaucus, claiming a human sacrifice.)

48. As does *The Angel of Pain*, insofar as Benson, like Blackwood, is concerned with an ecstatic vision of Pan's world. But Benson salvages his story by the astringency of the final terror; Blackwood throws his away by failing to develop what suggestions of terror he provides. Malevolence might have helped to give impetus to the plot.

CHAPTER VI. CULMINATIONS: D. H. LAWRENCE

1. Lawrence's poetry will be conspicuously omitted from this discussion; not even in those of the *Last Poems* in which Huitzilopochtli and Dionysus are included among the gods that might reside in man is there any mention of Pan. The period of the Pan cluster was in fact one in which Lawrence's main creative effort was going into prose works. "America and the East" were not propitious for poetry, as Richard Aldington says in the introduction to *Last Poems* (Florence, 1932), p. xvii, but America, at any rate, was highly propitious for Pan.

2. *Apocalypse* (London, 1932), pp. 205, 97.

3. First published in *Rhythm* (1913). *Phoenix: The Posthumous Papers of D. H. Lawrence* (London, 1936), p. 307. The connection between the section quoted and the book under review may seem obscure, and its context does little to clarify the matter: Lawrence's love of woman, joy in his work, and reverence for Pan can only be found in *Georgian Poetry: 1911–1912* by stretching a point. "Romantic, tinged with a love of the marvellous, a joy of natural things," comes much closer to, say, the pseudo-Meredithian Pan of woodland panic (Edmund Beale Sargant's "The Cuckoo Wood," *Georgian Poetry: 1911–1912*, London, 1920, p. 169) than does Lawrence's own Pan worship.

4. "The Novel," *Reflections on the Death of a Porcupine* (Philadelphia, 1925), p. 119.

5. "To Be, and To Be Different," section vi of "The Crown" (1915), first published in *Reflections on the Death of a Porcupine* (pp. 88–89). All six sections were written by October 2, 1915 (see *The Letters of D. H. Lawrence*, ed. Aldous Huxley, New York, 1932, p. 263), but only the first three were printed in *The Signature* (1915).

6. "The Novel," p. 121.

7. *The Wisdom of the Heart* (London, 1947), p. 10. Also quoted in H. M. Daleski, *The Forked Flame* (London, 1965), p. 21.

8. *Phoenix*, p. 61.

9. New York, 1921, p. 215 (chapter vi). This is a much more orthodox travel book than *Twilight in Italy* (written 1912, first published in 1916), which contains Lawrence's earliest developed Pan figure, Il Duro. Lawrence and John Addington Symonds were sensitive in a surprisingly similar way to resonances from the classical past: "the very word [Eryx] call[s] an echo out of the dark blood" (p. 67) is a pleasing combination of the traditional values with the Lawrentian idiom. Compare Lawrence's later remark (ca. 1926) quoted by Dorothy Brett in *Lawrence and Brett: A Friendship* (Philadelphia, 1933), p. 285: "Think . . . of Pan, of the mythical Gods; think of all that old mythology; of Lorenzo the Magnificent. That is what Italy and Greece mean to me."

10. *Phoenix*, p. 520; *Apocalypse*, p. 224. *Phoenix*, p. 296.

11. Other critics have used such terms as the Jungian "primordial image" or Maud Bodkin's "archetypes" to mean something approximating the "image cluster" (though I know of no discussion of the Pan figure under either of those rubrics). I prefer the neutral term which emphasizes technique and does not raise questions of literary psychology, at this point irrelevant.

Brewster Ghiselin, "D. H. Lawrence in Bandol," *Western Humanities Review*, Vol. 12 (Autumn 1958), as quoted in Edward Nehls, *D. H. Lawrence: A Composite Biography* (Madison, Wisconsin, 1959), III, 297.

12. The identification of Pan with the devil, available at least from the time of Eusebius if not before, has been more often, as here, stated as a fact (of theology or mythology) than exploited as a literary concept. Recent literary examples include Strindberg's "The Goat-God Pan and the Fear of the Pan-Pipes," and some of the Pan horror stories. Helen Beauclerk's short story "The Miracle of the Vineyard," *The Ways of God and Men* (New York, 1950), p. 215, might well be an elaboration of the sentence from "Pan in America" just quoted.

13. The argument is substantially the same as that in Lawrence's *Studies in Classic American Literature* (1923) where, however, he follows Whitman more closely in omitting the word "Pan," which Whitman never used to mean "Allness."

14. *Phoenix*, pp. 22–24. The essay was first printed in *Southwest Review*, vol. 11 (January 1926), but was at least partly written by May–June 1924.

15. See William York Tindall, *D. H. Lawrence and Susan His Cow* (New York, 1939), for a discussion of the Wordsworthian and Emersonian attitudes shown in Lawrence's writings on nature, despite his denial of his masters. Tindall could have made more use than he did of this essay, which proves his point admirably.

16. As he rejected Whitman and Wordsworth, so Lawrence bites the hands of the anthropologists who may have fed him: "What can men who sit at home in their studies, and drink hot milk . . . and write anthropology . . . know about the men of Pan?" He may have learned from them something about animism and primitive ritual, about the "men of Pan," but Sir James Frazer, Jane Harrison, and Leo Frobenius have very little of relevance to say about the Pan figure itself. His debts to modern researchers are of a more general nature: the Jungian overtones of "the god-demon Pan who can never perish, but ever returns upon mankind from the shadows" (*The Plumed Serpent*, Vintage edition: New York, 1959, p. 348) are much stronger than any evident influence of the anthropologists. See also Lawrence's definition of "Pan-creatures" in archaeological terms (*Reflections on the Death of a Porcupine*, p. 140) as religious (chiefly primitive) artifacts of living beings.

17. Chapter vi, "Il Duro" (London, 1927), pp. 134–140. Compare Cicio in *The Lost Girl*, or the faunlike Italian of *Etruscan Places*; both have the characteristic yellow, gleaming eyes, but neither transcends human limitations in the way "Il Duro" does.

18. John Middleton Murry (in *Son of Woman*, London, 1954) repeatedly identifies Dionys as a Pan figure and, with less justification, calls Mellors, too, a Pan-male. Irwin, following Murry, does likewise. Cicio, George in *The White Peacock*, and the Gypsy of "The Virgin and the Gypsy" are other Dark Heroes who have been called Pan figures by one critic or another.

19. Leyland and Sandbach in Forster's "Story of a Panic" are comparable in some ways. *St. Mawr* quotations are from the Vintage edition (New York, 1959).

20. Irwin ("The Survival of Pan," p. 164) equates the "wild spirit" of the ranch with a "survival of Pan." For once I find myself in agreement with an "implicit" Pan, because this one is demanded by the structure of the story and confirmed by the parallel scenes of "Pan in America." See especially p. 149 of *St. Mawr*.

21. Cipriano is more successful in obtaining this acknowledgment than is, for instance, Somers in *Kangaroo*. *The Plumed Serpent*, pp. 341–344 of chapter xx, "Marriage by Quetzalcoatl."

22. I have taken these terms from Robert B. Heilman's extremely useful article "Charlotte Brontë's 'New' Gothic," *Victorian Literature: Modern Essays in Criticism*, ed. Austin Wright (Oxford, 1961), esp. pp. 73–76. Like Charlotte Brontë, Lawrence uses "the relatively crude mechanisms of fear" to express "an integrity of feeling that greatly deepens the convention" (p. 73), "feeling that is without status in the ordinary world of the novel" (p. 75), "the extra-rational" (p. 76). See also Kingsley Widmer, *The Art of Perversity* (1962), for comments on Pan as a Gothic demon-lover figure in Lawrence.

23. Compare the phallic imagery of "The Border Line" (*Complete Short Stories*, New York, 1961, III, 595), and the unusually abstract formulation of "The Woman Who Rode Away": "the great primeval symbols were to tower once more over the fallen individual independence of woman" (*Tales*, London, 1934, p. 774).

24. *St. Mawr*, p. 149.

25. This is part of his negative comment on Sylvia Townsend Warner's *Lolly Willowes*, who "didn't know *how* to be a witch. Sabbaths and talks with satan are all beside the point." Quoted in Mabel Dodge Luhan's *Lorenzo in Taos* (New York, 1932), p. 312.

26. *After Strange Gods* (London, 1934), p. 59.

27. John B. Vickery, "Myth and Ritual in the Shorter Fiction of D. H. Lawrence," *Modern Fiction Studies*, 5 (Spring 1959): 68. Vickery almost sees the point here; the statement quoted is not a summary of "The Last Laugh," but it is a very fair summary of the Pan horror story in general. But Vickery abandons the idea and goes off in pursuit of Frazerian red herrings, confusing Pan with Frazer's dying and reviving gods. Lawrence's references to the death of Pan are as intellectually allegorical as Mrs. Browning's. As far as I know, Harry T. Moore, in *The Life and Works of D. H. Lawrence* (New York, 1951), pp. 248–250, is the only critic who has made the associations, correct as far as they go, with the stories of Machen and Forster.

28. As the memoirs of the time amply corroborate, as far as Taos is concerned. The letter is printed in *Lorenzo in Taos*, pp. 134–135. Both letters also relate closely to "Pan in America," part of which at least was finished in May

or June 1924 (see *Lorenzo in Taos*, p. 198), and to the Pan cluster in general. See Nehls, *Lawrence*, II, 320, for Dorothy Brett's account of a snowy evening in Hampstead, at about the time of the letters ("today a fall of snow," letter to Johnson, p. 598), and Nehls, p. 515, for a note pointing out the connection between this episode and "The Last Laugh." In a diary entry for September 30, 1924 (Nehls, p. 362), Lawrence reports that he has just sent the manuscripts of "Jimmy and the Desperate Woman" and "The Last Laugh" to the publishers.

29. *Letters*, pp. 598–601. See *St. Mawr* for a further development of the perfectly logical association of Pan and centaur: Lewis is "centaur" in his dealings with the horse St. Mawr. Piero Nardi comments that "come si vede, dire centauro era per Lawrence lo stesso che dire Pan" (It is evident that the word "centaur" was for Lawrence the same as the word "Pan"; *Vita di D. H. Lawrence*, Milan, 1941, p. 599) — a suggestive half-truth. The name of Willard Johnson's journal, *The Laughing Horse* (of which Lawrence had just received a copy), instigated most of the wordplay in this letter. Note the Swinburnian phrases here and again in *The Overtone*.

30. Lawrence is very fond of this proverbial phrase: apart from the cases discussed here, he uses it in "David" (1919) and in "Nathaniel Hawthorne" (*Studies in Classic American Literature*). Catherine Carswell (*The Savage Pilgrimage*, New York, 1932, p. 81) quotes Lawrence as saying that *Women in Love* was a book "that would laugh last."

31. The reactions of the two people most closely involved have come to light in the *Memoirs and Correspondence of Frieda Lawrence*, ed. E. W. Tedlock (London, 1961). Frieda begins by writing to Murry on November 16, 1955: "But for me you are always the old god Pan! You remember when Christianity came there was a voice heard crying: 'Pan is dead.' Maybe now Pan has come to life again" (p. 365). Murry's rejoinder (November 27) is: "Funny you calling me Pan. Lorenzo, you remember, used Pan to kill me off in one of his stories — a queer one which I have never quite understood — all about me and Brett and a policeman in snowy Hampstead. Quite a good picture of me . . . But I didn't and don't understand quite what, *in the story* [italics Murry's], I was supposed to have done that deserved death at Pan's hands . . . But employing Pan to kill me off was a bit steep. And why did he leave *you* out of that story?" (p. 367). Frieda concludes (December 10): "I don't like the Pan story and don't understand it. He really felt you as Pan and I fear envied you" (p. 368). Murry has clearly understood the story and pointed unerringly to its main structural weakness; Frieda cannot possibly "make sense" of it because she insists on identifying Pan with Murry rather than with Lawrence. The biographical basis of the story is hinted at by Catherine Carswell (p. 193) when, despite the caution of her direct statements (1932), she points to "The Overtone" as an "illuminating commentary" on the situation (or, in the London ed., p. 202, the much more illuminating "The Border Line"). F. A. Lea's *Life of John Middleton Murry* (London, 1959), p. 120, mentions "The Border Line" in this context. The relationship between Frieda and Murry remained Platonic during Lawrence's lifetime.

32. Compare Philip, in "The Border Line." Rather later, in a letter to Brett, July 29, 1926, Murry is again associated with a negative Pan principle: "In the *Adelphi*, the *Life of Christ* is relegated to the back pages, and our little friend is discovering he is a pantheist: without a Pan, however: fryingpantheist!" *Letters*, p. 676. "Thoughts on Pantheism" by The Editor appeared in the August issue of *Adelphi*, 4.2:77f. Lawrence foisted an equally dismal pun onto Lou in *St. Mawr*: "fallen Pan" and "pancake" (p. 56).

33. The scent of almond-blossom in midwinter (compare "Glad Ghosts") sets the mood of sexual awakening, as both Vickery and Moore point out (see note 27 above). Compare "Pan in America": "the nymphs . . . made the myrtles blossom more gaily." Her reaction to Pan — a delight in this world so great that it enhances what she sees into a vision of a new world — is comparable to Eustace's vision in "The Story of a Panic." I assume that this is the specific application that Moore has in mind when he refers to Forster as an analogue to this story.

34. "The Cuckoo Wood," by Edmund Beale Sargant, the only Pan poem in *Georgian Poetry: 1911–1912*, provides an interesting gloss to Lawrence's story:

"Doubt not Pan shall come at last
To put a leer within your eyes
That pry into his mysteries.
He shall touch the busy brain
Lest it ever teem again;
Point the ears and twist the feet,
'Till by day you dare not meet
Men, or in the failing light
Mutter more than, Friend, good-night!
Am I eager or afraid?
. . . Has Pan gone by?
Pan has but twain, Pan's eyes are bright!
. . . Pan himself is watching us" (p. 176).

35. Lawrence uses the same device again in the climax of "The Border Line": Philip (another Murry figure) "showed his big teeth in a ghastly grin of death . . . convulse[d] in strange throes . . . the sickly grin of a thief caught in the very act" (p. 604). Saki and Benson provide closer analogues to the plot than does Machen.

36. It is amusing to note that Dorothy Brett, as she herself recounts it, actually looked for Pans as she toured Italy: "you remember . . . how I wrote you that I found Pan on the cliff road down to the Piccola Marina?" *Lawrence and Brett*, p. 285.

37. *The Dark Sun* (New York, 1957), pp. 188, 190.

38. In the letter to Johnson, the possibility of using the usual formula appears to have passed through Lawrence's mind: "the Horse is dead: he'll kick his heels no more. I don't know whether it's the pale Galilean who has triumphed, or a paleness paler than the pallor even of Jesus"; and, a few sentences later, "when Jesus was born" Pan died. The phrase in the essay, "at the beginning of the Christian era," muffles even the tiny suggestion of cause-and-effect contained in the letter.

39. Compare Stephen, in *The Longest Journey*, who makes the same critically accurate remark, but draws the opposite conclusion from it. Stephen was sensitive and in touch with real experience and thus rejects a cliché; she is insensitively protecting herself from experience. Lawrence, unlike Forster, is attempting to revivify the symbol at this point.

40. See Hough, *The Dark Sun*, p. 226, for a discussion of Jungian parallels for Lawrence's dualisms, especially the dualism of light and dark, night and day.

41. Compare Piero Nardi's sensible statement "Cristo poteva identificarsi, esteriormente, con Osiride come già con Pan" (Christ could be identified, outwardly, with Osiris, as he had previously been with Pan; *Vita di D. H.*

Lawrence, p. 741), which I prefer to his more metaphorical "trapasso del Cristo crocifisso al redivivo Pan" (passing over from the crucified Christ to the resurrected Pan; p. 466). *St. Mawr and The Man Who Died* (Vintage: New York, 1959), p. 197.

42. *Lady Chatterley's Lover,* chapter xix. Compare "The Education of the People" (1917), *Phoenix,* p. 651: "scarlet trunk-hose" and much else in this essay parallel Mellors' remarks and fill out the details. James Stephen's Caitilin also replaces Pan's sort of love with Angus Óg's "tenderness."

43. The notion of a dialectical inner conflict in Lawrence is an extremely useful one, but again (as in the matter of the Dark Hero) I would prefer biographical terms for it, such as Daleski's father-mother opposition (*The Forked Flame,* p. 36). Of course a biographer is entitled to use thematic terms for the same reason that I prefer not to: to avoid begging the questions that he is setting out to answer.

44. He realizes that different Pan images have different functions (which no other critic has done), although he makes no attempt to supply the historical context. "Pan più demone che dio" (Pan more demon than god; a translation of a phrase from "Pan in America") corresponds to my "sinister Pan"; he distinguishes it from the more cheerful centaur-Pan; mentions the romantic Pan ("Pan l'eterno" — Pan the eternal), and deals with (and over-does) the Pan–Christ duality, in the course of his thirty-two references to Pan.

45. *Lawrence and Brett,* p. 286. The connoisseur of ceremonial Pans should not neglect Brett's other references in *Lawrence and Brett*: in New Mexico she once painted a picture of Pan at the Crucifixion (so, oddly enough, did Lawrence himself, in 1927) and "the heads of Pan and Christ are both your heads" (p. 288); "you look wicked and Pan-like" (p. 56); compare pp. 108, 118, 121. Pages 32, 51, and 109 use "faun" instead of Pan, but, as Nardi rightly observes, "per la Brett, dire Pan e dire fauno è tutta una cosa" (for Brett, "Pan" and "faun" were one and the same thing; p. 597). Lawrence himself distinguished the two more carefully. See also Nehls, *Lawrence,* III, 142; I, 438; II, 57; and Murry, *Son of Woman,* p. 306.

CHAPTER VII. AFTERMATH

1. *Cakes and Ale,* chapter xi.

2. O'Neill's phrase, from a self-interpretation quoted in Barrett O. Clark's *Eugene O'Neill: The Man and His Plays* (New York, 1947), p. 104.

3. *The Birth of Tragedy,* tr. Francis Golffing (Garden City, N. Y., 1956), pp. 59–60 (section ix). Subsequent Nietzsche references are to this edition.

4. *A Long Day's Journey into Night* (New Haven, 1956), p. 131. Written 1941. Within the realistic situation of *A Long Day's Journey into Night,* "metaphysical solace," in Nietzsche's phrase, must be provided by the play itself; the masks are no longer a possible or necessary symbolic device. "Dionysiac art . . . forces us to gaze into the horror of individual existence, yet without being turned to stone by the vision" (section xvii).

The positive visionary experience corresponding to Nietzsche's "objectification of a Dionysiac condition, tending toward the shattering of the individual and his fusion with the original Oneness" (section viii), is described by Edmund in terms of the sea fog (Act IV, p. 131), without reference to Pan.

5. "Death of a God," *Collected Stories* (New York, 1953), pp. 358–365.

Apparently first printed in 1941. Compare Walter de la Mare's *Memoirs of a Midget*: "Did he believe, perhaps, in the pagan Gods? — Mars and all that? Was there, even at this very moment, cramped up among the moss and the roots, a crazy, brutal Pan in the woods? And those delicious Nymphs and Naiads! What would he do if one beckoned to him? — or Pan's pipes began wheedling?" (New York, 1922, p. 234).

6. *Balthazar* (New York, 1958), pp. 200, 18; *Justine* (New York, 1957), pp. 99, 91, 194; *Mountolive* (London, 1958), p. 215. *Clea* (London, 1960), p. 13, gives a more traditional Pan in the nonurban "Grecian world" of a Mediterranean island. For an illustration corresponding to the intaglio described, see Herbig's *Pan der griechische Bocksgott*, p. 34.

7. Tr. James W. McFarlane (New York, 1956), p. 23. Compare Hawthorne and Browning for less suggestive, more explicit symbolic artifacts.

8. "The Novel," p. 109.

9. For example, Louis Bromfield's *The Strange Case of Miss Annie Spragg* (New York, 1928), Warwick Deeping's *Exile* (New York, 1930), and numberless allusions in semipopular fiction. Norman Douglas' "Locri Faun" in *South Wind* is perhaps a gentle spoof of this expatriate exoticism, found at its best, of course, in Forster.

10. See Giose Rimanelli, "The Conception of Time and Language in the Poetry of Cesare Pavese," *Italian Quarterly* 8.30 (Summer 1964): 14–34. Jean Giono called three of his best-known novels collectively "Pan" (*Colline, Un de Beaumugnes,* and *Regain*), but the symbolism of the fearful or harmonious integration of the human with the all-pervading nature spirit, Pan, is only made explicit in the essay *Présentation de Pan* (Paris, 1930) and the story "Prélude de Pan" in *Solitude de la Pitié* (Paris, 1932), pp. 25–29. Like Pavese, and unlike the English authors cited, he is trying to deal seriously with the romantic concept of a meaningfully surviving primitivism in both its "grandeur" and its "sauvagerie." Compare the other stories which are dependent on the specifically Provençal setting and tradition.

11. Jones, *On the Gods of Greece, Italy and India* (1784, and since revised), *Works*, III (London, 1807), 370, 384. Cox, *An Introduction to the Science of Comparative Mythology and Folklore* (New York, 1881), p. 193. Graves, *The Greek Myths*, especially I, 103 (for Pan's mother, Penelope, as a variety of striped duck); I, 81 (for Apollo's victory over Pan as the Hellenic conquest of Arcadia); II, 289 (for Pan as the offspring of a totemistic group marriage).

12. *Collected Poems* (London, 1960). Reprinted by permission of E. P. Dutton and Co., Inc., and Faber and Faber, Ltd. Compare Theocritus VII, 106–7. The passage from Ezra Pound reprinted by permission of New Directions and Faber and Faber.

13. "Professor Greywood as Pan," *Graffiti* (New York, 1959), pp. 74–76. See Guthrie's "Thessaly," "Paxos" ("pin your goat feet to the Cross"), and "I.R.T.: Rush Hour" ("Christ and Pan and Lucifer in one") in *A World Too Old* (New York, 1927), pp. 11–16, 24, for interesting reworkings of more typically Victorian themes. See also Edna St. Vincent Millay, "Doubt No More That Oberon" and the fourteenth sonnet from *Second April*; Edith Sitwell's fleeting, decorative Pan references scattered through her *Bucolic Comedies* ("goat-footed" is a favorite epithet); W. R. Rodgers' "Pan and Syrinx," *Europa and the Bull* (London, 1947); and Vernon Watkins' "Zacchaeus in the Leaves," *The Lady and the Unicorn* (London, 1958). Yeats catches the orgiastically lecherous associations of Pan's cavern (compare Aristophanes) in "News for the Delphic Oracle" (1939): "Foul goat-head, brutal arm appear . . .

nymphs and satyrs / Copulate in the foam." See Thomas Taylor on *The Cave of the Nymphs* (London, 1823), p. 185, for the neo-Platonic significance of Pan's cavern.

14. We have already mentioned Nelson Bond's pastiche of E. F. Benson and others, and imitations of Lord Dunsany and James Huneker (by Margery Lawrence and Lester del Rey). See also M. P. Dare's "The Demoniac Goat," *Unholy Relics and Other Uncanny Tales* (London, 1947), p. 106, for a close verbal imitation of lines from Machen's "The Great God Pan"; the Crowley-esque ceremony of Ngaio Marsh's detective story *Spinsters in Jeopardy* (New York, 1953); and William Miner's retelling of Saki's "Music on the Hill" in the setting of a New York penthouse apartment, *Cosmopolitan Magazine*, August 1961, pp. 83–85.

15. *The Hunger and Other Stories* (New York, 1959), pp. 74–86. First published in *Playboy* magazine, 1956. See Tom Kaye's *It Had Been a Mild, Delicate Night* for a more sophisticated treatment of Unholy Rape (Lawrence and Henry Miller are invoked on the jacket). The contrast with the coy, evasive sexuality of Norman Lindsay's *Pan in the Parlour* (London, 1934) provides an amusing clue to the development of pulp fiction in the last quarter-century. See Andreas Embiricos, "ARGO or the Voyage of a Balloon," in *Two Stories* (London Magazine editions, 1967), for a more serious version of Pan as a patron god of mindless virility, in both its violently destructive and its regenerative forms.

16. The phrase is found in E. C. Stedman's *Life and Letters* (New York, 1910), p. 402. It is a contemporary private comment on Stedman's poem "Pan in Wall Street" (1869), in which Pan, though dear and jolly, is scarcely amorous.

17. Robert Payne suggested, in his book on Charlie Chaplin called *The Great God Pan*, that the dream sequence of classical dance in Chaplin's *Sunnyside* (as well as a similar scene in *Modern Times*) represents Pan's dance. This is a good deal more plausible than Payne's extended metaphor of Chaplin as Pan (overlapping confusingly with Chaplin as Pierrot).

Mildly amorous Pans are a staple of the magazine cartoonist's stock. See *Playboy* and *Esquire*, *Punch* and the *Spectator*, to take a few examples at random, and (suitably bowdlerized) a Walt Disney comic book, where Pluto meets Pan and dances to his music in the forest breezes (Dell Giant no. 33, 1960).

18. Section iv of Nietzsche's introduction (1886) to *The Birth of Tragedy*, Golffing translation, p. 8. "Worauf weist jene Synthesis von Gott und Bock im Satyr?"

19. Osbert Burdett, *The Beardsley Period: An Essay in Perspective* (New York, 1925), characterizes Beardsley's art as "the return of Pan, the repudiation of authority" (p. 109), the "long-delayed revenge" of the grotesque, "Pan and Punch and Pierrot" (p. 113). I would prefer to apply this metaphor to a slightly later stage of Pan's development.

20. Williams, introduction to *The New Book of English Verse* (London, 1935), pp. 16–17. Knox, "The Greeks at Sea," *Literary Distractions* (New York, 1958), pp. 19–20. Italics mine.

21. Aldous Huxley, introduction to his edition of the *Letters of D. H. Lawrence*, p. xii. Compare Joseph Campbell's discussion, in anthropological terms, of classical Pan as a "dangerous presence dwelling just beyond the protected zone of the village boundary." *The Hero with a Thousand Faces* (Cleveland, 1956), p. 81.

INDEX

HARVARD STUDIES IN COMPARATIVE LITERATURE